GOD IS WITH YOU IN HARD TIMES WHEN YOU THINK THAT HE IS NOT

Elijah Paul

Elijah Paul Ministry

CONTENTS

ABANDONMENT

To be abandoned by another person is to be deserted and forsaken, whether you are a single female who was left alone by a man to raise children by yourself, left alone in a tough situation without kids, or whether you are a sick person, an inmate, an unemployed person, an outcast, a blackballed person, or someone else who was abandoned. Christ and the Apostle Paul were abandoned by family and friends, but God was with them, even when it did not seem like God was with them (Mark 14:37 – 50; John 1:10 – 14; Acts 13:26 – 31). Mary birthed biological children after Christ was born, and at one point they forsook him (John 7:1 – 8). The Apostle Paul said that at different times while he was in prison as an innocent man for Christ's sake, all people forsook him, but that Christ stood with him, and strengthened him (2 Tim. 4:9 – 18). Christ is the Son of God, but in his human state of mind, even Christ cried loudly and asked God, "Father why have you forsaken me" (Matt. 27:46). Therefore, at certain times it seems like God is not with us, and it seems like there is no sign from the Lord. God left Christ alone on the cross and watched Christ with a caring and compassionate eye from a distance. God also sees you and hears you, and will establish, strengthened, and settle you, but sometimes these blessings come after we have endured suffering, somewhat like Christ suffered (1 Pet. 5:10). Also remember that Christ was abandoned by the very disciples and apostles who told Christ that they would rather die than forsake him, but those same apostles ran away and left Christ alone to be arrested by soldiers, beaten, spat on, mocked, jailed, tried in court, condemned to death, nailed to a cross, stabbed with a spear, given vinegar to drink instead of water, and totally disowned by the Apostle Peter (Mark 14:10 – 72; John 1:10 – 14).

See also *BETRAYAL; OUTCAST; ALONE; WITH*.

ACCUSATIONS

A false charge, claim, or lawsuit against an innocent person. The Bible tells us that the devil falsely accuses righteous people night and day. The devil even goes before God to lie on righteous people (Job 1; 2; Rev. 12:10). The devil, his demons, his evil angels, and his human devils on earth also falsely accuse innocent people (Rev. 12:9-11; Job 1:1, 6 – 12; 2:1 – 7). But holy and righteous angels do not lie on anyone and do not falsely accuse anyone, so God fearing humans should not either (Jude 1:8 – 10; 2 Pet.2:9 – 14). If you are falsely accused, rebuke the person who falsely accused you, as the archangel rebuked the devil, and suffer for righteousness' sake if you must (Jude 1:9; 1 Pet. 3:8 – 18; Ps. 38:15 – 22). You can rebuke the devil and a human devil in silence if you must, especially if the human is your supervisor or boss. If you rebuke a human by speaking to them, it is not always necessary to use the word "rebuke" when you discreetly, humbly, and respectfully rebuke a person. But you should use Bible scripture and say the word "rebuke" when rebuking the devil, just as Christ and his angels do (Luke 4:1 – 8; Jude 1:9; Zech. 3:1 – 9).

Christ is acquainted with sorrow and grief (Isa. 53). With much wisdom also comes much grief to us as well (Eccles. 1:18). It may seem like sinners are not being punished by God, but God requires us to keep serving him and we will see who is punished and who is protected (Mal. 3:13 – 18; Deut. 23:6; Ps. 73:1 – 12). You shall be safe from slander and have no fear when destruction comes (Job 5:21). If you are falsely accused for Christ's sake, you are blessed, just as Christ himself and the Apostle Paul were falsely accused (Matt. 5:10 – 11; 1 Pet. 4:12

– 19). Therefore, do not feel unhappy, because many innocent and righteous people in the Bible were also falsely accused (Matt. 11:18 – 19; Mark 3:20 – 21; Luke 23:1 – 11, 13 – 26; John 18:29 – 32; Acts 24 and Acts 25).

Paul was beaten because the Jews assumed that he had brought a Gentile into their temple (Acts 21:26 – 32). The Apostle Paul was falsely accused and beaten several different times, and Christ told Paul that when his servants are weak, Christ is strong for them, and that when we feel alone in our problems, sometimes God is saying that his grace is sufficient for that moment or for that season of adversity (Gal. 6:17; 2 Cor. 11:24 – 33; 12:6 – 10; 1 Cor. 4:10 – 14). Before Stephen was stoned to death, his wise words caused some of the people to plot against him by finding other people to falsely accuse him of blaspheme, but many of them who sat on the council saw the Spirit of God in Stephen (Acts 6:8 – 15). If you are fighting a lawsuit or criminal case, you should fight it with all that is in heaven and all that is within you. When Christ says that we should turn the other cheek if someone hits us on one cheek, or the cheek of the court system, this only applies to when someone persecutes you for being a Christian and living according to Christ's Word. Just as Christ and his apostles, and the Old Testament prophets accepted their persecution, but accepting persecution does not mean that you should allow anyone to force you to do something against your religious beliefs. Just as Daniel, Shadrach, Meshach, and Abednego refused to go against God (Dan. 3; 6). And if anyone falsely accuses you in a natural sense or in a worldly manner, you should fight back like your life depends on it. Because in some cases, including in some divorce cases, a person could be fighting for their financial life or the life and custody of their children, for example.

False accusations at work should be defended because your career, name, and reputation could be at risk. The Lord is faithful, who shall establish you and keep you from evil (2 Thess. 3:3).

Obviously in a criminal case you would be fighting for your

life of freedom. People who are guilty of falsely accusing others are in trouble of hell's fire and may not be forgiven by God unless they first ask the victim for forgiveness, then ask God for forgiveness (Matt. 5:21 – 24). Jesus tells law officials and others not to falsely accuse people (Luke 3:14; Exod. 23:1 – 2, 7). God hates false accusations (Ps. 119:104, 128). Christians must have the same standards (Tit. 2:1 – 8).

ADDICTIONS

There is no high nor addiction like being addicted to the Holy Ghost who is from high in heaven. Apostle Paul said that some people in the Bible were addicted to the ministry, and that is good, if they are truly called by God to be ministers (1 Cor. 16:15). Many are called, but few are chosen, and many ministers are addicted to the money that church members give them but are not addicted to standing for the Word of God (Matt. 8:11 – 12; 20:16; 22:14).

The Bible says, "Addictions, drugs, alcohol, whorish women and men, enslave the heart" (Hos. 4:11). And some drugs cause paranoia which cause people to run or hide when no one is pursuing them (Prov. 28:1). Some people become paranoid without using drugs, because God causes them to be paranoid due to their sins (Lev. 26:36). If you have, or are currently on the verge of destroying yourself, God says there is help in him (Hos. 13:9). The best way to truly be free from addictions and seemingly hopeless situations is to bury those sins in water during baptism, leaving the addictions and problems in a watery grave while you rise out of the water as a born – again new creation filled with the power of the Holy Ghost. The Bible says that anyone who is in Christ is a new creation. Old things are passed away and all things are new (2 Cor. 5:17; 11:1 – 4). This happens when you are baptized in the name of the Lord Jesus Christ for the forgiveness of sins, and you will receive the gift of the Holy Ghost (John 3:1 – 7; Acts 2:36 – 39; 8:14 – 17; 10:47 – 48; 19:2 – 5). God gives the Holy Ghost, who is the Comforter who God sends in Christ's name, to people who obey him (Acts 5:32; Luke 11:13; John 14:13 – 18, 26 – 27 and John 1:1, 14; Col. 3:16; 1 John 2:5, 7, 14). And Christ gives eternal salvation to people who obey him (Heb. 5:7 – 9). Christ the Redeemer shall come to them who turn from sin, says the Lord (Isa. 59:20). If anyone says that they are in Christ but still walk in darkness such as being addicted to smoking cigarettes, overeating, and becoming unhealthy, sinful sex, drinking alcoholic drinks often, or using drugs, for example, they lie, and the truth is not in them (1 John 1:5 – 7).

Strength also comes from both fasting and praying at the same time (Matt. 17:14 – 21). Because addictions are sometimes demons, fasting and praying is needed to cast out certain demons (Matt. 17:14 – 21). Most people nowadays fast in a manner that allows them to drink fluids but not eat food, or to eat vegetables but not eat meet, or to drink water but not drink other fluids. That is a start, and that may be all that some people are able to do if they have health problems. But if a person does not have health problems, they should do without water, fluids, and all food for a set amount of time that they set. Just as Christ, Elijah, and Moses did when they fasted forty days and forty nights, but even most strong Christians nowadays cannot fast that long (Matt. 4:1 – 10; Exod. 34:27-28; Deut. 9:9; 1 Kings 19:8 – 9). If we can train ourselves to do without food and water even for short periods of time, we can certainly do without drugs, alcohol, sex, and gambling, among other addictive habits. We may think that we cannot live without those things, but we certainly cannot live without food and water, so to train ourselves to occasionally do without food and water strengthens us to do without everything else in the world, while leaning on the Spirit of God as we do without food and water, and continuing to allow God to carry us 365 days a year as we live our lives without addictions.

If you enable or provide for a person with addictions, they may never stop using and abusing (Jer. 23:14). You could be literally loving them to death while they put themselves at risk of dying from their addiction. People who strengthen the hands of evildoers are just as guilty as the people who are addicted to evil practices and are partaker and accessory to the addict's sins (2 Chron. 28:13). Drug selling, use of drugs, prostitution, pornography, gambling, excessive drinking of alcohol, and adultery are evil, among other addictions and ungodly acts. It is sin on the clean person's part to know to do good but not do it (James 4:17; Lev. 5:1; Prov. 3:27 – 29). David said, "I will set no evil thing before my eyes, I hate the work of them who turn aside, it shall not cleave to me. I will not know a wicked person" (Ps. 101:3 – 4). That could also pertain to drug users and drug dealers. The Bible says that an unjust person is an abomination to the righteous, and the righteous is an abomination to the wicked (Prov. 29:27). Drug dealers are wicked. If anyone is addictive to sex, pornography, or lust, Job said, "I made a promise with my eyes to not look at any woman other than my wife" (Job 31:1, 7 – 12). The book of Isaiah also tells us to not look at sinful things (Isa. 33:15 – 16). When your eye is good, your whole body is full of light, but when your eye is bad, your body also is full of darkness and evil (Luke 11:33 – 36). The Apostle Paul said it is best that a man not even touch a woman, unless the man is married to that same woman (1 Cor. 7:1 – 2).

The Bible teaches us to not be partaker of nor accessory to other people's sins and to keep ourselves pure (1 Tim. 5:22; Rev. 18:4). It is not wise to die for another person's sins (Num. 16:26; 11:11 – 17; 2 Cor. 6:14 – 18; Rev. 18:4; Gen. 18:20 – 33; 19:17, 24 – 26).

Some addictions are evil spirits that grow worse when addicts relapse or backslide. When one unclean spirit or one evil spirit leaves the inside of the human body, and the evil spirit is not replaced with the Holy Ghost inside of the human body, that evil spirit will return with seven more evil spirits. At this point the addict could be eight times worse than before (Matt. 12:43 – 45). If a person had two cocaine spirits which are also unclean and evil spirits for example, the clean, rehabbed, delivered, and victorious former addict could possibly receive sixteen cocaine spirits if they backslide or relapse.

And if a person had three addiction demons and God heals and delivers the person but that person does not replace the addictions with the Holy Ghost inside of them, the addictions could return twenty – four times worse than before (Matt. 12:43 – 45). Christ casted demons and evil spirits out of one man, and the Lord asked the unclean spirit what his name is, and the unclean spirit said, "My name is Legion, because we are many" (Mark 5:1 – 9). We wrestle not against flesh and blood, but against evil spirits in high places, therefore we must put on the whole armor of God, in righteousness on the right hand and on the left hand (Eph. 6:11 – 18). After you are filled with the Holy Ghost, the Bible says, "Greater is Christ the Holy Ghost who is in you, than they who are in the world (1 John 4:4). And greater is Christ inside of a person than the unclean spirits or addictions that would dwell inside of the person. Drug rehabilitation centers can be good, especially when they are faith based, but many addicts, users, and abusers overcome their addictions through Christ and consistent prayer, praise and worship, and occasional fasting, and by separating themselves from people and environments that are not spiritually, mentally, physically, or emotionally healthy. If a so – called friend or any human promises you freedom that does not involve total commitment to Christ, do not believe it, because by whom a person is overcome, by them also is the person brought back into bondage, and the latter end is worse than the first. It would be like a dog returning to eat its own vomit, and the misleading, fake and deceptive person would be your captain back to bondage (2 Pet. 2:18 – 22; Heb. 11:13 – 16; Exod. 13:17; Num. 11; 14:3 – 4; 16:8 – 15; Deut. 17:14 – 16; Neh. 9:9 – 19).

To clarify how clean and unclean spirits dwell inside of people, a person in the Bible had a spirit of deaf and dumb, and a spirit of sickness. This is not to say that all sicknesses are spirits (Mark 9:17 – 25; Luke 11:14; 13:11). There is also a spirit of having respect and fear of God, which is good to have. And there are spirits of meekness, quietness, wisdom, knowledge, understanding, sadness, jealousy, spirits of antichrist, and demonic and foul spirits (Num. 5:14, 30; Deut. 34:9; Isa. 11:1 – 5; Matt. 5:3; Gal. 6:1; Eph. 1:17; 1 Pet. 3:4; 1 John 4:3; Rev. 18:1 – 2).

The Bible also tells us to not believe every spirit but try the spirits to see if they are of God, because many false teachers, false preachers and false prophets have gone out into the world (1 John 4:1; Rev. 2:2; 2 Tim. 3). The devil makes himself and his angels look like angels of light (2 Cor. 11:13 – 15). Just as when he makes people feel good when they use cocaine and other drugs and narcotics, cigarettes, too much alcohol, and having sinful sex. Even casinos look lively and are illuminated with a multitude of lights, just like the devil, but behind those lights are sorrows and great disappointments for some people. The love of money is the root of all evil, and many people have sought and pursued ungodly money against God's will, and as a result have pierced themselves through with many sorrows. This includes drug dealers, thieves, greedy, and dishonest people (1 Tim. 6:6 – 12; 2 Kings 5:15 – 27; Matt. 13:3 – 9, 18 – 23).

Breaking promises to God cause life to be harder than before. If after you have escaped the pollutions of the world, and become entangled again in the world, your latter end will be worse than the beginning (2 Pet. 2:20; 1 John 5:4 – 5; Eccles. 5:4 – 6). Even earthly rehabilitation centers agree that when people relapse, they usually end up in worse shape than ever before.

Be not filled with wine or any mood – altering substance but be filled with the Spirit of God (Eph. 5:18). None of this will work if you do not truly want to be healed and delivered from your addiction. Lay aside every weight. Resist and strive against sin and addiction until you die in the Lord (Heb. 12:1 – 4; James 4:7; John 17:14 – 19; 1 Cor. 10:8 – 13).

Christ says, "Sin no more, or a worse thing will happen to you" (John 5:14). In other words, if you do not get filled with the Holy Ghost, a worse thing will happen to you someday. Christ says that without him we can do nothing (John 15:1 – 14; Mal. 4:1; Eccles. 9:1; Jer. 5:10). Some people are highly successful who are not Christians, but they still cannot breathe and function mentally and physically without the Lord allowing it to happen. But every knee must bow to Christ and every tongue must confess that Christ delivered them from the devil's diseases, an addiction is a disease (Rom. 14:11; Heb. 1:4 – 6; Deut. 5:9 – 10).

Come to Christ and he will give you rest. His yoke is easy, and his burden is light (Matt. 11:28 – 30. Another scripture says, "Ask for the old paths, where is the good way, and walk therein, and you shall find rest for your souls. But they said we will not walk therein" (Jer. 6:16). Denying that you have a problem and that you need Christ to heal you will only make addiction last longer, possibly for many more years, and addiction to drugs, alcohol, and cigarettes shortens the life of any person who continues to use. Cigarettes are also drugs according to drug rehabilitation centers, and they are correct when they say this.

Former addicts must be careful while trying to help current addicts. If a former drug addict, or anyone, decides to help a person who is currently using or selling drugs, they must be careful not to be tempted themselves. It is best for former addicts and users to never go around present – day drug dealers, users, abusers, and addicts. They are not your friends, and it is all right to not ever go around them again. The Bible says that they will speak evil of you because you do not run with them anymore (1 Peter 4:4; Jude 1:22-24; Gal. 6:1; Zech. 3:1 – 7; Matt. 17:14 – 21; Acts 19:14 – 18; Prov. 10:12; James 5:19 – 20; 2 Chron. 19:2 – 4).

Remember, your new condition will be worse than your former condition if you relapse, and sometimes the new condition could mean time in prison (John 5:14; 2 Pet. 2:20; Isa. 57:11 – 12; Matt. 12:43 – 45). We reap and gather what we plant. If we plant in the flesh, we shall reap corruption to the flesh, but when we plant to the Spirit, we reap life everlasting (Gal. 6:7 – 10, 14).

Some drug rehabilitation centers teach that any form of

addiction hurts the people around you. It can be an addiction to drugs, alcohol, sex, buying too many clothes or shoes, pornography, eating too much food, gambling, watching too much television or spending too much time on social media and the internet. Too much of almost anything, even good things, can be bad for you. Some people spend more time or money using or getting what they desire than they spend time or money on the significant people in their life, or they neglect God and loved ones to fulfill addictions and habits. In some cases, the addiction causes them to hurt the people around them to fulfill their desire. If an addiction causes an addict to become unhealthy or to die sooner rather than later, to be incarcerated, or to lose their job or their inheritance, they would have also hurt the people in their lives as a result.

Esau sold his birthright for a piece of food (Gen. 25:33; Heb. 12:13 – 16). That is the same as a person selling property or selling their body for drugs.

Addictions do not discriminate or have respect of persons. Addictions have destroyed kings (Prov. 31). Christ says, "If your hand, foot, or eyes cause you to sin, spiritually cut them off, because it is better to live a life without hands, feet, and eyes than to have your whole body casted into hell" (Matt. 18:8 – 9). This parable applies to whatever you are addicted too. You should cut the addiction out of your life before you allow them to get you thrown into hell's fire, or to harm you or your family members, or to lose a job (Matt. 19:2 – 12; Rev. 14:1 – 5). And what profits does a person have if they gain the whole world and lose their soul, or what will a person give in exchange for their soul (Mark 8:36 – 38; James 1:8 – 27; Job 27:8 – 23). David said that he would rather be a doorkeeper in God's house than to dwell in the house of wickedness (Psalm 84:10). The same applies to dwelling in the house of drug users, drug sellers, dangerous gambling houses or whore houses.

They who love pleasure sometimes become poor, and they who love alcohol and drugs shall never be rich, unless they are already rich, but they could still lose their riches or their life to addiction (Prov. 21:17). Addiction also causes mental illness and other health problems.

Addictions are sweet when you get what you want, but according to the Bible fools hate to turn away from it (Prov. 13:19; 18:1 – 2). The Bible tells us that some things from the devil seem to be good to us but are evil (2 Cor. 11:12 – 15). Some people like what is good to them but is bad for them. Sweet foods can be good to us but bad for us. Vegetables may not taste good to kids but are good for kids. Worldly music, gangster music, sex music, and lust music can be good to us but bad for us. Drugs, cigarettes, and alcohol are good to people but bad for them. Some people do what is good to them, but it may not be right in the sight of God. We must do what is good and right in the sight of God. Just as preachers must teach the good, right, and true way whether people like it or not (1 Sam. 12:23; 2 Chron. 31:20 – 21).

Christ says that our spirit is often willing to do right, but the flesh is weak (Matt. 26:41). But if you allow Christ to do so, he will strengthen and settle you (1Pet. 5:6 – 11; Ps. 3:5; 55:22). The Spirit of God is against the flesh, and the flesh is against the Spirit of God (Gal. 5:13 – 26; 1 Pet. 2:11 – 12). People who are in the flesh cannot please God, and when people feed their addictions, they are fulfilling fleshly desires and the lusts of the flesh (Rom. 8:8). We must put on Jesus Christ, and make no provisions for the flesh, to fulfill the lusts of the flesh (Rom. 13:14). Flesh and blood cannot inherit the kingdom of heaven, but walking and living in the Spirit while you are alive, and being changed to a heavenly spirit on judgment day is the only way to enter heaven (1 Cor. 15:42 – 52; Gal. 5:16, 24 – 25; 1 Thess.4:14 – 17).

We reap what we sow, in every aspect of life, good or bad (Rom. 2:4 – 11; Gal. 6:7 – 10). Christ says that we must be born of the water and of the Spirit, or we cannot go to heaven (Joh. 3:3 – 7). Therefore, we must worship God in spirit and in truth, and not in the flesh nor as a lover of the world (Joh. 4:23 – 24; Zech. 8:1 – 8). Because the world loves its own and a friend of the world is an enemy of God (James 4:2 – 4; Joh. 1:10 – 12; 15:18 – 19; 1 Joh. 2:15 – 17; 3:13; Phil. 3:16 – 21). Christ says, "I have overcome the world." Greater is Christ in you than they who are in the world (Joh. 16:33; 1 Joh. 4:4). You too can overcome the world of sin and addiction through God Almighty.

Minister's abuse of wine and alcohol goes back thousands of years in the Bible, and some of them even vomited on the tables in the house of God (Isa. 28:7 – 18).

Addicts are slaves of sin, and the addiction is the addicts' slaveholder and idol god. Some people even cry about their idol, whether it is an idol god or an idolized human (Ezek.8:14). Whatever or whoever controls you or whoever you obey instead of God, or whatever you place equal to God, or desire more than or the same as God, is your god (Rom. 6:16; 2 Pet.2:18 – 22; 1 Sam. 15:24; 2 Kings 17:7 – 8, 13 – 14, 20; Isa. 57:10 – 13).

In some ways we must suffer like Christ suffered, and they who have suffered in the flesh have ceased from sin (1 Pet. 4:1 – 5). She, or he, who lives in pleasure is dead while they live (1 Tim.5:6; Eccles. 7:15; Matt. 8:19 – 22; 23:27; Rev. 3:1 – 3; Jude 1:12; James 2:20).

Be dead to sin, but alive to righteousness (Rom. 6:1 – 15; 1 Pet. 2:23 – 25; Col. 3:1 – 4). Christ says, "They who the Son set free are free indeed" (Joh. 8:34 – 36; Rom. 6). Where the Spirit of Christ is, there is freedom (2 Cor. 3:17). But do not use your God given freedom to sin on occasion (Gal. 5:13). We should not make plans to sin, to fulfill the lusts of the flesh, because a little sin defiles the whole body, but using drugs and abusing alcohol is a lingering long – lasting defiling (Rom. 13:14; Gal. 5:9, 13; Ps. 19:12 – 14; Mic. 2:1).

If you live in the flesh you shall die, but if you live in the Spirit, you put to death the deeds of the body, and you shall live (Rom. 8:13). Therefore, allow God to order your steps, and do not allow sin and addiction to rule you (Ps. 119:133). But some people seek their own, and not the things that are of Jesus Christ (Phil. 2:21; 1 Tim.6:9 – 10; James 3:13 – 16; Joh. 5:41, 44;

1 Cor. 13:5).

Some people say that former drug users, addicts, and alcoholics are never healed but are recovering addicts until they die. This is not true, because who Christ set free are free indeed. What we allow God to do for us is forever (Eccles. 3:14, Jer. 29:4 – 9; Joh. 8:34 – 36; Rom. 6). People who Christ heal are made perfectly whole (Matt. 14:35 – 36). Some people say that they tried hard to be free from addictions, but still cannot beat it. They must cry out to God while he is near (Isa. 55:6; Ps. 75:1; 78:32; 118:17.) If you do not accept God while he is calling you, he may withdraw himself from you until you repent (2 Chron.12:5 – 8; Hos. 5:3 – 6, 15; Judg. 16:16 – 31; Isa. 54:5 – 8). That same scripture says that in your affliction you will seek him early. You must not turn to "a higher power," but to the highest power in heaven, earth, hell and the whole universe, who is God Almighty in the name of Christ (Joh. 15:5; Eccles. 5:8; Rom. 13:1; Ps. 91:1 – 2). If it seems like you cannot get through to God, you must do like the people who could not reach Christ with a sick person due to Christ being in a crowded house. Those people tore the roof off the house and lowered the sick person in through it (Mark 2:1 – 5). Sometimes you must break down whatever obstacle that is keeping you from Christ, like they tore off the roof. Often, we must wait on God. Psalms 130:6 says that we must sometimes wait on God like we wait on the morning. We must wait on God like drug addicts wait on the morning when they are expecting a check, or money, or their next hit or next fix (Ps. 130:6). Without faith it is impossible to please God. They who come to God must first believe that God exists, and that the Lord is a rewarder of them who diligently seek him (Heb. 6:1 – 6; 11:6). If you are currently risen with Christ, seek those things which are above, where Christ sits on the right hand of God. Set your affections on things above, not on things of the world (Col. 3:1 – 2). The way of life is above to the wise, that they may depart from hell beneath (Prov. 15:24). A scripture in the book of Psalms says, "Who do I have in heaven besides you Lord, and there is none on earth that I desire beside you" (Ps. 73:25). Seek ye first the kingdom of God, and his righteousness, and all necessities shall be added unto you. Where your treasure is, there will your heart be also. If your treasure is not godly, you will be found with the ungodly. If your treasure is drugs you will be found with drugs, and if your treasure is alcohol or cigarettes, you shall be found with alcohol or cigarettes. If your treasure is God Almighty, you shall be found with strong holy and sanctified Christians, and one day you shall be found in heaven (Matt. 6:19 – 21, 24 – 33; 19:16 – 30; Rom. 2:6 – 11; 8:5; Phil. 2:21; 1 Kings 3:7 – 15; Heb. 11:24 – 27).

Concerning people who love being addicted to drugs or alcohol, Christ says that they who find their worldly life shall lose their life, and they who lose their worldly life for Christ's sake shall find their life, and they who do not carry their own cross for Christ's sake, is not worthy of Christ (Matt. 10:34 – 39; 1 Joh. 5:12; 2 Tim. 2:9 – 13). Christ suffered for us, leaving us an example, that we should follow his steps (1 Pet. 2:21). But some people love to get high on drugs and alcohol. To them Christ says that if anyone comes unto him and does not deny themselves of all sinful desires, that person is not worthy of the Lord. And if anyone walks with Christ and look back, they are not fit for the kingdom of heaven (Luke 9:57 – 62; Heb. 11:13 – 16; Phil. 3:20; Num. 13:25 – 33; 14:1 – 24).

Know ye not that unrighteousness shall not enter the kingdom of God? Be not deceived, neither fornicators, idolators, adulterers, thieves, covetous people, nor people who love to get high on drugs and overuse of alcohol shall inherit the kingdom of God (1 Cor. 6:9 – 11). David said to God, "When you say, 'seek my face,' my heart said unto you, your face Lord, I will seek" (Ps. 27:8). Otherwise, God says, "I will go and return to my place until they acknowledge their sins, and seek my face, in their affliction they will seek me early" (Hos. 5:3 – 6, 15; Ps. 78:34).

Moses was raised by the daughter of an Egyptian king, but he refused to be called a prince of Egypt and chose to suffer with God's people, and like Christ, instead of enjoying the pleasures of sin for a season (Heb. 11:24 – 27). We must deny ourselves of addictions and sin just as Moses denied himself of riches and royalty (Luke 9:23 – 26). Therefore, church goers should not smoke cigarettes, because cigarettes slowly destroy the human body and people who inhale secondhand smoke.

True religion is to go unspotted from the world and to help people who need necessities, and to not help someone support their addiction (James 1:26–27; Isa. 1:15 – 20). The Apostle Paul said that he was crucified from the world and the world from him (Gal. 6:14). The fruit of the Spirit of God is goodness, righteousness, and truth, and it is a shame to even speak of in a glorifying manner the fleshly sins that sinners do. This also means that it is a shame to brag about the prosperity or power of drug dealers (Eph. 5:9 – 12).

According to the Bible, people are foolish who love their sins including loving to get high on drugs, smoke cigarettes, or drink alcohol excessively. The Bible says, "Why is there in the hand of a fool the purchase price of wisdom since they have no heart for godly wisdom" (Prov. 17:16)? A person who isolates themselves to feed their addiction, will oppose all wisdom, if they get what their heart wants (Prov. 18:1 – 2). God told one hard working rich man that he was a fool and will die that same night, because the man worked hard for earthly possessions and was not equally rich towards God (Luke 12:16 – 21; Isa. 40:21 – 25). King Solomon asked God for wisdom instead of riches, long life, and vengeance upon his enemies, therefore God gave him wisdom and riches, and rest and peace in the land (1 Kings 3:10 – 12; 10:21, 27; 1 Chron. 22:9).

Most people will not seek God to help them get rid of addictions, but still hope to be set free Prov. 18:1 – 2). After you are full of the Holy Ghost you cannot do the things that you would do if you were not full of the Holy Spirit (Rom. 7:15 – 25; Gal. 5:17). Some people make themselves rich but have nothing because they are spiritually empty, blind, miserable, and unsaved, but some poor people are rich with salvation, sanctification, holiness, happiness, good health, good children, peace, wisdom, necessities, strength, safety, and protection (Prov. 13:7; Rev. 3:15 – 22). Some of God's people live like Christ lived, in tribulation and poverty, but are spiritually rich (Rev. 2:9). God fills the hungry with good things but sends the rich away spiritually empty (Luke 1:53). Notice that the scripture does not say that the hungry were filled with food, but with good things, whatever their souls' hunger and thirst for. But sometimes we must seek God and not simply wait on him to show up, seek and you shall find (Luke 11:9 – 10; Matt. 11:28 – 30; Jer. 6:16). Blessed are they who thirst and hunger after righteousness, for they shall be filled (Matt. 5:6; Ps. 42:1 – 3; Prov. 15:8 – 9). Christ says, "I am the bread of life. They who come to me shall never hunger, and they who believe in me shall never thirst," nor desire alcohol on a regular basis, and never desire drugs or cigarettes (Joh. 4:13 – 15; 6:35; 7:37). Former drug addicts must remember that after being a drug addict, it is best to never drink alcohol again, because alcohol causes relapses and a desire for a stronger high. God loves people who follow righteousness (Prov. 15:9). But people who are full of sinful things shall hunger, and shall seek God but not find the Lord, and shall call on God but not receive an answer, until they repent (Luke 6:25; Prov. 1:28 – 30). God knows that some people prefer to thirst for sin, cigarettes, drugs, alcohol, addictions, and sinful sex like a thirsty person seeks a drink of water (Job 15:16). We all should be addicted to doing spiritual things for the Lord and for his people (1 Cor. 16:15 – 16).

Your body does not belong to you, it belongs to God and is a temple of God. They who abuse or defile their body with sin including drugs, defile the temple of God. This causes God to destroy that person if that person does not destroy themselves first (1 Cor. 6:9 – 20; and 1 Cor. 3:16 – 23; Eph. 2:19 – 22; Heb. 3:4 – 19; 4:1; Rom. 6:23).

Christ, Paul, and Peter said that their bodies were temples of God (Joh. 2:19 – 21; 2 Cor. 5:1; 2 Pet. 1:12 – 15; Heb. 9:11).

God does not dwell in temples made with hands, but in holy and sanctified humans (Acts 7:48; 17:24). Someone might say that if another person endured drugs and alcohol, they will also endure. This is true in some cases. Paul was a chief sinner but obtained mercy to be an example to us (1 Tim.1:15 – 16). Christ says that sometimes people who sin only on occasion die before people who sin often (Luke 13:2 – 5). This is because some people are punished for their sins soon after they sin, and others are punished for their sins later (1 Tim. 5:24 – 25). People do not retire from using drugs, abusing alcohol, and smoking cigarettes. They either quit and live a healthy life or refuse to quit and shorten their life after they live a life of sickness and sometimes poverty and time in prison.

The reason that a person cannot get enough drugs, alcohol, cigarettes, or sinful sex, or they keep using and abusing after being satisfied, is because they are empty inside. There is an absence of being full of the Holy Ghost also known as the Holy Spirit, and when we are empty the devil will attempt to fill us with anything that is not good for your temple of God. Some people who do not use drugs find themselves not feeling fulfill even after reaching many of their goals in life. They need to be full of the Holy Ghost with their academic, financial, athletic, personal, or profession success (Matt. 12:43 – 45; 1 Cor. 6:9 – 20; and 1 Cor. 3:16 – 23; Eph. 2:19 – 22; Heb. 3:4 – 19; 4:1; Rom. 6:23; Joh. 2:19 – 21; 2 Cor. 5:1; 2 Pet. 1:12 – 15; Heb. 9:11).

Below are additional holy scriptures about sin and addiction and the fulness and joy that comes with allowing the Lord to set you free. They who the Son of God set free shall be free indeed (Joh. 8:34 – 36; Rom. 6).

Selling property and inheritance (Gen. 25:30 – 34; Heb. 12:12 – 17).
God has pleasures forever (Ps. 16:11).
The path of life (Ps. 16:11).
Fullness of joy (Ps. 16:11).
Addiction causes loss of friends (Prov. 17:9).

Addiction is deceitful (Prov. 20:1).

Addiction can cause you to be poor (Prov. 21:17).

Foolish people spend their money on drugs and alcohol (Prov. 21:20).

Addicts are never satisfied (Prov. 27:20).

Self – destruction (Prov. 27:20).

Destruction from God (Prov. 27:20).

Using and abusing early in the morning (Isa. 5:11 – 12).

Disregarding Christ (Isa. 5:11 – 12).

God's help is free (Isa. 55:1 – 2).

Spending money in vain (Isa. 55:1 – 2).

Hear God and allow your soul to live (Isa. 55:3).

Change your ways and choose life (Isa. 55:6; Ps. 75:1; 78:32; 118:17 – 19).

Desiring drugs or alcohol everyday (Isa. 56:10 – 12).

Excessiveness and disorder (Ezek. 23:11; Col. 3:5).

Selling your children (Joe. 3:3, 7).

God bless the child that has their own God given prosperity (Luke 16:10 – 13).

Lacking self – restraint (1 Cor. 7:5; 2 Tim. 3:1 – 5).

Do not lust after evil (1 Cor. 10:6 – 12).

Addiction to the ministry of the Messiah (1 Cor. 16:15).

Be not drunk (Eph. 5:18).

Be filled with the Spirit of God (Eph. 5:18).

Addiction can cause damnation (2 Thess. 2:12).

Former addicts should never hang with people who they used to do drugs with (1 Pet. 4:1 – 5).

See also *ALCOHOL*.

ADOPTIONS

To legally accept someone that is not your biological child and to love, nourish, develop, educate, and carefully lead and guide them throughout life (Exod. 2:2 – 10). When you are baptized properly, God adopts you (Gal. 4:1 – 9; Acts 2:36 – 39; 8:14 – 17; 10:47 – 48; 19:2 – 5; Joh. 3:3 – 7).

You may say that we all are already God's creation. That is true, but God himself says that we must all become a born – again new creation (1 Pet. 1:23; John 3:1–6; 2 Cor. 5:17; Rom. 6; 8:5–18; 1 John 2:29; 5:4).

The Apostle Paul spiritually adopted Timothy by becoming Timothy's mentor (1 Tim. 1:1 – 2). When you spiritually adopt someone in the church, you do not have to call them godparents or godchildren unless you choose to do so. But children who are in foster care can benefit greatly from being part of a good church family who will help the foster children secure good foster parents, or at least good godparents, making a child their godchild. No man in the church should be called "father," as Christians of the Catholic Church address their priests and popes, because Christ says that God is our only spiritual Father, and this is why most churches do not have godfathers, even though there are good and acceptable titles of godmothers and godparents (Matt. 23:9).

Esther was adopted by her older adult cousin, and she obeyed him as if he was her biological father (Est. 2:7, 20). David basically became King Saul's godson, and Saul's biological son loved David as his own soul. David obeyed Saul and Saul rewarded him. However, Saul ended up going against David and tried to kill him because the people of Saul's kingdom favored David (1 Sam. 18:1 – 11). This is one reason that it is very important to screen people who want to adopt kids or who want to become godparents nowadays. Even in the Bible, Abraham's wife Sarah became so desperate to have a child that she arranged for their maid to become pregnant by Abraham (Gen. 16:1 – 10; 30:1 – 24). But notice that Sarah ended up despising her maid after the maid became pregnant (Gen. 16:4 – 6). There should be no sexual encounters with adopted children, foster children nor godchildren between them and the people who support them or who become their adopted mothers, fathers, sisters, cousins, uncles, aunts, and grandparents. The relationship between adopted children, foster children, godchildren, and their new family should be strictly family based with daily God – fearing family values. Adults are perverted and spiritually sick who molested a foster child, orphan or adopted child and should be incarcerated in prison for abusing children. It should not matter that a foster child, orphan, or adopted child is not the same race as the people who adopted them if their new parents are God – fearing people.

See also *FOSTER CARE*.

ADVERSITY

A condition of suffering or affliction. When Christ suffered, he committed himself to God, and so should we (1 Pet. 2:19 – 25). God brings you out of adversity to bring you into a better situation (Deut. 6:23 – 24). You must go through something to become good at something. Often you must pass God's test, to have a testimony. God puts us through adversity so he can bring us out. Regarding us causing adversity or trouble ourselves, Nehemiah told God, "You are right in all that is bought upon us, for you have done right, but we have done wrong" (Neh. 9:33). David said, "Your righteousness O God, is very high, even though you have sent great trouble my way" (Ps. 71:19 – 20). The righteous shall flourish like a tree planted beside water, and in hard times, like a palm tree in hot climates (Ps. 92:12; Jer. 17:8; Num. 24:6).

The Old Testament and the New Testament both tell us that we must not live by bread alone or any earthly thing alone, but by every Word of God (Deut. 8:2 – 3; Luke 4:1 – 4). Even if we happen to not obey every Word of God, we must accept the entire Word of God. We must not reject the Word of God nor support anti – biblical laws, practices, and lifestyles. Christ was tested by God in the wilderness, and God allowed the devil to tempt Christ (Luke 4:1 – 4). And God says that he led the Hebrews through the wilderness to humble and test them. God allowed them to suffer hunger, so that he could know their heart, whether they would keep his commandments or not, and to teach them that they must not live by bread nor earthly possessions alone, but by the Word of God (Deut. 8:2 – 3). Therefore, if God never allows or causes us to suffer or to live through adversity, that would be like an athlete never running at practice but expecting to be strong enough to run in a game while everyone on the other team is competing against him or her. It takes both sunshine and rain to grow crops, and there must be rain in our lives to appreciate the sunshine. Sometimes we need to stop, realize, and appreciate the fact that the sun does not need to be shining every day for it to be a nice and pretty day. Some cloudy days are beautiful days with very nice temperatures. And on hot sunny days the shady places are not always shady. Adversity is also caused by God to prevent us from predicting everything that will happen in our lives (Eccles. 7:10, 14). And to protect us from our own will that is opposite of God's will (Num. 22:24 – 27, 32). But adversity is sometimes one of God's mysteries, and we know that God works in mysterious ways (Eph. 1:9 – 11). Also, sometimes God causes adversity to move us out of our comfort zone, forcing us to move to a better place that he has in store for us.

There is no wisdom, understanding, nor counsel against God, neither has anyone taught him, nor counseled him (Prov. 21:30; Isa. 40:12 – 17, 28 – 31). But the way of sinners is harder (Prov. 13:15). God allowed adversity in the life of Paul to keep him humble (2 Cor. 12:7 – 10). God in his grace and mercy, blesses ungodly people, but they still make plans against him (Hos. 7:15). God's blessings fall on the just and the unjust, the good, the evil, and the unthankful, even though they do not serve him in holiness and sanctification. God blesses them because they are part of his creation, but to be blessed does not mean that a person is saved (Deut. 9:4 – 7; 10:17 – 22; Ezek. 29:17 – 20; Matt. 5:43 – 48; Luke 6:35; Acts 14:8 – 18; Ps. 17:13 – 15; Neh. 9:35 – 39; Ps. 145:9 – 10).

God even sometimes causes evil to happen, to punish or to test certain people (Prov.16:4; Jer. 44:27; Isa. 45:7; Job 1:6 – 22; 2:1 – 10; 42:11; 1 Sam. 16). If only praising God would cause us to be delivered and saved, people would praise God while continuing to be a hypocrite, but God's way of being pleased requires us to do many different things, including righteous service toward him and humanity, raising our children the right way, being a good and godly spouse, passing God's tests, being patient, denying ourselves for Christ's sake, and being a living sacrifice. To those of us who feel that all the good we do is still not good enough, and that no matter how righteous we try to live we are still faced with and witness much adversity, the following scriptures are for you, "The Lord is with you, while you are with him, and if you seek him, he will be found by you, but if you forsake him, he will forsake you. In those times there was no peace to people who went out, nor to them who came in, but great vexations were upon all the inhabitants of the nations. And nation was destroyed of nation, and city of city, for God did vex them with all adversity. Be strong therefore and let not your hands be weak, for your work shall be rewarded" (2 Chron. 15:1 – 8; 24:20; 1 Chron. .28:9; Ezra 8:21 – 23; 2 Thes. 3:13; Gal. 6:9 – 10; Ps. 37).

No matter how you look at life, God has done right but we are wrong at times, or God is right and simply wanted to do his will, because he is God Almighty and can make everything all right whenever he chooses to do so (Neh. 9:33 – 35; Ps. 33:4; 119:128, 137, 138; Lam. 1:18).

If you are suffering and tried while living a righteousness life like Job lived, God is still right, because the devil asked God for permission to afflict Job (Job 1; 2; 4:3 – 8; 32:1 – 10; 34:34 – 37; 42:7 – 9).

The devil cannot do more to us than God allows, but God does sometimes allow us to cause trouble for our own lives, because it was our desire, our choice, and our decision, and God gave us our own mind to choose right or wrong (Job 1:1, 6 – 12; 2:1 – 10; 29:7 – 25; 31:1; Zech. 3:1 – 2; Matt. 26:44 – 54; Luke 22:31 – 32; Joh. 19:10 – 11; 2 Cor. 12:6 – 10; Heb. 2:14 – 15; Rev. 1:18; 2:10; 13:5 – 8).

God Almighty is the only one who can kill and make alive, and who can accept us into heaven or send us to hell. Therefore, when a situation is sad or pitiful and God refuses to change it, the ultimate reward is that God sends those same people to heaven (James 4:12; Deut. 32:39; 1 Sam. 2:6 – 7; 2 Kings 5:7; Joh. 14:1 – 3; Matt. 8:11 – 12).

Weeds and tares grow on their own but crops and pretty lawns must be maintained and sustained, or they will die, have stunted growth, or suffer from diseases (Matt. 13:1 – 23, 24 – 30, 36 – 43). Anything good must be cared for, but bad things can often grow on their own and they get worse and worse. God can even wink his eye or move just one of his fingers to shape and reshape the earth's landscape, but he chooses to use volcanos, rain, floodwater, and earthquakes, for example, which can cause us adversity while he refreshes and reshapes the earth. Even a seed must break open and die before it can sprout into a plant (Joh. 12:24 – 26). Just as most of us must first die before we can inherit the kingdom of heaven.

There will be some dark days in our lives (Eccles. 11:8). When trouble happens, you are not the only one going through something, even though it may seem like it (1 Pet. 5:6 – 11). When we think that God has done or allowed plenty of suffering or trouble in our lives, he will show you that he has caused or allowed someone else to suffer worse than you (Ezek. 14:22 – 23). God believes in hard work and sacrifice as when he made the earth, but some people think that good things are supposed to happen overnight (Isa. 66:7 – 8). God even caused Christ to suffer before he died, rose from the dead, and went back to heaven. Christ had the power to lay down his life at any time, but he did God's will by suffering first in his life of poverty, standing for the truth, not speaking the wrong things, sometimes remaining silent, resisting temptation, resisting wealth when the devil tempted him, and setting excellent examples for us all (Joh. 10:17 – 18; Matt. 26:52 – 54). Christ could have made any kind of gesture such as winking his eye or waving his hand just once to save us, but God requires hard work and sacrifice. God strengthens us for future trouble by causing us to endure current and present trouble. Thus, some adversity is practice, preparation, and training to be able to handle greater adversity. If God never allows us to suffer a cold which is a virus, our immune system would not be strong enough to fight off greater illnesses and threats to the body. David would not offer anything to God without it costing him something (2 Sam. 24:24). So, it is plain to see that God believes in hard work and some sacrifice and suffering, to go along with his grace and prosperity.

There was a person in the Bible who had an impediment, and the people sought Christ so that Christ could lay his hand on the person while praying to Father God (Mark 7:32). We should never forget God while suffering adversity (Ps. 44:13,17 – 22). Job did not sin while suffering (Job 1:6 – 22). And Job received the bad news of the death of his children and the loss of his wealth and property all in a very short time (Job 1:6 – 22). Job continued to trust in the Lord and to stand for the Word of God even though his friends accused him of suffering due to being punished by God for sinning, and his wife would not come near him at times due to the odor of his breath. She also told him to go ahead and curse God so that he could die and end his suffering, and probably so she would not have to deal with his sickness anymore. But Job told her that she talked like a foolish woman, and that even though he felt that God was killing him, he still trusted in the Lord (Job 2; 13:15 – 16; 19:13 – 22; 27:1 – 12). Job's friends cried when they first saw how sick he was, and they sat with him seven days without speaking, but they later falsely accused him and condemned him, but God was with Job, healed Job, restored his money and property and gave him more biological children. The children who Job lost to death went to heaven (Job 4:1 – 8; 32:1 – 10; 34:34 – 37; 42:7 – 9).

God does not allow us to swear anymore, but if you obey all the following scriptures except the part about swearing, you will never be moved (Ps. 15; 24:4; Matt. 5:33 – 37; James 5:12).

If you do the things in the following scriptures, you shall never fall (1 Cor. 10:12; 2 Pet. 1:2 – 10; Phil. 3:13 – 15).

If you should happen to fall, God will uphold you (Ps.

37:23 – 24; 94:18 – 19). If you are weak in the day of adversity, your strength in the Lord is small (Prov. 24:10; Heb. 12:1 – 14). We must always pray, and not grow weak (Luke 18:1). They who wait upon the Lord shall renew their strength. They shall run and not be weary, they shall walk and not grow weak (Isa. 40:27 – 31; Am. 2:10 – 16).

God is not mocked, for whatsoever a person sows and plants, that shall they also reap (Gal. 6:7 – 8; Rom.2:6). David in the Bible once said, "I am this day weak, though anointed king, and my enemies are too hard for me, but the Lord shall reward the doer of evil according to their wickedness" (2 Sam. 3:1, 39).

Be not weary in well doing, for in due season we shall reap if we do not grow weak (Rom. 2:6 – 11; Gal. 6:6 – 10; 2 Thess. 3:13 – 16; 1 Pet. 2:13 – 25; 3:13 – 17; 4:17 – 19; Heb. 6:10; Ps. 37).

If you suffer for righteousness' sake, you should be happy and are blessed. Do not be afraid of the enemy, neither worry (1 Pet. 3:14 – 17; Ps. 38:15 – 22). It may seem like sinners are not being punished by God, but God says keep serving him and we will see who is punished and who is protected (Mal. 3:13 – 18; Deut. 23:6; Ps. 73:1 – 12).

Some people are so unwise that they think they can cheat death and avoid the grave, but death comes when God says so, not when mankind, witchcraft, or an angel of the devil says so, and God says Christ came to prevent us from suffering from the wrath that he sends and from death (Isa. 28:15 – 19). God bruises, binds, and wounds, but his hands also make people whole (Job 5:18). Christ says, "Be not afraid of people who can kill the body, and after that can do no more to you. But I forewarn you whom you shall fear. Fear God, who after he has killed, has power to cast you into hell, yes, I say unto you, fear God" (Luke 12:4 – 5).

It is by the Lord's mercies that we are not consumed, because his compassions fail not, they are new every morning, great is his faithfulness, whether he afflicts us, or whether we afflict ourselves (Lam. 3:22 – 26). Christ will return unexpectedly on judgment day like a thief in the night, but he also cuts off the life of people unexpectedly like a thief in the night (1 Thess.5:1 – 11; 2 Pet. 3:10 – 18; Luke 12:13 – 21; Job 24:13 – 17).

Our dying day is our judgment day, because we will rise from the dead the same way that we died, either righteous or unrighteous (Rev. 22:10 – 13; Acts 24:15; 1 Pet. 3:18; Dan. 12:1 – 3; Ezek. 18:19 – 32; 2 Thess. 1:4 – 12).

The Apostle Paul said that God had mercy on a man who was sick nearly unto death while serving the Lord in righteousness, so again, if you wake up in the morning, God has already had mercy on you (Phil. 2:25 – 30). Just as God's mercy is new every morning, when we are in trouble, God's grace and strength is new every morning to them who ask him for help and wait on him (Isa. 33:2). Psalm 119:126 – 128 says, "It is time for you, Lord, to work, because they have voided your Word. Therefore, I value all your Word concerning all things to be right, and I hate every false way." We must always confess and admit that God is right and that we are wrong (Exod. 9:27; Hos. 14:9; Judg. 16).

God's judgments are right, and he is faithful to us, but in his faithfulness, he sometimes afflicts us (Ps. 119:75 – 77). God is right in all his judgments and actions, but some people would rather suffer, die, and go to hell before they accept that God is always right (Rev. 16:5 – 11; 1 Pet. 2:23; Jer. 11:20; Ps. 67:4; 96:10; Dan. 9:14).

Again, no matter what happens, God is always right (Ezek. 18:19 – 32; 2 Thess. 1:4 – 12. Christ says that even if someone could go to hell and come back to warn others, some of them still would not repent (Luke 16:20 – 31). As for God, his way is perfect (Ps. 18:30). The scriptures listed below offer additional spiritual guidance on adversity.

God causes some adversity (Deut. 32:39; Job 5:17 – 19; Ps. 44:13, 17 – 22; 71:20).
My soul out of all adversity (2 Sam. 4:9).
God did vex them with all adversity (2 Chron. 15:6).
God is right and we can be wrong (Neh. 9:32 – 33).

The righteous man Job (Job 1:13 – 19).

Accepting the good with the bad (Job 2:9 – 10).

Adversity does not simply happen, it comes from God, you, Aomeone else, or the devil (Job 5:6 – 7).

We are born into adversity (Job 5:6 – 7).

Adversity tests the saints (Job 23:10 – 12).

Foolishly saying, "I shall never be in adversity" (Ps. 10:6).

The Lord is my shepherd, I shall not want (Ps. 23).

In my affliction they rejoiced (Ps. 35:15).

It seems like you are alone but you are not alone (Ps. 71:9 – 14).

Adversity is a part of life (Ps. 90:9 – 10).

Rest from the days of adversity (Ps. 94:13).

Must have God in your plans (Ps. 127:1).

Real friends and brothers are born to help you in your adversity (Prov. 17:17).

If you grow weak in the day of adversity (Prov. 24:10).

Present – day adversity makes us happier in the future (Eccles. 7:1 – 4).

In the day of adversity consider (Eccles. 7:14).

Some of our leaders cause adversity (Isa. 9:13 – 17).

God causes us to wait (Isa. 30:18 – 20).

God will lead you out of your adversity (Isa. 30:18 – 20).

The Lord gives you the bread of adversity and water of affliction (Isa. 30:20).

God will help (Isa. 50:5 – 9).

Backsliders have plenty of adversity (Jer. 5:6).

Our ways sometimes cause adversity (Hag. 1:6 – 11).

Keep your eyes Christ (Matt. 14:25 – 31).

Trouble comes to people who cause adversity (Matt. 18:7).

Those who cause adversity (Luke 18:1 – 8).

Adversity turned to joy (Joh. 16:20 – 22).

Adversity of the apostles (1 Cor.4:9 – 14; 2 Cor.4:7 – 18; 6:1 – 10).

Adversity of the Apostle Paul (2 Cor. 11:20 – 33).

Do not be afraid of adversity (Phil. 1:28).

Adversity of God's people (Heb. 11).

They who suffer adversity (Heb. 13:3).
Adversity is not strange or uncommon (1 Pet. 4:12 – 19).
The devil causes some adversity (1 Pet. 5:8).
Mark of the beast (Rev. 13:15 – 18; 14:9 – 12).
Victory over the beast (Rev. 15:1 – 4).

ALCOHOL

It is all right to occasionally drink intoxicating drinks, especially if the drink does not contain manmade harmful chemicals (Est. 5:6; Ps. 104:15; 1 Tim. 3; Tit. 2:3). But if a person is offended because you drink in their presence or in their home, it is best to not drink at all, for peace's sake (Rom. 12:18; 14:14 – 23). The reason drinking alcohol, or any intoxicating beverage is sometimes sinful is because they can be addictive, or they may contain chemicals that harm the body. Our body is the temple of God that should not be defiled. Drinking can cause people to be in danger while swimming, driving, and operating machinery. Drinking on a regular basis or at inappropriate times causes a person's judgment and thinking to be impaired, and it causes emotional and mental problems including depression, because alcohol like marijuana is a depressant. Cocaine is a stimulate that includes deadly manmade chemicals, but even in its natural form, cocaine is extremely addictive and anything that is extremely addictive is sinful. Therefore, some drugs including cocaine, fentanyl, meth, and all narcotics are highly lethal, deadly, or addictive and are sinful to use. Alcohol is not nearly as addictive nor lethal as certain drugs and narcotics, but alcohol is classified as a drug, therefore even though some preachers and ministers do not believe that any Christian should drink alcohol occasionally, there is nothing wrong with a drink on occasion if the person can handle being a little intoxicated. And if the alcoholic drink does not cause the person to relapse into using drugs again. Former drug addicts should not drink alcohol at all.

When Paul told Timothy the minister to drink no more

water, but to drink wine for his stomach's sake and for frequent infirmities, he did not mean to never drink water, but he meant that wine sometimes improves certain illnesses of the stomach (1 Tim. 5:23). But too much of anything, except Christ, is bad for you. One of the holy and godly qualifications of being a church minister is to not drink much wine nor intoxicating drink (1 Tim. 3; Tit. 1:5 – 16). And the same applies to all church members, young and old, male, and female (Tit. 2). Some drunkards have and still do persecute the righteous with their spoken words against them (Ps. 69:12).

People have been purposely getting other people drunk for sexual reasons for thousands of years. And the practice of people who have sold their children or prostituted their children for drugs did not start in recent centuries, but even when the Old Testament of the Bible was written, God spoke of people who sold a boy to get prostitute services and sold a girl so that they could get wine (Joe. 3:3). The Bible clearly states that we must not sell our children into prostitution, nor to obtain prostitution services (Lev. 19:29). Not only is it a sin to get a person drunk or drugged to have sex with them, but to drug or intoxicate them to simply look at their nakedness is sin, and God will turn the offender's glory into shame. The same applies to people who look at the nakedness of people who got drunk on their own (Hab. 2:15 – 16; Gen. 9:18 – 29).

A very unpleasant example of people using alcohol for sexual purposes is when Lot's daughters got him drunk so that they could have sex with him to produce his grandchildren to extend the family lineage, (Gen. 19:32). But that was not necessary, because God does not need sin to fulfill his purpose, just as he did not need Abraham's wife to force Abraham to sleep with their maid to produce a son after God had already promised them a son even though they were an elderly couple (Gen. 16). Lot was Abraham's nephew. Nowadays, whether the victim is a family member or not, people still use drugs and alcohol to weaken other people, so that they can rape them, therefore be very careful and never drink a beverage that you have not kept in your hands the entire time after it was opened.

Politicians, princes, and kings were warned against drinking excessively or they could pervert the administration of justice of those who are suffering from affliction and adversity, and drugs and alcohol does not discriminate, but can brings down even kings and queens (Prov. 31:1 – 9; 1 Kings 16:8 – 9). Unless a person is already rich, the Bible tells us that drinking excessively and being sexually immoral can prevent a person from becoming rich, and they who love pleasure will be poor (Prov. 21:17; Hos. 4:11).

Drunkards and gluttons can reduce themselves to poverty, to wearing rags, to having red eyes, to seeing things that are not there, to saying inappropriate things, to having health problems, to having sorrows and troubles, to disrespecting parents and to getting involved with whorish people (Prov. 23:19 – 35). In the Old Testament, the punishment for rebellious children and children who were drunkards and even gluttons, was death, but Christ died so people like that, and other sinners, will not have to die until God says so (Deut. 21:18 – 21).

We must not live the rest of our lives in the flesh nor in lust and craving for alcohol, but for the will of God, and not in drunkenness, partying, and abominable idolatries. People may think it is strange that you no longer run with them, speaking evil of you, but you must serve God Almighty who is the judge of the living and the dead (1 Pet. 4:1 – 5).

The Bible tells us to not mix with winebibbers, unless you are teaching them about Christ, or at least modeling good Christian behavior (Prov. 23:20; Luke 7:34). When Christ sat with wine drinkers, he was teaching them about God Almighty and how to get to heaven (Matt. 11:18 – 19).

Alcohol on a regular basis also causes physical health problems and mental health problems. God says that our bodies are his temple for him to dwell in (Luke 17:20 – 21). And that if we defile our body, God shall destroy the body, if we do not destroy our own body (1 Cor. 6:9 – 20; and 1 Cor. 3:16 – 23; Eph. 2:19 – 22; Rom. 6:23; Heb. 3:4 – 19; 4:1; Rev. 21:22 – 27).

It is not good to drink around children because you would be modeling behavior that could hurt them in several ways.

Christ says that John the Baptist was the second greatest man to ever live, and John the Baptist did not drink any wine nor strong drink (Luke 1:15). Thus, it is best to not drink alcoholic beverages at all, or not drink them on a regular basis. Jesus Christ himself drank wine, and he was even accused of being a winebibber, which is a person who drinks plenty of wine (Matt. 11:18 – 19; Luke 7:34). Obviously, Christ was not a winebibber, wine-o, nor an alcoholic, but he did drink some wine, and teaches us to drink wine while accepting the Lord's Supper (Matt. 26:26 – 29). But we must not eat and drink the Lord's Supper if we are not living a sanctified and holy life separate from willful and habitual sin. Because when eating and drinking the Lord's Supper while living in sin causes sickness and even death (1 Cor. 11:23 – 30; and 1 Cor. 5:6 – 8). Some people provide grape juice instead of wine when administering the Lord's Supper. Former drug addicts and alcoholics may also want to drink grape juice instead of real wine if they think that they may relapse. It is not true when people say that it is alright to drink often if you do not stagger, waddle, wallow, or wobble, because drinking often hurts something about your life even if you can still walk a straight line.

Christ tells us to watch for his coming, and to not forget to beware of his coming while eating and drinking with drunkards. Christ will return and he will fine a lot of people not prepared to go to heaven whether they sin with alcohol or drugs, or some other sin (Matt. 24:45 – 51). Christ tells us to watch for his return, and not be drunk and consumed with the cares of this life and the many forms of sin (Luke 21:25 – 34).

Christ's mother Mary forced him to turn water into wine because they ran out of wine at a large festive gathering (Joh. 2:1 – 11).

In the Bible fermented grape juice (yayin) was strong

drink, and (shekar) was various kinds of intoxicating drinks (1 Sam. 1:15; Prov. 20:1; Isa. 29:9). Unfermented grape juice was called new wine (Neh. 13:5; Prov. 3:10; Isa. 65:8; Zech. 9:17; Acts 2:13). The new wine put into wine skins was unfermented and when fermented would burst the old skins, indicating that it was ready for their purpose (Matt. 9:17).

Priests were forbidden to engage in strong drink before engaging in holy duties, to separate holy from unholy and clean from unclean, and to set examples for children (Lev. 10:8 – 11; Ezek. 44:21). God tells us about preachers and ministers who could not teach the truth nor warn others because they were often partying and intoxicated, even vomiting in holy places (Isa. 28:7 – 13; 56:9 – 12 and Isa. 19:14. God says that not only do some people love those kinds of ministers, but they are like that themselves (Mic. 2:11). A Nazarene was a person from the town of Nazareth where Christ grew up. A Nazarite was a man or woman who was separated unto the Lord). The Nazarite's vow committed men and women to total abstinence from strong drink, wine, grapes, liquor, and vinegar. (Num. 6:1 – 3, 20; Judg. 13:1 – 7; Luke 1:15). But it was alright for priests to drink new wine from time to time, which was not very strong (Num. 18:11 – 14).

Pregnant women were instructed by God to eat right and to not drink wine, intoxicating drinks, or alcoholic beverages (Judg. 13:1 – 7, 13).

The Bible teaches us to not be drunkard, but to be filled with the Holy Ghost (Eph. 5:18). Power and strength come with being filled with the Holy Ghost (Luke 24:49; Acts 1:8; 10:38; 1 Thess. 1:5; Rom. 15:13). Drunkenness is a sin and is compared to being a child of the devil (1 Sam. 1:14 – 17). According to the Bible, drunkards shall not inherit the kingdom of God, and we must not allow intoxication nor sinful sex acts to cause us to not go to heaven (1 Cor. 5:11; 6:9 – 11; Gal. 5:16 – 26; Rom. 13:13; Hos. 4:11).

Some sinners will go to heaven after God has mercy on them, but counting on judgment day mercy is risky. On judgment day, God will say, "They who are unjust, let them be unjust still; they who are filthy, let them be filthy still; they who are righteous, let them be righteous still; and they who are holy, let them be holy still. And behold, I come quickly; and my reward is with me, to give everyone according to their works." All we can do is hope that God has mercy on rebellious people (Rev. 22:10 – 13; Acts 24:15; 1 Pet. 3:18; Dan. 12:1 – 3; Ezek. 18:19 – 32; 2 Thess. 1:4 – 12).

Hell has opened its mouth wide beyond measure for all sinners who do not repent and turn from their sins (Isa. 5:11 – 25; 2 Tim. 3:1 – 7).

We must not live by bread, other foods, and water alone, and we must certainly not depend on alcohol and wine to survive. Just as in the wilderness when God provided food, water, clothes, and shoes that never wore out in forty years, but he did not provide them with wine nor intoxicating drink, but some of them made it themselves (Deut. 8:2 – 3; 29:2 – 6; Luke 4:1 – 4 and Ex.17:7; Num.20:7 – 13, 27:14; Deut. 6:16; Ps. 106:32 – 33).

Whomever allows wine and intoxicating drinks to get the best of them is not wise (Prov. 20:1). Trouble comes to people who disregards God's Word and get up early in the morning to drink, mixing drinks, and who drink from morning until night, even with music, who call good things evil and evil things good. They are self – righteous, accept bribes to justify the wicked, and persecute the righteous. Saints and holy and sanctified Christians do not drink in the morning (Acts 2:13 – 15).

ALONE

Regardless of what you go through, you are not the only one going through it (1 Pet .5:6 – 11. God never leaves us nor forsakes us (Heb. 13:5 – 6; Isa. 42:16 – 21; 54:4 – 10).

In addition to the scriptures listed below, please see also *WITH; FORSAKE; PROTECTION; VICTORY; TEST; KEEPER; OUTCAST.*

The Lord alone led him (Deut. 32:9 – 14).
No helper for Israel (2 Kings 14:26 – 27).
God left him, to try him (2 Chron. 32:31).
God never hides from trouble (Ps. 10).
I shall dwell in the house of the Lord (Ps. 23).
Sometimes we feel left alone (Ps. 31:22).
Loved ones, friends, and kinfolk staying away (Ps. 38:11).
Friends sometimes leave (Ps. 88:8 – 9).
Loved ones and friend leave (Ps. 88:18).
My enemies are against me (Ps. 102:7 – 10).
Being in need of comforting (Ps. 119:81 – 82).
No one cared for me (Ps. 142:4 – 6).
Two are better than one (Eccles. 4:7 – 12).
God will come (Isa. 46:12 – 13).
Call God while he is near (Isa. 55:6; Ps. 75:1; 78:32; 118:17).
God will show up (Isa. 57:13 – 21).
I sat alone because of your (Jer. 15:17).
God is always with us (Jer. 15:15 – 21).
Mocked and persecuted for God's sake (Jer. 20:7 – 9).
Sometimes we have grief while serving the Lord (Jer. 45:4 – 5).
God sees all sin (Ezek. 8:12).

Deliverance from trouble (Mic. 4:9).

The Father has not left me alone (Joh. 8:29).

The Holy Ghost comforts us (Joh. 14:16 – 26).

Christ was left alone by his disciples, but the Father was with him (Joh. 16:32).

Access to God (Eph. 2:10 – 22).

The Apostle Paul was left alone (2 Tim. 4:6 – 22).

Cast all your cares upon God and he will lift you up in due time (1 Pet.5:6 – 11).

ANXIETY AND DEPRESSION

Anxiety can be a fearful concern or interest or uneasiness of mind due to anticipation. It is a sin to fear anyone or anything other than God (Rev. 21:8, 27; 22:14 – 15; Heb. 11:24 – 27; Neh. 6:13; Phil. 1:28; Isa. 8:11 – 13).

It is, however, understandable to have anxiety when faced with pressure or things that can be detrimental to you. Even Christ had a moment of anxiety before he was taken by the guards to be tried, crucified, and killed (Luke 22:39 – 46). Christ said that he was in deep sorrow and distress, even extreme sorrow, unto death, but he concluded that God's will shall be done, and not his own will, while sweat rolled from his body to the ground like drops of blood (Matt. 26:36 – 39; Luke 22:42 – 44).

Christ was despised and rejected, a man of sorrows, acquainted with grief, and even though most people run from Christ, he carries our sorrows, and he was wounded for our transgressions, and bruised for our iniquities. God laid on him the sin of us all, and he was oppressed and afflicted (Isa. 53).

It is all right for Christians to take doctor prescribed medication for anxiety, and for depression. Taking the medicine is better than suffering or battling the feeling of anxiety and depression alone and is better than having emotional problems that lead to more mental conditions. Anxiety and depression are metal conditions, but no one should be ashamed of the diagnoses, even though there is also no need to broadcast your personal conditions. Untreated anxiety or depression can lead to sleep disorders, nervousness, family problems, problems at work, problems socializing, problems making decisions, and depression. Treated anxiety and treated depression makes life a lot better and a lot easier.

See also *MENTAL HEALTH; WORRYING.*

BETRAYAL, DECEPTION, AND TRUST

To deceive or forsake. A traitor (1 Chron. 12:17; Acts 7:52). Some people speak peace to their neighbors but have evil intentions in their heart at the same time (Ps. 28:3 – 5). But the Bible tells us to build our neighbors up in the Lord (Rom. 15:2; Lev. 18:19 – 20). A neighbor is everyone in society including bosses, supervisors, coaches, teachers, preachers, police, doctors, lawyers, auto mechanics, and all other people. The Bible says that we should speak truth to our neighbor and love our neighbor as we love ourselves (Eph. 4:25; Lev. 19:18; Matt. 5:43 – 45; Mark 12:31). The Bible also says that we must not think evil in our hearts against our neighbor, neither speak a false oath, because God hates those type of things (Zech. 8:17).

People who betray good people shall be punished by God (1 Chron. 12:17). In these last days, dangerous times have come, and many people shall be traitors, among other evil things, and are lovers of pleasures more than lovers of God, ever learning but still not able to come to the knowledge of the truth, while deceiving people and being deceived themselves by crooks who are just as evil as them. What goes around comes around, and we reap what we sow (2 Tim. 3:1 – 7, 12 – 13; Rom. 2:4–11; Gal. 6:7–10; Ezek. 14:6 – 11; Heb. 3:7 – 13).

No weapon formed against you shall prosper if you are a servant of the Lord and live a righteous life (Isa. 54:17; Jer. 29:1

– 11; 1 Chron. 12:17; Ps. 109:1 – 13).

Eve deceived Adam, and Delilah deceived Samson (Gen. 2:16 – 17 and Gen. 3; 1 Tim. 2:13 – 14; Judg. 16). We know that Eve did not have another man, and maybe Delilah did not either, so a woman can deceive and betray a man in more ways than by having an affair with another man. Esau's and Jacob's mother tricked her husband Isaac into giving the larger part of the family inheritance to Jacob instead of Esau, even though Esau was the oldest. It was prophesized that the elder shall serve the younger, Jacob being the younger of the twins, but God does not need trickery to fulfill his prophesies (Gen. 25:19 – 34; 27:30 – 45). God tells us to not trust people, that a person's enemies shall be of their own household, and to not tell certain things to untrustworthy spouses who sleep beside you every night (Matt. 10:33 – 39; Mal. 7:5 – 10; Ps. 101:1 – 4, 7; Prov. 30:11). This could be a case of not sharing information with the spouse until a better time to talk, or in an untrustworthy or failed relationship it may be best to not share certain information at all. In the case of Adam obeying his wife Eve, he should have obeyed God instead, and he would have saved all of us from trouble and death. Adam told God that the wife who God gave him deceived him. Therefore, even a God sent spouse can deceive you, but often the spouse who people chose without God's guidance is much more trouble (Gen. 3:1 – 13; 1 Tim. 2:13 – 14). Noteworthy, no – good men deceive women just as often as women deceive men, but in the Bible, women were much more deceptive. Men are often bold and overconfident like a loudmouth barking dog, and women are more curious, slick, sneaky and quiet like a cat who attacks in silence at the right time.

David's son Absalom killed one of his half – brothers for raping his half –sister who was Absalom's whole sister (2 Sam. 13). Absalom killed his half – brother two years after the rape took place, thus being guilty of pre – meditated murder, and hatred (2 Sam. 13:23). Absalom fled for three years and did not see his father David the whole time (2 Sam. 13:37 – 39).

David mourned and wept daily because of the death of his son who Absalom killed, even though the son who raped his sister disappointed and embarrassed David. Notice that Absalom lied to God and David by saying that he would serve the Lord if God would deliver him back home after being a fugitive (2 Sam. 15:1 – 12). After a long time, David desired to see his son Absalom who had done the killing (2 Sam. 13:34 – 39; 14:1). After David forgave Absalom, David and Absalom still did not see each other for another two years after David allowed him to come back to Jerusalem (2 Sam. 14:23 – 33). When David sent his men to bring Absalom out of hiding as a fugitive for three years, even though David desired to see him, David still did not want to see his face for two more years. After years of David dealing with the death of one son and the raping that he committed, and the pain and embarrassment that his daughter suffered as a victim of rape, David finally allowed himself to see Absalom and he kissed Absalom (2 Sam. 14:23 – 33). Notice that David's nephew who was Absalom's first cousin, initiated the process to get Absalom back home from banishment, so it was a family effort to heal a family problem (2 Sam. 14:23 – 33). However, Absalom did harm to his cousin Joab after Joab would not honor a certain request, just like people nowadays do things to hurt us after we help them (2 Sam. 14:1 – 3, 19 – 23). Absalom betrayed David again too after David finally forgave him. Absalom caused a mutiny against his father David and forced David to run for his life and to vacant his throne as king (2 Sam. 15). Absalom forced David's wife and concubines to sleep with him. Absalom used his army that used to be David's army to overthrow David. This is an example of how families pray together and stay together, but it is also an example of how family members and friends can betray and hurt you after you have done all you can for them, and after you have forgiven them for evil and cruel violations, then they hurt you again.

Regarding Absalom, God had the last word, and Absalom was killed by his cousin Joab in a military style battle (2 Sam.

18:14, 32 – 33). But David still loved Absalom and wept when he heard the news of Absalom's death, and David said that he wish he had died in place of his rebellious son Absalom (2 Sam. 18:14, 32 – 33). David's army became jealous about David's weeping concerning Absalom and asked if they had died and Absalom had lived, would he be happy (2 Sam. 19:1 – 7). That is true love for a rebellious child, but the child and the father still reaped what they sowed, because David had sinned too when he impregnated a married woman and killed her husband (2 Sam. 11; 12:1 – 24; 15:1 – 30; 16:5 – 14, 21 – 22; 17:15 – 22; 18; 1 Kings 15:3 – 5; Ps. 118:18; Isa. 55:3; Acts 13:34).

Jacob forgave his eldest son Reuben after Reuben had sex with his stepmother, but while Jacob was on his death bed, Jacob reminded Reuben that he was unstable as water, and that he would never prosper (Gen. 35:22; 49:3 – 4; 1 Chron. 5:1 – 2; James 1:5 – 8).

God does not trust his servants, whether they are angels or holy humans, but we must trust God (Job 4:18; 15:15; Rev. 12:1 – 9, 13, 17; Luke 10:17 – 18).

We should not trust in idols (Isa. 42:8, 17). It is best to not trust any human, not even human idols, and God says cursed are they who trust in humans, adding sin to sin, but blessed are they who trust in the Lord, and whose hope is the Lord (Jer. 2:13 – 14; 17:5, 7; Isa. 30:1 – 3; Judg. 10:10; 1 Sam. 12:19; Ps. 2:12; Ps. 31; Ps. 52).

You may be able to trust a sanctified virtuous spouse (Ps. 31:10 – 31). The Bible tells us to not trust politicians, friends, siblings, spouses, or neighbors (Jer. 9:4; Mic. 7:5 – 7; Matt. 10:33 – 39; Ps. 118:8 – 9 and Ps.146).

Christ said that he did not need anyone to tell him about humans, because he already knows what is inside of humans (Joh. 2:23 – 25). Jacob's son Joseph was entrusted with the entire kingdom of ancient Egypt in the Old Testament while being a slave, and when the king's wife attempted to sexually seduce Joseph, he refused (Gen. 39). Most humans cannot be trusted that much, but Joseph had godly, holy, and spiritual integrity, not the integrity of the world. A friend of the world is an enemy of God (James 4:2 – 4; Joh. 1:10 – 12; 15:18 – 19; 1 Joh. 2:15 – 17; 3:13; Phil. 3:16 – 21).

The devil is the deceiver of the whole world, but it is impossible to deceive God's elect, holy, and sanctified people (Matt. 24:24; Rev. 12:9; 20:3, 8, 10; Luke 4:1 – 21).

We must be doers of the Word of God, and not just hearers only, otherwise, we deceive ourselves (James 1:22). Some people's mouths are full of deceit and fraud (Ps. 10:7; 59:12). Christ teaches us to pray for people who deceitfully betray us and persecute us, but this does not mean that we should allow them in our lives, heart, or space again, and the prayer can also be a request to God to punish the violators, offenders, liars, and betrayers (Matt. 5:44; Luke 6:28; 11:46).

Like Christ, God's true people do not speak deception nor guile to other people (Ps. 32:2; 34:13; 55:11; Isa. 53:9; Joh. 1:47; 1 Thess. 2:3; 1 Pet. 2:1; 2:22; 3:10; Rev. 14:5).

When friends, family members, church members, teammates, or employees part ways with their counterparts and former leaders, they must be careful not to burn the bridge. As the following scripture indicates, they may end up needing someone who they thought that they would never need again (Judg. 11:7).

See also *FRIENDS; FORSAKE; ENEMIES.*

Thou shalt not raise a false report. God shall not justify the wicked (Exod. 23:1, 7).
God traps the worldly wise in their own craftiness (Job 5:13; 1 Cor. 3:19).
Worldly counsel (Job 18:5 – 8,17 – 18, 21).
Friends and family (Job 19:13 – 22).
Job & Zacchaeus helped the poor, didn't defraud or falsely accuse (Job 30:25-26; Job 31; Luke 19:8).
People you cared for (Ps. 35:11 – 21).
Friends who you feed (Ps. 41:4 – 9).
Against your brother (Ps .50:20).

So-called friends (Ps. 55:12 – 17, 20 – 21).

Siblings and family (Ps. 69:8 – 12).

We should hate very false way (Ps. 119:104, 128).

God delights in us conducting business fairly, but unfairly is an abomination (Prov. 11:1).

Lying about giving to the church, the needy, and to charity (Prov. 25:14).

Nation against nation (Isa. 19:2).

False ministers see false visions (Jer. 14:14; 23:32; Lam. 2:14; Ezek. 21:23).

Some people love a false oath (Zech. 8:17).

Christ condemned by the Jews and betrayed by the Apostle Peter (Mark 14:56 – 72).

Christ's sister and brother (Joh. 7:5).

False preachers handle the Word deceitfully and lay in wait to deceive (2 Cor. 4:1 – 2; Eph. 4:14).

False apostles (2 Cor. 11:13).

Turned from Paul (2 Tim. 1:15 – 18).

Paul forsaken (2 Tim. 4:6 – 22).

Do not falsely accuse anyone (Tit. 2:3).

BLESSINGS

To bless God is to praise and glorify God, even during our adversity or affliction (Job 1; 2:1 – 3; Ps.103:1; 104:1). All humans should bless God (Ps. 145:21). The Bible says that every creature that God made glorifies him except certain humans (Ps. 148; Isa. 43:7, 20 – 22).

One way that God blesses people spiritually is when he sanctifies and set apart certain people unto himself for holy use (Gen. 2:3; Joh. 17:17-19; Isa. 29:23; Heb. 2:11; 11:16; 12:14 – 15; Ps. 4:3 – 5; Rom. 12:1 – 2; Eph. 5:5 – 10, 25 – 27;2 Tim. 2:19 – 26).

When humans bless other people, they pronounce blessedness towards those people (2 Sam. 6:18).

When humans ask to be blessed by God, they request salvation, care, happiness, protection, or prosperity from God (Num. 6:23 – 27). When we obey the Lord, things go well for us, and he blesses, leads, guides, and protects us. Again, sometimes we need to stop, realize, and appreciate the fact that the sun does not need to be shining for it to be a nice and pretty day. There is an old saying that says, "Learn to count your blessings." This means that we should learn to appreciate God when it seems like he is not near and remember all the times when he was near and totally with us. Many O Lord my God are your wondrous works, and your thoughts towards us cannot be recounted in order. If I would declare and speak of them, they cannot be numbered (Ps. 40:5. Joh. 21:24 – 25).

All people are blessed in one way or another, but few people are anointed, and there are more people who are ordained than there are anointed, because both God and humans can ordain a person to do something, but only God can anoint a person to have a spiritual gift, purpose, talent, skill, or mission. An anointed person is destined to fulfill a purpose for God, and it cannot be prevented by mankind. Spiritual anointings from heaven are not the same as mankind anointing another person with holy oil, but sometimes the two are done simultaneously by instructions from God.

Jacob's father in – law was blessed tremendously after Jacob started living with him (Gen. 30:25 – 30). And if only one spouse is saved in a marriage, the sanctified spouse causes their children and the unsaved spouse to be blessed and protected, but rebellion can cause God to end his grace (1 Cor. 7:14; 2 Cor. 6:1 – 10; Rom. 6:1, 14 – 15, 23; 2 Sam. 7:15; Rev. 20:6; Heb. 12:14 – 15; Gal. 1:6; Jude 1:4; 2 Tim .2:1; Ezek. 18).

The unsaved person must work out their own salvation with God, with trembling and fear of God (Phil. 2:12 – 15). God says, "Let us have grace, but we must still serve God acceptably with reverence and godly fear, because our God is a consuming fire, and a jealous God" (Deut. 4:24; Exod. 34:14; Heb. 12:26 – 29; Ezek. 8:5 – 18).

When people work against God's sanctified and holy Christians, and even against some weak or newly converted Christians, God turns the curse into a blessing (Deut. 23:5 – 6; Gen. 50:14 – 21; Neh. 13:1 – 2; Est. 9:24 – 25; 2 Sam. 16:5 – 13; 1 Chron. 12:17; Jer. 31:25 – 34).

Paying tithes will cause a person to be blessed, but this does not mean that they are necessarily saved (Mal. 3:8 – 10). Your good works can cause you to be blessed with earthly things, but they cannot save you (2 Sam. 22:20 – 27; Eph. 2:8 – 9). Just because a person is called to do a service for the Lord does not mean that they are saved. The Bible says, "Many are called but few are chosen" (Matt. 8:11 – 12; 20:16; 22:14). A person is not crowned by God unless they strive lawfully and in holiness (2 Tim. 2:1 – 5). Blessed are they who read and later die in the Lord (Rev. 1:3; 14:13). Obeying God causes both blessings and salvation forever (Deut. 11:27 – 28; 30:19; Ps.

18:17 – 27; 115:13; 119:1 – 2; Mal. 2:2).

If God is to keep blessing America or any nation, those nations must also bless God. King David and King Solomon said that they will bless the Lord at all times (Ps. 34:1; Prov. 3:5 – 10). Blessed is the nation whose God is the Lord (Ps. 33:12). In every nation they who fear Christ, and work righteousness is accepted by Christ (Acts 10:35). God has mercy on them who fear him (Luke 1:50). God's wrath towards us is according to our fear towards him. If we have little fear of God, he has great wrath towards us (Ps. 90:11). The Bible describes many nations in the following scripture, "God you are just in all that is brought upon us. You have done right, but we have done wickedly. Neither have our leaders and politicians kept your word. They have not served you in their nation, in the large and prosperous land that you gave them, neither turned they from their wicked works (Neh. 9:33 – 35).

A very popular Bible scripture says, "If my people who are called by my name, shall humble themselves, and pray, and seek my face, and turn from their wicked ways, then will I hear from heaven and heal the land" (2 Chron. 7:14; Luke 19:37 – 42; Hos. 5:3 – 6, 15; Ps. 78:34).

Sometimes God changes his mind about blessing us, due to sin, and we do not even know what God had planned for us (Num. 24:11; 33:55 – 56; Hos. 7:1 – 2). Even holy and sanctified people do not always know what God has planned for them. Eyes have not seen, nor ears heard, neither has it entered the heart of mankind, the things that God has prepared for them who love the Lord (1 Cor. 2:9; 1 Pet. 1:8; Phil. 4:4 – 7; 1 Cor. 2:9; Isa. 64:4 – 8; Ps. 31:19; Luke 19:33 – 42; Jer. 33:3).

Sometimes God prevents others from doing good towards us (Num. 24:11). And sometimes our blessings are right in front of us, but we will not accept and embrace them (Josh. 18:2 – 4). There are times when God would heal or bless people, but their sins prevent him (Hos. 7:1 – 2; Jer. 18:8 – 10; Jon. 2:8; Luke 19:41 – 42; Acts 13:46; 1 Pet. 3:7; Prov. 5:7 – 12; Matt. 11:20 – 24).

God has mercy on us all, and blessings shine on the just and the unjust, the unthankful and the evil, according to God's will (Matt. 5:44 – 48; Luke 6:34 – 35; Eccles. 9:1 – 3). Even humans give to their good children, and on occasion to the disobedient children because parents love all their children. The same applies to God and his creation, but this does not mean that God is pleased with unjust, unholy, evil, and unthankful people. Christ had not been born into the world yet when the Hebrews left slavery in Egypt, and later wandered in the wilderness due to sin. But while in the wilderness they served the same God, ate the same spiritual meat, drank the same spiritual drank, and drank of the same spiritual Rock that followed them, that Rock was Christ, but God was not pleased with most of them, and they were destroyed by God (1 Cor. 10:1 – 13 and 1 Cor. 3:5 – 17). Not even every so-called Christian is a sanctified servant of the Lord, because some people only benefit from God's protection and prosperity while not standing for the Word of God (Luke 4:4; Exod. 24:7; Deut. 8:3; and Deut. 4:1 – 9). Christ says that he will say to those people on judgment day, depart from me, you worker of iniquity (Matt. 7:22 – 23).

Individuals, couples, groups, races of people, and organizations who have been blessed with plenty are commanded by God to do plenty towards God, and towards other people (Luke 12:42 – 48; 2 Cor. 1:3 – 4). While Job was suffering, his wife told him to curse God and die, to end his suffering. But Job told her that we must accept good from God and adversity too, and that although it seemed like God was killing him, Job said, "Yet will I still trust in the Lord" (Job 2:8 – 10; 13:15 – 16). Job was one of the most righteous men on earth when God allowed the devil to kill his children, take his health, and his wealth. But Job said, "God gives, and God has taken away, blessed be the name of the Lord (Job 1; 2:1 – 3; 31:13 – 23). God took the life of Job's children after Job prayed regularly for their safety (Job 1:1 – 5). After Job passed God's test, the Lord gave Job more children and more wealth, and restored his health. God blessed the latter days of Job more than the beginning of his life (Job 42).

To be afflicted or face adversity from God can sometimes be a blessing. David said it was good that he was afflicted, so that he could learn God's ways, through humility and patience (Ps.119:71). Jeremiah said he received affliction from God because of God's wrath on other people, and that his affliction made his skin, flesh, and bones old (Lam. 3:1 – 4). Sometimes the good suffers with the bad. They who endure to the end shall be saved (Matt. 10:20 – 22; 24:13; Heb. 3:7 – 19; Joh. 6:26 – 29; Eccles. 9:11 – 12).

Neither the devil nor any other evil spirit, evil person, or idol can bless you. They give people things, but they are not blessings (Matt. 4:5 – 8; 12:25 – 26; Judg. 11:24; Jer. 44:15 – 19). And God does not help sinners commit sin, neither does he uphold them in their sin (Job 8:20). Sometimes people obtain things through sin according to their own will, including through black magic or voodoo, like money, fame, a mate, or new – born babies. But God does not bless you through sin. God asks, "What sin have you found in him that causes you to sin" (Jer. 2:5)? God and Christ have never sinned (Deut. 32:4; 2 Chron. 19:6 – 10; Ps. 18:30; 92:15; Heb. 4:15 and Heb. 2:16 – 18; Gal. 2:17).

If a person conceives a child without being married, God did not give that child to the parent, but they did that on your own through sin. The Lord is often with people while they are pregnant and while they are delivering babies, but God did not help them conceive the babies in sin. In life when we receive good or bad, either God did it, you did it, someone else did it, or the devil did it. The Bible says, "Fear the Lord, take heed to the Word of God and do it, and there is no sin with the Lord our God" (1 Chron. 19:7). Superstar singer and dancer Beyonce' once said immediately after a dance routine in front of a large crowd that God was with her out there on stage. God woke her up in the morning and gave her the strength to move and do whatever she chose to do, but God was not with her, neither did he assist her in dressing half naked, nor in moving her body in obscene ways, and dancing an unholy dance.

Christ says that the devil was not in him nor over him (Joh. 14:30). And God said there is no other god with him (Deut. 32:12, 39). If you are a sinner, the devil will not go against sinners, nor against himself. He will give you what you want to keep you serving him, even if you do not know that you are serving him (Mark 3:22 – 27). Some of the devil's gifts may seem good, but good and perfect gifts come from Christ, and there is no variation with gifts from God (James 1:13 – 17). If you desire blessings, desire spiritual gifts, and not only material gifts and prosperity (Eph. 1:3; 1 Cor. 12:28 – 31; 14:1).

Do not be quick to bless someone to be a preacher (1 Tim. 5:22). They may not be called to do what they or you think that they are called to do. You will be partaker of their sins if God did not call them. Many are called, but few are chosen by God (Matt. 8:11 – 12; 20:16; 22:14). Blessed are they who wait on their ministry (Rom. 12:6 – 7; Isa. 30:18).

What we say while blessing or cursing a person could come true, if it is God's will, or if God allows it (Prov. 11:11). Thus, we can sometimes speak things into existence (Prov. 11:11). So, watch what you say to your children. Telling them that they will be a failure, or that they are like the other parent who may not be a good person, could cause them to be what you said they will be. Death and life are in the power of the tongue, and people who love life shall reap the fruits of it, but they who speak negativity which is a form of death, such as hindrance, regression, stunted growth, discouragement, instilled low confidence and instilled low self – esteem can cause problems in life for the person who hears and accepts the negative comments (Prov. 18:21 and Prov.12:18). People can bless you in conversations by just saying, "God bless you." In return, you may want to bless them and the good advice that they gave you (1 Sam. 25:32 – 33; Prov. 11:11). And people may be able to curse you by speaking a curse into existence (2 Sam. 16:5 – 10). Some people bless you with their mouth and curse you in their heart at the same time, so not all encouraging words are genuine (Ps. 62:4). When a person blesses you openly, it could cause other people to persecute and curse you, due to jealousy, hate, and spite, but all true servants of Christ experience this and God protects, leads, and guides them (Prov. 27:14). God turns curses into a blessing (Deut. 23:5; Neh. 13:2; Est. 9:24 – 25; 2 Sam. 16:5 – 13; Jer. 31:25 – 34; Zech. 8:13).

God will turn your enemies' prayers into curses against themselves (Ps. 109:7). God will bless people who bless the saints and curses people who curse the saints (Gen. 12:3). But Christians should bless people who curse and persecute them, and the reward is a blessing for you from God because you blessed your enemy (Matt. 5:44; Luke 6:27 – 28; Rom. 12:14; Job 29; 30). And the Bible does say, "As some people love cursing, so let curses come to them, and as some people do not delight in blessing, so let blessings be far from them" (Ps. 109:17). When God blesses people, they are blessed indeed, but when God curses people, they are cursed beyond what they can change, unless they repent (Num. 22:6; Deut. 11:29; 27:9 – 26; 28).

Blessing and cursing should not come from the same mouth. This also pertains to profanity that should not be spoken from the same mouth as someone who confesses Christ, praises God, and blesses people (James 3:10). Water fountains do not produce both fresh water and salt water, and wise people with knowledge should show with good conversation their works with meekness of wisdom, without envying and strife. They do not lie against the truth. Otherwise, that wisdom does not come from heaven, but from earth and from the devil. But wisdom from heaven is first pure, and without hypocrisy (James 3:8 – 18).

Children should be blessed after birth, just as Christ and others were blessed as infants (Luke 2:21 – 23). Baptism should not be performed on most kids until they understand that they are not being baptized to only cover their sins by the blood of Christ, but to commit to living free of willful sin the rest of their lives. Christ was not baptized until he was 30 years old (Luke 3:21-23). He was blessed as an infant, but he was not baptized as a child at all (Luke 2:21 – 23; Matt. 3:13 – 17). It is alright to have a child christened as in the practice that originated in the Catholic Church, but to cause them to be baptized because an adult wants them to be baptized, and when an adult repeats the words of a minister on the behalf of an infant, is not proper baptism. The child would grow into adulthood having never been baptized properly and never spoken their own vows to the Lord during baptism. Christ prayed to God at his baptism (Luke 3:21 – 23). Christ says if anyone dedicates their life to him and then looks back at their past sinful lifestyle, they are not fit for heaven (Luke 9:57 – 62; Heb. 11:13 – 16; Phil. 3:20; Num. 13:25 – 33; 14:1 – 24).

One of the main problems young people have is that they were baptized too young. The Bible says that after we are baptized or give our life to the Lord, if we break that promise, our lives get worse, and that it is best to not make a promise to God, than to make it and break it (Eccles. 5:1 – 7; Deut. 23:21 – 23; Num. 30:2; Prov. 20:24 – 25; Jer. 42:1 – 6, 21 – 22; 2 Pet. 2:23).

The Bible says, "If we sin willfully after we have received the knowledge of the truth, there remains no more sacrifice for sins, but there is only a fearful expectation of judgment and fiery punishment. They who broke Moses' law died without mercy by the testimony of two or three witnesses. How much sorer punishment for people who have trodden underfoot the Son of God, and have counted the blood of his covenant, wherewith he was sanctified, an unholy thing, and did it despite the Spirit of grace? It is a fearful thing to fall into the hands of the living God" (Heb. 10:26 – 31; Exod. 20:18 – 19; Deut. 5:23 – 26; Mic. 2:1; Ps. 19:12 – 14).

Parents should bless their children, and occasionally greet them with a holy kiss (Gen. 31:55; Rom. 16:16; 1 Cor. 16:20; Job 1:5). Parents before death should also bless their children, while the kids are young, and again before parents die, giving them authority, guidance, and inheritance. This is done by anointing them with holy oil and laying a hand on them while praying in Christ's name. If no holy oil is available, or because of health reasons a parent cannot lay their hand on the child, then speaking to the child and praying to God in Christ's name will fulfill the blessing, in Christ's name. Christ simply raised his hands when he blessed the apostles as he was lifted back up to heaven (Luke 24:49 – 51). When Moses lifted his hands the people prevailed in battle, but when he lowered his hands, the enemy prevailed, so the people propped up Moses' hands (Exod. 17:10 – 12). When you bless someone, it cannot be reversed, so be careful not to take away the birthright of an older child or bless a certain child with something that another child would have had, unless you are sure that is the best decision to make for everyone involved (Gen. 27; 48; 49; Deut. 33; 1 Chron. 5:1). God quickly reverses his curses on people if it is his will, or after a cursed person repents for their sins or cries out to God for help (Deut. 23:5; Neh. 13:2; Est. 9:24 – 25; 2 Sam. 16:5 – 13; Jer. 31:25 – 34; Zech. 8:13).

The children also need to bless their parents in their hearts and verbally, and to not curse them or wish that harm happens to them (Prov. 30:11 – 12). Momma may have, father may have, but God blesses the child who has their own. Christ says people who manage a little money well will manage a lot of money well, and people who do not manage a little money well will not manage a lot of money well. Furthermore, Christ says that if a person does not manage another person's property well, why should he or a human give that person property that they can call their own (Luke 16:10 – 12)?

We must thank the Lord for the food that he provides for us (Rom. 1:21; 1 Tim. 4:1 – 5; Col. 3:15). Blessing food causes it to be purified from all uncleanness (1 Tim. 4:1 – 5). In the Old Testament, certain meats were unclean to eat, but Christ purged all meats, making it possible to eat after it is blessed and cleansed in prayer in Christ's name (Mark 7:14 – 20; 1 Tim. 4:1 – 5; Rom. 14).

There is no such thing as luck, fate, karma, fortune, or misfortune. Because God only ordains or allows blessings, adversity, and curses. Either God did it, you did it, someone else did it, or the devil did it. There is nothing else (Deut. 32:39; Joh. 15:5; 1 Pet. 5:8; Rev. 12:7 – 17; Job 1; 2; 5:6 – 7, 17 – 19; 2 Cor. 2:10 – 11; Eccles. 8:14).

When the devil afflicted Job, God allowed that to happen after the devil asked God for permission to test, try, and tempt Job. God told the devil how much trouble he could cause Job, and nothing more (Job 1:6 – 22; 2:1 – 10; 42:11). When Eve allowed the devil to entice her, that was the work of the devil through Eve, because it was not her idea (Gen. 3). Some people think that Judas betrayed Christ according to Judas 'own will (Joh. 12:3 – 6). But the Bible tells us that the devil entered Judas, so the devil caused him to betray Christ (Luke 22:3 – 6; Joh. 13:27). When David seduced a married woman, impregnated her, and killed her husband, David himself did that (2 Sam. 11; 12; 1 Kings 14:8; 15:3 – 5). When David conducted a census of the people without God's approval, the devil provoked David to do that (1 Chron. 21:1, 14 – 17; 2 Sam. 24:1). The devil wanted to sift Peter like wheat, destroying him, but Christ did not allow it (Luke 22:31 – 32). Peter still disowned Christ three times before Christ was crucified. Peter did that on his own (Matt. 26:66 – 75). Christ says that the devil has no more power than God allows (Job 1:1, 6 – 12; 2:1 – 10; 29:7 –25; 31:1; Zech. 3:1 – 2; Matt. 26:44 – 54; Luke 22:31 – 32; Joh. 19:10 – 11; 2 Cor. 12:6 – 10; Heb. 2:14 – 15; Rev. 1:18; 2:10; 13:5 – 8).

There is no wisdom, understanding, nor counsel against God, neither has anyone taught him, nor counseled God Almighty (Prov. 21:30; Isa. 40:12 – 17, 28 – 31).

Christ is the head of all powers and principalities (Matt. 28:18; 1 Cor. 15:24 – 28; Eph. 1:21 – 23; Phil. 2:9; Ps. 8; Heb. 2:5 – 9; Joh. 16:15).

Even hell belongs to God. Christ has the keys to hell and death, and just as the devil will not work against himself, he will not build a hell for himself either (Rev. 1:18; 20:10; Luke 17:19 – 26; Matt. 12:22 – 28). In Christ dwells all the fullness of God, and you are complete in him, who is the head of all principalities and powers (Col. 2:9 – 10).

BROKENHEARTED

To be downcast, sorrowful, or hopeless (Isa. 61:1 – 3; Jer. 23:9 – 11; Luke 4:16 – 21). The Bible says, "And when he had opened the book, he found the place where it was written, The Spirit of the Lord is upon me, because he has anointed me to preach the gospel to the poor; he has sent me to heal the brokenhearted, to preach deliverance to the captives, and recovering of sight to the blind, to set at liberty them who are oppressed and bound, to preach the acceptable year of the Lord.' And he closed the book, and he gave it again to the minister, and sat down. And the eyes of all of them who were in the synagogue were fastened on him. And he began to say unto them, 'This day is this scripture fulfilled in your ears'" (Isa. 61:1 – 3; Jer. 23:9 – 11; Luke 4:16 – 21).

CARE

To feel interest or concern (Deut. 11:12; Eph. 1:16 – 19). Lack of concern. Neglect (Ps. 142:4). The Bible says, "Cast all your cares upon the Lord God because he cares for you" (1 Pet. 5:7).

See also *WITH; PROTECTION; HELP; FRIENDS.*

CHILD ABUSE

It cannot be said enough, Christ says that if anyone abuses, neglects, or hurts a child that believes in him, that person would be better off if they put a weight around their neck and jump into the sea, and that children have special angels just for them who visits God face to face often on behalf of children (Matt. 18:3 – 6, 10). Christ embraced a child in his arms and said to his disciples, "Whosoever shall receive a child in the name of Christ, receives Christ" (Mark 9:36 – 37). In other words, all child abusers and child molesters will suffer in this world and in hell. People who are involved with child pornography or lusts after a child are child molesters, even if they never commit a sex act with a child. Because the Bible says that as a person thinks in their heart and mind, so are they (Prov. 23:6 – 7; Matt. 5:27 – 29; Ps. 14:1; 53:1; Jer. 17:9 – 11).

God casts down imaginations and thoughts that are not holy and righteous (2 Cor. 10:3 – 5). The Word of God says, "For this is the will of God, your sanctification, that you should abstain from sexual sins, and that no one should take advantage of a person in this manner, because the Lord is the avenger of all such sin, offenses, and violations, as we also forewarned you. For God did not call us to uncleanness, but to holiness. Therefore, they who reject this does not reject mankind, but they reject God" (1 Thess. 4:3 – 8).

People are commended because of their wisdom, but they who are of a perverted heart shall be despised (Prov. 12:8). Even if a child tempts a grown person or consents to having sex, it is still wrong to have any kind of sex with a child. If anyone knows about a child being molested or abused and does not report it to the police, they are just as guilty as the person who is doing the abusing (James 4:17). God sees and regards everything (Jer. 29:23; 2 Sam. 12:7 – 14; Num. 32:22 – 23; Rom. 2:16; Matt. 10:26; Luke 12:2 – 5; Isa. 59:12; Ps. 44:20 – 21; 90:8; Nah. 3:4 – 6; 1 Cor. 4:5; Ezek. 16:36; 23:18, 29, 35; Prov. 15:3; Eccles. 5:8; Heb. 4:12 – 13; Hos. 7:2).

The law of the land is right when it forces child molesters to make themselves known when they move into a community (Prov. 21:10). And the law of the land is right when it sometimes takes children out of the custody of unfit and unsafe parents. Some parents forsake their kids and allow their kids to be sexually abused, but God will not forsake us (Isa. 49:13 – 15).

Some people refuse to know God's ways (Job 21:14). Some parents do not live sanctified nor have high moral lifestyles, but most of them still love their children (1 Kings 3:16 – 28). Those same scriptures highlight a woman mistakeably killing her newborn baby by sleeping on top of the baby while they slept. And some parents who are fit, or perceived to be fit, but are not God fearing, still love their kids and give them gifts, but being God fearing adds an omnipotent level of protection from heaven (Luke 11:13; Matt. 18:3 – 6, 10; Mark 9:36 – 37).

To spoil a child with excessive amounts of gifts or by allowing a child to have their way a lot is also child abuse, or to not properly discipline your child, because you would be setting your child up for future hardship. There is nothing like tough love. Even God uses tough love on us.

In the Old Testament, before Christ died for everyone's sins, people who did not report sin were killed without mercy (Lev. 20:4 – 5). Now that Christ has changed the rules, child abusers and molesters are still subject to God's wrath, even though we should not kill them, but if a child molester is caught in the act, the child must be protected and defended. Remember, they are better off if they jump into the sea with a weight tied around their necks (Matt. 18:3 – 6). The same applies to people who know about a child being abused and not telling the police, and the principal of the school, if the abuse involves an educator. The same applies if abuse happens in church settings (James 4:17; Lev. 5:1; Prov. 3:27 – 29; Matt. 23:23)

Nowadays when a child reports that a parent has abused them by spanking them, a law official will respond immediately. But if a child reports that they have been sexually molested, people including many law officials, care providers, teachers, counselors, school administrators, church members, and social workers are slow to act and often assume that the child is lying. Children should always be given the benefit of the doubt.

The Bible says that there shall be offenses, but trouble comes unto them who cause the offenses (Matt. 18:7). Thus, children who do not believe in Christ, they will reap what they sow, and if anyone should abuse them, that person shall also reap what they sow, but in a far worse manner than the kid who God punishes in one way or another for not believing in Christ (Matt. 18:3 – 7, 10; Ezek. 35:5 – 6).

The Bible says that we should not provoke children to anger (Eph. 6:4; Col. 3:16). This also means to not provoke children by abusing, neglecting, or discouraging them. It also means to not provoke children to disrespect parents because they are ashamed of the parents' actions, words, or bad reputation. We must not drown our children in sorrow, because sorrow of the heart breaks the spirit (Prov. 15:13; 18:14). The Bible says, "A merry heart does good like medicine, but a broken spirit dries the bones" (Prov. 17:22; 18:14). And life and death are in the power of the tongue, and people who love life shall seek life and give life with the tongue (Prov. 18:21 and Prov. 12:18).

CHILD SUPPORT

To not pay child support makes a Christian worse than an infidel (1 Tim. 5:8; James 1:26 – 27; Jer. 5:28 – 31). Parents are required to provide for the children, not the children for the parents, unless there are situations of hardship (2 Cor. 12:14). And when parents pay child support, whether it is paid by mothers or fathers, that is their responsibility anyway, and they should not brag about it (Luke 17:7 – 10). It is often hard for a parent, mostly good fathers, to accept paying child support while already giving their children plenty, or they have been paying child support but now realize that they must give much more, or that the children will do without more expensive necessities that the other parent cannot afford. It can be very discouraging and even depressing for a working – class or middle – class father to give sometimes two to three times the amount of child support. But the father should dig deep into his heart, pocket, and bank account and invest in his children and God will give back all that the father sacrificed for his children. If a kid does not deserve more than the amount of child support, or if they are lazy, disobedient, or spoiled, then they do not always deserve extra benefits, but sometimes they will still need at least some extra benefits. This is usually a result of the mother spending the child support on herself, and sometimes on another man too, or because the mother does well towards the children, but she does not make enough money to provide a certain lifestyle for the kids, or to buy vehicles, or to pay for college. At that point, if the biological father is able, he should give much more money, time, and benefits if he is able to do so. The extra provisions, spending, and sacrifice will not last forever because kids grow up fast, but it is understandable that it can be hard for the father to accept, especially if another man is benefiting from what the biological father is providing. Fathers should consider that rich fathers pay hundreds of thousands and even millions of dollars to the household of their children and their mother, and if another man lives there with the mother, that man is benefiting from the monthly contributions of the biological father. It is a very uncomfortable situation, but it is reality, and nothing can be done about it. Nothing.

God blesses fathers, and mothers, who invest and sacrifice both money and time with their children, and he protects them from other burdens in life, because God never puts more on us than we can bear (1 Cor. 10:12 – 13; 1 Pet. 4:12 – 19; 1 Thess. 3:3).

It is well worth the extra spending and investing when it keeps the kid out of trouble, off the streets, out of jail, and from conceiving a baby themselves. It is good when noncustodial parents spend time with kids, but it is great when a noncustodial parent help raise their children, coparenting, which requires much more time and consistency. Simply spending time usually means occasional time together, but occasional time is not nearly enough time. God says that even if a person did not have children, they still would not be satisfied with their extra money (Eccles. 4:8). Give, and it shall be given back to you, like it is pressed down in a basket and running over out of the basket (Luke 6:38).

Christ turns the heart of the fathers to their children and the heart of the children to their fathers, and if either refuse, God curses them (Mal. 4:6; Luke 1:17).

Lastly, John 3:16 tells us that God gave his only begotten Son, that we shall not perish, but have ever lasting life. And 1 John 3:16 tells us that Christ laid down his life because he loved us, and that we are to lay down certain parts of our life for our loved ones, our spiritual brothers, and sisters, and for people in need (1 Joh. 3:16 – 23).

See also *FATHERLESS; CHILD ABUSE.*

CHILDREN'S PRAYER

As I lay me down to sleep, I pray the Lord my soul to keep. If I should die before I wake, I pray the Lord my soul to take. If I should live another day, I pray the Lord to guide my way, in Christ's name, Amen.

The following prayers can be used by adults as well. Psalm 3:5 and Psalm 4:8 speak of us laying down to sleep with God being our protector.

Additional prayers that are good for both children and adults are the Lord's Prayer (Matt. 6:6 – 13); the Benediction (Num. 6:23 – 27); and Psalm 23. All prayers must start with, "God or Father," and end with, "in Jesus Christ's name," or in "Christ's name," or in the "name of the Messiah," or in the "name of Yeshua Messiah." Then say, "Amen," which is a statement of sincerity towards God (Col. 3:17, 23). Otherwise it does not mean anything to God, because to not pray in the name of Christ could mean you are praying to anyone or anything, or to an idol god. And some prayers require both fasting and praying to get your desired results (Mark 9:17 – 29).

Christ protects all kids, especially kids who believe in him, and he greatly punishes people who take advantage of them. Children have special angels just for them who speak face to face with God on the behalf of children (Matt. 18:3 – 6, 10). Christ embraced a child in his arms and said to his disciples, whosoever shall receive a child in the name of Christ, receives Christ (Mark 9:36 – 37). Ephesians 6:1 – 4 teaches kids to obey and honor their parents so that they can live a long life on earth. Parents should teach their children about Christ from birth, so it will never depart from them (Deut. 6:4 – 9;

Prov. 22:6).

CLASS (SOCIOECONOMIC STATUS)

A word that labels people according to their socio-economic status and how they behave (1 Sam. 9:21). There is really no such thing as class. A sanitation truck driver may make more money than a secretary who works for a C.E.O. Therefore, class cannot be defined by salary or position. A millionaire professional football player earns more money than doctors and social workers who help people, but the football player mainly entertains people. It is possible for people without a college degree to be the richest person in the world. Also, just because a person is rich or educated does not mean that they know how to behave.

A schoolteacher makes a lot less money than a medical doctor and a professional athlete, but if it was not for the schoolteacher the doctor and the professional athlete would not exist. Regarding the professional athlete, the world can do without their talents, but the world cannot do without school-teachers, doctors, and people who pick up and haul away our trash. Some sanitary workers have good employer provided benefits such as medical and dental insurance, and retirement plans, while some highly paid consultants in certain professions make a lot of money but must purchase their own insurance and be self – disciplined enough to save for retirement. There are many professions that allow people to earn a high yearly income, but they are not required to help anyone. Helping people is not part of their job description. But there are high paying professions and low paying professions that require their employees to help people, and it is part of their job description. The latter is higher – class than people who make a lot of money but do not help poor people and working – class people. Christ left his riches in heaven to live a poverty – stricken life among poor people and working – class people so that he could be like most people on earth and not like the few rich, powerful, and politically correct people on earth (2 Cor. 8:9; Phil. 4:19; Lev. 12:6 – 8; Luke 2:21 – 24; Rom. 15:1 – 3).

What we really have is poor people thinking that middle – class people have a high level of buying power, middle – class people thinking that rich people have an even higher level of buying power, and rich people trying to keep up with each other. Regarding poor people, middle – class people, and working – class people, having good consumer credit causes a person to appear to have a lot of money, which is good, but they may not have the amount of money that other people think that they have. Good credit goes farther than having plenty of money with bad credit. Therefore, having good credit can be classier than being rich, reckless, and irresponsible. There are also people with what is called "old money," who are families that have been rich for generations.

Christ favors people from low socioeconomic levels, and not many so – called high – class people are called by God (1 Cor. 1:19 – 31). People from all different backgrounds are called to salvation, but not many worldly – wise people are called to lead in a holy and sanctified manner (Acts 17:2 – 4, 12).

David was from an average family, and he was a little boy who tended to livestock (1 Sam. 16:1, 13, 19 – 23). Esther was told by her adopted father not to reveal her family name, because that could have placed her at a disadvantage while competing with other beautiful women who were attempting to be chosen by a king (Est. 2:8 – 11). When Gideon was called by the Lord to do a service, Gideon told God that he was from a poor family and that he was the least of his family members, but that did not matter to God, and God still chose him (Judg. 6:14 – 16).

Christ also teaches us how to handle not being physically attractive, and the Bible tells us that Christ was not physically attractive nor was he handsome (Isa. 52:13–15, 53; Heb. 2:16–18; 4:15; 1 Pet. 2:22). God the Son chose not to visit the earth as a handsome man because people would have favored him for good looks and not because he is the Son of God. And he did not visit the earth as a middle – class person, a rich person, or a powerful politician because people would have favored him for those reasons. Christ left his riches in glory to live on earth with people who have regular jobs and with poor people (2 Cor. 8:9; Phil. 4:19; Lev. 12:6 – 8; Luke 2:21 – 24; Rom. 15:1 – 3).

See also COMMON PEOPLE.

COMFORT

God is the God of all comfort, and we should comfort people who need comforting, just as God has comforted us (2 Cor. 1:3 - 4; 1 Thess. 5:11). The Lord gives the Holy Ghost, also called the Holy Spirit, to people who obey him (Acts 5:32; Luke 11:13; Joh. 14:13 – 18, 26 – 27 and Joh. 1:1, 14; Col. 3:16; 1 Joh. 2:5, 7, 14).

God fills them with the Holy Ghost, which means that God the Holy Ghost dwells inside their bodies and he is called the Comforter, and God sends the Holy Ghost in the name of Christ. Even people who are not obedient or righteous enough to be filled with the Holy Ghost still receive comfort from God when the Holy Ghost dwells with them outside their bodies. The Bible says that we should walk in the fear of the Lord and in the comfort of the Holy Ghost (Joh. 14:16 – 26; 15:26 – 27; 16:7 – 16; Acts 9:31; 2 Pet. 2; Ps. 94:19; 2 Thess. 2:16 – 17; Jude 1).

A good spouse comforts their mate after the mate's parents die (Gen. 24:67).

People indebted and distressed followed King David (1 Sam. 22:1 – 2).

God's rod of righteousness comforts you (2 Sam. 7:13 – 15; Ps. 23:4; 45:6; 89:30 – 34; 2 Thess. 2:8; Isa. 11:1 – 5; Heb. 1:8; Rev. 12:5; 19:15).

Hezekiah spoke comfortably to the Levites (king spoke comfortably to ministers (2 Chron. 30:22).

Spoke comfortably to them, be strong and courageous, don't be afraid (2 Chron. 32:6 – 8).

Don't cry nor be sorrowful, because joy in the Lord is your strength (Neh. 8:9 – 12).

Job's family, friends, and acquaintances comforted him after God revived him (Job 1; 2:1 –3, 8 – 10; 13:15 – 16; 31:13 – 23; 42:11).

Job said that his friends were not good comforters during tribulations (Job 2; 4:1 – 8; 16:2; 27:1 –12; 32:1 – 10; 34:34 – 37; 42:7 – 9).

The righteous man Job comforted mourners (Job 29:25).

Helping the poor (Job 36:15).

While thinking you should conclude that God's comfort delights the soul (Ps. 94:19).

My comfort in my affliction (Ps. 119:50).

I remember God's past judgments, and have comforted myself (Ps. 119:52).

Kindness be for my comfort (Ps. 119:76).

When will thou comfort me? (Ps. 119:82).

A good word (Prov. 12:25).

A soft answer (Prov. 15:1).

Resting in the grave brings more comfort than that of oppressors & the oppressed (Eccles. 4:1 – 3).

God's anger is turned away, and he comforts me (Isa. 12:1).

Comfort my people, says the Lord (Isa. 40:1).

Speak comfortably to Jerusalem, they received double punishment for their sins (Isa. 40:2).

Lord has comforted his people after they said that God had forgotten them (Isa. 49:13 – 15).

Parents may forsake and forget you, but God will never forsake nor forget you (Isa. 49:13 – 15).

God says, "Be not afraid of man, I, even I, am he who comforts you (Isa. 51:12).

I have seen his ways, and will heal and lead him, and comfort him and his mourners (Isa. 57:18).

Comfort all who mourn (Isa. 61:2).

As a good mother comforts you, so will God Comfort you (Isa. 66:13).

So will I comfort you (Isa. 66:13).

Being in trouble with God causes great discomfort (Jer. 16:5, 7 – 8).

Mourning into joy, and will comfort them, rejoice from sorrow, being satisfied (Jer. 31:13 – 14).

Lovers and friends become enemies, and no one to give comfort (Lam. 1:2 – 3, 8 – 9, 16 – 17).

God finds comfort when he keeps his promise to punish and destroy (Ezek. 5:13; Ps. 119:126; Job 37:7; Hos. 4:1–2; Isa. 14:24; 46:9–10; 55:10–11; Jer. 23:20; Ezek. 5:13; 6:9–10; 12:21–28; 22:14; 24:13–14; Dan. 9:12–14; Matt. 24:32–44; 2 Pet. 3:6–14; 2 Kings 10:1).

God comforts us after he destroys, and he does not destroy without cause (Ezek. 14:22 – 23).

God cause people to be ashamed after they provide sinful sexual comfort to others (Ezek. 16:54).

Speak comfortably to her, a door of hope (Hos. 2:14 – 15).

Good words and comfortable words (Zech. 1:13).

Blessed are they who mourn, for they shall be comforted (Matt. 5:4).

Comfort of the Holy Ghost (Acts 9:31).

Comfort of the scriptures (Rom. 15:4).

Prophecies are for both warnings and comfort (1 Cor. 14:3).

The God of all comfort (2 Cor. 1:3).

Be able to comfort them (2 Cor. 1:4).

Forgive him, and comfort him (2 Cor. 2:7).

I am filled with comfort, exceedingly joyful, in all our tribulation (2 Cor. 7:4).

We were comforted in your comfort (2 Cor. 7:13).

Be of good comfort, be of one mind, live in peace (2 Cor. 13:11).

He might comfort your hearts (Eph. 6:22).

If any consolation in Christ, if any comfort of love, if any fellowship of the Spirit (Phil. 2:1).

I also may be of good comfort, when I know your state (Phil. 2:19).

Their hearts may be comforted, being knitted together in love

(Col. 2:2).

Comfort you concerning your faith (1 Thess. 3:2).

Comfort one another with these words regarding judgment day (1 Thess. 4:13 – 18).

Comfort yourselves together (1 Thess. 5:11).

Comfort the feebleminded (1 Thess. 5:14).

Comfort your hearts and establish you in every good word and work (2 Thess. 2:17).

See also *SORROW; JOY; HAPPINESS; PROTECTION; COUR-AGE.*

COMMON PEOPLE

Christ calls common people more often than he calls the rich, powerful, and politically connected people, because working class, middle – class, and poor people are usually humbler and trust in the Lord more often (1 Cor. 1:19 – 31; Jer. 9:23 – 24). Christ says that if we are not nice, helpful, gracious, and merciful to people who do not have a high socioeconomic status, it is the same as neglecting the Lord (Matt. 25:35 – 45). Some of the apostles were working – class people (Matt. 4:18 – 22). And so – called common people in many cities heard Christ gladly (Mark 12:37).

Ungodly people in the Bible considered it to be a disgrace for people of royalty or high social status to be buried in graveyards with common people, or to be put in prison with them (Jer. 26:23; Acts 5:18). But Christ was buried alongside common people, poor people, working class people, wicked people, and rich people, because Christ the Son of man and God are not high – minded nor arrogant (Isa. 53; Matt. 27:57 – 60). Let not the powerful glorify their power. Let not the highly intelligent glorify their intelligence. Let not the rich glorify their wealth, but let them who glorifies, glorify this, that they know and understand that the Lord exercises lovingkindness, justice, proper judgment, and righteousness on earth, and that God delights in these things (Jer. 9:23 - 24).

Some common people in the Bible were simply sinners who sinned but were not evil or wicked people, and people of low social status (Lev. 4:27; Ezek. 23:42). The Bible uses the words "common people" in some scriptures to refer to sinners, evil, wicked, base, and low – level people, but are not the same as the common people who the Bible identifies are working class, middle – class, and poor people (Acts 17:5; Job 30:8; Isa. 3:5; Mal. 2:9).

See also *CLASS*.

CONFIDENCE

Full of trust. Let they who think they stand take heed to God's warnings, least they fall (1 Cor. 10:12). Therefore, do not be overconfident, and do not get yourself into anything that you cannot get yourself out of, in Christ's name. If adversity does happen due to over confidence, do not quit, unless it was a bad idea from the start. Christians walk in spiritual darkness who claim to love, fear, and trust God while also having low confidence, fear, low self – esteem, and lack of courage (Isa. 50:10; 2 Kings 17:20 – 41. So, whether you lack confidence or are overconfident, you can do nothing for long without Christ (Joh. 3:27; 15:1 – 14; Dan. 11:33 – 35; Jude 1:24). And you can do all things through Christ who strengthens you (Phil. 4:11 – 13; 2 Cor. 6:3 – 10).

See also *WITH; HELP; HOPE; ALONE; KEEPER; MORE THAN YOU CAN BEAR; ADVERSITY; SUCCESS; CONQUEROR; COURAGE*.

CONQUERORS (OVERCOMERS)

People who stand for God's Word are not simply conquerors, but "more" than conquerors, with Christ who loves them (Rom. 8:37; Rev. 6:2; 2 Cor. 2:14; Prov. 16:32; Eccles. 7:19).

They conquer more than battles of military warfare, but also of evil and wicked spiritual warfare in high ranking dark evil principalities, in addition to conquering drug addiction, sex addiction, cigarettes, alcohol, hate, lust, being outcasted, fatherless, motherless, being a convict, being an ex – convict, being on trial facing criminal conviction, financial problems, and all problems known to the entire history of mankind (Matt. 28:18; 1 Cor. 15:24 – 28; Eph. 1:20 – 23; Phil. 2:9; Ps. 8; Heb. 2:5 – 9; Joh. 16:15).

Therefore, we must put on the whole armor of God, including the breastplate of righteousness (Eph. 6:10 – 18; Rom. 13:12; 2 Cor. 6:7; 1 Thess. 5:6 – 11; Ps. 3:3; 119:114).

See also *VICTORY*.

COURAGE

Strength, heart (2 Chron. 32:7; Am. 2:16). God told Moses to encourage Joshua before he became the successor of Moses (Deut. 1:38; 3:28). When people persecuted Elijah for serving the Lord, God told him that he was not alone and that he was in the presence of God and angels (1 Kings 19:1 – 18; 2 Kings 6:14 – 17. Jeremiah was persecuted so much that he said he would not speak again in God's name, nor mention the name of God, but Jeremiah could not resist openly praising God (Jer. 20:8 – 9). God encourages us continually in the Bible to be strong and of good courage, and to fear not, and that the Lord will be with you wherever you may go. And that Christ will not fail you nor forsake you, and Christ will fulfill his purpose in you and fulfill your desires that are not anti - God desires (Num. 13:20; Deut. 31:6 – 7, 23; Josh. 1:6, 9, 18; 10:25; Isa. 41:6; 1 Chron. 22:13; 28:20; Ezra 10:4).

God sometime takes courage out of the hearts of your enemies and even causes some of them to do good things for you (Josh. 2:8 - 16).

One Bible scripture says to males, be strong and of good courage, and be men for our people and for the cities of our God, and let God do what is good in his mind (2 Sam. 10:12; 1 Chron. 19:13). All things work together for good to people who love God and are called according to his purpose (Rom. 8:28). God reveals the mystery of his will to us according to his pleasure and his purpose (Eph. 1:9 – 11). It also takes courage to teach and preach the strict true Word of God to people in churches, preaching it in season and out of season, even though most people refuse to accept sound and strong doctrine, turning away from the truth. And have hired weak preachers to tell them only what they want to hear (2 Tim. 4:1 – 5; 2 Chron. 15:8). God has saved us and called us with a holy calling, not according to our works, but according to his own purpose and grace through Christ before the world was even created (2 Tim. 1:9). This grace involves more than some people going to heaven when they do not deserve to go to heaven, but also to receive gifts and desires on earth that we sometimes do not deserve. The Bible also says to deal courageously, and the Lord shall be with the good that you do (2 Chron. 19:11). Delight yourself in the Lord and he shall give you the desires of your heart (Ps. 37:4; 145:19). Wait on the Lord and he shall strengthen your heart, all you who hope in the Lord (Ps. 10:17; 20:1 – 4; 21:2; 37:4 – 8; 145:16, 19; Mark 11:24; Eccles. 11:9).

For more encouraging scriptures, please read the books of Psalms and Proverbs. See also *WITH; HELP; ENCOURAGEMENT; COMFORT; HOPE; CONFIDENCE.*

CRYING

When some people say that men should not cry, they are incorrect, because even good strong men in the Bible cried while repenting unto God, while in pain, while in joy, when a family member or friend died, and at numerous other times, including many times in the books of Psalms, Jeremiah, and Lamentations (Heb. 12:13 – 16; Gen. 27; 33:1 – 17; 35:29; 2 Sam. 1:17).

If men do not live for Christ and serve him, they will cry either before they die, or on judgment day when it will be too late to cry (Matt. 13:36 – 43; Rev. 22:10 – 13; Acts 24:15; Dan. 12:1 – 3; Ezek. 18:19 – 32; 2 Thess. 1:4 – 12).

God is the God of all mercies, and he has compassion for people who genuinely cry (Joh. 11:33; 2 Cor. 1:3 – 4; Ps. 106:7; Isa. 49:13). Especially when we cry with a contrite heart and in repentance towards God, having godly fear and godly sorrow for our wrong doings (Isa. 57:15; 66:1-2; Ezra 9:6; 2 Cor. 7:9 – 10; Ps. 34:15 – 18; 38:15 – 18; 51:17; 85:8; Ezek. 18:21 – 22.)

God asks, "When will you cry out to me, the guide of your life from your youth? You have spoken and done evil things" (Jer. 3:3 – 5). Just as we should sometimes pray in private and not always openly, we should also cry in private but sometimes among true family members and true friends. Crying out to God does not always involve tears, but making loud appeals to God for help is also a form of crying out, but it still must be sincere. And it is best to not hold back tears when appealing to God. If a person chooses to hold back tears while talking to humans, that can be all right (Matt. 20:30 – 34; Gen. 21:14 – 20; Exod. 3:7). Whether you cry alone or cry in the presence of others, God says, "When you sow and plant in tears, you shall reap and gather in joy. They who weep while bearing precious seeds shall without any doubts have joy in the future (Ps. 126). David said, "I have been young and now I am old, but I have never seen the righteous forsaken, nor their children begging for bread" (Ps. 37:25; 71).

When we need help, we should not be ashamed or too hardhearted to cry out to Christ (Mark 10:46 – 52). Christians who do not occasionally cry out to Christ are either hard-hearted, hypocrites, or lacking knowledge (Job 36:13; 27:8 – 10; Isa. 57:13). However, just because you do not see a person cry out does not mean that they are not doing so in private (Matt. 6:6). Sometimes we do not get what we need because we simply ask, instead of crying out (2 Chron. 20:9). Sometimes we must cry out like a pregnant woman suffering from labor pain (Isa. 26:16 – 17. Jer. 4:31; 5:1). Some people's sins are so great that God will not hear their cry in terms of what they want, but he gives them what he knows that they need (Jer. 30:15; Ezek. 8:18; Matt. 5:43–48; Luke 6:35; Acts 14:8–18; Ps. 17:13–15; Neh. 9:35–39; Ps. 145:9–10; Deut. 9:4–7; 10:17–22; Eccles. 9:1 – 3).

When this happens, they need to repent, not for what they want, but to save their soul (Acts 17:29 – 31; 2:36 – 42). We must cry out for knowledge sometimes, and hope in the Word of God (Prov. 2:3 – 5; 119:145 – 148). Cry out daily if necessary, and God will answer (Ps. 55:16 – 17; 84:2; 86:3; Isa. 30:19; 58:9). But it is impossible to please God without faith (Heb. 6:1 – 6; 11:1, 6; Luke 18:1 – 8). Bible scripture says, "Let my soul live, and it shall praise thee, and let thy judgments help me. I have gone astray like a lost sheep. I do not forget your commandments" (Ps. 119:173 – 176). God sometimes does not hear our cry because we chose to do things that he told us not to do (1 Sam. 8:4 – 18). The Bible says, "Exercise justice, and have mercy and compassion on people, and oppress not the widow, fatherless, outsider, nor the poor. They refused to obey and would not listen and made their hearts as adamant as stone. Therefore, it came to pass that as God cried out to them, and they would not hear, God did not hear when they cried out to him" (Zech. 7:8 – 14).

DIGGING DITCHES

It has been said that when your enemy digs one ditch, they should dig two, because they will fall into one themselves, but the Bible tells us that the wicked are sunk down in the same one ditch that they made for someone else. They are caught in their own net that they laid for someone else, and they are snared by the work of their own hands (Ps. 7:15; 9:15 – 16; 10:2; Prov. 26:27; 28:10). The Prophet Jeremiah asked God to remove his wrath from upon the people who were rebellious towards God, but those same people dug a pit, a grave, for Jeremiah (Jer. 18:20). And when the blind leads the blind, they both fall into a ditch. This means that spiritually ignorant people and unwise people lead each other into a ditch (Matt. 15:13 – 14).

See also *ENEMIES*.

ENCOURAGEMENT

To strengthen by urging to go forward, even during adverse or very challenging times (Deut. 1:38; 3:28; Judg. 20:22; 1 Sam. 30:6; 2 Sam. 11:25; 1 Chron. 28:19 – 20; 2 Chron. 31:4; 35:2; Ps. 64:5; Isa. 41:7; Job 22:29).

God is the lifter up of our heads (Ps. 3). We should encourage others to do good, and not to do bad (Ps. 23; 64:5). We must not drown ourselves in sorrow, because sorrow of the heart breaks the spirit (Prov. 15:13). The spirit of a person will sustain them in sickness, but who can bear a broken spirit (Prov. 18:14). The Bible says, "A merry heart does good like medicine, but a broken spirit dries the bones" (Prov. 17:22; 18:14).

See also *COURAGE; HELP; COMFORT; HOPE; WITH.*

ENEMIES

An adversary, an opponent, an oppressor (Ps. 78:61). God can be an enemy to certain people when they live in sin, or are anti – Christian, or do evil things (Jer. 21:5; Lam. 2:5; Ps. 106:42). God sometimes sends our enemies against us when we sin willfully (2 Chron. 12:1 – 2; Num. 14:11 – 20; 24:11; Josh. 7:7 – 13).

Sometimes our enemies feel that they are doing nothing wrong when they afflict Christians, because those Christians have sinned against God and did not appear to be Christians based on their actions (Jer.50:7). Concerning God's people, "Rejoice not against me, O my enemy, when I fall, I shall arise. When I sit in darkness, the Lord shall be a light unto me. I will bear the indignation of the Lord because I have sinned against him. Until he pleads my cause, and executes judgment for me, he will bring me forth to the light, and I shall behold his right-eousness. Then she and he who is my enemy shall see it and be ashamed" (Mic. 7:8 – 9).

Christ did not come to condemn the world, but people who do not believe in him are already condemned, because they condemn themselves due to hating the light of truth and loving darkness. Their ways are evil, and coming to the light would expose their sinful ways. But when people repent, the light exposes their righteousness, and they have nothing to hide (Joh. 3:17 – 21). Christ told people and he is telling us, "I am the light of the world. They who follow me shall not walk in darkness but have the light of life" (Joh. 8:2 – 12 and John 1:1 – 14). Although one of Job's friends was wrong when he accused Job of being sick due to sin, he was right when he said that the wicked are driven from the light by God because they hate the light anyway, and that they are chased into darkness and out of the world, meaning into the grave (Job 18:17 – 18). God shall protect his saints, but the wicked shall be ashamed and silent in a cold dark grave (1 Sam. 2:9; Ps. 31:17).

God makes us stronger than our enemies (Ps. 105:24). But we must not rejoice in the presence of our enemies when they are punished by God, or God will ease their punishment and take away his wrath from them, because he is "just" and "merciful" to everyone (Prov. 24:17 – 23; Matt. 5:44 – 48; Luke 6:34 – 35; Deut. 10:17 – 22; Eccles.9:1 – 3).

Job said he did not rejoice at the destruction of people who hated him, neither did he allow his mouth to sin by wishing a curse upon his enemies (Job 31:29 – 30). Job also said that he wept when others were in trouble, and for the poor, but when he became afflicted and expected good, evil came to him (Job 30:25 – 31). People who are glad when they see others in trouble shall not go unpunished (Prov. 17:5). We should not rejoice when our enemies fall in the future (Prov. 17:5; 24:17 – 20; Job 31:29 – 30). However, there is another scripture that says that the righteous shall rejoice when they see God's vengeance on the wicked, and that they will wash their feet in the blood of the wicked. This scripture means that we can sometimes rejoice when we defeat our enemies in battle, or while fighting for our lives in self – defense (Ps. 58:10; 2 Chron. 20:27). Obviously, God has often allowed the enemies of Christians to rejoice in their presence as punishment for disobeying his Word (Lam. 2:17; 1 Sam. 2:1; 30:16). But David prayed and asked God to not allow his enemies to continue to rejoice in his presence (Ps. 35:18 – 28). And most certainly, it is totally alright to thank the Lord for your blessings in the presence of your enemies and heathens (2 Sam. 22:50; Ps. 18:48 – 49; Isa. 61:6). David said, "Thou prepared a table before me in the presence of my enemies" (Ps. 23). And because God blesses us in the presence of our enemies and non – believers, we must certainly stand for his Word and bless Christ openly (Ps. 31:19 and Ps.

23; 1 Pet. 3:15).

Wait on the Lord, and keep his way, and he shall exalt you, and when the wicked are cut off, you shall see it or hear about it (Ps. 37:34). But God's way is to not rejoice at them being cut off, because God has no pleasure in killing sinners and backsliders, but because it is impossible for God to lie, or to speak something that will not happen, he has to keep his Word to send death due to sin (Ezek. 18:19 – 32, 33:11, 19 – 20; Matt. 18:11 – 14; Lam. 3:31 – 33; 1 Tim. 2:4; 2 Pet. 3:9).

God also has no pleasure in Christians who draw back and who backslide (Heb. 10:35 – 39). Remember, regarding life and death, blessings and adversity, prosperity, and affliction, and regarding everything, everyone, and every place, it is impossible for God to lie (Heb. 6:18; Num. 23:19; Deut. 32:4; 1 Sam. 15:29; Ps. 89:35; 92:15; Jer. 15:18; Tit. 1:2).

Christ tells us to love our enemies and bless people who curse us (Matt. 5:43 – 48). Smile at your enemies in a non-provocative way (1 Sam. 2:1). Christ blessed his enemies when he said during his crucifixion, "Forgive them Father for they know not what they do" (Luke 23:34; Acts 3:12 – 17). Christ went against his own mother at one point for something that she had done outside of the will of God, and he went against his younger brothers and sisters, the children who Mary birthed after Christ was born, because they did not believe in him during the same time that the Jews sought to kill him for speaking against the evil practices of the world (Matt. 12:46 – 50; Joh. 7:1 – 5). King Asa removed his mother from being queen because she practiced sin and idolatry (1 Kings 15:13). Levi did not show respect of persons to his father, mother, brother, or own children, but he demanded that they observe the Word of the Lord (Deut. 33:9). True religion is to go unspotted from worldly affairs, and to help the poor, widows, and the fatherless (James 1:26–27; Isa. 1:15 – 20). Christ says, "I have overcome the world," and greater is Christ in you than they who are in the world (Joh. 16:33; 1 Joh.4:4). But if after you have escaped the pollutions of the world, and become entangled again in the world, your latter end will be worse than the beginning (2 Pet. 2:20; 1 Joh. 5:4 – 5). The world loves its own people, and worldly people sometimes do not love the true people of God because God's real people stand with him and for his Word regardless of anything (James 4:2 – 4; Joh. 1:10 – 12; 15:18 – 19; 1 Joh. 2:15 – 17; 3:13; Phil. 3:16 – 21; Rom. 8:7).

The Bible says that Christ's friends tried to physically harm him and accused him of being evil (Mark 3:20 – 35). Notice, this scripture begins with his friends trying to harm him and ends with his mother and younger siblings offending him. The Bible tells us to not put our trust in a friend, and do not tell a certain type of spouse certain things, because a person's enemies shall be of their own household (Matt. 10:33 – 39; Mal. 7:5 – 10; Ps. 101:1 – 4, 7; Prov. 30:11). A lot of people know that the world loves its own, but they do not know that the Bible also says that a friend of the world is an enemy to God (James 4:2 – 4; Joh. 1:10 – 12; 15:18 – 19; 1 Joh. 2:15 – 17; 3:13; Phil. 3:16 – 21; Rom. 8:7).

Apostle Paul said that he was crucified from the world and the world from him (Gal. 6:14). Christ tells us to love our enemies, just as Christ loves his enemies, and he even asked God to forgive the people who killed him (Luke 23:34; Acts 3:12 – 17). And it is possible to be blessed and still be an enemy of God. Blessings come to the just and the unjust, the unthankful and the evil, because God is perfect in his wrath but also in his grace and mercy, but people should not expect to ride grace and mercy all the way to heaven. That will not work for most people (Deut. 9:4 – 7; 10:17 – 22; Ezek. 29:17 – 20; Matt. 5:43 – 48; Luke 6:35; Acts 14:8 – 18; Ps. 17:13 – 15; Neh. 9:35 – 39; Ps. 145:9 – 10).

People who thank, praise, and glorify God receive blessings from God, and glorifying and praising God is a form of sacrifice, but obedience is better than sacrifice (1 Sam. 15:22; Matt. 9:10 – 13; 23:23; Prov. 21:3; Ps. 4:5; 40:6 – 8: Hos. 6:6; Mic. 6:7; Heb. 13:15).

Not everyone who praises and glorifies God will go to heaven, but they who obey God will inherit the kingdom of God (Matt. 7:21 – 23; Mic. 3:11). Psalms 34:1 says, "I will bless the Lord at all times, his praise shall continually be in my mouth." But anyone can praise God and say Lord, Lord (Matt. 7:21 – 23; Mic.3:11). This is one reason another scripture says, "Blessed are they who keep justice, and who does righteousness at all times" (Ps. 106:3; 119:20). Be doers of the word and not just hearers only (James 1:22 – 27; Matt. 13:1 – 23; Acts 17:11 – 12; Ps. 81:10 – 16; Jer. 15:15 – 21; Rev. 10:9 – 11).

We must receive the Word of God in our hearts after we hear it, and people usually do what is in their heart, because where your treasure is, there shall your heart be as well (Ezek. 3:10; Luke 12:32 – 34; Rom.2:6 – 11; 8:5; 1 Kings 3:7 – 15; Heb. 11:24 – 27).

They who live godly in Christ Jesus shall suffer persecution like Christ suffered from his enemies (2 Tim. 3:11 – 13; Ezek. 14:6 – 11; Heb. 3:7 – 13; Ps. 38:9 – 22; Jer. 15:15 – 21 Joh. 16:20).

If you are a Christian who is not persecuted, that means you are not living according to the Word of God, and you are not standing for the Word of God, therefore the devil has no reason to cause you to have enemies who would hinder you.

See also *ADVERSITY; FRIENDS; BLESINGS; DECEPTION; BE-TRAYAL; ENVY.*

ENVY

Painful or resentful awareness of another person's power, possessions, success, or advantage with a desire to possess that same power, possessions, success, or advantage (Ps. 37:1; 73:3; 106:16; Num. 12; Prov. 24:1; Eccles. 4:4; 1 Pet. 2:1).

Love does not envy (1 Cor. 13:4 – 5). One reason that Christ was killed was because certain people envied him (Matt. 27:18). A sound heart is life to the body, but envy is rottenness to the bones (Prov. 14:30). We should not envy nor seek sinners' peace or prosperity (Deut. 23:6; Ps. 37).

See also *ENEMIES*.

FAILURE

If you sin willfully or habitually, or join with sinners, God may cause you to fail or allow you to fail (2 Chron. 20:35 – 37; Luke 2:34; Rev. 2:1 – 5). Because we can do nothing effectively, efficiently, and consistently without Christ (Joh. 3:27; 15:1 – 14; Dan. 11:33 – 35; Jude 1:24).

Without Christ we eventually fail or have plenty of trouble with our success, either spiritually, earthly, carnally, and certainly worldly (2 Pet. 1:10; 3:17; 1 Cor. 10:12; Isa. 31:3; Heb. 6:1 – 6; Jer. 23:12; Hos. 4:14).

Enemies and persecutors cannot cause saints and true and real Christians to fail (Mic. 7:8; Rom. 8:31). Nothing good shall fail (Josh. 23:14). When God allows one door to close, he opens another (1 Cor. 10:12; 2 Pet. 1:2 – 10; Phil. 3:13 – 15). People who obey the Word of God, including what is in the following scriptures, shall never be moved, and God will uphold them (Ps. 15; 24:4; 94:18 – 19; Matt. 5:33 – 37; James 5:12).

The steps of a righteous person are ordered by the Lord, and they delight in Christ. Even though they may fall, they shall never be totally and utterly cast down, because God upholds them with his mighty and powerful hand (Ps. 37:23 – 24).

See also *FALL; ADVERSITY; SUCCESS; COURAGE; CONFIDENCE.*

Not fail you, nor forsake (Deut. 31:6, 8).
I will not fail you, nor (Josh. 1:5).
Walk before me in truth with all their heart and with all their soul, there shall not fail (1 Kings 2:4).

Eyes of the wicked shall fail, and they shall not escape (Job 11:20).

My eyes fail from searching your Word, when will you comfort me (Ps. 119:82).

Shall fall down, and they shall fail together (Isa. 31:3).

Search from the book of the Lord, and read: Not one of these shall fail (Isa. 34:16).

Not fail nor be discouraged (Isa. 42:4).

Neither will I always be angry, for the spirit would fail before me, and the souls that I (Isa. 57:16).

And every vision fails (Ezek. 12:22).

Easier for heaven and earth to pass away than for one tittle of the law to fail (Luke 16:17).

Prophesies, they shall fail (1 Cor. 13:8).

You are the same, and your years shall not fail (Heb. 1:12).

Fail the grace of God (Heb. 12:15).

FAITHFULNESS

Loyal. Firm in keeping promises (1 Sam. 26:23; Ps. 40:10; 92:2; Isa. 11:5; 25:1). God's mercy is new every morning, and his compassion never fails. Great is His faithfulness (Lam. 3:22 – 23). God's faithfulness never fails while he protects us from our enemies, and if our children rebel against the Lord, he will punish them and keep loving them (Ps. 89:20 – 33). God is faithful to do all the good things towards us that he promises (1 Thess. 5:24; Jer. 32:37 – 44). But scripture says that God is faithful, and righteous (Isa. 11:4 – 5). Which means that we must be righteous as well, because although he is faithful to protect and bless us, he is also right when he chastises us for unrighteousness (Isa. 55:10 – 11 and Isa. 14:24; 46:9 – 10; Jer. 23:20; Ezek. 6:9 – 10; Matt. 24:32 – 44; 2 Pet. 3:6 – 14).

God is faithful to us, and we must be faithful to him (Deut. 7:9; Ps. 31:21 – 24). However, the Bible says that God is also faithful and truthful about sending people to hell (Rev. 20:5 – 8, 27; 22:14 – 15).

When God says something, he shall do it (Isa. 55:11; 46:9 – 10; Jer. 23:20; Heb. 6:18; Num. 23:19; Deut. 32:4; 1 Sam. 15:29; Ps. 89:35; 92:15; Jer. 15:18; Tit. 1:2).

The Bible even says that whoso is wise, and will observe God's mercy, goodness, and his punishments, they shall under-stand the lovingkindness of the Lord (Ps. 107). When God holds his peace through grace and punishes us lightly, that does not cause some people to fear him (Rom. 2:4 – 6; Isa. 57:10 – 11). Most people want to hear that God is good and that he does not punish us. The Bible says that God is good, and does good, and that we should ask him to teach us his Word and his ways (Ps. 119:68). However, God himself says that his goodness towards us does not cause us to fear or obey him, but that it should (Isa. 57:11 – 13; Hos. 3:5).

Judgment from God on judgment day will begin with people who claim to be Christians, and if the righteous scarcely go to heaven, where shall the sinner, ungodly, and the hypocrite appear? Let them who suffer according to the will of God commit the keeping of their souls to Christ in well doing, as unto a faithful Creator (1 Pet. 4).

God says that he will forgive our sins and cleanse us of our sinful acts if we allow him to do so, and when people hear the good that God does towards us, people shall fear God for his goodness and the prosperity that he provides (Jer. 33:8 – 9). Thus again, God's goodness and grace should not be taken for granted and should cause us to fear God. His goodness does not give us a path to disobedience.

An Egyptian king asked the Israelite women to kill all male babies to extinguish the Hebrew population, but the ladies feared God and not man, so God gave them houses for their fear of him (Exod. 1:8 – 21). Not fearing God causes us to suffer on earth and fall short of heaven (Heb. 4:1; Deut. 28). The Bible says, let them who think they stand take heed, or they too will fall (1 Cor. 10:1 – 14). God is good, but how good are you to God? We were created to serve and to glorify God (Isa. 43:7, 20 – 22). When we serve God in holiness, on judgment day, God will say, "Well done, my good and faithful servant" (Matt. 25:23). And you shall receive a crown of life because those of us who are with Christ even in hard times, are called, chosen, and faithful (Rev. 2:10; 17:14).

God will test us by putting us through trials, but he never tempts us. We are tempted by humans, human's inventions, our own desires, or the devil, but God is faithful and will not allow us to be tempted above what we are able to withstand (1 Cor. 10:12 – 13). The Lord is faithful, who will establish you and keep you from sin and evil (2 Thess. 3:3). God made all of us righteous, but mankind seeks many evil inventions (Eccles. 7:26 – 29; Ps. 33:13 – 15). While we use those evil inventions, God punishes us, but he is ready to forgive if we repent and turn away from the evil practices of those inventions (Ps. 106:29, 39 – 43). The Bible says, "You answered them, O Lord God, you are God who forgave them, though you punished them for their inventions" (Ps. 99:8). God says that people who participate with evil inventions are worthy of death (Rom. 1:21 – 32). And they will die if they do not repent and live a righteous life, because the consequences and wages of sin is death (Rom. 6:23; Ezek. 7:13; 18:4).

The Bible says let us not tempt Christ as idolaters, fornicators, complainers, and other sinners did in the wilderness who died for their sins. Those are examples and warnings to us (1 Cor. 10:5 – 11). People are tempted when they are drawn away by their own lust and enticed. When lust is conceived, it brings forth sin, and sin brings forth death (James 1:12 – 16; Rom. 6:23). This is one reason that the Bible tells us to not consent when sinners try to entice us (Prov. 1:10 – 19). God once changed his mind about destroying Jerusalem because the people humbled themselves and acknowledged that God is righteous (2 Chron. 12:6 – 8). If we confess our sins, admit that God is right, and that we are wrong, God is faithful to forgive our sins and cleanse us from all unrighteousness. But if we say that any sin is not sin, we call God a liar, and the truth is not in us (Exod. 9:27; 1 Joh. 1:9 – 10). We are not destroyed daily because God's mercy and compassions are new every morning, great is His faithfulness (Lam. 3:22 – 23; Ps. 92:1 – 2; Isa. 33:2).

Christ tells us that he will allow the devil to put some Christians in prison to try them, and there will be tribulations, but be faithful unto death, and Christ shall give you a crown of life (Rev. 2:10). We are partakers with Christ, if we hold the beginning of our confidence steadfast unto the end (Heb. 3:14; Rev. 2:2 – 5; Matt. 13:1 – 23).

Paul while in prison was faithful until he died, and he believed until he was murdered that he would be set free (2 Tim. 4:9 – 18). When people persecute Christ and Christians, they who are with Christ are called, chosen, and faithful (Rev. 17:14).

See also *WITH.*

My servant Moses, he is faithful in all my house (Num. 12:7).

He is God, the faithful God (Deut. 7:9).

He was a faithful man, and feared God more than many (Neh. 7:2).

Help Lord, the godly man ceases. The faithful disappear (Ps. 12:1).

The Lord preserves the faithful (Ps. 31:23).

A faithful person shall abound with blessings (Prov. 28:20).

He was faithful, nor was there any error or fault found in him (Dan. 6:4).

Judah still walks with God, even with the Holy One who is faithful with the saints (Hos. 11:12).

Good and faithful servant (Matt. 25:21 – 23).

They who are faithful over a few things shall be faithful over plenty (Matt. 25:21; Luke 16:10 – 12).

God is faithful, who will not allow you to be tempted 1 Cor. 10:13).

Faithful is he who calls you, who also will do it (1 Thess. 5:24).

The Lord is faithful, who will establish you and keep you from evil (2 Thess. 3:3).

He counted me faithful, putting me into the ministry (1 Tim. 1:12).

This is a faithful saying that Christ came into the world to save sinners (1 Tim. 1:15).

Faithful to God who appointed him, as also Moses was faithful in all his house (Heb. 3:2 – 5).

If we confess our sins to God, he is faithful and just to forgive and to cleanse us (1 Joh. 1:9).

Be faithful until death, and I will give you a crown of life (Rev. 2:10).

They who fight spiritual war against the devil with Christ are called, chosen, and faithful (Rev. 17:14).

Called Faithful and True, and in righteousness he judges and make war (Rev. 19:11).

I make all things new. Write, for these words are true and faithful (Rev. 21:5; 22:6).

FALL

When righteous people fall, that does not necessarily mean they have sinned, because a righteous person may fall seven times, but still pick themselves up. Just as a toddler falls while learning to walk (Prov. 24:16 – 17). In these last and evil days God shall allow some people who understand him to fall, to try them, and to purge them of all impurities and iniquities (Dan. 11:35). The Bible also says that the birth of the Messiah is for the fall and rising again of many people (Luke 2:34). Rejoice not against me, my enemy. When I fall, I shall rise. When I sit in darkness the Lord shall be my light (Mic. 7:8). The Bible says that it is sometimes good that we are afflicted, so we can learn God's ways (Ps. 119:64 – 72). Job fell and was afflicted by God when God took all of Job's children and destroyed most of his property, but Job did not sin, and he learned even more of God's ways (Job 1; 2; 42:7). Job said to God, "Even though you slay me, I still trust in you" (Job 13:15 – 16). Notice that God took the life of Job's children's after Job prayed regularly for his children's safety, but those kids went to heaven because they were not rebellious, and they died by God testing their parent (Job 1:1 – 5).

The Bible warns us when it reminds us that 23,000 people fell in one day due to fornication. In this scripture the word "fell" means that God took their lives, they died (1 Cor. 10:8).

The Lord upholds everyone who falls and lifts everyone who is bowed down (Ps. 94:18 – 19; 145:14). However, even though righteous people fall and rise, evil and wicked people fall into trouble when they fall (Prov. 24:16 – 17). People do not need to look like a witch or a drug dealer to be wicked.

Christ says, "Beware of wolves in sheep's clothing" (Matt. 7:15 – 23; Acts 20:29 – 30). Some hypocrites outwardly appear to be righteous, but within they are full of hypocrisy and sin (Matt. 23:28). And the devil makes himself appear to be good, like a minister of light, and his ministers appear to be ministers of righteousness but are deceptive devils (2 Cor. 11:13 – 15). The Bible teaches us to not rush to be a young minister who may become spiritually arrogant because of their anointing, or one who is not viewed as a holy and sanctified person by sinners, because all such cases can cause a person to fall into the snare and condemnation of the devil (1 Tim. 3:1 – 7). Ministers and any person who loves money too much shall fall into temptation and foolish and hurtful lusting for material and fleshly things, and fall into the snare of the devil, and pierce themselves through with many sorrows (1 Tim. 6:6 – 12). If they fall away from the Word of God, they crucify over again the Son of God and put Christ to an open shame (Heb. 6:1 – 6). Let them who think they stand for God's Word take heed, or they too will fall (1 Cor. 10:12). Beloved, considering that some of you already know these things, while others wrestle with the scriptures, beware, or you also could be led away with the error of the wicked and fall from your own steadfastness (2 Pet. 3:16 – 17).

Finally, the Bible says, "Grace and peace be multiplied unto you through the knowledge of God, and of Christ our Lord. As his divine power has given to us all things that pertain to life and godliness, through the knowledge of him who has called us to glory and virtue. Whereby are given unto us exceeding great and precious promises: that by these you might be partakers of the divine nature, having escaped the corruption that is in the world through lust. And beside this, giving all diligence, add to your faith virtue; and to virtue knowledge; and to knowledge temperance; and to temperance patience; and to patience godliness; and to godliness brotherly kindness; and to brotherly kindness love and charity. For if these things be in you, and abound, you shall neither be barren nor unfruitful in the knowledge of our Lord Jesus Christ. But they who lack these things are blind, and cannot see afar off, and has forgotten that they were purged from their old sins. Sisters and brothers, be diligent to make your calling and election sure, and if you do these things, you shall never fall" (2 Pet. 1:2 – 10).

See also *FAIL; SUCCESS.*

You will not prevail against him but will surely fall before him (Est. 6:13).

O God, let them fall by their own counsels (Ps. 5:10).

Workers of iniquity have fallen and cannot rise (Ps. 36:12).

Though he falls, he shall not totally cast down. For the Lord upholds him with his hand (Ps. 37:24).

They who trusts in riches shall fall but the righteous shall flourish (Prov. 11:28).

They who help sinners shall fall. They shall fall together (Isa. 31:3).

Young men shall completely fall (Isa. 40:30).

Justice stands afar off, and truth is fallen in the streets (Isa. 59:14).

And fall, for I shall bring evil upon them (Jer. 23:12).

Shall instruct many, yet they shall fall by the sword (Dan. 11:33).

Some of them of understanding shall fall, to try them (Dan. 11:35).

You shall fall in one day, and the prophet also shall fall (Hos. 4:5).

They who do not understand shall fall (Hos. 4:14).

Ephraim fall in their iniquity: Judah also shall fall with them (Hos. 5:5).

O Israel, return to the Lord your God, for you have fallen by your iniquity (Hos. 14:1).

Not the least fall to the ground (Am. 9:9).

I will rise up the tabernacle of David that is fallen (Am. 9:11; Acts 15:16).

Rejoice not against me my enemy: When I fall, I shall rise (Mic.

7:8).

Great was the fall of it (Matt. 7:27).

This child is for the fall and rising again of many in Israel (Luke 2:34).

God allowed the temporary fall of black Jews so salvation can also come to Gentiles (Rom. 11:11).

FAVOR

The soul of the wicked desires evil. Their neighbor finds no favor from them (Prov. 21:10). But when a person's ways please the Lord, God causes even their enemies to be at peace with them (Prov. 16:7). If God does not cause your enemies to favor you, he will at least cause them to be at peace with you, even though they are still against you, but this happens when God is pleased with your actions and your lifestyle (Ps. 41:11). When God favors you over your enemies, he has no favor in them, unless you celebrate their fall. Then he withdraws his wrath from them (Josh. 11:20; Prov. 24:17 – 23; Job 31:29 – 30). Good godly understanding causes God to favor you, but the way of sinners is hard (Prov. 13:15). When King Saul became jealous of young David, Saul would not allow David to return to his father. Saul's son and others favored David and helped to protect him from Saul, and Saul's daughter loved and supported David, even though Saul gave her to David in marriage to hinder David. Also noticed how God caused Saul, David's enemy, to place David in high – ranking positions while he hated David (1 Sam. 18). Obviously, God will cause your real friends to favor you too, as was the case when King Hiram of Tyre highly favored David (1 Kings 5:1).

God caused the enemies of Jeremiah to favor him after he was released from prison for speaking God's Word. God also showed favor for the godly poor people of the land who slaveholders did not take into slavery after everyone else was taken (Jer. 15:10 – 11; 39:8 – 18; 40:1 – 7; Ps. 106:41 – 47).

Moses was hidden by his mother when he was an infant because the king of the land attempted to kill all the first – born males to ensure that Moses would not become an adult and deliver the slaves out of bondage. When his mother sent the infant down river in a floating basket while Moses's older sister followed from a distance to ensure that the baby Moses would be found by a caring person, the baby was found by the king's daughter who adopted Moses. The king's daughter unknowingly hired Moses's biological mother who was a slave but was now being paid to be Moses 'nanny (Exod. 2:1 – 15; 7:1; 11:2 – 3). Hallelujah. Glory be to God Almighty. God caused Moses to lead his people out of slavery from Egypt, and God showed the Egyptians openly how much he favored the Hebrews (Exod. 11:3; 12:36). Sometimes, as ended up temporarily happening to Moses, our service to God becomes seemingly so hard that we think God no longer favors us, but God does not withdraw his favor unless we rebel against the Lord (Exod. 17:7; Num. 11:11; Ps. 78:10 – 72; Heb. 3:7 – 19; 4:1 – 2).

God will protect you from your enemies by causing the public to favor you so much that your enemy will be afraid to persecute you (Mark 14:1 – 2; Gen. 26:26 – 31; Acts 4:21; 5:26).

When Joseph, Jacob's son, was a slave in Egypt, the Lord blessed the slaveholder's house for Joseph's sake because Joseph was righteous, and Joseph would not sleep with the king's wife after she tried hard to seduce him daily (Gen. 39). Notice that the king who was also the slaveholder favored Joseph, so the king's house was blessed for Joseph's sake, and because the king favored Joseph. Even after the king's wife lied and said that Joseph tried to rape her, Joseph was casted into prison, but the inmates and the prison guards favored him as well, because God was with Joseph (Gen. 39). Joseph continued to be favored after he was released from prison (Gen. 40 and Gen. 41). When Paul was in jail, the Jews said that they would not eat until they had killed Paul, and if they did not kill him, may a curse fall upon them, but God caused the jailers to move Paul with an escort of hundreds of soldiers versus just forty Jews (Acts 23:11 – 24). God at other times also caused Paul to be favored by his enemies and prison guards (Acts 27:2 – 3; 28:16).

God says that he will cause one child of God to chase away a thousand enemies, and two of God's people will put ten thousand enemies to flight (Lev. 26:8; Deut. 32:30; Josh. 23:10). But if you rebel against the Lord, he will cause people to chase you like being chased by bees (Deut. 1:44). David said that he would not be afraid of tens of thousands of people (Ps. 3:6).

Some of Daniel's enemies favored him because the Lord loved Daniel and God said that Daniel was "greatly beloved" by the Lord (Dan. 1:3 – 6, 9; 6:2 – 3; 9:23; 10:11, 19).

God favored Hezekiah's prayer and granted Hezekiah fifteen more years to live after he was on his death bed, and after God healed him, an enemy king sent him gifts (2 Kings 20:1 – 7; Isa. 39:1).

Esther served the Lord in holiness and spoke out against the evil king who persecuted her people, and she said if her stance caused her to be killed by the king, then let her perish (Est. 2:17; 5:2; 8:1 – 2, 7; 9:1 – 3). The heathen king of the land ended up favoring the Jews and told them to do whatever was necessary to protect themselves from their enemies, even if the enemies were women and children, and many non – Jews became Jews because they feared the Jews (Est. 8). Some other people in the Bible who God caused to be favored by their enemies include, Ezra (Ezra 7:6); Nehemiah (Neh. 13:6); and Jehoiachin (2 Kings 25:27 – 30; Jer. 52:31).

God took the promised land from the heathen and gave it to Israel, not because the people of Israel were so righteous, but because the native people of the land were even worse sinners (Deut. 9:4 – 7).

Not obeying God allows people to sometimes obtain things but not live long enough or be in position to use those things (Deut. 28). God told Israel while traveling through the wilderness on their way to the promised land that they must not rebel against him, and to not fear the native people of the land. Because they were the Hebrews bread and that their defense had parted from them, and that God was with the Hebrews (Num. 14:9). Sometimes good people benefit from what evil people have done, because God gives it to the good people, and sometimes evil people benefit from what good people do, because God's people often carry heavy burdens of different people under them and help people who do not deserve help (Eccles. 8:14).

Christ promises, "Blessed be the poor, for their's is the kingdom of God" (Luke 6:20). Some people make themselves rich but have nothing, because they are empty, blind, miserable and unsaved. But some poor people are rich with salvation, sanctification, holiness, happiness, good health, good children, peace, wisdom, necessities, safety, and protection (Prov. 13:7; Rev. 3:15 – 22).

God will give his people houses and property that they did not have to build, but sinners built and formerly owned them before God gave them to his people (Num. 14:9; 21:25; Ezra 7:21 – 23; Exod. 3:21 – 22; 11:2 – 3; 12:35 – 36; Ps. 105:42 – 45; Prov. 21:18; 28:8; Josh. 24:13 – 17; Hab. 1:6; Isa. 61:6; Deut. 3:5 – 7; 6:4 – 12; 19:1; Neh. 9:9 – 19, 25 – 26, 36 – 37; Job 27:16 – 17).

Favor is not the same as "respect of persons," which is a sin. If you always put God first, he will favor you. Many people have said that they do not favor one of their children over their other children, but most people do favor one child or one person at their place of employment over another person. If they deserved to be favored in certain situations, that is all right, but to all ways favor a person or to favor them most of the time is "respect of persons," which is a deadly sin. God even favors some of us more than others, but God himself says that he does not have "respect of persons" for anyone, rich or poor, black or white, male or female, and we as humans should be the same way, especially in our legal and court systems and in all manner of business deals (Rom. 2:4 – 11; Matt. 12:46 – 50; Mark 3:31 – 35; Deut. 33:9; 1 Kings 15:13; Eccles. 9:11 – 12.)

Many people seek human's deceitful favor, including the favor of human rulers, but God is the judge (Prov. 29:26; 31:30). The Word of God says, "A good name is to be chosen rather than great riches, loving favor rather than silver and gold. The rich and the poor have this in common; 'The Lord is the maker of them all.' A wise person foresees sin and evil and separates themselves from it, but simple – minded people embrace it and are punished. Train up a child in the way that they should go, and when they are older, they will not depart from it. By humility and the fear of the Lord are riches, honor, and life" (Prov. 22:1 – 6). We should mainly seek favor from God only, but most people seek honor from humans more so than from God (Joh. 5:41, 44; 7:18; 12:43; 2 Cor. 3:1 – 4; 1 Thess. 2:4 – 6).

The Bible says that even rich people must seek to be rich towards God and not rely so much on their earthly riches, or they will be in jeopardy of dying suddenly and going to hell (Luke 12:16 – 21; (Isa. 40:21 – 25). Serving God will cause you to be favored by the Lord and by humans, while also gaining a good godly understanding (Luke 2:52; 1 Sam. 2:26; Isa. 61:9; Acts 2:46 – 47; Prov. 3:1 – 4; 22:11).

In God's favor is life, but willful and habitual sinners' sin against their own souls (Ps. 30:5; Prov. 8:35 – 36; Mic. 2:1; Ps. 19:12 – 14; Rom. 1:18 – 32; 2 Thess. 2:10 – 15).

Job's prayer for other people was better than their own prayers for themselves, because God favored Job (Job 42:8). Some other people in the Bible who received favor from God are Lot (Gen. 19:14 – 21); Elisha and the widow (2 Kings 8:1 – 6); Mary (Luke 1:28 – 30); Ruth and Naomi (Ruth 1:3 – 14; 4:13 – 17); Ebedmelech the Ethiopian (Jer. 39:15 – 18); Israel in the wilderness (1 Chron. 16:18 – 22); Nehemiah (Neh. 2:1 – 7); and all virtuous women (Prov. 12:4; 31:10 – 31; Ps. 144:12; 2 Pet. 1:2 – 11). This is because they were righteous, and God protected them because they were righteous (Ps. 5:12; Prov. 14:9).

He who finds a godly wife, and she who finds a godly husband, finds a good thing, and obtains favor from God. Houses and riches can be inherited from your earthly father, but a good spouse comes from the Lord, who is your heavenly Father (Prov. 18:22; 19:13 – 14; Ps. 128).

Marriage is honorable in all, and the bed undefiled, but

whoremongers and adulterers shall be judged by God (Heb. 13:4; 1 Tim. 1:9, 10; Rev. 21:5 – 8, 27; 22:14 – 15). The Word of God says that God's judgment on rebellious sinners will be hell if God does not have mercy on them, and we cannot keep getting by on mercy (Eph. 5:5; Rev. 21:8, 27; 22:14 – 15).

The body is not for fornication, but for the Lord, and our bodies belongs to God, not to us (1 Cor. 6:13, 19 – 20). In the Bible God killed 23,000 people at one time because of fornication (1 Cor. 10:8 – 13. Therefore, flee fornication, and adultery (1 Cor. 6:18). This means to run from fornication and adultery if you must, like Joseph did in the Old Testament (Gen. 39). And in the New Testament another man named Joseph did not have sex with Mary the mother of Christ while being engaged to marry her (Matt. 1:18 – 21; Luke 1:27). Elijah lived with a widow for a while during a great drought and famine, but they did not have sex (1 Kings 17:1, 8 – 24).

If you are married, you are one body with your spouse (Matt. 19:5 – 6; Gen. 2:24). God does not dwell in temples made with hands, but in holy humans (Acts 7:48; 17:24). Thus, the body is the temple of God (Joh. 2:19 – 21; 2 Cor. 5:1; 2 Pet.1:12 – 15). And God destroys whoever defiles the temple (1 Cor. 6:9 – 20; and 1 Cor. 3:16 – 23; Eph. 2:19 – 22; Heb. 3:4 – 19; 4:1; Rom. 6:23).

Godly, holy, and sanctified Christians who have sinned willfully must repent and God will still favor them (Isa. 60:10). Habitual and willful sinners receive blessing from God from time to time, but that does not mean that God is pleased with them (Matt. 5:43 – 48). Everyone sins, but we must not make excuses for willful sin, even if we are not able to immediately stop sinning willfully, but to make excuses is to also speak against the Word of God (Ps. 119:58; Prov. 3:4 – 8). People of that nature have pleasure in unrighteous and love their sinful ways, and they are slaves of sins (Rom. 1:18 – 32; 2 Thess. 2:10 – 15; 1 Chron. 29:17; Ezra 10:11; Ps. 40:8; 62:4; 103:21; 119:14 – 16, 24, 33 – 36; 44 – 47; 119:75 – 77; Jer. 6:10 – 14; 2 Pet. 2:13).

God asks, what sin have you found in him that causes you

to sin (Jer. 2:5)? We must do all we can to not use our God given freedom and grace to sin willfully, not even during special occasions (Gal. 5:13). We are justified by Christ, but Christ is not the minister of sin (Gal. 2:17). The Bible says, "If we sin willfully after we have received the knowledge of the truth, there remains no more sacrifice for sins, but there is only a fearful expectation of judgment and fiery punishment. They who broke Moses's law died without mercy under the testimony of two or three witnesses. How much sorer punishment for people who have trodden underfoot the Son of God, and counted the sanctified blood of Christ's covenant an unholy thing, and did it despite the Spirit of grace? It is a fearful thing to fall into the hands of the living God" (Heb. 10:22 – 31; Exod. 20:18 – 19; Deut. 5:23 – 26; Mic. 2:1; Ps. 19:12 – 14).

Remember, the people in Moses's time begged to hear Moses, because if God had instead spoken to them in person, they would have surely died (Exod. 20:18 – 19; Deut. 5:23 – 26). God sent Ezekiel to warn the people, but God said that the people would not listen to Ezekiel, and that they would not even listen to the Lord (Ezek. 3:4 – 21). Holy scripture says, "God's voice shook the earth in the Old Testament, but during these last and evil days God will shake both heaven and earth. Therefore, we must serve God with reverence and godly fear. For our God is a consuming fire, and a jealous God, whose name is Jealous" (Deut. 4:24; Exod. 34:14; Heb. 12:26 – 29; Ezek. 8:5 – 18).

God also reminds us of him destroying the entire world except eight people in the days of Noah, and how he destroyed the cities of Sodom and Gomorrah at another time in history, and that when he returns this time, in some marriages one spouse will be taken to heaven and the other left behind (Luke 17:20 – 37). Christ says if a person could come back from hell to tell the world how bad hell is, some people still would not believe that they can go to hell too. This scripture also says that if people did not believe Moses and the prophets, some people nowadays will not believe that they can go to hell (Luke

16:19-31; Acts 13:41. This is true, because people did not and do not believe after Christ came from heaven to warn the people of the earth, while simultaneously saving the souls of people, healing them, and delivering them. Christ even asked one man how can he believe heavenly things if he did not even believe what Christ said about earthly things (Joh. 3:12 – 13. In terms of suffering and dying in sins, sometimes seeing is not believing (Jer .3:8).

Righteousness delivers us from death (Prov. 10:2; 11:4). But grace does not allow us to continue in sin, and the wages of sin is death (Rom. 6:23 and Rom. 1:18 – 32; 2 Thess. 2:10 – 15; 8:13 – 14; 1 Kings 13:11 – 24; 1 Cor. 11:23 – 30; Ezek. 7:13; 18:4; 33:11, 19 – 20; Deut. 30:19 – 20; Job 20:11; 24:19; 36:5 – 13; Ps. 1:5 – 6; Prov. 19:5, 9; 21:16; 27:20; 30:15, 16; Isa. 5:14; 13:9; Josh. 7:1 – 13; 1 Chron. 10:13 – 14; Rev. 2:23; Matt. 18:11 – 14; Lam. 3:31 – 33; 1 Tim. 2:4; 2 Pet. 3:9; Luke 13:1 – 5).

A good person deals graciously and lends to others, and they guide their business and lending with discretion, therefore most people do not receive a loan, and good people are not obligated to be a lending tree (Ps. 112:5). God will make you the head and not the tail, above and not beneath, and to lend and not borrow (Deut. 15:5 – 6; 28:12 – 14; Ps. 18:43; 105:43 – 45; 2 Sam. 22:44).

When people backslide from God, they often end up being the tail, and God says it is like a dog returning to eat its own vomit (2 Pet. 2:18 – 22). First shall be last, and last shall be first. God puts down one person and lifts up another (Matt. 19:29 – 30; 20:15 – 16; Luke 2:34; 13:23 – 30; Ps. 75:6 – 7; Isa. 60:22; Deut. 6:10 – 12 and Deut. 28; Lam. 5; Ezek. 33:10 – 16; Job 27:16 – 17; Est. 3:8 – 15; 4:1 – 3, 13 – 17; 6:13; 8; Zech. 10:6).

Another example of the first being last and the last being first is when Esau and Jacob were twins in their mother's womb. Jacob grabbed the heal of Esau and tried to prevent him from being born first, but Esau was still born first. Later in life, Esau foolishly sold his birthright to Jacob for one simple meal of food, making Esau last, and God even counted it as foolishness and said that the older brother would serve the younger. But Jacob ended up needing Esau's help, desperately, and Jacob voluntarily bowed down with his whole family before Esau, and Esau welcomed him and helped him, making Esau first again. But ultimately, Jacob is first because he was chosen by God to be the patriarch of the nation of Israel. And because God loves all his children, especially those who serve him, Esau is also special to God because God in his grace and mercy caused Esau and his descendants to prosper as well, to not be last in the world, and to have a chance of eternal life in heaven (Gen. 25:19 – 34; 27:30 – 45; 33:1 – 17; Heb. 12:13 – 16). People who have become last can someday be first again spiritually, and in earthly matters, but if a person dies unsaved, they have a great chance of being both last and lost for eternity. They who endure until the end shall be saved (Matt. 10:20 – 22; 24:13; Heb. 3:7 – 19; Joh. 6:26 – 29; Eccles. 9:11 – 12).

Ask the Lord to shine his face upon you. One prayer from the Bible simply says, "The Lord bless you and keep you. The Lord makes his face shine upon you and be gracious to you. The Lord lifts up his countenance upon you and give you peace" (Num. 6:24 – 27; Ps. 31:16; 67:1).

David said, "God, make your face shine on your servant. Save me for your mercy's sake" (Ps. 31:16; 67:1; 80:3, 7, 19). The book of Psalms also says, "God, make your face shine on your servant and teach me your Word" (Ps. 119:135). But some people allow the god of this world to blind them from the light of Christ who is trying to shine on them (2 Cor. 4:4 – 6). The Prophet Daniel said, "There shall be a time of trouble, more than there has ever been, more than in any nation of the past. And at that time the true people of God shall be delivered, everyone who shall be found with their names written in the Book of Life. And the dead in graves shall awake and rise, some to everlasting life, and some to shame and everlasting contempt. They who are wise shall shine like the bright sky, and they who turn many people to righteousness shall shine like stars forever and ever (Dan. 12:1 – 3). The Bible says that true and real Christians who are blameless and harmless children of God without fault, shine like a light in the world as examples to a crooked and perverted generation of people (Phil. 2:15). Christ says that the righteous shall shine in heaven like the sun. They who have an ear to hear let them hear (Matt. 13:43).

See also *FRIENDS; BLESSINGS; WITH.*

FORSAKE

To abandon, to leave. Sometimes it seems like God has forsaken us (Lam. 5:20; Jer. 20:7 – 9; Ps. 22:1; 77:10 – 11; Matt. 27:46; 2 Cor. 4:8 – 11).

Sometimes sinners keep sinning because they think God has forsaken the earth (2 Pet. 3:3 – 4, 9 – 10; Ezek. 8:12; 9:9; Jer. 12:4; 16:17 – 18; Isa. 40:27; Ps. 94:1 – 11).

People who forget what God has done for them are hard-hearted (Mark 6:48 – 52; 8:15 – 21; Ps. 37:24; 78). Christ says that he will not totally forsake us nor fail us (Deut. 4:31; 31:6; Josh. 1:5; Heb. 13:5; Isa. 42:16 – 21).

The Lord God Almighty says, "For a moment I forsook you, but with great mercies I will gather you" (Isa. 54:7). Christ asked God to take away his pain, and God did not respond at all, but God did send an angel to strengthen Christ before he was arrested and while Christ worried and sweated so hard while praying that the sweat hit the ground like drops of blood. Christ concluded that it was not his will, but God's will that matters (Matt. 26:36 - 39; Luke 22:39 - 46; Isa. 53). Even Christ the Son of Man while dying on the cross felt that God had forsaken him, because God would not answer him and showed no presence at all with Christ while Christ was on the cross, but Christ ended up being crowned King of heaven, earth, hell, and the entire universe (Matt. 27:46; Mark 15:34 – 39; 28:18; Luke 23:46; Joh. 19:30; 1 Cor. 15:24 – 28; Eph. 1:21 – 23; Phil. 2:9; Ps. 8; Heb. 2:5 – 9; Joh. 16:15).

Even when Christ first started his ministry, God sent Christ into the wilderness alone but full of the Holy Ghost, to be tempted, tested, and tried by the devil. Every time that the devil tempted Christ, he responded by speaking holy scripture to the devil, and when Christ won the victory and passed the test, the Bible says that the devil departed from Christ only for a season (Luke 4:1 – 21; 1 Pet. 1:6). And when the Apostle Peter was in prison God sent an angel to help Peter, but the angel later departed (Acts 12:6 – 11). The Bible says that God will not always dwell with us, and this means that God must allow us to experience some growing pains on our own, just as we allow our own children to leave home and grow up while hopefully making good godly decisions and not ungodly decisions (Gen. 6:3). This is why God the Father sends God the Holy Ghost who is also the Comforter to dwell with us, because God the Father is in heaven and God the Son shall not return until judgment day (Acts 5:32; Luke 11:13; John 14:13 – 18, 26 – 27 and John 1:1, 14; Col. 3:16; 1 John 2:5, 7, 14).

Sometimes Christ leaves us to try us (2 Chron. 32:31; 1 Pet.4:12 – 19). And if we live in sin, Christ will totally reject our ways (Lam. 5:22).

Family and friends will forsake you, but Christ will not forsake you (Joh. 16:32; Matt. 26:56; Ps. 27:10; Isa. 49:13 – 15; 2 Tim. 1:15 – 18; 4:10, 16).

God will cause our enemy's defense and confidence to depart from them, and make it clearly known that God is with you as your defense and guide, so fear not (Num. 14:9). Sometimes your enemies hope and believe that God has forsaken you and forgotten about you so that they can pounce on you (Ps. 71:11; Isa. 49:14). You may be persecuted but not forsaken, cast down but not destroyed (2 Cor. 4:9). Just before the Apostle Paul was about to be executed, he said, "Demas forsook me because he loves this present world. Alexander did much evil to me, and no man stood with me while I was being tried in court, but the Lord stood with me, and strengthened me" (2 Tim. 4:6 – 18). Alexander the coppersmith did much evil to Paul and Paul said may the Lord reward Alexander according to his works (2 Tim. 4:6 – 8, 14). When Paul went to court the first time, no one stood with him, and everyone forsook him. Paul prayed that God did not punish them for abandoning him (2 Tim. 4:16). So, he prayed for people who deserted and forsook him. Christ tells us to love our enemies, bless them who curse you, do good to them who hate you, and pray for them who despitefully use you and persecute you (Matt. 5:43 – 48). Christ blessed his enemies when he said during his crucifixion, "Forgive them Father for they know not what they do" (Luke 23:34; Acts 3:12 – 17). If you find that hard to do, consider how David forgave his son Absalom after Absalom killed another one of David's sons (2 Sam. 13:20 – 29, 37 – 39; 14:30 – 33). Absalom later caused most of David's kingdom to go against David, and forced David into exile while Absalom ruled the kingdom and slept with David's maids and concubines (2 Sam. 15). Absalom even tried to kill his father David (2 Sam. 16:10 – 12). But David still forgave Absalom and wept painfully when Absalom was killed, and David said that he wished that he could have died in the place of Absalom (2 Sam. 18:32 – 33; 19:1 – 7).

The Bible also tells us to bless them who persecute you, bless and not curse (Matt. 5:44; Luke 6:27 –28; Rom. 12:14; Job 29; 30; 31). That is what Paul did. Paul did not curse Alexander for treating him badly, but he simply said that God will punish him. The Bible does say, "As some people love cursing, so let curses come to them, and as some people do not delight in blessing others, so let blessings be far from them" (Ps. 109:17).

Paul also said, "The Lord give mercy unto the house of Onesiphorus, because he often refreshed me, and was not ashamed of my prison chains" (2 Tim. 1:8, 16).

The righteous have never been forsaken by God, neither have their children and grandchildren begged for food (Ps. 37:25). If you are slack with God, he will withdraw himself from you until you repent (Hos .5:3 – 6, 15; Isa. 54:5 – 8; Judg. 16:19 – 31). Just as God departed from King Saul who failed the Lord (1 Sam. 18:12; 16:14; 28:15). The Lord also departed from Samson until he repeated (Judg. 16:20). King David said that he kept the ways of the Lord and did not wickedly depart from God (2 Sam. 22:22 – 23). Josiah was the greatest king to ever live, second under King Christ, and the people of the land never departed from following the Lord in holiness all the days of King Josiah's life (2 Chron. 34:33). We should depart from evil and do good, seek peace, and pursue peace, and you will dwell with God forevermore (Ps. 34:14; 37:27). The way of life is above to the wise, so that they will depart from hell beneath (Prov. 15:24). By mercy and truth iniquity and sin are purged, and by the fear of the Lord people depart from evil (Prov. 16:6). God says that his people are persecuted for departing from evil, and that most people depart from God and lie about God being pleased with them while claiming that they can still live an ungodly life, while their sins testify against them. God says regarding his true saints that his Word will not depart out of their mouths, neither out of the mouth of their children and grandchildren (Isa. 59:12 – 21). The Bible says that many people have departed from the Christian Faith while lusting after worldly things and ungodly money and have pierced themselves through with many painful sorrows (1 Tim. 4:1 – ; 6:6 – 12; 2 Kings 5:15 – 27; Matt. 13:3 – 9, 18 – 23). Nevertheless, the foundation of God stands sure, having this seal; the Lord knows people who are truly his, and let everyone who confesses Christ depart from iniquity and sin (2 Tim. 2:19; Matt. 7:21–23; Mic. 3:11). If you forsake God, he will forsake you and he will do harm to you after he has done good to you in the past (1 Chron. 28:9; 2 Chron. 15:2; 24:20; Deut. 31:6 – 8, 16 – 17; Josh. 24:15 – 25; Judg. 10:13; 1 Kings 9:8 – 9; Jer. 23:39; 5:7, 19; Ps. 50:22 – 23; Ezra 8:22 – 23, 31; Lam. 5:20).

When you turn your back on God, you commit at least two sins, turning your back on God, and serving another person, god, or thing, adding sin to sin (Jer. 2:13 – 14; Judg. 10:10; Isa. 30:1; 1 Sam. 12:19).

Christ does say that he will never leave us nor forsake us, but this means that Christ will not allow things to get worse while we are having a hard time, and if things do get worse, Christ will not leave nor forsake us, and it refers to when Christ is fighting your battles while you live a righteous lifestyle (Deut. 31:6 – 8; Heb. 13:5; Isa. 42:16 – 21; 54:4 – 10). Some people have forsaken the right way, and have gone astray, and love the wages of unrighteousness (2 Pet. 2:15). Some of them do not know, and others have forgotten that the wages of sin is death (Rom. 6:23 and Rom. 1:18 – 32; 2 Thess. 2:10 – 15; 8:13 – 14; 1 Kings 13:11 – 24; 1 Cor. 11:23 – 30; Ezek. 7:13; 18:4; 33:11, 19 – 20; Deut. 30:19 – 20; Job 20:11; 24:19; 36:5 – 13; Ps. 1:5 – 6; Prov. 19:5, 9; 21:16; 27:20; 30:15, 16; Isa. 5:14; 13:9; Josh. 7:1 – 13; 1 Chron. 10:13 – 14; Rev. 2:23; Matt. 18:11 – 14; Lam. 3:31 – 33; 1 Tim. 2:4; 2 Pet. 3:9; Luke 13:1 – 5).

When Solomon was anointed by God to build the house of God, his father David told him to be of good courage, that God was with him, and that God would not forsake him while following God's plans to build the house of the Lord (1 Chron. 28:19).

God says that the sins of some people are written with an iron diamond tipped pen upon the tables of their hearts (Jer. 17:1). God is asking us in these last days to write his Word in our hearts and minds (Prov. 3:3; Jer. 31:33; 2 Cor. 3:2 – 3, 7). And that all who forsake the Lord shall be ashamed, and they who depart from the Lord shall be written in the earth, meaning in the grave, and not written in the Book of Life, because they have forsaken the Lord who is the fountain of living water (Jer. 17:13). Christ gives us the fountain of living water, which is the Holy Ghost, and he says that people who are not born again of the water and of the Spirit cannot go to heaven (Joh. 3:3 – 7; 7:37 – 39). Meaning, we must be baptized in water in the name of Christ and be filled with the Holy Ghost, also known as the Holy Spirit (Acts 2:36 – 39; 8:14 – 17; 10:47 – 48; 19:2 – 5). Christ gives the Holy Ghost to people who obey him (Acts 5:32; Luke 11:13; Joh. 14:13 – 18, 26 – 27).

People often forget God who formed them (Deut. 32:18; Prov. 31:5). And they forget God who delivered them (Luke 17:11 – 19). God says that they are unmindful of him and have forgotten him who fathered them (Deut. 32:18). People who forsake God, praise the wicked (Prov. 28:4). This can sometimes happen when people become fat with earthly gain and material things (Deut. 32:15).

God's punishment and destruction because people forsake him (Deut. 28:20).
Forsaken the covenant of the Lord God of their fathers (Deut. 29:25).
Forsook the Lord and served idols and decorated trees (Judg. 2:13).
Now the Lord has forsaken us (Judg. 6:13).
Have forsaken our God (Judg. 10:10).
You have forsaken me, and served other gods (Judg. 10:13; 1 Sam. 8:8; 1 Kings 11:33).
We should not forsake the Lord to serve idols (Josh. 24:16).
God will not forsake his people (1 Sam. 12:22; 1 Kings 6:13).
Forsook the Lord their God (1 Kings 9:9).
Forsaken your covenant, torn down your altars and killed your prophets (1 Kings 19:10).
I will forsake rebellious people and turn them over to their enemies (2 Kings 21:14).
They have forsaken me, and (2 Kings 22:17).
You have forsaken me, and therefore I have left you (2 Chron. 12:5).
Lord is our God and we have not forsaken him (2 Chron. 13:10).
We keep the commandments of God, but you have forsaken him (2 Chron. 13:11).
Because you have forsaken the Lord, he has also forsaken you (2 Chron. 24:20).
Refused to obey and made a captain to return to bondage but God did not forsake them (Neh. 9:17).
Put their trust in you, for you Lord have not forsaken them who seek you (Ps. 9:10).
God, why have you forsaken me (Ps. 22:1)?
Neither forsake me, O God (Ps. 27:9).
When my father and my mother forsake me, the Lord will take care of me (Ps. 27:10).

Do not cast me off in old age, forsake me not when my strength fails (Ps. 71:9).

God forsook the tabernacle of Shiloh because of sinful humans (Ps. 78:60).

If your children forsake God, he will punish them and then continue to love them (Ps. 89:20 – 33).

I will obey your Word, please do not forsake me totally (Ps.119:8, 136).

Do not forsake the works of your hands (Ps. 138:8).

They have forsaken the Lord (Isa. 1:4).

These things I will do for them, and not forsake them (Isa. 42:16).

The Lord has called you like a woman forsaken in her youth (Isa. 54:6).

You shall no longer be called forsaken (Isa. 62:4).

Have forsaken the Lord thy (God Jer. 2:19).

How shall I pardon you for this? Your children have forsaken me (Jer. 5:7).

Like you have forsaken with strange gods, you shall be sent into a strange land (Jer. 5:19).

I will forsake you, says the Lord (Jer. 23:33).

I, even I, will forget you, and I will forsake you (Jer. 23:39).

Why do you forget us forever and forsake us so long (Lam. 5:20)?

Forsake the holy covenant (Dan. 11:30).

Forsake the idols of Egypt (Jon. 2:8).

The apostles forsook all to follow Christ at first (Matt. 19:27 – 29; Luke 5:11).

Then the disciples forsook him and fled (Matt. 26:56).

By faith Moses forsook being a rich politician in Egypt (Heb. 11:27).

Be content with what you have, for God says, "I will never leave you, nor forsake you" (Heb. 13:5).

See also *WITH; FRIENDS; TEST; ENCOURAGEMENT.*

FOSTER CARE (AND FATHERLESS CHILDREN)

The Bible addresses orphans and mostly uses the word fatherless to describe these very delicate and sensitive situations. A fatherless child in the Bible was a child who was an orphan or a child who had only a mother, or who had a deadbeat father or absent father. The definition of the word orphan is a child who has two dead parents. A foster child is a child who was taken by the state from their biological parents due to abuse or neglect. A ward of the court is a child or adult person with a disability who is protected by the court system and placed with a caregiver. God is very critical of and punishes people who mistreat and who do not help the fatherless, motherless, orphans, wards of the court, foster children, poor people, and widows, and to help them is the standard, expectation, and definition of true religion (Isa. 1:17, 23; 10:1 – 2; Ezek. 22:7, 29; Mal. 3:5; James 1:26–27; Isa. 1:15 – 20).

There are several sad realities to being fatherless or a foster child. In addition to being a foster child growing up while knowing that no one really wants them, foster care usually ends between the ages 18 and 21. If the children are not adopted by that age, they age out of the foster care system. Most kids who have two parents are not even mature enough to make it on their own between the ages of 18 and 21. Therefore, it is a very sad situation, especially if the foster child's childhood involved abuse and neglect. When the Bible was written, fatherless children were mainly a result of fornication and fathers being killed in war. Nowadays due to drugs, neglect, and bad stepfathers, we now also have motherless children. To be a 30-year-old grandparent is not good, especially if the grandparent does not set good examples for their grandchild. But even though being a grandparent between age 30 and 40 is not ideal, if the young grandparent cares for the grandkids in a godly manner, that is better than the grandkids moving from one foster home to another their entire childhood. Grandchildren are the crown of elderly people, and parents are the glory and pride of children (Prov. 17:6). Therefore, parents must live up to their responsibility so their kids will not have to be placed in foster care or be pushed upon grandparents who should be finished raising children.

Many fatherless kids were conceived in the sin of their parents but when the kids serve the Lord, they become more blessed. God is a Father to the fatherless and a husband to widows, especially those who love and fear him (Ps. 68:4 – 5 and Ps. 66:16 – 20; 130:3 – 4; 145:17 – 21). The Bible tells us to ask God to establish his Word in us as servants, and that we must be devoted to fearing God (Ps. 119:33 – 38). God takes pleasure in people who fear him and hope in his mercy (Ps. 147:10 – 11; 119:132). God's mercy is with people who love and fear him from generation to generation (Luke 1:50; Deut. 7:9; Heb. 12:26 - 29; Ps. 66:16 – 20; 130:3 – 4; 145:17 – 21; Prov. 16:6).

The beginning of wisdom is to fear God (Ps. 111:10; Isa. 66:1 – 2). We must love, and fear God (Eccles. 12:13; Luke 12:16 – 21; Prov. 16:6; Mal. 2:5 – 6; Ps. 103:11, 17 – 18; 111:10; 115:11 – 18; Isa. 50:10; 66:1 – 2; 2 Kings17:20 – 41).

God orders communities, societies and nations all over the world to find out why children become orphans and foster children, and to work diligently to prevent it from happening again, while also ensuring that children who are already in foster care and adoptive homes are not neglected, abused, or harmed (Jer. 5:28). Fatherless children were taken from mothers during the slave trades in the Bible and in the recent American and European slave trades (Job 24:9). Job was one of the most righteous people to every live, and he helped poor people, fatherless and parentless children, and widows (Job 29:12 – 25). The Lord says, "Learn to do good, seek justice, relieve the oppressed, defend the fatherless, and plead for the widow" (Isa. 1:17).

God says, "Can a woman forget her sucking child, that she should not have compassion on the child of her womb? Yes, they may forget, yet will I not forget you" (Isa. 49:13 – 15). Christ is the helper of the fatherless (Ps. 10:14). And God has always instructed us to care for the fatherless and the motherless (James 1:26 – 27; Ps. 82:3; Est. 2:7, 20). The same applies to widows, outsiders, and the outcasted (Deut. 15:11; 24:19 – 21; Prov. 29:7; 31:9; Jer. 22:16). When we do not care for, provide for, and protect orphans, foster children, widows, outsiders, and outcasted people, God will punish us and not hear our prayers, because we would not have answered when he instructed us to help the needy (Zech. 7:8 – 14). Cursed be they who pervert the justice of the fatherless, the widow, the outsider, and the outcasted, and all the people shall say, Amen (Deut. 27:19). The Lord preserves the outcasted and outsider, and he relieves the orphan and foster child, but God turns wicked people upside down (Ps. 146:9). Social workers, foster parents, adoptive parents, biological parents, educators, judges, law enforcement officials, legislators, and the Department of Human Service are evil and wicked if they neglect, abuse, or harm foster children. God is with people who do not oppress and harm the fatherless, outcasted, outsider, and widow (Jer. 7:5 – 7). To those who abuse, neglect, harm, and even kill orphans, widows, and the fatherless, and think that God does not see them, the Bible says, "O Lord, to whom vengeance belongs. Understand, you senseless among the people, and you fools, when will you be wise? God who planted the ear, shall he not hear? God who formed the eye, shall he not see?

God who instructs the nations, shall he not correct" (Ps. 94; Rom. 12:19 – 21; Nah. 1:1 – 3; 2 Thess. 1:7 – 9; 1 Sam. 25:2 – 39; Deut. 2; 25:17 – 19; 32:35 – 43)?

If parents do not turn their hearts toward their children, and their children do not turn their hearts towards their good and fit parents, God will curse the parents and the earth (Mal. 4:6). Kids are supposed to be the pride of fathers (Prov. 17:6). Christ says that if anyone hurts a child who believes in him, that person would do better to tie a weight around their neck and jump into the sea, rather than suffer what God has for them, and that children have special angels specifically for them who visit God face to face often on behalf of the children (Matt. 18:3 – 6, 10). Christ embraced a child in his arms and said unto his disciples, whosoever shall receive a child in the name of Christ, receives Christ (Mark 9:36 – 37).

God himself will punish widows and fatherless children that are hypocrites, sinners, evildoers, and foolish, because they refuse to return to him (Isa. 9:13 – 17). Disobedient children and adults will not live out half their days on earth, unless they repent (Ps. 55:23; Prov. 20:20; 30:11; Exod. 21:17; Lev. 20:9; Matt. 15:3 – 9).

Not enough is done to help orphans and foster children, and too many of them end up homeless, pregnant, in prison, or working as prostitutes or as criminals such as drug dealers after they become adults. If they are not adopted by age 18, or 21 in some states, they become too old to remain in foster homes according to most laws of the land, which is very, very sad. Because they spend most of their innocent childhood being unhappy, abused, or neglected, and then spend large parts of their remaining life, or all their remaining life, homeless, in prison, or out of prison with the same hard situations that they grew up in. This can be prevented when the people who were paid to be foster parents care enough to allow the foster children to stay in their homes even after age 18 or 21 just as they would do for their own biological children, but the foster children must be respectful and obedient.

Foster parents and state officials should plan a career path and some type of post high school education for foster children, and this will not only educate them, but this gives them a few more years to mature before they enter a mean and cold-hearted world. The foster children will qualify for Pell Grants and government assistant for one-, two-, or four-year education programs after high school. The foster parents can also allow the foster children to live with them after high school while they work their first full time job, even if the foster child is required to help pay bills in the home due to them being employed full time. These are options that God – fearing, God – loving, caring, compassionate, and kindhearted people would do even though they are no longer being paid to be foster parents. Foster parents who do it only for the money are not Christ – like and they are not godly. Christ said if we do not visit, help, protect, and provide for people who are sick, in prison, hungry, or in need of clothes, we have failed to do those same things unto Christ (Matt. 25:31 – 46; Job 13:15 – 16; 24:1 – 11; 29; 31. Paul's friend Epaphroditus labored so hard for the Lord that he made himself sick nearly to death, while also supplying Paul's need in prison that others did not supply (Phil. 2:25 – 30).

Some foster parents only provide housing to foster children to get the money that is paid to them by the state agency, and that is not good. And what is even more evil is that some foster parents neglect and emotionally, physically, and sexually abuse foster children.

The Department of Human Services in the state of Florida, USA lost a child and did not know that the child was missing until someone prompted them to check the foster home for the child. When they went to the foster home, the child was nowhere to be found. That is a very sad case, but our society became even more neglectful and evil when we learned that not only do some foster kids get sold into the Sex Slave Trade, but some of them were murdered and their organs such as their heart, liver, kidneys, and lungs were transplanted into a sick person who paid plenty of money for the organs of an innocent child. This should be sad and disturbing for any human to hear or read. People who participate in, or are accessory to these sins are evil and wicked. Some people say that all sins are the same, but that is not true. Evil and wicked sins are not simply sins. Some prostitutes were killed, and their dead bodies were found in dumpsters with some of their organs missing out of their body. Some of those prostitutes may have been former foster children, but if not, no person deserves to be treated that way, and anyone who would want the organs of another person inside their body that they took from another human being who was killed, are evil, wicked, mentally, and spiritually sick, and spiritually dead. The Bible says that God is angry everyday with wicked people, which means that the recipients of the organs and the people who partook and participated in the murdering will suffer worse than they ever suffered in their entire life (Ps. 5:4 – 7; 7:11; 11:5; 34:16; and Ps. 94; Isa. 5:20 – 25; 13:6 – 13; Rev. 9:20 – 21).

Four very good options for foster children and orphans who have aged out of the foster care system is first, the church. Even if a foster child had foster parents who did not belong to a church or who did not attend church on a regular basis, young adults leaving foster care cannot go wrong if they join a good church and become very active in the church such as being in the choir, the music ministry, and the youth ministry. Noteworthy, Catholic priests have molested young boys, and that must be mentioned here. Secondly, joining the military allows a young person to serve their country and to travel around the world. But the military also provides very stable and safe housing, three meals a day every day of the week, clothing allowances, job training, and college classes. The third option could be the United States Job Corp where young adults live on a campus and are paid to learn a trade or a skill that will lead to employment after graduation. These campuses have at times not been as safe as a military base, fort, camp, or post, nor as safe as college campuses, and students are not required to practice as much self – discipline, self – motivation, and self – determination as in the military. But the United State Job Corp is a good choice. The fourth option is a one – year trade school or a four – year college where the young adult can live in the dorm all year and only need to find a place to go for holidays.

Below is a prayer for all young people but specifically for orphans, foster children, wards of the court, fatherless kids, and motherless kids, followed by additional holy scriptures to read. Remember, true and undefiled religion is to not harm people and to care for orphans, widows, and foster children (James 1:26–27; Isa. 1:15 – 20).

Lord God Almighty in the name of Jesus Christ, please protect and provide for all children, especially the parentless, foster children, orphans, and victims of neglect and abuse. And Lord God, please prevent children who have not been violated, abused, or neglected from ever being harmed or neglected. Lord God, please bless all parents including godparents, grandparents, foster parents, guardians, enemies, friends, and family members to always do the right thing towards all kids. In Christ's name we pray, forever. Amen.

Afflicting widows and fatherless children (Exod. 22:22).
Of the fatherless and widow (Deut. 10:18).
The outsider and the fatherless (Deut. 14:29; 24:17 – 21; 26:12; 27:19).
Drive away the mule of the fatherless (Job 24:3).
Pluck the fatherless from their mother's breast (Job 24:9).
Poor that cried, and the fatherless (Job 29:12).
Fatherless has not eaten (Job 31:17).
Hand against the fatherless (Job 31:21).
Helper of the fatherless (Ps. 10:14).
The fatherless and oppressed (Ps. 10:18).
Defend the poor and fatherless (Ps. 82:3).
And murder the fatherless (Ps. 94:6).
Let his children be fatherless and his wife a widow (Ps. 109:9).
Favor his fatherless children (Ps. 109:12).
Relieves the fatherless and (Ps. 146:9).

Into the fields of the fatherless (Prov. 23:10).
Fatherless plead for the widow (Isa. 1:17).
They do not defend the fatherless (Isa. 1:23).
Neither have mercy on their fatherless (Isa. 9:17).
The cause of the fatherless (Jer. 5:28).
The outsider, the fatherless (Jer. 7:6).
The fatherless, nor the widow (Jer. 22:3).
Leave your fatherless children and widows, I will preserve them (Jer. 49:11).
We are orphans and fatherless (Lam. 5:3).
They vexed the fatherless (Ezek. 22:7).
In you the fatherless finds mercy (Hos. 14:3).
True and undefiled religion is to not harm people and to visit the fatherless and widows (James 1:27).

FRIENDS

We are friends with Christ when we obey his Word, otherwise we are simply a liability who he must provide for and protect (Joh. 14:15; 15:14 – 15). If people want real, honest, God-fearing and God loving friends who they can trust, they must also show themselves as being friendly (Prov. 18:24; Judg. 19:3; Ruth. 2:13). This does not mean that people should be fools for other people to gain a fake friend. King David said, "Depart from me, you evildoers, for I will keep the commandments of my God!" (Ps. 119:115). There are friends who stick closer than some brothers and sisters, but the ultimate friend who sticks closer than any biological or church sister or brother is Christ (Prov. 18:24). We must love our neighbor as ourselves, and a good neighbor nearby is better than a brother far away (Prov. 27:10; Rom. 13:9 – 10). However, a true friend always loves, and a brother and sister is born to stick with you through adversity (Prov. 17:17). Thus, a real friend on earth is hard to find. Christ was a friend to Moses, Abraham, and the apostles (Exod. 33:11; James 2:23); and Christ will be our true friend if we obey him (Joh. 15:13 – 14). The Bible tells us to put our trust in Christ only (Mic. 7:5 – 7).

Some people avoid poor people and do not favor them, while the rich has plenty of friends, and also fake friends, mainly because they are rich (Prov. 14:20).

If people hang around you because you give freely, or because you are rich, this does not mean that they are your friends (Prov. 19:6; 14:20). Friends scratch each other's back and lifts them up when they even appear to be down or feeling down (Prov. 27:17; 18:24). Real friends may have problems, but they are still better than the kisses of an enemy (Prov. 27:6). It is all right to remind a friend that they owe you (Ph'm. 1:18 – 19); or about what you have done for them, if they seem to have forgotten or are being neglectful towards you (2 Cor. 11:7 – 9; 12:15 – 19); and if they get offended, then they have a problem. Earthly friends may betray or forsake you, as Christ was betrayed when he was on earth, even by his family (Mark 3:21; 14:65 – 72; Joh. 7:5; Mic. 7:4 – 7). Family and friends will forsake you, but Christ will not forsake you (Joh. 16:32; Matt. 26:56; Ps. 27:10; Isa. 49:13 – 15; 2 Tim. 1:15 – 18; 4:10, 16).

Other people in the Bible were also betrayed by their friends (Judg. 14:20; Ps. 31:9 – 12; 35:13 – 15; 41:9; 55:12 – 17; 88:8 – 9, 18; Job 19:14 – 22; 2 Tim. 1:15; 4:6 – 18; 2 Cor. 11:26; Gal. 2:4).

Christ was betrayed by Judas (Matt. 26:14 – 16, 25, 47 – 56; 27:3 – 8; Acts 1:16 – 19). Christ was also forsaken by Peter (Matt. 26:66 – 75); and abandoned by all the disciples (Mark 14:44 – 50; Matt. 26:66 – 75.) Thousands of people turned their back on Christ, but after the resurrection, all the apostles eventually believed. And John was considered the disciple who Christ loved (Joh. 13:23; 19:26; 20:2; 21:7, 20). Although Job's friends accused him of bringing his sickness upon himself because of sin, they were supportive initially and they made an appointment to see him. And when they saw how sick he was, they cried, prayed to God, and sat with him seven days without talking. Job's wife and friends are also a good example of how sick people, and people who have been victimized, can have more faith than their supporters who are not suffering or are not victimized (Job 2; 4:1 – 8; 27:1 – 12; 42:7). Job's friends eventually criticized him more than they comforted him (Job 4:1 – 8; 6:11 – 15; 32:1-10; 34:34 – 37; 42:7 – 9). God tells us to comfort those who are in any trouble, because God has comforted us (1 Cor. 1:3 – 4).

David and Jonathan were the best of friends (1 Sam. 18:1 – 11; 19:1 – 3; 2 Sam. 1:26). David said that his enemies were against him but especially his neighbors, acquaintances, lover, friends, and kinsmen (Ps. 31:11; 38:11); even his brothers and sisters (Ps. 69:8; 88:8). Do not seek revenge, because vengeance belongs to God (Nah. 1:1 – 3; Rom. 12:19 – 21; 2 Thess. 1:7 – 9; Ps. 94; 1 Sam. 25:2 – 39; Deut. 2; 25:17 – 19; 32:35 – 43).

People who are friends with a fool shall be destroyed (Prov. 13:20). After we are saved, it is all right to help former friends, if possible, but we should not hang with them if they are living a sinful, reckless, high risk, or irresponsible lifestyle (1 Pet. 4:1 – 5; Prov. 22:24). Make no friends with an angry person, and with a furious person do not go (Prov. 22:24). Friends of the world are enemies of God (James 4:2 – 4; Joh. 1:10 – 12; 15:18 – 19; 1 Joh. 2:15 – 17; 3:13; Phil. 3:16 – 21).

See also *ENEMIES; BETRAYAL; FORSAKE; WITH.*

HAPPINESS

If you suffer for Christ's sake, you should be happy (James 5:10 – 11; 1 Pet. 4:12 – 16). A person should be happy when God corrects and chastises them, therefore do not despise the chastening of the Lord Almighty (Job 5:17). God chastises people who he loves, so if you are not being chastised by God, it is highly likely that God has allowed you to punish yourself when the consequences of your sinning causes pain and problems in your life. Your sins will find you out, and your sins will testify against you (Jer. 14:7 – 12; Num. 32:22 – 23; Isa. 59:12; Nah. 3:4 – 6; Ezek. 16:36 – 38; 23:18, 29, 35).

God also turns people over to the devil for punishment, but the devil is not allowed to kill them until God allows it, and if God allows it (1 Tim. 1:18 – 20; 1 Cor.5:1 - 7; 2 Cor. 12:6 - 10). King David said that God chastised him sorely, but God did not give him over to death (Ps. 118:18). David said that he was happier with the joy of the Lord than when other people brought in plenty of crops and wine (Ps. 4:7). Happy are the people whose God is the Lord (Ps. 144:15).

They who find a godly spouse find a good marriage, but death as in discouragement, and life as in encouragement are in the power of the tongue (Prov. 18:21 – 22). It is not best to have a lot of children nowadays, but the Bible tells us that having children make us happy (Ps. 127:3 – 5). A virtuous woman is blessed and respected by God, her husband, her children, and many people in the community. But a shameful and untrustworthy spouse is rottenness to the bones of the other spouse (Prov. 12:4; 31:10 – 31; Ruth 3:11). Seek ye first the kingdom of heaven and everything else will be added to your life (Matt.

6:19 – 21, 24 – 33; 19:16 – 30; Rom. 2:6 – 11; 8:5; Phil. 2:21; 1 Kings 3:7 – 15; Heb. 11:24 – 27; Ps. 73:25). See also *JOY; SORROW; MORE THAN YOU CAN BEAR; ANXIETY AND DEPRESSION.*

When you eat the labor of your hands, you shall be happy (Ps. 128:2).

Happy are they who hope in the Lord their God (Ps. 146:5).

Happy is everyone who finds wisdom and who gains understanding (Prov. 3:13 – 18).

They who have mercy on the poor shall be happy (Prov. 14:21).

Happy are they who fear the Lord always (Prov. 28:14; and Prov. 3:5–8; 2 Chron. 31:21; Num. 15:39–41; Jer. 29:11–13).

Where there is no vision the people fail, but they who obey God shall be happy (Prov. 29:18).

Do not seek the prosperity and short-lived peace of ungodly people and arrogant people (Jer. 12:1 – 3; Mal. 3:13 - 18; Deut. 23:5 - 6; Ps.73:1 - 12; Prov. 23:17).

Pursuing ungodly money causes many painful sorrows (1 Tim. 6:6 – 12; 2 Kings 5:15 – 27; Matt. 13:3 – 9, 18 – 23).

People are happy and saved who endure being a living sacrifice (James 5:11; Matt. 10:20 – 22; 24:13; Heb. 3:7 – 19; Joh. 6:26 – 29; Eccles. 9:11 – 12; Luke 17:7 – 10; Rom. 12:1; Eccles. 12:13 – 14; Deut. 10:12–14; Heb. 12:26–29).

HELP

To assist, to aid (1 Chron. 15:26; Est. 9:3; Ps. 37:24; 2 Cor. 1:11, 24; Rev. 12:16). If you feel helpless, you must accept that without Christ you can consistently do nothing. People who do not trust in the Lord must understand that if God does not wake them up every morning, they can do nothing (Luke 12:25 – 26; Joh. 15:1– 14; Mal. 4:1; Isa. 26:12; Jer. 5:10).

Our help is in the name Christ (Ps. 124:8). If you feel that you have destroyed or messed up your life, or if a loved one of yours is destroying or messing up their life, God says that there is help in him (Hos. 13:9). Bible scripture says, "Let my soul live, and I shall praise thee; and let your judgments help me. I have gone astray like a lost sheep. But I do not forget your commandments" (Ps. 119:175 – 176). God knows people who trust in him (Nah. 1:7). The battle is not ours, but God's, and he does not need humans' devices to win (2 Chron. 20:15; Deut. 3:22; Josh. 23:10; Exod. 14:25; Eccles. 9:11 – 12; Hos. 1:7; 2 Cor. 10:4 – 6; 1 Sam. 17:43 – 54; Ps. 20:7; 60:11; Isa. 31:1).

God does not need our help (Act 17:25; Joh. 2:25; 16:30; Ps. 50:12; Num. 22:18; 24:13; 1 Chron. 21:1 – 17; 27:23 – 24).

God only requires us to live righteously, because even if God was hungry, he would not tell us (Ps. 50:12). But some people do not want God's help (1 Sam. 8:20). Happy is the person whose help and hope is the Lord (Ps. 146:5 – 7). We must sometimes go boldly before the throne of God in prayer to obtain help in our time of need (Heb. 4:15 – 16; Isa. 33:2; 1 Sam. 2:8 - 10; Eph. 3:20 – 21).

Only a fool refuse to ask Christ for help (Isa. 22:11; 47:10 – 15; Ps. 14:1). It is very easy for God to help (2 Chron. 14:11).

We should help all people, especially members of the church, because God has helped us through problems and tribulations and had mercy on us while providing comfort and guidance (Gal. 6:10; Rom. 15:26; 1 Chron. 12:22; 1 Joh. 3:17 – 18; 2 Cor. 1:3 – 4; Matt. 5:41 – 42; Prov. 27:17; 2 Tim. 1:15 – 18).

Helping must also be mutual when possible (2 Cor. 8:11 – 15; 12:13 – 18; Phil. 2:30). The Prophet Jeremiah said that he received affliction from God because of God's wrath on other people (Lam. 3:1 – 4). Jeremiah stood before God to ask God to turn his wrath away from the people. Those same people later wanted to kill Jeremiah. The Prophet Jeremiah then asked God, "Are you rewarding me evil for doing good" (Jer. 18:19 – 20. That is how people treat leaders sometimes. This is why the Bible says, "With much wisdom comes much grief" (Eccles. 1:18). Christ is very acquainted with sorrow and grief (Isa. 53:3).

In the Old Testament a certain race of people was cursed for not helping God's people (Deut. 23:3 – 6; Neh. 6:9 – 15). And when anyone attempts to curse a true child of God, God turns the curse into a blessing (Neh. 13:1 – 2).

Do not brag after you help someone (Matt. 6:1 – 4). And sometimes we must clean up our own act before we can help others (Matt. 7:1 – 5). Helpers in the church rank higher with God than members of the church government (1 Cor. 12:28). Church and family members must realize that they are one, and that if one suffers all suffer (1 Cor.12:12 – 26). We should support the weak, and bear one another's burdens (Acts 20:33 – 35; 1 Thess. 5:14; Rom. 15:1 – 5; Gal. 6:2; Heb. 13:3; Num. 11:16 – 17).

Iron sharpens iron, so we must sharpen and support each other (Prov. 27:17). Love suffers long (1 Cor. 13). The body of Christ is one, so if one suffers, all suffer (1 Cor. 12:12 – 28). One reason that we have the term "Good Samaritan" is because the Samaritans did not have a reputation of doing good, but the one Samaritan who helped the wounded and half dead man who was laying by the roadside proves that there is good in everyone regardless of their background or race (Luke 10:30 – 37). But notice that the priest and Levite who were supposed to be holy ministers of the Lord did not help the man. If we refuse to help people when we are able, God will cause us to cry and not be heard (Prov. 21:13; 29:7; Luke 10:30 – 37; James 4:17; Prov. 3:27 – 29; Job 29:16).

However, we must be careful how we help people who have addictions, because they may cause us to fall (Jude 1:22 – 23; James 5:20). People who do not trust in God should cry out to whatever they trusted in to help them, and they will see that ungodly things will fail them in due time, and God Almighty will say, "Where is your idol now" (Deut. 32:36 – 43; Judg. 10:14; Jer. 2:28; Isa. 57:13; Judg. 5:8; Zech. 7:13; 1 Sam. 17:43 – 54)?

Where are their gods, idols, and anti – God resources when they need them? Are they dead, asleep, or on a journey (1 Kings 18:25 – 39; Isa. 26:13 – 14). God helps all people (Matt. 5:45)? God Almighty does not help sinners commit more sin (Job 8:20); and neither should we (2 Chron. 19:2).

Pastors often need help in the church, but as many helpers as possible should be called by God and filled with the Holy Ghost (Acts 6:1 – 6; 1 Tim. 5:22; 1 Cor. 12:23 – 28; Luke 10:38 – 42; 2 Kings 22:4 – 7; Exod. 18:13 – 26; Num. 11:16 – 25; Jer .20:1; 1 Chron. 6:48; 9:11, 26 – 27; 23:4 – 5; Ezra 8:15 – 23).

It is hard to help people without sacrificing something, whether it be time, money, resources, or hard work. When you sacrifice your own goods to help the sick, needy, imprisoned, and hungry people, God has for you in heaven a better and enduring substance (Heb. 10:34). But if you do not help those same people, Christ says that it is as though you did not help him (Matt. 25:31 – 46; Job 13:15 – 16; 24:1 – 11; Job 29 and Job 31). Paul's friend Epaphroditus labored so hard for the Lord that he made himself sick nearly to death, while also supplying Paul's need in prison that others did not supply (Phil. 2:25 – 30). We must do all things in the name of Christ, wholeheartedly, as unto the Lord, and not as unto humans (Col. 3:17,

23). John 3:16 tells us that God gave his only begotten Son that we shall not perish but have everlasting life. And 1st John 3:16 tells us that Christ laid down his life because he loves us, and that we should lay down certain parts of our lives for our loved ones, spiritual brothers, and sisters, and for people in need (1 Joh. 3:16 – 23).

God tells us to forgive people seven times seven times (Luke 17:3 – 4; Matt. 18:21 – 22; Prov. 17:9). It requires that much forgiveness to deal with some people, because they are always doing something wrong. And if you find that hard to do, consider how David forgave his son Absalom after Absalom killed another one of David's sons, and later took the whole kingdom from David (2 Sam. 13:20 – 29, 37 – 39; 14:30 – 33; 15; 16:10 – 12; 18:32 – 33; 19:1 – 7).

We should be fellow – workers together (2 Cor. 8:23; Phil. 4:3; 3 Joh. 1:8; Col. 4:11); fellow – laborers (1 Thess. 3:2; Ph'm. 1, 24); fellow – servants (Rev. 6:11; 19:10; 22:9); fellow – soldiers (Phil. 2:25; Ph'm. 2); and if in prison or in jail, inmates who become born again Christians should be fellow – prisoners, praying for one another and protecting one another, just as when Christ and the Apostle Paul were in jail (Rom. 16:7; Col. 4:10; Ph'm. 23). But no one helped Christ. He was totally abandoned and forsaken by everyone (Mark 14:44–50; Matt. 26:30–31, 66–75). Most of the Apostle Paul's friends abandoned and forsook him too (2 Tim. 4:6 – 18).

Do unto others as you would have them do unto you or treat them better than you treat yourself. We must also be careful how we treat people because we may need those same people again one day (Judg. 11:7; Gen. 37; 39; 40; 41; 42; 43; 44; 45; 46; 47; 48; 49; 50:1 – 2). And God sometimes causes resourceful people to not help sinful people (Jer. 15:5).

See also *FAVOR; MORE THAN YOU CAN BEAR; PROTECTION; WITH; HOLD ON; SORROW; COURAGE; HOPE; VICTORY.*

When it is safe do not turn a blind eye to people who need help Deut. 22:4).

Fake friends and deceptive help (1 Chron. 12:17).

Sometimes God sends so much help that we know it is a host of help from God (1 Chron. 12:22).

God sends help from powerful people and from people who do not have power (2 Chron. 14:11).

Helping the ungodly and anti – Christians will cause wrath on you from God (2 Chron. 19:2).

Sometimes we must gather as one to ask help of the Lord (2 Chron. 20:4; Matt. 18:19 – 20; 2 Chron. 26:3 – 21; Acts 12:12; 20:36; 21:5; 2 Chron. 20:13 – 14; Zep. 3:17).

God's help in times of evil, affliction, hunger, famine, and disease)2 Chron. 20:9).

Rest knowing that your enemies are flesh and blood but God fights your battles (2 Chron. 32:8).

Do not be ashamed to ask a human for help after bragging on God (Ezra 8:22).

Job helped the fatherless, the poor and people who had no helper (Job 29 and Job 26).

God helps his troubled people but enemies say there is no help for you in God (Ps. 3:1 – 2).

when it seems like God and humans will not help you (Ps.22:1 – 19).

God delivers and saves his people from the wicked because they trust in him (Ps. 37:40).

It is all right to ask God to help quickly, right now (Ps. 40:13 – 17).

Lord, I am poor and needy, please do not delay helping me (Ps. 40:17).

Give us help from trouble, the help of humans is useless (Ps. 60:11).

Help us, O God of our salvation, forgive our sins for your name sake (Ps. 79:9).

The Lord is our defense (Ps. 89:18 – 19).

Unless the Lord had been my help, my soul would be dead (Ps. 94:17).

Your helpers and your enemies (Ps. 118:7).

My help comes from the Lord (Ps. 121:1 – 2).

Our help is in the name of the Lord who made heaven and earth (Ps. 124:8).

Let your hand help me, for I have chosen your Word (Ps. 119:173).

Put no trust in humans who die like everyone else, but trust in God who helps the needy (Ps. 146).

Try not to grow old without children and a spouse because you need help (Eccles. 4:7 – 13).

Trusting in ungodly people for help will cause both of you to fall (Isa. 31:1 – 3).

The Lord God shall help me, I shall not be ashamed (Isa. 50:7 – 9).

Help from angels (Dan. 10:13).

In the last days God's help of his people but some shall die in righteousness (Dan. 11).

But in me is your help (Hos. 13:9).

Lord, I believe, help my lack of faith…help often comes with Fasting and praying (Mark 9:14 – 29).

Ministering to small and great with help from God (Acts 26:22).

Help in times of need (Heb. 4:16).

HOLD ON

See also *PATIENCE; HELP; STAND STILL; WAIT; HOPE; VICTORY; WORRYING.*

After your strength is gone (Deut. 32:36).
And become stronger (Job 17:9).
To righteousness (Job 27:1 – 6).
Until you die (Job 27:1 – 6).
The race is not given to the swift (Eccles. 9:11 – 12).
Renew your strength (Isa. 40:27 – 31).
Patience saves souls (Luke 21:6 – 19).
Your crown (1 Cor. 9:24 – 27; Rev. 3:7 – 13).
Bear your burdens (Gal. 6:2 – 10).
Until judgment day (Phil. 1:6, 10; 2:16).
Hold on to the good (1 Thess. 5:20 – 23).
Hold on to the truth (2 Thess. 2:7 – 17).
Until the end (Heb. 3:6, 14).
Hold on to our profession (Heb. 4:14 – 16; 10:22 – 28).
Until Christ comes (Rev. 2:24 – 29).
After repentance (Rev. 3:1 – 6).

HOPE

We should hope in the Word of God (Ps. 119:147). The resurrection of Christ from the dead gives us a lively hope (1 Pet. 1:3). Happy is the person whose help and hope is the Lord (Ps. 146:5 – 7). We must not only hope in the midst of adversity, but we must rejoice in the fact that there is hope, and sometimes be patient in prayer (Rom. 12:12). King David said that he would have fainted if he did not believe that he could see the goodness of the Lord in the land of the living. Wait on the Lord, be of good courage, and Christ will strengthen your heart, wait, I say, on the Lord (Ps. 27:12 – 14). When it looks like hope is gone, the heart becomes discouraged, but when prayers are answered, hope changes to a tree of life (Prov. 13:12). If things do not look good, that does not mean that it will not turn out good. All things work together for good if you love the Lord and are called according to God's purpose, and we are more than conquerors in Christ Jesus, but if you are not called by the Lord to do a certain thing, maybe even the thing that got yourself in trouble, it may not work out (Rom. 8:28 – 39; 2 Cor. 2:14). However, God has mercy on people who got themselves in trouble if they call on him and repent for their sins. Josiah was the second – best king in the Bible (2 Kings 23:19 – 25). But he was killed due to not obeying God's will, although God still accredited him with righteousness after his death, because he lived a holy and sanctified life. So, Josiah is going to heaven, but he died prematurely due to disobedience (2 Kings 18:4 – 7; 23:25; 2 Chron. 35:20 – 27). People who are called must endure hardness as a good soldier, while knowing that they will not be crowned unless they work truthfully for the Lord in holiness and sanctification (2 Tim. 2:1 – 5).

Look again unto a holy and sanctified church, even if God has cast you out of his sight, the Lord will receive you back again (Jon. 2:4). If you are alive, even if you cannot walk or are confined in any way including prison, if you are alive there is hope. Faith is the substance of things hoped for, and the evidence of things not seen (Heb. 11:1). Faith without works is dead, and faith without works cannot save you (James 2:13 – 26; Matt. 7:7; Mark 2:1 – 5). Hope that is seen is not hope, (Rom. 8:24). And for people who would rather be dead than alive, the Bible says, "There is hope for people who are joined to all the living, and a living dog is better than a dead lion. For the living know that they shall die but the dead know nothing, neither have they anymore a reward. Eat and drink with a merry heart, for God now accepts your works, while you are alive" (Eccles. 9:4 – 7). On judgment day God will say, "They who are unjust, let them be unjust still. They who are filthy, let them be filthy still. They who are righteous, let them be righteous still. And they who are holy, let them be holy still. Behold, I come quickly, and my reward is with me, to give everyone according to their works," (Rev. 22:10 – 13; Acts 24:15; 1 Pet. 3:18; Dan. 12:1 – 3; Ezek. 18:19 – 32; 2 Thess. 1:4 – 12).

God certainly blesses and protects his servants, even until old age and death, and he bears them, because he made them (Isa. 46:4). God in his grace and mercy, blesses ungodly people, but they still make plans against him (Hos. 7:15). God gives blessings to the just and the unjust, and to the good, the evil, and the unthankful, because they are his creation too (Deut. 9:4 – 7; 10:17 – 22; Ezek. 29:17 – 20; Matt. 5:43 – 48; Luke 6:35; Acts 14:8 – 18; Isa. 57:15 – 21; 64:4 – 8).

But on judgment day and on the day of their death, it will be too late for the unjust, the unthankful, and the evil to change and join Christ (Rev. 22:10 – 13). There will be a resurrection of the dead, both the just and the unjust (Acts 24:15). And the holy and just shall forever remain holy and just, but the unjust and filthy shall remain unjust and filthy forever

(Rev. 22:10 – 13). The righteous shall rise to everlasting life and the sinner shall rise to everlasting damnation (Dan. 12:1 – 3; Matt. 13:47 – 50; 25:31 – 46; Acts 24:15; Joh. 5:24 – 29).

People in the grave cannot praise God, neither can death celebrate God, and they who go down into the pit cannot hope for God's truth. The living, the living, they shall praise God (Isa. 38:16 – 20; Ps. 6:5; 63:3 – 4; 88:10 – 12; 115:17; 116:1 – 2, 9). The devil and his demons have bowed to Christ (Mark 3:9 – 11). Although they must bow to Christ, it is too late for them to seek salvation. They are more than simply condemned, they are damned (2 Pet. 2:4). But the worst living human sinner has hope if they repent, because help for even the worst person is in the Lord (Hos. 13:9).

God upholds the righteous, and he upholds the statements and words of his servant (Ps. 37:17; Isa. 44:24 – 26). Even the Word of his Son and servant Jesus Christ (Isa. 42:1 – 8). David said, "Uphold me according to your Word, that I may live, and let me not be ashamed of my hope" (Ps. 119:116).

See also PATIENCE; ADDICTIONS; ADVERSITY; TODAY; HELP; SORROW; ENCOURAGEMENT; VICTORY.

JOY

We must serve the Lord with joyfulness about being free from willful sin, or we shall have trouble (Deut. 28:47 – 48; Mic. 2:1; Ps. 19:12 – 14; Rom. 1:18 – 32; 2 Thess. 2:10 – 15).

To people who do not believe in Christ or who believe but insist on rebelling against the Lord, God says, "Because you refuse to serve the Lord with joyfulness and gladness of heart, for the blessings and abundance of all things, therefore you shall serve your enemies who the Lord shall send against you, in want of all things" (Deut. 28:47 – 48).

We are hardhearted if we do not serve the Lord with gladness and go before his presence with singing (Deut. 28:47 – 48; Ps. 100:2). Sometimes we must be filled with the Holy Ghost to receive godly joy while going through affliction and adversity (Rom. 15:13; 1 Thess. 1:6). Paul did not mind dying for Christ if he could finish his adversity and affliction filled course with joy (Acts 20:24). We sometimes sow and plant in tears, but we reap in joy (Ps. 126:5). Christians must count it all joy when they are faced with temptations (James 1:2). The joy of the Lord is your strength (Neh. 8:10). Paul said, "I am filled with comfort, I am exceeding joyful in all our tribulations" (2 Cor. 7:4). Christ has the power to present you to himself faultless and with joy (Jude 1:24 – 25). If we walk in the Spirit, we will not fulfill these temptations (Gal. 5:16). Because the fruit of the Spirit is love, peace, longsuffering, faith, goodness, gentleness, and joy (Gal. 5:22; Col. 1:11; Prov. 12:20). Sin is a joy to people who lack God's wisdom (Prov. 15:21); and the parent of a foolish sinner has no joy (Prov. 17:21). Sinner's joy must be turned to godly sorrow, that is, repentance (James 4:8

– 10; 2 Cor. 7:9 – 10). Receiving the Word of God with joy but failing to continue to seek God will not work (Matt. 13:20 – 23). The world rejoices in sin, but real Christians must sometimes cry and suffer as Christ did. Christians' tears and sorrow shall be turned to joy (Ps. 126:5; Joh. 16:20). Just as a pregnant mother's labor pains are turned to joy after the baby is born (Joh. 16:21). We should rejoice in being partakers with the suffering of Christ (1 Pet. 4:12 – 13). Weeping may endure for a night, but joy comes in the morning (Ps. 30:5). This sometimes means the very next day. At other times it means that trouble is darkness, and deliverance is light. Ask and it shall be given, if you ask in Christ's name, your joy shall be full and fulfilled (Joh. 16:24). But for your joy to be full you must obey the Word of God, otherwise joy from God and joy from the world is only temporary (Joh. 15:10 – 11). Peace often brings joy, and Christ says, "Peace I give unto you, not as the world gives to you, but as God gives to you. Let not your heart be troubled, neither let it be afraid" (Joh. 14:27).

It helps to become full of the Holy Ghost, because power comes with the Holy Ghost (Luke 24:49; Acts 1:8; 10:38; 1 Thess. 1:5; Rom. 15:13).

Christ gives the Holy Ghost to people who obey him (Acts 5:32; Luke 11:13; Joh. 14:13 – 18, 26 – 27 and Joh. 1:1, 14; Col. 3:16; 1 Joh. 2:5, 7, 14).

God has not given us the spirit of fear; but of power, and of love, and of a sound mind (2 Tim. 1:7). Ask God to create in you a clean heart, and to renew a right spirit within you (Ps. 51:10). Ask God to restore the joy of his salvation, and to uphold you by his free Spirit (Ps. 51:12; 94:18 – 19). Christ gives eternal salvation to people who obey him (Heb. 5:7 – 9). God's commandments are not grievous (1 Joh. 5:3). In God's presence is the fullness of joy, and pleasures for evermore (Ps. 16:11). The Christians in 2 Cor. 8:2 suffered deep poverty but were still filled with joy. In the day of prosperity be joyful, but in the day of adversity we must consider that God may have allowed or caused adversity so that we cannot always predict what he will do next (Eccles. 7:14). Even though we have not seen Christ, we must rejoice with joy unspeakable (1 Pet. 1:8). Blessed are they who have not seen Christ but still believe (Joh. 20:24 – 31).

.

KEEPER

God will keep you as the apple of his eye and hide you under the shadow of his wings (Ps. 17:8).

A scripture in the Bible asks, "Am I my brother's keeper" (Gen. 4:9)? Moses asked God, "Did I conceive all these people that I must carry them in my bosom" (Num. 11:11 – 17)? Even though it is our duty to help God keep people saved, even good preachers who plant and water are nothing, because God gives the increase (Jude 1:21 – 25; 1 Cor. 3:1 – 15; Gal. 6:1; 1 Pet. 4:8; James. 5:20). Ultimately, God is your keeper (Ps. 121:5). Everything that God did not plant shall be uprooted by the Lord and destroyed (Matt. 15:13). Christ is the Good Shepard and Bishop of our souls, and no one can pluck us out of God's hands (Joh. 10:1 – 17, 24 – 29; 1 Pet. 2:21 – 25). Being confident of this very thing, that God who has begun a good work in you will perform it until the day of Jesus Christ (Phil. 1:6). So that God can keep us, we must keep the Word of God, especially after we are warned (Ps. 19:11; 119:9 – 16, 116; 1 Pet. 4:19). Christ will keep us in the palm of his hands, even if the devil is standing at our right hand to resist us (Zech. 3:1 – 7; Isa. 49:15 – 16; Ps. 121). But the devil will only leave you for a season (Luke 4:13; 1 Pet. 1:6). If you put God first always, he will preserve you (Isa. 26:3; 1 Thess. 5:23; 2 Tim. 4:18; 2 Sam. 8:6, 14; Ps. 37:28).

God keeps the feet of his saints (1 Sam. 2:9). Cast your burdens upon the Lord, and he shall sustain you, he shall never allow the righteous to be moved (Ps. 3:5; 55:22; Neh. 9:21; Isa. 59:16; 1 Kings 17).

God will keep them in perfect peace whose mind is stayed

on him (Isa. 26:3; Ps. 3:5 – 10). God says, "Everyone who is called by my name, whom I have created for my glory, I have formed them, yes, I have made them. You are my witnesses, says the Lord, and my servants whom I have chosen, that you may know and believe me, and understand that I am He. Before me there was no God formed, nor shall there be after me. I, even I, am the Lord, and besides me there is no Savior. Therefore, you are my witnesses, says the Lord, that I am God. And there is no one who can deliver out of my hand. I work, and who will reverse it" (Isa. 43:7 – 13)? Pray about everything and the peace that surpasses all understanding shall keep your hearts and minds through Christ Jesus (Phil. 4:6 – 7).

Ask God to guard over your mouth and the words of your lips (Ps. 141:3). God who keeps us will not allow our feet to be moved. God who keeps you will not slumber (Ps. 121:3 – 5). The Lord shall preserve you from all evil. He shall preserve your soul. The Lord shall preserve you going out and coming in, from this time forth, and even forevermore (Ps. 121:7 – 8). If the Lord does not build the house the laborers labor in vain, and if the Lord does not keep the city the watchman watches in vain (Ps. 127:1). Keep me Lord from the hands of the wicked, preserve me from the violent person whose purpose is to make my steps stumble (Ps. 140:4). Keep me from the snares that they have laid for me, and from the traps of the workers of iniquity (Ps. 141:9).

The Holy Bible says, "The Word of God is perfect, converting the soul. The testimony of the Lord is sure, making wise the simple. The statutes of the Lord are right, rejoicing the heart. The commandments of the Lord are pure, enlightening the eyes. The fear of the Lord is clean, enduring forever. The judgments of the Lord are true and righteous altogether, more desired than gold, yes, than much fine gold, sweeter also than honey and the honeycomb. Moreover, by the Word of God is your servant warned, and in obeying the Word of God is great reward. Who can understand their errors? Cleanse thou me from secret faults. Keep back your servant also from presumptuous sins, let them not have dominion over me. Then shall I be upright, and I shall be innocent from the great transgression. Let the words of my mouth, and the meditation of my heart, be acceptable in your sight, O Lord, my strength, and my redeemer" (Ps. 19:7 – 14).

Furthermore, the Bible says, "Wherefore let them who suffer according to the will of God commit the keeping of their souls to him in well doing, as unto a faithful Creator" (1 Pet. 4:19). We are also kept by faith, but by faith unto salvation, not faith while living in willful and habitual sin, faith unto salvation, ready to be revealed in the last time (1 Pet. 1:1 - 5).

If you love God, keep his commandments and live (Joh.14:15, 21; 15:10; Rev. 12:17; 14:12; 22:9; Exod. 16:28; 20:6; Lev. 22:31; 26:3; Deut. 5:10, 29; 1 Kings 3:14; 6:12; 9:6; 11:38; 2 Kings 17:13; 1 Chron. 29:19; Neh. 1:9; Ps. 89:31; 119:115; Prov. 3:1; 4:4; 7:1 – 2; Dan. 9:4).

Keep me from evil, so that it will not grieve me (1 Chron. 4:10). We keep the charge of the Lord, but you have forsaken him (2 Chron. 13:11).

Keep them, O Lord, you shall preserve them from this generation forever (Ps. 12:7).

Kept me from the path of the destroyer (Ps. 17:4).

All the paths of God are mercy and truth to people who keep his Word (Ps. 25:10).

O keep my soul, and deliver me. Let me not be ashamed. I put my trust in you Lord (Ps. 25:20).

Wait on the Lord, and keep his way, and he will exalt you (Ps. 37:34).

God will give his angels charge over you to keep you in all your ways (Ps. 91:11).

Discretion shall preserve you, understanding shall keep you (Prov. 2:11).

We should keep the godly values that our godly parents taught us (Prov. 6:20).

When you sleep it shall keep you, when you awake it shall talk to you (Prov. 6:22).

They who forsake the Word praise the wicked. They who keep it contends with them (Prov. 28:4).

God called you in righteousness and will hold your hand, and will keep you (Isa. 42:6).

Christ asked God to keep us through the name of Christ (Joh. 17:11 – 12).

Not take them out of the world but keep them from the evil (Joh. 17:15).

If you keep yourself from fornication, you do well (Acts 15:29).

God keeps your heart and mind through Christ Jesus (Phil. 4:7).

The Lord is faithful who will establish you and keep you from evil (2 Thess. 3:3).

Keep by the Holy Ghost in you that which God has *committed* to you (2 Tim. 1:12 – 14).

Keep yourselves from idols (1 Joh. 5:21).

Keep yourselves in the love of God, looking for the mercy of our Lord (Jude 1:21).

To Him who is able to keep you from falling and present you faultless (Jude 1:24).

Keep those things that are written because the time is at hand (Rev. 1:3).

I will keep you from the hour of temptation that will come upon all the world (Rev. 3:10).

Keep the sayings of the prophecy of this book (Rev. 22:7).

Keep the sayings of this book, worship God (Rev. 22:9).

See also *WITH; PROTECTION; VICTORY*.

MENTAL HEALTH

Just as everyone has physical illnesses at times, most people also have mental illnesses, whether they know it or not, even if it is temporary. And some mental illnesses allow people to still be productive in their careers and professions, but they still have mental problems. People with OCD – Obsessive – Compulsive Disorder often do a better job on projects than people without OCD because they never settle for a job not well done. They love to excel and to perform on a high level. And when OCD becomes to obsessive, they should ask a doctor for medication or make other adjustments to balance their disorder that caused them to be very successful in the past.

God tells us to comfort the feeble – minded (1 Thess. 5:14). Some people are born with mental problems and/or physical illnesses (Mark 9:17 – 25). And there are people who develop chronic mental problems years after birth. Healthy minds become ill sometimes just like healthy bodies sometimes become ill. When the mind becomes ill, the body may follow, because the mind manages the body (Pr.17:22; 18:14. This refers to depression and sadness too, and the Bible says, "A merry heart does good like medicine, but a broken spirit dries the bones" (Prov. 17:22; 18:14). We must not drown ourselves in sorrow, because sorrow of the heart breaks the spirit (Prov. 15:13). Just before Christ was crucified, he was in deep anxiety, and his disciples' sorrow caused them to sleep (Luke 22:39 – 46). The spirit of a person will sustain them in sickness, but who can bear a broken spirit (Prov. 18:14). There are people who create their own mental and emotional problems through drug, alcohol, other substance abuse, and bad decisions. To those people, the Bible says that God has not given us the spirit of fear, but of power, of love, and of a sound mind (2 Tim. 1:7). Do not take anything for granted and do not assume anything but pray about everything and the peace that surpasses all understanding shall keep your hearts and minds through Christ Jesus (Phil. 4:6 – 7). God will keep you in perfect peace if you trust in him and keep your mind stayed on him (Isa. 26:3). God gave King Saul an evil spirit, a sad emotional spirit, that resulted in depression, and the only thing that made him feel better was holy music (1Sam. 16:14, 23). Then there were times when even holy music did not help, because God was against him (1 Sam. 18:10 – 12; 19:9 – 11).

The Criminal Justice system should reconsider certain people with mental problems before they are punished unfairly This does not mean that they should always be set free, because they may be dangerous. Incarcerating them may only make their situation worse through neglect and abuse. Executing the mentally ill is sinful and cruel punishment, even though the convicted person may have committed a sinful and cruel crime. But Christ died for their sins as well, even though sometimes a life sentence is appropriate for anyone who commits certain types of crimes. They should be confined but not executed (Matt. 1:21; Acts 26:18; Gal. 1:4; 1 Joh. 2:2).

Mental illness is nothing to be ashamed of, and people who try to hide it or refuse to seek help are harming themselves even more. Anyone with mental illness, anxiety, depression, emotional problems, phycological problems, obsessive disorders, or problems with alcohol or drugs should not refuse to take doctor prescribed medicine when necessary, and counseling when necessary. If being admitted into a mental health facility is necessary, then do it. It is best to manage mental illness than to suffer for years, months, weeks, or days. And sometimes when mentally ill people do not seek help, they suffer in silence. Others suffer while displaying loud outburst or violent acts, and they should face the fact that they have a problem before they end up in jail, prison, or without a spouse and family, some even becoming homeless due to family members not wanting to tolerate the extreme behavior any longer. Sadly, in some cases death happens when another person kills a mentally ill person who may have been violent or using or seeking narcotics in an unsafe environment. There is also the case of suffering the consequences of drinking and driving.

The Bible says that a double minded person is unstable in all their ways, therefore being a highly intelligent double-minded person causes some of the same problems that mentally ill people cause (Gen. 35:22; 49:3 – 4; 1 Chron. 5:1 – 2; James 1:5 – 8; 2 Pet. 3:14–17).

The Bible's definition of "sober" does not always refer to alcohol but also to having a balanced, stable, self – controlled, self – disciplined, self – driven, self – determined, self – motivated mind with self – restraint and temperance, and help from Christ who strengthens us, and who makes us more than conquerors (Rom. 8:28 – 39; 2 Cor. 2:14; Acts 26:25; Rom. 12:3; 2 Cor. 5:13; 1 Thess. 5:6, 8; 1 Tim. 3:2, 11; Tit. 1:8; 2:2, 4, 12; 1 Pet. 1:13; 4:7; 5:8).

The Bible says that a person who controls their own spirit and behavior, who are slow to speak and quick to listen, and are slow to become angry are stronger than a soldier who conquers a city (Rom. 8:28 – 39; 2 Cor. 2:14; Rev. 6:2; 2 Cor. 2:14; Prov. 16:32; Eccles. 7:19; Isa. 53:7; Mark 15:4 – 5; James 1:19 – 27; Prov. 14:29; 15:18; 21:23 – 24; 25:8 – 10; Eccles. 3:1 – 8; 5:1 – 7).

Without Christ we can do nothing for long (John 15:1 – 14; Mal. 4:1; Jude 1:12; Matt. 3:10; Eccles. 9:1; Jer. 5:10).

God the Father sends us God the Holy Ghost to comfort us, and he is our Comforter who is the God of all comfort (Joh. 14:16 – 26; 15:26 – 27; 16:7 – 16; 2 Cor. 1:3 - 4; 1 Thess. 5:11; Acts 9:31; Ps. 94:19; 2 Thess. 2:16 – 17; 2 Pet. 2; Jude 1; Acts 5:32; Luke 11:13; Joh. 14:13 – 18, 26 – 27 and Joh.1:1, 14; Col. 3:16; 1 Joh. 2:5, 7, 14).

See also WORRYING; ADDICTIONS; ANXIETY; SORROW; ALCOHOL.

MORE THAN YOU CAN BEAR

God never puts more on us than we can bear (1 Cor. 10:12 – 13; 1 Pet. 4:12 – 19). Therefore, if it seems like things are overwhelming, we are either losing faith in God, or we put more on our own selves than we can bear. The Bible says that if you build a house without first counting the cost, and you cannot finish building, people will mock you and say that you started to build but could not complete it (Luke 14:28 – 30; Prov. 24:27). You would have done that on your own, not God, and not anyone else. You would have given yourself too much to bear. Just as when a person puts an overwhelming load on themselves when they marry or have kids by the wrong person.

Christ says, "Come unto me, all you who labor and are heavy laden, and I will give you rest. Take my yoke upon you and learn of me, for I am meek and lowly in heart. And you shall find rest unto your souls. For my yoke is easy, and my burden is light" (Matt. 11:28 – 30). But if you are a sinner, God's burden is heavy, and your own self – inflicted burden is heavy (Isa. 30:27 Zech.12:1 – 3; Ezek. 14:22 – 23. Another scripture says, "Ask for the old paths, where is the good way, and walk therein, and you shall find rest for your souls. But they said, 'We will not walk therein'" (Jer. 6:16).

God is merciful, just as he was merciful when Cain said that his punishment from God was more than he could bear, but God protected Cain (Gen. 4:1 – 17). Sarah put more on herself than she could bear when she did not believe that God would give her a son in her old age. She instead told her husband Abraham to sleep with their maid, but later Sarah despised the son that was conceived from Abraham sleeping with the maid (Gen. 16; Heb. 6:15).

Christ never puts on us more than is right (Job 34:23). God never puts on us more than we can bear, and there has no temptation taken you but such as is common to humans (1 Cor. 10:1 – 13; Joh. 17:14 – 19; Rev. 3:10 – 13; James 4:7; Luke 4:1 – 13).

Notice that the first part of the scriptures says, "Let them who think they stand take heed lest they fall" (1 Cor. 10:12 – 13; 1 Tim. 4:16). Sometimes we reap what we sow, we reap what we plant and grow (Gal. 6:7 – 10; Jer. 31:9). The same applies to people who persecute the saints. The wrong that they did is returned upon their own head (Gal. 5:10; Acts 18:6; 1 Sam. 25:39; 1 Kings 2:32, 37, 44; 2 Chron. 6:23; Neh. 4:4; Est. 9:25; Job 5:13; Ps. 7:16; 140:9; Ezek. 11:21; 17:19; 22:31; Joel 3:4 – 7; Oba. 1:15).

People are tempted when they are drawn away by their own lust and enticed. When lust is conceived, it brings forth sin, and sin brings forth death (James 1:12 – 16; Rom. 6:23). This is one reason that the Bible tells us to not consent when sinners try to entice us (Prov. 1:10 – 19). God gives his angels charge over us, to bear us up in their hands, otherwise we sometimes harm ourselves (Ps. 91:11 – 12; Matt. 4:5 – 7). God will carry and bear the righteous as a daughter and son, even to their old age (Isa. 46:4; Deut. 1:31). When they are afflicted, God is afflicted too (Isa. 63:8 – 9). Cast your burdens upon the Lord, He shall never allow the righteous to be moved (Ps. 55:22; 81:5 – 6). Christ bore our sins on the cross, by his stripes are we healed (Isa. 53:5; 1 Pet. 2:24). However, God gets tired of bearing with our rebellious and habitual sin, and he will sometimes allow people to suffer from those sins until they die, unless they repent (Num. 14:27 – 34). God also gets tired of people who repent and go back (Jer. 15:6). If your sins are too heavy for you, ask God to relieve you of the sins and to not punish you in his wrath (Ps. 38:1 – 4). Paul said that he bore in his body the marks of the Lord Jesus (Gal. 6:17; 1 Pet. 5:1). Paul lived as we must all live, like Christ, which requires some suffering, affliction, and adversity (2 Cor. 11:24 – 33; 1 Cor. 4:10 – 14). We must suffer some of the things that Christ suffered (Isa. 53). When times get hard, God's grace is sufficient, even if He caused the adversity in your life, or if you caused it in your own life (2 Cor. 12:6 – 10; 11:24 – 33; 13:3 – 9; 1 Cor. 4:10 – 14; 2 Sam. 3:31 – 39; Est. 4:3; Neh. 1:4).

Evidently, God did not put more on Christ than He could bear, but during his last hours Christ sure felt that God had put too much on him to bear (Matt. 26:36–42; Luke 22:39–46). A quote from the Bible says, "Woe to me for my hurt! My wound is grievous, but I said, truly this is grief, and I must bear it" (Jer. 10:19). We must all bear grief, because Christ was despised and rejected, a man of sorrows and acquainted with grief (Isa. 53:3 – 4. Christ was rejected in his own hometown (Luke 4:16 – 32; 9:51 – 58). Christ's own biological brothers did not believe in him (Joh. 7:1 – 8). Christ came unto his own, including the black Jews, and his own received him not (Joh. 1:10 – 14; Acts 13:26 – 31; Luke 24:44 – 49). Christ bears the sins of many (Isa. 53:12; Heb. 9:28). No matter how you are suffering or resisting, if you are still alive you have not resisted unto blood striving against sin, as Christ did (Heb. 12:4; James 4:7; Joh. 17:14 – 19; 1 Cor. 10:8 – 13). No matter what anyone goes through, it is not as hard as what Christ went through. One scripture says, "The Lord has chastened me sore, but he has not given me over unto death" (Ps. 118:18). Hezekiah said, "Thou in love for my soul delivered me from the pit of corruption, for thou have casted all my sins behind your back. For the grave cannot praise you, death cannot celebrate you. They who go down into the pit cannot hope for your truth. The living, the living, they shall praise you, as I do this day. The father to the children shall make known your truth. The Lord was ready to save me, therefore we will sing songs all the days of our life in the house of the Lord. I will call on the Lord as long as I live. I will walk before the Lord in the land of the living" (Isa. 38:16 – 20; Ps. 6:5; 63:3 – 4; 88:10 – 12; 115:17; 116:1 – 2 , 9).

Christ says that people who have truly repented for a lot of sins and a very sinful lifestyle, love him much and serve him greater in labor for the Lord, and people who have repented for a few sins and a less sinful lifestyle, love him not as much (Luke 7:36 – 48). Christ said that people who do not bear their cross cannot be his disciple (Luke 14:26 – 35; Matt. 10:33 – 39; 16:24 – 27).

Apostle Paul desired to live like Christ and also to suffer like Christ when he said, "Things that were gain to me, I counted as a loss for Christ's sake, and I count all things as a loss for the excellency of the knowledge of Christ Jesus my Lord, for whom I have suffered the loss of all things, and do count them as dung, that I may win Christ. Not having my own righteousness, but the righteousness that is of God by faith, that I may know him, and his suffering" (Phil. 3:7 – 11).

Another person in the Bible said, "I will wait on the Lord of my salvation and bear the indignation of the Lord, because I have sinned" (Mic. 7:8 – 10).

Being filled with the Holy Ghost provides us with Comfort while we are going through trials, tribulation, adversity, and affliction (Joh. 14:16 – 26; 15:26 – 27; 16:7 – 15). But we must be obedient to God to be filled with the Holy Ghost (Acts 5:32; Luke 11:13; Joh. 14:13 – 18, 26 – 27 and Joh. 1:1, 14; Col. 3:16; 1 Joh. 2:5, 7, 14; Isa. 59:20).

Notice that Christ said that they could not bear the things that he was saying until they received the Holy Ghost (Joh. 16:12 – 15; Luke 24:49; Acts 1:8; 10:38; 1 Thess. 1:5; Rom. 15:13).

This is why Christ feeds some of us spiritual milk instead of spiritual meat. Some of us are not mature enough or strong enough to handle spiritual meat but are still sucking a spiritual bottle of milk like a baby in the Christian Faith (Heb. 5:11 – 14; 1 Cor. 3:1 – 2; 10:1 – 13; 1 Pet. 2:2; Isa. 28:9 – 12). But after some time, Christ expects those of us who are on milk to be able to bear meat (Heb. 5:11 – 14).

Christ gives eternal salvation to people who obey him (Heb. 5:7 – 9). After punishing the disobedient, Christ told the obedient group who had endured their adversity and tribulation that He would put no other burden on them (Rev. 2:24).

Christians should bear one another's burdens (Gal. 6:2; Heb. 13:3; Num. 11:16 – 17). Love bears all things (1 Cor. 13:7 – 8. Iron sharpens iron, and we must sharpen each other (Prov. 27:17). Moses told God that he could not bear leading all the people in the wilderness, so God gave him helpers (Exod. 18:13 – 27; Num. 11:11 – 17; Deut. 1:9 – 16). Other Levites including Ezekiel had to bear the burdens of the people because they were men of God (Num. 18:1, 23; Ezek. 4:4). Nowadays God says be not many ministers, because they receive the greater condemnation if they do not teach holiness (James 3:1; 1 Cor. 9:16). Ministers must bear the burdens of church members, but the ministers should not put burdens upon the people, not even the burdens of false doctrine and overpaying money to the ministers (Acts 15:25 – 28; 1 Pet. 5:1 – 11). God no longer punishes children for the sins of the parents, but that could have been more than you could bear (Ezek. 18:19 – 20).

While asking God to forgive the people for their sins Daniel told God, "Your city and your people are called by your name" (Dan. 9:3 – 19). God says, "If my people, who are called by my name, (Christians) shall humble themselves, and pray, and seek my face, and turn from their wicked ways, then will I hear from heaven, and will forgive their sins, and will heal their land" (2 Chron. 7:14; Isa. 6:8 – 10; Ezek. 33:31; Matt. 13:14 – 15; Luke 19:37 – 42; Deut. 29:2 – 6).

But God also that says the sinners of his people will die, just as heathens and infidels die in their sins (Am. 9:10). Which means again, that there are Christian sinners who are wretched and hypocritical, and there are heathens who confess Christ, but are still heathens (Am. 9:10). David said to God, "When you say, 'Seek my face,' my heart said unto you, your face Lord, will I seek" (Ps. 27:8). Otherwise, God says, "I will go and return to my place until they acknowledge their sins, and seek my face, in their affliction they will seek me early" (Hos .5:3 – 6, 15; Ps. 78:34). The Bible also says, "The Lord knows them who are his, and let everyone who confesses the name of Christ depart from sin" (2 Tim. 2:19). Flee youthful lusts, and follow righteousness, faith, love, and peace with them who call on the Lord with a pure heart daily (2 Tim. 2:22; Job 27:8 – 23; Ps. 1; Prov. 3:5 – 8).

The judgment of God starts at the church, with church people (1 Pet. 4:17). When God used the prophet Amos to warn the people of destruction, they said Amos had conspired against them and that the land was not able to bear his words (Am. 7:1 – 10). Notice, first God was patient with them and did not punish them for a long time. Secondly, they said the land could not bear it. But the land would have been healed if they would have just turned from their sinful ways (2 Chron. 7:14; Luke 19:37 – 42). Again, God never puts more on us than we can bear (1 Cor. 10:12 – 13). Therefore, if it seems like things are overwhelming, we are either losing faith in God, or we put more on ourselves, than we can bear. The Lord tells us, "Do not think it is strange when you are faced with a fiery trial that is to try you, as though some strange thing happened to you. But rejoice because you are partakers of Christ's suffering. If people speak evil of you because you are a sanctified Christian, you should be happy, because the Spirit of God rests upon you. On their part Christ is blasphemed, but on your part, he is glorified. But do not suffer as a murderer, thief, evildoer, or busybody in other people's business (1 Pet. 4:12 – 19; 1 Thess. 3:3).

Again, if anyone suffers as a Christian, let them not be ashamed" (1 Pet. 4:12 – 19; 2 Tim. 1:12). We must also bear our own cross of adversity (Mark 8:34 – 38). And if we are ashamed of Christ and the Word of God in this evil adulterous generation, Christ will be ashamed of us before God (Mark 8:38; 1 Thess. 2:2; 2 Tim. 1:12; Rev. 3:1 – 6; Hos. 7:1 – 4.

If you deny Christ, he will deny you (2 Tim. 2:12; 3:11

– 12). Blessed are they who are not offended in Christ (Matt. 11:6).

Mankind is either full of the Holy Ghost, full of themselves, full of the devil, or empty. When we are full of the Holy Ghost, we are strengthened from sinful activity and from pain, and we are comforted (Joh. 14:16 – 26; 15:26 – 27; 16:7 – 16; Acts 9:31; 2 Thess. 2:16 – 17; Ps. 94:19; 2 Pet. 2; Jude 1).

Christ says that some people are like a tomb that is beautiful on the outside and made of pretty white marble, but inside are the bones of a dead person (Matt. 23:27). When we are empty, we can be everything from lonely, to suicidal, to having a need to be fulfilled in various ways. This is why some people are depressed, or drink alcohol, smoke, use drugs, buy things that they do not need, or commit fornication and adultery. But when people are empty, God will enter them if they allow him to do so (Luke 11:13; Joh. 14:13 – 18, 26 – 27; Acts 5:32 and Acts 2:36 – 39.

Our bodies are temples of God (Joh. 2:19 – 21; 2 Cor. 5:1; 2 Pet. 1:12 – 15). And if we defile our body with drugs, too much alcohol, too much eating, eating the wrong foods, sex outside of marriage, pornography, or dressing in a revealing manner, for example, God will not dwell in us, because God does not dwell in an unclean temple, and they who defile the temple of God, which you are, God eventually destroys that person and that temple (1 Cor. 6:9 – 20; and 1 Cor. 3:16 – 23; Eph. 2:19 – 22; Heb. 3:4 – 19; 4:1; Rom. 6:23; Rev. 21:22 – 27).

God does not dwell in temples made with hands, but in holy humans (Acts 7:48; 17:24). If you are empty and not full of the Holy Ghost, the devil could enter you and cause you to do things that are against God, against yourself, against your family, and against others. Even after God casts out the devil from your body, and you do not allow the Holy Ghost to enter and dwell within you, you are still empty and the one demon that you had inside of you will return with seven more. And if you had two demons casted out of you by the Lord, those two will return with fourteen more (Matt. 12:43 – 45; 2 Pet.

2:19). Thus, for every one demon that God casts out of a person's body, seven more will enter them if they do not allow God to fill them with the Holy Ghost and fulfill their every need. Some people are possessed with demons that cause them to be a murderer, child molester, adulterer, or fornicator, among other things. Christ casted demons out of one man, and there were so many demons in the man that they were called Legion (Mark 5:1 – 20). Christ says that this is an evil, adulterous, and demonic generation (Matt. 12:39 – 45. Demons do not always reveal themselves as evil, but as wolves who look like sheep, and as angels who are really devils (Matt. 7:15 – 29; 2 Cor. 11:14 – 15).

When things happen in life, either God did it, you did it, someone else did it, or the devil did it, and sometimes we put too much on ourselves or another person messes up our life, even if it is temporary. In Christ dwells all the fullness of God, and you are complete in him, who is the head of all principality and power (Col. 2:9 – 10; 1 Cor. 15:24 – 28; Eph. 1:21 – 23; Phil. 2:9; Ps. 8; Heb. 2:5 – 9; Joh. 16:15; Matt. 28:18;).

See also *HELP; ADVERSITY; ADDICTIONS; WITH; TEST; PATIENCE; SORROW; ALONE; VICTORY; FATHERLESS; WORRYING.*

OUTCAST

In the Old Testament people were outcasted for various reasons (1 Sam. 26:19; 2 Chron. 11:14 – 16; Ezra 2:59 – 63; 7:26; Neh. 7:61 – 64; Lam. 2:14; Ps. 31:11; 38:11; 69:8; 88:8).

New Testament scriptures tell us to put people out of the church if they refuse to obey the Word of God to the point that it is intolerable and hurting others (1 Cor. 5; 1 Tim. 1:19 – 20). However, if a person is unfairly driven away from a family, place of employment, church, team, or any organization, they should be asked to return (2 Sam. 14:13 – 14; Ezek. 34:1 – 10). Because if a person is outcasted wrongfully, God will be with them, and against the person who unfairly sent them away (Ps. 147:2; Mic. 4:6). Just as God was with Ishmael when Abraham's wife caused Abraham to outcast his son and his son's mother into a barren desert land (Gen. 16; 17:20; 21:9 – 21). It is God's desire to bring back all his outcasted people (Ps. 147:2; Isa. 11:12; 56:8; Jer. 49:36). Especially when the outcasted repent for their sins, just as the people who casted them out should repent for their sins (Job 8:4 – 7; Jonah 2:4).

Sometimes the very person who is driven away is the same person who is desperately needed in the future (Judg. 11:1 – 11). At another time Jacob who was renamed Israel had a younger son named Joseph who the older sons envied, and they abandoned him in a desert land and left him there to die. A group of people found him and sold him into slavery in Egypt where he eventually became the second highest ranking person in the whole kingdom. When a famine struck the land that Jacob and his sons lived in, his sons went to Egypt to seek food, but they did not know that they were negotiating with their younger brother who they thought was dead by now. When Joseph finally revealed his identity to them, they were ashamed and condemned in their own sight. They desperately needed their brother to help them prevent their families including their father Israel from starving to death (Gen. 37; 39; 40; 41; 42; 43; 44; 45; 46; 47; 48; 49; 50:1 – 2)

Christ was an outcast and knows how people feel who are wrongfully casted away from the church, home, organization, team, school, or affiliation. It is their loss, not the person's who was driven away. (Matt. 3:21; 13:57 – 58; Luke 4:14 – 32; Joh. 1:11; 7:1 – 14).

Christ knows just how we feel and was tempted at all points, but still did not sin (Heb. 4:15 and Heb. 2:16 – 18). Just as his Father God Almighty is perfect and has never sinned (Deut. 32:4; 2 Chron. 19:6 – 10; Ps. 18:30; 92:15; Gal. 2:17; 1 Pet. 2:22; Heb. 4:15).

Christ even died, but most people do not want to die, or are afraid to die, but Christ knows how we feel in that area too (Luke 22:39 – 42; Mark 15:34; Heb. 4:15). Because he died, and rose from the dead, defeating death forever (1 Cor. 15:50 – 58; Joh. 12:24; Dan. 12:1 – 4; 1 Thess. 4:13 – 18; Rev. 22:10 – 11).

We should bow to God in prayer while confidently kneeling before the throne of grace as though we are in heaven bowing before the throne of God, to obtain mercy, and find grace to help in times of need (Heb. 4:14 – 16). If you go unto Christ with a desire to live righteously, he will not cast you out nor cast you away (Joh. 6:37). The Bible says that God will not cast away a righteous person, but that he will not help an evil or wicked person, and that God is angry with wicked people every day (Joh. 9:31; Job 8:20; 35:13; Ps. 66:16 – 20; Isa. 1:15; 59:1 – 2; Rom. 1:18 – 32; 2 Thess. 2:10 – 15).

There are people who cast away others and think that they do service unto God by casting them away (Joh. 16:1 – 3). But it is better to be an outcast from one place where you would eat meat, and instead live where love is and eat herbs (Prov. 15:17). Christ says, "Rejoice when you are put out of the presence of some people, because your reward is great in heaven" (Luke 6:22 – 24).

David's son Absalom caused a mutiny against his father David and forced David to run for his life and to vacant his throne as king, and he slept with David's maids (2 Sam. 15). Absalom's mutiny ended up failing, and he was outcasted by his father David after Absalom ran away for his life. Absalom lied to God by saying that he would serve the Lord if God would deliver him back home after being a fugitive (2 Sam. 15:1 – 12 and 2 Sam. 13). When David allowed Absalom to return home, Absalom sinned against God and went against David again, and some people nowadays work against us again after they are forgiven (2 Sam. 14:1 – 3, 19 – 23).

God says, "I will restore health unto you, and I will heal you of your wounds, says the Lord; because they called you an outcast who no one wants" (Jer. 30:17).

See also *FOSTER CARE; ABANDONMENT; ALONE; KEEPER.*

Marrying heathens before Christ died for all people (Ezra 10:7 – 17).
God is your Father (Isa. 63:16).
The original apostles were outcasted by Jews, Greeks, and Romans (Acts 13:44 – 52).
The devil is an outcast of God (Rev. 12).

PATIENCE

There may come a time in the life of holy, sanctified, praying faithful, and spiritually laboring Christians when God will delay giving them the desires of your heart, as the Bible says that God will give us (Ps. 10:17; 20:1 – 4; 21:2; 37:4 – 8; 145:16, 19; Mark 11:24; Eccles. 11:9).

It may seem like your dreams and goals are fading fast, that time is running out, that you are aging out, or that your time has passed. You know that God has always been with you and helped you to overcome great deficits, win great battles, reach high goals, rise from deep depths and from deeply burned ashes, but this time it seems like God is not with you, and you may feel that he never was with you concerning one specific goal that is so hard to reach. You may feel like giving up, but God keeps pushing you and driving you to labor for him in other areas of life. Just as when the Prophet Jeremiah said that he would no longer speak in the name of the Lord, but Jeremiah could not resist the urge to still labor and speak for the Lord. It was like fire shut up in his bones that he just had to let out. Jeremiah had felt that God's enemies and his enemies were stronger than him, and everyone laughed at Jeremiah because he trusted in the Lord (Jer. 20:7 – 9; 38: 6 – 11). After having patience and suffering through adversity and affliction, God caused Jeremiah, and certain children, women, men, and poor people to not go into slavery with the rest of the nation, and God caused Jeremiah's enemies to favor him, and they released him to live the rest of his life in freedom (Jer. 15:10 – 11; 39:8 – 18; 40:1 – 7).

God expects strong Christians to not complain and to totally understand that God will test them and even allow the devil to test, try, and temp them (Rev. 2:10; 3:10). Just as Job did not curse God nor lose faith in God, nor stop trusting in God after God gave the devil permission to destroy Job's property, children, wealth, and health (Job 1; Job 2 and Job 42). The patience of Job in sickness, and with loss of his children, and loss of his property and money was still being talked about thousands of years later (James 5:11). Sometimes, in the life of strong, knowledgeable, and wise Christians, God may not give them what they want until later, even after they pass God's tests and resisted the temptations of the devil. Sometimes God literally says, "Well done, you passed the test, now wait on your reward, your prize, and your heart's desire" (Ps. 10:17; 20:1 – 4; 21:2; 37:4 – 8; 145:16, 19; Mark 11:24; Eccles. 11:9).

It is totally like achieving a college degree and passing the test to become certified with a license but still having a hard time obtaining the job that you want. But one day you will get exactly what you want, what you worked extremely hard for, and what you deserve.

God says that the earth, or even a single nation, was not made in one day (Isa. 66:7 – 8). God often does things in his own time (Isa. 60:22). Since the beginning of the world, people have not heard, nor perceived by the ear, neither has the eye seen, O God, besides you, what is prepared for people who wait on the Lord and who love the Lord (Isa. 64:4; 1 Cor. 2:9). Sometimes no matter what the blessing is from God, it would have been greater if we could have just had more patience (Luke 18:1 – 8).

Be careful how you ask God to give you the gift of patience, because the only way that God can give you patience is to also put you through something and make you wait for a very long time for relief and success, but after enduring you inherit the promises of God (James 1: 2 – 8; 5:10 – 11; Heb. 6:12).

The following scriptures says, "And we ought to always pray, and not faint. If you faint in the day of adversity, your strength in the Lord is small" (Prov. 24:10). We must serve the

Lord with joyfulness, or we shall have trouble (Deut. 28:47 – 48; Mic. 2:1; Ps. 19:12 – 14). We are hardhearted if we do not serve the Lord with gladness and go before his presence with singing (Deut. 28:47 – 48; Ps. 100:2). God says what glory shall we receive when we suffer after doing wrong? But when we suffer after doing good and take it patiently, that is acceptable with God (1 Pet. 2:19 – 25). Therefore, do not become tired of doing good (Gal. 6:9; Ps. 37). If you suffer for righteousness' sake, you should be happy and you are blessed, and do not be afraid of the enemy, neither worry (1 Pet. 3:14 – 17; Ps. 38:15 – 22). It may seem like sinners are not being punished by God, but God says keep serving him and we will see who is punished and who is protected (Mal. 3:13 – 18; Deut. 23:6; Ps. 73:1 – 12).

Therefore, being justified by faith, knowing that tribulation works patience; and patience works experience; and experience works hope, and hope makes us not ashamed (Rom. 5:1 – 4; Isa. 49:23). The Bible says, "Let not anyone be ashamed who waits on the Lord. Let them be ashamed who transgress against the Lord. Let integrity and righteousness uphold me, for I wait on you Lord." (Ps. 25:3, 21). Faith without works is dead, and faith without works cannot save you (James 2:13 – 26; Matt. 7:7). Tribulation causes patience (Rom. 5:1 – 3; 12:12). We are saved by hope, and hope that is seen is not hope. But if we hope for what we cannot see, then we wait with patience (Rom. 8:24 – 25). For we walk by faith, not by sight (2 Cor. 5:7; Heb. 11:1). The trying of your faith works patience. But let patience have its perfect work, that you may be perfect, wanting nothing (James 1:3 – 4). When God showed John the revelations in the book of Revelation, John said that he was our brother and companion in tribulation, and in the patience of Jesus Christ (Rev. 1:9). When we keep the Word of God's patience, he will keep us from the hour of temptation that shall come upon all the earth to try them (Rev. 3:10). It is not strange nor uncommon for Christians to have fiery trials to try us (1 Pet. 4:12 – 19; 1 Thess. 3:3). We should rejoice and be happy that we suffer like Christ, for great is our reward in heaven

(Acts 5:40 – 42; Luke 6:22 – 24; Matt. 5:10 – 12). Some people who choose not to suffer like Christ are impatient and break man's law, and this does not please God (1 Pet. 4:12 – 19). The patient person in spirit is better than the proud person in spirit (Eccles. 7:8). Remember the patience of Job during his suffering (James 5:10 – 11). The apostles and prophets ministered in much patience, afflictions, lack of necessities, and in distress, stripes, imprisonments, watching, and fasting (2 Cor. 6:3 – 10; James 5:10 – 11). Hold on to what you have and let no one take your crown (Rev. 3:11; Rom. 2:6 – 11).

The Lord will direct your hearts into the patient waiting for Christ (2 Thess. 3:5). Christ says that when we are being persecuted for his sake, even to death for some people, and when family and friends betray you, continue to stand for the Word of God, and in your patience, you shall save your soul (Luke 21:15 – 19; James 1:21).

Be steadfast, unmovable, always abounding in the work of the Lord, knowing that your work is not in vain in the Lord (1 Cor. 15:58).

We should serve God without being afraid of any enemy (Luke 1:74; Lev. 26:6; Heb. 11:23 – 29; Ps. 119:134). When you believe, you must also speak the truth (2 Cor. 4:13). David said that he loves God's Word, because it is very pure (Ps. 119:140). The Lord is good to people who wait on him, to the soul who seeks him (Ps. 33:20; Lam. 3:25). It is good that a person should both hope and quietly wait for the salvation of the Lord (Lam. 3:26). Blessed are they who wait on the Lord (Isa. 30:18). They shall not be ashamed (Isa. 49:23; Ps. 25:3; 1 Pet. 4:16). God will favor you, and your time shall come (Ps. 102:13). After you have suffered a while, God will make you perfectly rewarded, and establish, strengthen, and settle you (1 Pet. 5:10). In yet a little while, in a little moment, God will show up with peace and prosperity (Isa. 10:24 – 25; 26:20). Cast not away your confidence, which has great recompence of reward. For you have need of patience, that, after you have done the will of God, you will receive the promise. For yet a little while, God who shall come will come, and will not tarry. The just shall live by faith, and it is impossible to please God without faith (Rom. 1:16 – 18; Hab. 2:4; Gal. 3:11; Heb. 10:36 – 39; 11:1, 6; and Heb. 6:1 – 6; Joh.16:16).

Lay aside every weight and the sin and let us run with patience the race that is set before us (Heb. 12:1 – 2, 4). Call upon God with a pure heart (2 Tim. 2:21 – 22; Job 27:8 – 23; Ps. 1; Prov. 3:5 – 8).

When you have a pure heart, God will answer, unless it is not his will, or you ask for something you do not need (James 4:1 – 3). Devil worshippers in the Bible called upon their idol god, and when the idol could not answer, Elijah mocked them by saying, is he sleep, is he on a journey (1 Kings 18:25 – 29? The only way to get to the one and only living God is through Christ (Joh. 14:1, 6. There is no salvation in any other name (Acts 4:12; 1 Tim. 2:5; Joh. 5:20 – 27; 1 Joh. 2:1). You will die in your sins if you do not believe in Christ (Joh. 8:21 – 24). All other gods are dead, or are living devils, and they will never answer you unless you sell your soul to them and serve them (Luke 4:1 – 13).

Being "persistent" in prayer and going boldly before the throne is good when you are desperate or have a sense of urgency (Luke 11:5 – 13; 18:1 – 8; Heb. 4:16; Eph. 3:20 – 21); but if not, be patient (Matt. 6:7). Even when it comes to getting revenge on enemies and adversaries, wait on God and he will punish them for you (Prov. 20:22; Luke 18:1 – 8; Rom. 12:19). Wait on the Lord and keep his way, and you shall see wicked people cut off (Ps. 37:34). Let integrity and uprightness preserve you (Ps. 25:21).

In the "Parable of the Sower" several people planted seeds on different kinds of ground and their crops failed. But the one person who planted his seeds on good ground and grew a good crop brought forth fruit with patience (Luke 8:15; Matt. 13:1 – 23; Acts 17:11 – 12; James 1:22 – 27; Ps. 81:10 – 16; Jer. 15:15 – 21; Rev. 10:9 – 11).

Here is the "patience" of the saints. Here are they who

keep the "commandments" of God, and the "faith" and "patience" of Christ (Rev. 13:10; 14:12; 2 Thess. 3:5). We inherit the promises of God through faith and patience (Heb. 6:12).

Christ waited 30 years before he started his ministry, even though his mother forced him to turn water into wine before it was his time to start working miracles. He told his mother Mary that it was not his time yet. But Mary and Christ must be given credit for knowing why Christ was born and still being patient for 30 years (Joh. 2:1 – 11).

Noah was in the Ark one year and seventeen days, including five months floating in flood waters, and seven months stuck on a mountain waiting for God to give them instructions to leave the ark that was surrounded by mud, dead animals, dead humans, and dangerous waterborne wildlife (Gen. 7:4, 10 – 12, 24; 8:3 – 4, 13 – 19).

After Abraham patiently endured for 25 years and already in old age, he obtained the promise from God to conceive a son by his elderly wife Sarah (Heb. 6:15). But Sarah laughed at God concerning the promise and did not have patience and demanded that Abraham sleep with a female slave to produce a son (Gen. 16; 18:13). Sarah ended up despising the son and his mother and sent them away into the wilderness (Gen. 21:9 – 21). God kept his promise, but Sarah caused herself problems by not believing.

Isaac was the son of Abraham and Sarah who God promised to them. Isaac's twin sons were Esau and Jacob. God renamed Jacob and called him Israel. Jacob worked seven years for a man for the right to receive his wife of choice who was the man's daughter. Her name was Rachel. But Jacob ended up working another seven years before Rachel's father finally decided to give her to him, which was a case of deception and trickery. And even after receiving his new bride, he worked an additional seven years for his very unfair father in-law (Gen. 29:18 – 30).

Joseph of the Old Testament, who was the 17 – year – old son of Jacob, was abandoned in a desert land by his brothers due to their jealousy of him. He was later found and sold into slavery in Egypt by another group of people. He was eventually given more power in the nation of Egypt where he was enslaved than everyone except the king of Egypt, but he suffered, including when he served two years in an Egyptian prison, and waited a total of 13 years for this unexpected blessing to happen. Even more years pasted before he finally saw his father and brothers again (Gen. 37; 39; 40; 41:41; 45; 46; 47; 48; 49; 50:1 – 2).

Moses was a high ranking Egyptian official and prince in Egypt while Jacob's and Joseph's descendants were enslaved in Egypt. Moses himself was a descendant of Jacob but was raised by an Egyptian princess. Moses' mother put him in a basket and sent him down river to prevent him from being murdered when the Egyptian king was killing all male Hebrew babies of enslaved parents, to try to prevent Moses from being born. Moses grew up and killed a slave overseer for being cruel to slaves. To escape possible prosecution, he fled from Egypt and into the wilderness where he waited for years before God sent him back to Egypt to lead the Hebrews out of slavery. God totally defied and embarrassed the Egyptian pharaoh by working miracles through Moses. Egyptian pharaohs would have been equivalent to kings nowadays (Acts 7:23-24; Exod. 2; 7:7 – 20; and Exod. 8; 9; 10; 11; 18:8; 29:2).

God delivered the Israelites out of slavery in Egypt and promised them a land flowing with milk and honey, but they had to cross a desert to get there, and the journey took 40 years, partly because they did not believe and were rebellious and complained (Exod. 15:24; 16:2; 17:3; Num. 11:1; 14:2, 29; 16:41; Deut. 1:27).

The journey out of slavery should not have been a problem because God showed them miracles and wonders to support and comfort them (Neh. 9:16 – 17). They stayed at Mount Sinai eleven months without traveling (Exod. 19:1; Num. 10:11). So sometimes we must wait on God to tell us to move. They who wait on the Lord shall renew their strength, and mount up with wings like eagles, run and not be weary, walk and not faint, but even young strong sinners shall fall (Isa. 40:27 – 31; Am. 2:10 – 16). The Israelites complained in the wilderness within three days of leaving Mount Sinai (Num. 10:33; 11:1 – 3). This is the same Sinai in which Moses received and delivered to the people the Ten Commandments. They saw the thundering and lightning, and acknowledged that God could kill them, but they still complained (Exod. 19:20; 20:1 – 17, 18 – 19). But they learned to follow God at his command. He provided a cloud for them to follow by day and an appearance of fire to follow by night. God instructed them to move only when the cloud moved, whether it was two days, a month, or a year (Num. 9:15 – 23). There were times when they probably felt like moving, or maybe there was a pretty day and they wanted to move, but they did not. We must have that same patience to not move until God leads the way. Faith is followed by virtue, knowledge, temperance, patience, godliness, brotherly kindness, and love. If these things are in you and abound, you shall never be barren nor unfruitful. But they who lack these things are spiritually blind (2 Pet. 1:5 – 9).

The Israelites were in the wilderness for 40 years before they reached the Promised Land, until all the adults died except Caleb and Joshua due to lack of faith and lack of patience (Josh. 5:5 – 7; Heb. 3; 4:1 – 12; Num. 14:33 – 38). But when the Israelites were in the wilderness, they lacked nothing (Deut. 2:7). Their clothes did not become old, neither did their feet swell, for 40 years (Deut. 8:4; 29:5). God caused them to wander 40 years to dispose of the disobedient adults, but also to humble the children and teenagers, to prove them, to know what was in their hearts, whether they would keep God's commandments or not (Deut. 8:2 – 4; Judg. 2:20 – 23; 3:1 – 4). They ate manna 40 years, the same meal everyday (Exod. 16:35). Except when God gave them birds to eat with the manna which was bread, because of their complaining (Num. 11:1 – 6; Exod. 16:9 – 13). But God killed the adults while the meat was still in their teeth before they could chew it, because he was displeased with their rebellious, unthankful. and complaining attitudes (Num. 11:33 – 34; Ps. 78:17 – 18, 27 – 32; Job 20:23). The bread that we must patiently eat now is the Word of God because we cannot live by food alone, but by every Word of God (Matt. 4:4; 6:11; Joh. 6:31 – 35; Deut. 8:2 – 3; Luke 4:1 – 4).

Jeremiah said that God made the whole universe, but because the people were guilty of sin, the people would have to wait on the Lord's deliverance in time of trouble (Jer. 14:22).

A thousand years to God is one day, and one day to God is a thousand years. Therefore, Christ rose from the dead only two days ago in God's time (Ps. 90:4; 2 Pet. 3:4 – 8). In humans' time Christ was born of a virgin thousands of years after Adam and Eve, but only a few days after Adam and Eve in God's time. Believers in the Old Testament lived and died waiting on Christ to be born, therefore we should live and die waiting on the second coming of Christ (Isa. 7:10 – 16; 8:8; 9:6; Matt. 1:23; Deut. 18:15; Acts 3:20 – 22; Dan. 9:25 – 26).

God accredited them as being righteousness because they had faith in God and the promise of salvation in Christ who had not been born yet (Heb. 11:30 – 39). David lived and reigned as king more than a thousand years before the birth of Christ. Job prophesied about Christ and about going to heaven (Job 14:14; 19:25 – 27). In addition to Isaiah, some others who prophesied about the first coming of Christ hundreds and thousands of years before the birth of Christ were Isaiah (Isa. 60:18 – 22; 65:17 – 20; 66:22); Balaam (Num. 24:15 – 17); David (Ps. 23:6); Job (Job 14:14); and Solomon (Prov. 14:32). Their works and patience are accounted unto them for righteousness because they died in righteousness and died waiting for the Lord to be born (Gal. 3:6; Heb. 11:13, 39; 1 Pet. 4:6; Rev. 22:10 – 13; Ps. 106:6 – 31).

One day Christ did come as a baby, and one day soon he shall come a second time (Heb. 9:28; Joh. 14:3); like a thief in the night, when no one knows (2 Pet. 3:10; Rev. 16:15); to take away his people and cast other people into hell.

It took thirteen years for Solomon to build his home and

palace (1 Kings 7:1 – 2). And it took forty – six years for the temple to be rebuilt during the time of the Roman invasion and occupation of Israel (Joh. 2:20 – 21). David, Solomon's father, said that his soul waited on the Lord and that he hoped in God's Word (Ps. 130:5; Rom. 15:4 – 5). He also said that he waited on the Lord more than people who watch for the morning (Ps. 130:6). And we know how impatient or excited people anticipate the next day approaching. We must also wait for the return of the Lord like a farmer patiently and eagerly waits for rain for their crops (James 5:7 – 8). Sometimes people forget what God has done and wait not for his counsel (Ps. 106:13). But David asked God to lead him in the Lord's truth, and to teach him. David said that he waited all day on the God of his salvation (Ps. 25:5). King David said that he waited patiently for the Lord, and God heard his cry (Ps. 401). There were also times when David asked God to, "Deliver speedily. Be my strong rock, a house of defense to save me. Hide not your face from your servant. I am in trouble. Hear me speedily. O remember not against us former iniquities. Let your tender mercies speedily help us, for we are brought very low. Hide not your face from me in the day when I am in trouble. Incline your ear unto me. In the day when I call answer me speedily. Hear me speedily, O Lord, my spirit fails. Hide not your face from me, lest I be like them who go down into the pit." The Prophet Zechariah said, "And the inhabitants of one city shall go to another, saying, let us go speedily to pray before the Lord, and to seek the Lord of hosts. I will go also" (Ps. 31:2; 69:17; 79:8; 102:2; 143:7; Zech. 8:21).

Be of good courage, wait, I say, on the Lord (Ps. 27:14; Isa. 35:3 – 4). Rest in the Lord and wait patiently for him. Fret not because of them who prosper in their sinful ways (Ps. 37:7; 40:1). Because evildoers shall be cut off, but they who wait on the Lord shall inherit the earth (Ps. 37:9 – 10). The meek shall inherit the earth (Ps. 37:11; 25:12 – 14; 149:4; Matt. 5:5). That is, the "new earth," called heaven (Rev. 21:1). Sometimes God inflicts people with adversity. If they do not have the faith and patience to wait on the Lord, they may live to see a better day, but may not live long enough to reap the full benefits of the Lord (2 Kings 6:30 – 33; 7:1 – 2). Just as on judgment day God will allow some people to go to heaven to see it, but then cast them out to hell (Matt. 8:11 – 12; Luke 13:24 – 30. We should wait on the Lord until he has mercy on us (Ps. 123:2 – 3).

Regarding earthly, personal, and professional goals, if you feel that you have done all that you can do, leave it in God's hands because at this point you need to rest and wait.

Goals are what we pursue with faith, and God tells us that faith without working hard makes faith dead. Even though a dream can become a goal after we start pursuing the desires of our heart, if we do not have faith with consistent and dedicated works, then our dream is simply a dream that may never come true. Also remember that just because God says that he will give us the desires of our heart, that does not mean that it will come easily (Ps. 10:17; 20:1 – 4; 21:2; 37:4 – 8; 145:16, 19; Mark 11:24; Eccles. 11:9). Because when we desire something, we work hard and will do almost any godly and legal thing to get it. Be patient, but in times of need, desperation, or urgency, be persistent in prayer to get your prayers answered (Luke 18:1 – 8; 11:5 – 13; Gen. 32:24 – 30; Hos. 12:2 – 3; Mic. 7:7).

Whenever there is another option and whenever there is hope, do not give up (Matt. 6:7; 1 Kings 18:43; 2 Kings 5:10; Josh. 6:15 – 16; Heb. 11:30).

The Lord is good to them who wait for him, to the soul who seeks him (Lam. 3:25 – 26). Trust no one. Trust only God.

David said, "I have been young and now I am old, but I have never seen the righteous forsaken, nor their children begging for bread" (Ps. 37:25; 71). If you sow and plant in tears, you shall reap and gather in joy. They who weep while bearing precious seeds shall doubtlessly come again in joy (Ps. 126).

Finally, if anyone thinks that they are called by God to preach, or if someone is trying to convince another person to preach, the Bible says, "Wait," and not run into the ministry (Rom. 12:7); Jer. 23:20 – 22; 2 Pet. 2:1 – 5). Even if their calling becomes certain, they must still be patient and grow in the wisdom and love of the truth of God (1 Tim. 3:3; 2 Tim. 2:24; 1 Thess. 5:14). In the book of Revelation, God says that he knew the labor and patience of his saints and how they did not become weary while dealing with false apostles and fake Jews, but that they still needed to go back to the first works, which was the first time that they repented and gave their life to God, and regain the first love that they had for Christ (Rev. 2:1 – 7). God also talks about how one church's patience and works were better in the present time than when they first gave their life to the Lord in the past, but that he still had something against the church because they allowed sexual sins to happen (Rev. 2:18 – 29).

See also *MORE THAN YOU CAN BEAR; ADVERSITY; TODAY; TESTS; HOPE; WORRYING.*

PROTECTION

Defense, hiding, guard, security, refuge (Job 1:8 – 10; Ps. 62:7; 125:2). God protects, directs, and corrects us. The Lord is our shelter and strong tower from the enemy (Ps. 61:3). Often the long way to anything is the safest or smoothest way (Exod. 13:17). The Word of God says, "Many O Lord my God are your wondrous works, and your thoughts towards us cannot be recounted in order. If I would declare and speak of them, they cannot be numbered" (Ps. 40:5; Joh. 21:24 – 25).

The fear of mankind is a snare, but they who trust in the Lord shall be safe (Prov. 29:25). We must be careful, cautious, discreet, and discerning, but to fear anything or anyone other than God, is a sin (Rev. 21:8; Neh. 6:9 – 14; Ezra 8:22 – 23, 31; Phil. 1:28; 1 Joh. 4:18).

You should boldly say, "The Lord is on my side, he is my helper. I will not fear what humans can do to me" (Ps. 118:6; Heb. 13:5 – 6; Isa. 42:16 – 21). The devil is roaming the earth seeking whom he may devour, because he knows that it will not be long before he spends eternity in hell (1 Pet. 5:6 – 9; Rev. 12:7 – 17; Job 1; 2:1 – 10; 3:16 – 22; 13:15 – 16; 42:11).

The eyes of the Lord run to and from throughout the whole earth, to show himself strong on behalf of people whose heart is loyal to him (2 Chron. 16:7 – 10). The devil desired to shift Peter like wheat, but Christ prayed for Peter (Luke 22:31 – 34). Not everyone who is protected, blessed, and favored by God is anointed, but to people who are indeed anointed, God says, "Touch not my anointed, and do my prophets no harm" (1 Kings 13:4 – 10; 1 Chron. 16:18 – 22; Ps. 105:14 – 15). In the Bible, God literally did not allow a person to touch a righteous prophet in a harmful manner, but God killed that same righteous prophet because the prophet obeyed a lying preacher instead of obeying the Word of God (1 Kings 13:4 – 10). God nearly killed Moses for being disobedient, and God still did not allow Moses to enter the promised land, even though Moses was anointed (Exod. 4:24 – 31; Num. 20:12; Deut. 3:23 – 28). But again, even if you are not anointed in one way or another, you are still protected by God if you live righteously in Christ Jesus. Because the Bible says, "They who touch the righteous, touch the apple of God's eye" (Zech. 2:8).

They who control their own spirit is stronger than they who conquers a city (Prov. 16:32). Wisdom strengthens a wise person more than rulers in a city (Eccles. 7:19). If God be for us, who can be against us? In all these things we are more than conquerors through Christ who loves us (Rom. 8:28 – 39; 2 Cor .2:14). Notice, the scripture did not say that we are conquerors, but we are more than conquerors (Rom. 8:31, 35 – 39). No weapon formed against you shall prosper. And every tongue that speaks against you in court or in judgment shall be condemned. This is the heritage of the servants of the Lord. The Lord says, "Their righteousness is of me" (Isa. 54:17; Jer. 29:1 – 11; 1 Chron. 12:17; Ps. 109:1 – 13).

What most people do not say is this scripture also says, "And their righteousness is of me, says the Lord" (Isa. 54:17). We must also live right. However, all things work together for good if you are called according to God's purpose, but if you are not called by the Lord, all things may not work out every time (Rom. 8:28 – 39). People who are called must endure hardness as a good soldier, while knowing that they will not be crowned unless they labor righteously for the Lord (2 Tim. 2:1 – 5).

When people do not live right and are stubborn towards God's Word, he may not protect them like he would have (Judg. 2:11 – 23). The Bible says, "The Lord is on my side, I will not fear. What can humans do to me? The Lord is for me. Therefore, I shall see my desire on those who hate me. It is better to trust in the Lord than to put confidence in humans," including politicians (Ps. 56:4; 118:6 – 9. The Lord tells us to, "Put on the whole armor of God in righteousness, on the right hand and on the left hand, so that you may be able to stand against the wiles of the devil. For we wrestle not against flesh and blood, but against spiritual wickedness in high places. Therefore, take unto you the whole armor of God. Clothe yourself with truth and the breastplate of righteousness. Above all, taking the shield of faith, the helmet of salvation, and the sword of the Spirit, praying always" (Eph. 6:10 – 18; Rom. 13:12; 2 Cor. 6:7; 1 Thess. 5:6 – 11; Ps. 3:3; 119:114).

The Word of God is a light unto your paths (Ps. 119:105; Prov. 4:18). If you are faced with trouble or harm after all these instructions from God, then in love for you and punishment of your enemies, God himself will put on the breastplate of righteousness, the helmet of salvation, and clothes of vengeance (Isa. 59:17). It is a righteous thing for God to punish people who trouble the saints (2 Thess. 1:6). Concerning the spiritual wickedness in high places, those devils, and demons tremble at the name of Christ (James 2:18 – 20; Mark 1:23 – 28; 3:9 – 12; Luke 10:17).

God rarely allows us to run into deep trouble when we trust in him. He leads us from the front and protects our back. Just as in the wilderness he led the people with a cloud by day and fire by night (Exod. 13:21 – 22; Ps. 78:13 – 14). God leads us not into temptation (Matt. 6:13); he leads us beside the still waters (Ps. 23:2); he leads us in the path of righteousness (Ps. 23:3). The breastplate is worn on the front (Eph. 6:14); and God led the children of Israel through the Red Sea on dry ground while he protected their backside and prevented the Egyptians from catching up to them (Exod. 14:9 – 22). Notice that the angel of the Lord went from in front of them to behind them (Exod. 14:19). Christ also tells the devil to get behind him, and we should boldly rebuke the devil in Christ's name with faith and confidence and command that the devil get behind us as well. Notice that Christ was talking to the Apostle Peter in a scripture when he commanded that the devil get behind him, so sometimes the devil tries to get to us through someone close to us who is a solid Christian (Matt. 16:21 – 26; Luke 4:1 – 21; Zech. 3:1 – 3; Jude 1:9; Matt. 17:18).

We must be careful how we accuse or how we start feeling that a spouse cannot be trusted, because if we are wrong about the spouse, we could have problems in the marriage moving forward. But sometimes a person's enemies are them of their own household. And God tells us that certain spouses cannot be trusted, even though they sleep beside their mate every night (Matt. 10:33 – 39; Mal. 7:5 – 10; Ps. 101:1 – 4, 7; Prov. 30:11).

Submit yourself therefore to God. Rebuke the devil in the name of the Lord Jesus Christ and he will flee from you (James 4:7). God told the Hebrews that he would send his fear before them and make all their enemies flee from them (Exod. 23:27). However, if we do not obey God's Word, he could remove his right hand from holding back the enemy (Lam. 2:3).

When Paul was in jail, the Jews said that they would not eat until they had killed Paul, and if they did not kill him, may a curse fall upon them, but God caused the jailers to move Paul with an escort of hundreds of soldiers versus just forty Jews (Acts 23:11 – 24). God fights for you, but he does not always use weapons. In the Old Testament God told the people that he would fight for them (Exod. 14:12 – 14; Josh. 23:10; Deut. 3:22). And that he would have mercy on them and save them, but not with bow and arrow, sword, nor in a military battle (Hos. 1:7). However, there is a scripture in the Bible that says God fights with stars from heaven (Judg. 5:20). Nehemiah reminded the people that God is great and terrible and had fought for their brothers, sons, daughters, wives, and houses (Neh. 4:14). Job was one of the most righteous men to ever live, but he still said that the destruction of God was a terror to him (Job 1:1, 6 – 8; 2:1 – 3; 31:13 – 23; James 5:10 – 11). God hides us in his secret place, and sometimes the secret place is in plain sight of humans who do not know the difference but still cannot harm us (Ps. 31:20; 119:114; Jer. 36:26).

God's eyes are running to and from throughout the whole earth to show himself strong on behalf of people who have a perfect heart towards him (2 Chron. 16:9). For the eyes of the Lord are over the righteous, and his ears are open to their prayers, but the face of the Lord is against people who do evil (1 Pet. 3:12). Plus, angels are encamped around the righteous, and children, and there are more angels with us than there are devils and evil humans with our enemies (2 Kings 6:17; 2 Chron. 32:7 – 8; Ps. 34:4 – 15; Act 12:10 – 11; Num. 22:24 – 27, 32; Luke 24:15 – 16). If God had not given angels to us for protection, we would be in danger and destroyed daily (Ps. 91). Daniel said that the reason God helped him in the lion's den was because he was innocent of sin (Dan. 6:22). Sometimes God gives us a legion of angels and plenty of people to help us (Matt. 26:53; Acts 18:9 – 11; 2 Kings 6:17; 2 Chron. 32:7 – 8).

To people who do not obey God and do not trust in him, but trust in other people and in people who are idolized, God says, "Let them rise up and help you, and be your protection" (Deut. 32:35 – 39). God will keep you in perfect peace if you trust in him and keep your mind stayed on him (Isa. 26:3). Some people try to trust in God, and in idol gods including voodoo, sorcery, and witchcraft, and in human idols, and in other people at the same time, but that does not please the Lord (2 Kings 17:33 – 39). God sometimes causes our enemies to help us, and other people to favor us, but we must remember to trust only God. After bragging on God, sometimes we must fast and pray instead of asking for help from people who doubt God (Ezra 8:21 – 23). Because they are saying in their heart and mind, "Where is your God in whom you trusted" (Ps. 79:10; and Ps. 22:6 – 11; Isa. 66:5; Mic. 7:10; Ezek. 9:9 – 10).

People who are against God's people must be careful because God could cause them to turn against each other (2 Chron. 20:23).

When Christ said that we shall pick up snakes, and drink poison without dying, he was not speaking to us in this generation, but to the original apostles more than 2000 years ago

(Mark 16:16 – 18; Luke 10:19). Paul was bitten by a viper and did not die, but again, that power was given to them, and not necessarily to us. Paul simply shook off the viper without thinking twice about it (Acts 28:1 – 6).

We must pray over our food before we eat, not only to thank God for providing it but also to cleanse it of anything that can harm us in the present or in the future, but we must still use good judgment and be wise enough to not eat something that we know is unhealthy or dangerous (1 Tim. 4:4 – 5; Matt. 16:15 – 18). In terms of washing hands before we eat, Christ says that it is not what goes into a person that defiles them, but what comes out, because what is in us will come out in the form of actions or words, good or bad (Matt. 12:34; 15:15 – 20; Prov. 23:6 – 7; Ps. 51:1 – 6; Joh. 2:24 – 25; Jer. 17:9 – 10; Gen. 6:5 – 8).

What we put into our bodies do not always defile us in terms of sin, but it could still make us sick or even kill us, depending on what we put into our bodies. But concerning the bad things that come out of people towards us, the Spirit of God and Word of God which are the same, helps us to discern the thoughts and intentions of others (Heb. 4:12; 1 Cor. 12:10; Eph. 6:17). The Bible also says, "The Word of God is sharper than any two – edged sword, cutting deep into the bone marrow, soul, and spirit of mankind, and is a discerner of the thoughts and intentions of the heart" (Heb. 4:12).

In terms of Christians using weapons for protection, Christ told the apostles to take nothing on their journey but a staff, which was basically a long stick, that could be used for protection (Mark 6:8). He later told them to go get swords (Luke 22:35 – 38). And the Apostle Peter cut off the ear of a Roman soldier to protect the Lord. Christ eventually told the apostles to put away the swords because they who live by weapons shall die by weapons (Matt. 26:50 – 52; Joh. 18:10). We must not live by bread alone, nor by a weapon, but by every Word of God (Deut. 8:2 – 3; Luke 4:1 – 4; Matt. 6:11). But it is not a sin to own a gun. In some nations it is a crime to own a gun, but in the United States almost everyone is allowed to purchase or own a gun. Many people in the United States say that they have a right to own a gun according to the 2nd Amendment of the United States Constitution. But they speak as though the Constitution is the Word of God or is greater than the Word of God, but it is not. Sometimes amendments need to be amended.

Pastors, leaders, and the head of families should also protect their flock, including with guns, if necessary, even in churches. But the church members who are chosen to have a gun in church and in the parking lots must be Holy Ghost filled, God fearing, led by God and would not use the gun against innocent people. Moses was willing to be blotted out of the Book of Life for the people's sake (Exod. 32:31 – 32; Ezek. 20:13 – 17). This was after they wanted to stone him to death two different times (Num. 14:10; Exod. 17:4). That was an uncommon example of turning the other cheek (Isa. 50:6; Matt. 5:38 – 39; 2 Cor. 11:20 – 33; 1 Pet. 2:23).

God did not allow Moses to enter the Promised Land because of the people who he led and stood in the gap for (Num. 20:12; Deut. 3:23 – 28). Moses reminded God that if the Lord killed all the Hebrews in the wilderness, heathen nations would mock and say that the Lord killed them because the Lord could not deliver them to the promised land (Num. 14:11 – 20; 24:11). And Joshua asked God why he was allowing his people to die in battle against heathen nations, causing heathen nations to mock, but God told him that their enemies were defeating them because they were sinning (Josh. 7:7 – 13). David sinned and caused a multitude of people to be killed by the wrath of God. David then told God, "I have sinned, and I have done wickedly, but these sheep, what have they done?" David was willing to accept God's wrath instead of letting the people die because of his sins (2 Sam. 24:12 – 17).

There was a righteous prophet in the Bible who encountered an old prophet who seemingly was not active in the Lord anymore, and the righteous prophet promised God that he would follow his instructions to not visit, eat, nor drink with anyone in a certain place. But the old prophet told the righteous prophet that he too is a prophet and that an angel said it was alright for him to go and eat with him. God killed the righteous prophet for obeying the word of a lying prophet instead of obeying the Word of God (1 Kings 13:7 – 26). The Bible is perfectly aligned with supporting scriptures if you know where to find them. This is why the Bible says search the scriptures daily to see if they are true, and you will find that they speak of the first and second coming of Christ, and that even Moses wrote about Christ (Joh. 5:39 – 47; Acts 17:11; Ps. 119:82).

The prophets of the Old Testament also wrote about Christ (Joh. 5:39 – 47; Luke 24:24 – 27, 32; Acts 10:43; 17:11).

Christ was also with the Hebrews and Moses in the wilderness while they journeyed from slavery in Egypt (1 Cor. 10:1 – 17; Exod. 14:19 – 20; Deut. 32:4, 15, 18, 30 – 31, 37; Ps. 66:12).

New Testament scripture tells us that even if an angel or an apostle tells you to do something that is contrary and opposite to what is already written in the Bible, let them be cursed, and do not obey them (Gal. 1:8). Otherwise, you in all your righteousness could die like the righteous prophet who obeyed a lying preacher instead of obeying God (1 Kings 13:7 – 26). Because the Bible says that when we repent, God does not remember our past sins anymore, but even when you are righteous like the righteous prophet was, when you disobey God, it is possible that God will not remember your past righteousness anymore. But God would now remember your current rebellion. And when a preacher tells you the truth, he saves himself from death as well. But if a preacher does not tell the truth, people die in their sins, and the lying preacher dies in their sins too, and with the blood of the people on their hands (Ezek. 3:16 – 21; 18:19 – 32; 33:12 – 20; James 5:19 – 20).

Again, not every blessed person is anointed, but God says touch not my anointed and do my prophets no harm (1 Chron.

16:18 – 22; Ps. 105:15). They who touch the righteous, touches the apple of God's eye (Zech. 2:8). God literally did not allow a person to touch the righteous prophet in a harmful manner, but God killed that same righteous prophet because he obeyed a lying preacher instead of obeying the Word of God (1 Kings 13:4 – 10).

God will preserve you when you go out into the public and into hostile environments (2 Sam. 8:13 – 14). God protected David's mother, father, and family members while Saul sought to kill David (1 Sam. 22). When you trust in God, he will bless your coming in and your going out and keep and preserve you (Deut. 6:4 – 9; 11:18 – 21; Ps. 3:5 – 6 and Ps. 23; Ps. 121; Mark 16:15 – 16).

God says, "I know the thoughts that I have for your life, thoughts of peace and not of evil, to give you an expected end" (Jer. 29:11 – 14). But notice, God had already punished those people very hard before he said those very supportive words (Jer. 29:10). Yet again, God told those same people, "You shall call unto me, and pray unto me, and I will hear you, and you shall seek me and find me, when you seek me with your whole heart" (Jer. 29:12 – 14). God appeared to Abraham in a vision while his name was still Abram, and God told him to not be afraid, and that the Lord is his shield and his exceedingly great reward (Gen. 15:1).

King David in the Old Testament spoke about the future new heaven of the New Testament, and about the first coming of Christ, but also about God's protection when he said, "The Lord is my shepherd, I shall not want. He makes me lie down in green pastures; he leads me beside the still waters. He restores my soul. He leads me in the paths of righteousness for his name's sake. Yes, though I walk through the valley of the shadow of death, I will fear no evil, for you are with me. Your rod and your staff comfort me. You prepare a table before me in the presence of my enemies. You anoint my head with oil, my cup runs over. Surely goodness and mercy shall follow me all the days of my life and I shall dwell in the house of the Lord forever" (Ps. 23).

When power is gone (Deut. 32:30 – 43).
Saved from my enemies (2 Sam. 22:4).
Delivered from enemies (2 Kings 17:39).
Rest at ease while knowing that God fights your battles (2 Chron. 32:7 – 8).
While working for God (Neh. 4:7 – 23).
Protection for the poor (Job 5:15 – 16; Ps. 35:10).
Of animals (Job 38:39 – 41; 39).
From thousands of enemies (Ps. 3).
When we lie down (Job 11:19).
While we sleep (Ps. 3:5; 4:8).
God defends us (Ps. 5:11).
Take you rest in safety (Ps. 11:18).
No one shall make you afraid (Ps. 11:19).
Hold up my goings (Ps. 17:5).
Saved from my enemies (Ps. 18:1 – 3).
Whom shall I be afraid (Ps. 27:1 – 6).
Protection of humans and animals (Ps. 36:6).
God is my defense (Ps. 59:9).
Under God's wings (Ps. 17:8; 61:4).
Protection of God's anointed and his promise to them (Ps. 105:11 – 45).
If you praise the Lord (Ps. 107).
Prayers of safekeeping (Ps. 140 – 143).
For those who listen to God and wise people (Prov. 1).
While sleeping (Prov. 3:24).
Of animals (Prov. 12:10).
Of righteous people (Prov. 12:21).
Of those who fear God (Prov. 19:23).
Safety is of the Lord (Prov. 21:31).
Of the righteous (Prov. 24:15 – 16).
Protection to stay away from whorish women (Eccles. 7:26 – 29; Ps. 33:13 – 15).
Protection of us for God's sake (Isa. 37:33 – 35).

After repentance (Isa. 38:5 – 6).
Of humans and animals (Hos. 2:18 – 23).
From God's anger (Zep. 2:3).
Humans and animals (Matt. 10:29 – 31).
Of children (Matt. 18:1 – 6, 10).
From the world (Joh. 17:13 – 19).
From mobs (Acts 23:1 – 3, 12 – 25).
Weather (Isa. 4:6; 32:2; Acts 27:20 – 24).
God shall supply (Phil. 4:19).
Pray for protection (2 Thess. 3:1 – 5).
Of people who do good (1 Pet. 3:8 – 22).

REJECTION

As most of us know, Christ was despised, rejected, and acquainted with grief and sorrow, even though he had done no wrong, loves everyone, and died for everyone (Isa. 53; Acts 8:32 – 33; Matt. 26:62 – 64; Luke 22:39 – 46; Deut. 10:17 – 22).

Christ was rejected in his hometown (Luke 4:16 – 32; 9:51 – 58). Christ's own biological brothers did not believe in him (Joh. 7:1 – 8). His own race and religion rejected him (Joh. 1:10 – 14; Acts 13:26 – 31; Luke 24:44 – 49). They even sought to kill him before his time, so he did not walk in the land of the Jews anymore but instead walked in Galilee (Joh. 7:1). And when it was time for Christ to be crucified, the procurator Pilate according to Roman law was willing to release one so – called criminal, but the Jews rejected Christ and chose to release Barabbas who was a notorious criminal (Matt. 27:16 - 26; Luke 23:18). They denied the Holy One and the Just One and desired a hardened criminal (Acts 3:14).

In the Old Testament when the people desired a king like the surrounding heathen nations instead of allowing God to be their one and only eternal King, God told Samuel that they had not rejected Samuel the prophet who was against the idea, but they had indeed rejected God. They did not want to listen to God's Word through the mouth of a righteous human (1 Sam. 8:7). For example, when people tell other people that they should not fornicate or commit adultery and they reject the advice, they do not reject the person who offered the wise advice, but they reject God (1 Thess. 4:1 – 8). King Saul who they chose was later rejected by God because Saul rejected the Word of God when he obeyed the people instead of obeying

God (1 Sam. 15:23 – 26, 1 Chron. 10:13 – 14). They wanted a king whom they could tell what to do and what to say, just as a lot of people nowadays desire with itching ears a preacher who preaches only what they want to hear and fail to preach the true Word of God (2 Tim. 4:1 – 5). God chose David, a righteous person, who was also very young and not very tall (1 Sam. 16:1). Saul was a big and tall man (1 Sam. 9:2; 16:7). And when the Prophet Samuel sought Saul's successor, he looked upon men of great stature within David's family, but God refused them and said that he looks at the heart of humans and not the size, height, and stature (1 Sam. 16:7). After David there were some good kings, but most were corrupted and displeased God, so the Lord rejected them, and in the process, he rejected the tribe of Joseph and Ephraim, but chose the tribe of Judah which was the tribe in which David was born (Ps. 78:67 – 72). As Israel continued to crown human kings, they continued to reject God, so he temporarily rejected the whole nation of Israel (2 Kings 17:13 – 23; Jer. 7:15). In the New Testament, Christ says that if we reject him, he does not need to judge us on earth, but the words that he spoke will judge us (Joh. 12:46 – 48). Our sins testify against us (Jer. 14:7 – 12).

God rejects arrogant people (James 4:6). And in the Old Testament, God rejected the sacrifices at certain times and told the people to let proper treatment of one another run down as water, and righteousness as a mighty stream (Am. 5:21 – 24; Isa. 66:3).

We all should accept rejection without becoming angry, offended, ashamed, or discouraged, especially when seeking a person to date with hopes of them becoming your mate. If you are ever rejected after applying for a job, admission into a college, or acceptance in some other type of organization, do not allow yourself to feel unhappy or discouraged, but move on to the next opportunity in life. God will order your steps if you sincerely ask him. If God causes you to wait, he will not allow you to be ashamed even though competitors, haters, jealous people, rivals, adversaries, and enemies may think that you should be ashamed. God will eventually show up and show out in your life in the presence of family, friends, and enemies (Ps. 23; 119:80, 133; Rom. 5:5; 9:33; 10:11; 2 Thess. 3:14; 2 Tim. 1:8; 1 Pet. 4:16).

The Lord has rejected your confidences, and you shall not prosper (Jer. 2:37).

God brings evil unto the people because they reject his Word (Jer. 6:19).

God rejects people who have reprobate minds (Jer. 6:30; Rom. 1:18 – 32; 2 Thess. 2:10 – 15; 8:13 – 14; 1 Pet. 2:6 – 8; 1 Pet. 2:6 – 8; 2 Tim. 3:1 – 8; Tit. 1:16; Ps. 81:10 – 12, 15).

Have you utterly rejected Judah (Jer. 14:19).

Thou have utterly rejected us (Lam. 5:22).

Because you rejected knowledge, I will also reject you (Hos. 4:6).

Nor rejected me, but received me like an angel of God (Gal. 4:14).

REWARD

The Bible says that people who despise the Word of God will be destroyed, but people who fear God shall be rewarded (Prov. 13:13). Peter told Christ that they had left all and followed him. Christ replied, "There is no one who has left houses, brothers, sisters, father, mother, wife, children, or homeland for my sake, and the gospel's sake, who will not receive one hundred times more rewards in this life, but with persecutions" (Mark 10:28 – 31; Job 1; 2:1 – 10; 13:15 – 16; 42; 1 Cor. 7:25 – 34; Luke 14:25 – 27, 33).

Because they who live godly in Christ Jesus shall suffer persecution (2 Tim. 3:11 – 13; Ezek. 14:6 – 11; Heb. 3:7 – 13; Ps. 38:9 – 22; Jer. 15:15 – 21; Rev. 12:7 – 17; Joh. 16:20).

The scriptures also say that after we are rewarded a hundred times more on earth, we will receive eternal life in heaven (Mark 10:30). People who inherit eternal life in heaven where there will be no pain, suffering, tears, nor sickness, shall enter heaven after plenty of tribulation on earth (Acts 14:21 – 22; Rev. 21:1 – 8; Luke 22:39 – 46).

Blessed are they who are persecuted for righteousness's sake and are spoken against for Christ's sake. Apostle Paul wrote, "We boast of you among the churches of God for your patience and faith in all your persecutions and tribulations that you endure, which is the manifest evidence of the righteous judgment of God, for which you also suffer, since it is a righteous thing with God to repay with tribulation those who trouble you. And to give you who are troubled rest with us when the Lord Jesus is revealed from heaven with his mighty angels, in flaming fire taking vengeance on those who do not know God, and on those who do not obey the gospel of our Lord Jesus Christ. These shall be punished with everlasting destruction when Christ comes in that day, to be glorified in his saints. Therefore, we also pray for you that our God will count you worthy of this calling" (2 Thess. 1:4 – 12).

Christ is acquainted with sorrow and grief (Isa. 53:3). With much wisdom also comes much grief (Eccles. 1:18). Rejoice and be glad, because great is your reward in heaven (Luke 6:22 – 23; Matt. 5:10 – 12). Christ promises, "Blessed be the poor, for theirs is the kingdom of God" (Luke 6:20). Some people make themselves rich but have nothing because they are empty, blind, miserable, and unsaved, but some poor people are rich with salvation, sanctification, holiness, happiness, good health, good children, peace, wisdom, necessities, safety, and protection (Prov. 13:7; Rev. 3:15 – 22). No one knows everything. Poor people often have more wisdom than rich people and politicians, but the poor person's wisdom is despised and rejected (Eccles. 9:15 – 16; Isa. 53; 1 Cor. 1:26). Christ also says, "Woe unto certain rich people, because they have their reward on earth" (Luke 6:24; Ps. 17:13 – 14). All lovers of the world have their portion in this life (Ps. 17:13 – 15; Matt. 6:2, 5, 16; Eccles. 7:15). However, God is kind and gracious and gives to the good, the just, unjust, unthankful, and the evil, but that does not mean that God is pleased with the unjust, the evil, and the unthankful (Matt. 5:45; Luke 6:35; Deut. 9:4 – 7; 10:17 – 22).

We must abstain from fleshly lust that war against the soul (1 Pet. 2:11). The spirit is willing, but the flesh is weak (Matt. 26:41). But if you allow Christ to do so, he will strengthen and settle you (1 Pet. 5:6 – 11). They who are in the flesh cannot please God (Rom. 8:8). Because the Spirit is against the flesh and the flesh is against the Spirit (Gal. 5:16 – 26; 1 Pet. 2:11 – 12). Flesh and blood cannot inherit the kingdom of heaven, but walking and living in the Spirit while you are alive, and being changed to a heavenly spirit on judgment day is the only way to enter heaven (1 Cor. 15:42 – 52; Gal. 5:16, 24 – 25;

1 Thess. 4:14 – 17). We must be born of the water and of the Spirit, or we cannot go to heaven (Joh. 3:3 – 7; Acts 2:36–39; 8:14–17; 10:42–48; 19:1–6; John 3:3–7; Mark 16:16; Rev. 21:8, 27; 22:14 – 15).

They who plant in the flesh shall of the flesh reap corruption, but they who plant to the Spirit shall of the Spirit reap everlasting life (Gal. 6:7 – 8, 14). We reap what we sow, in every aspect of life, good or bad. This includes people who have been proud against God (Rom. 2:4 – 11; Gal. 6:7 – 10; Jer. 50:29). Therefore, we must worship God in spirit and in truth, and not in the flesh or as a lover of the world (Joh. 4:23 – 24; Zech. 8:1 – 8). Because the world loves its own and a friend of the world is an enemy of God (James 4:2 – 4; Joh. 1:10 – 12; 15:18 – 19; 1 Joh. 2:15 – 17; 3:13; Phil. 3:16 – 21).

Christ says, "I have overcome the world." Greater is Christ in you than the devil who is in people who love the world (Joh. 16:33; 1 Joh. 4:4). But if after you have escaped the pollutions of the world, and become entangled again in the world, your latter end will be worse than the beginning (2 Pet. 2:20; 1 Joh. 5:4 – 5). True religion is to go unspotted from the world (James 1:26–27; Isa. 1:15 – 20). Apostle Paul said that he was crucified from the world and the world from him (Gal. 6:7 – 8, 14). When we abstain from fleshly lusts and desires, we cease from sin, like Christ (1 Pet. 4:1 – 6). The fruit of the Spirit is goodness, righteousness, and truth. It is a shame to glorify the fleshly sins that sinners commit (Eph. 5:9 – 12). We must please God, believe that he exists, and diligently seek him (Heb. 11:6). If sinners do not repent, they shall not receive a reward, and their light of life shall be put out (Prov. 24:20). To be worldly minded is death, but to be spiritually minded is life and peace, and if anyone does not have the Spirit of God, they do not belong to God (Rom. 8:5 – 10).

God gave Nebuchadnezzar all of Egypt and its riches because he labored hard according to the will of God, but he was not a child of God (Ezek. 29:17 – 21). Just as God called Cyrus his servant because he too destroyed and chastised other sinners like God asked him to do, but he did not know God (2 Chron. 36:22 – 23; Isa. 45:1 – 14. God used Cyrus to punish Nebuchadnezzar, like he used Nebuchadnezzar to punish Israel, Tyrus, and Egypt. Notice that God gave Cyrus treasures too, for God's sake and for God's people sake (Isa. 45:3 – 7). Therefore, some sinners my receive rewards from the Lord because he used them to punish other sinners, just as God uses Muslims to punish sinful Christians, false Christians, and hypocrites, but neither sinner will be saved unless they repent (Acts 17:30 – 31).

God also gives wealth to some people so that they can give it to others. Before Christ died, rose from the dead, and ascended back to heaven, he only ministered to the Jews. He sent Paul to the Gentiles and asked Peter to accept them, but that was after Christ went back to heaven. Before that time, an unsaved woman approached Christ and asked that he heal her daughter. Christ told her that he did not come to minister to people who were not Jews, and that why should he take from God's children and give to dogs. The woman told Christ that even dogs eat of the crumbs that fall from the children's table, so Christ granted her request (Matt. 15:21 – 28). As you can see, just because a sinner is blessed, that does not mean that God is pleased with them or that they are saved. Now that Christ is calling all people to repentance, why wouldn't he bless sinners sometimes as well? Do you give only to your best behaving child? The child who is more obedient to God and to parents should receive the most and on a more regular basis, but you cannot totally disregard the disobedient child, even though you may not be pleased with them.

To whomever keeps God's Word and take heed to his warnings, there is great reward (Ps. 19:7 – 11). Evil people do deceitful work, but to them who plants righteousness shall be a sure reward (Prov. 11:18).

Preachers' primary reward should not be money (1 Cor. 9:16 – 18), but if they are hard laborers, they should receive a monetary reward (1 Tim. 5:18). Hopefully no one will be too proud to accept this message because God rewards the proud according to their sinful works (Ps. 31:23). The world loves its own (Joh. 1:10 – 12; 15:18 – 19); and many worldly people do what it takes to obtain worldly possessions and worldly rewards (Isa. 1:23). When a heathen king promised Daniel gifts and rewards to interpret a message from God, Daniel told him that he can give the gifts to someone else, and that he will still tell him what the Lord said (Dan. 2:1 – 6; 5:13 – 17).

Lastly, when there is plenty of adversity, even on a global or national level, seek God and he will be with you if you stand with him and for his Word. Be strong and your work shall be rewarded (2 Chron. 15:1 – 7; Ezra 8:21 – 23).

SAFETY

Security and freedom from arm or danger (1 Kings 4:25; Ezek. 39:26). Please see the scriptures listed below for more about safety in the arms of the Lord.

God gives safety to powerful people, but his eyes are upon their ways (Job 24:22 – 25).
I will lie down in peace and sleep, for you alone Lord make me dwell in safety (Ps. 4:8).
Hold me up, and I shall be safe, and I will obey your Word (Ps. 119:117).
Whoever listens to me will dwell safely, and will be secure, without fear of evil (Prov. 1:33).
Safety is of the Lord (Prov. 21:31).
They shall dwell safely, and no one shall make them afraid (Ezek. 34:28).
Make them to lie down safely (Hos. 2:18).
When they shall say, "Peace and safety," then sudden destruction (1 Thess. 5:3).

See also *PROTECTION.*

STAND STILL
AND KNOW THAT
I AM GOD

Faith without works is dead (James 2:13 – 26; Matt. 7:7; Mark 2:1 – 5). This means that we must sometimes literally and physically do something to reach our goals while having faith. But works also include fasting and praying, hoping, meditating, listening to and singing Gospel spiritual songs, giving, and helping others. God says that sometimes our strength while having faith and works, is to stand still (Isa. 30:1 – 3, 7). Elijah became discouraged to the point that he asked God to kill him after laboring for the Lord and thinking that he was one of only a few servants of the Lord in the land. The Lord then passed by him and there was a great strong wind, but God was not in the wind, and then an earthquake, but God was not in the earthquake, and after the earthquake a fire, but the Lord was not in the fire, and after the fire, "A still small voice." God quietly comforted Elijah and told him that there were 7000 holy and sanctified people in the land who had not served sin nor honored an idol (1 Kings 19).

God is gracious and merciful when he hears our cry, a God of justice, blessed are they who wait for him. And though the Lord gives us the bread of adversity and the water of affliction, God gives us truthful pastors according to God's own heart who will feed us knowledge and understanding. God will provide a word behind us saying, "This is the way, walk in it" (Isa.

30:18 – 21; Jer. 3:15). Sometimes when we are looking for God to speak to us in a loud and clear voice, he is speaking to us in a small low voice. Nowadays, God speaks from within people in the form of the Holy Ghost who dwells inside people who obey him (Acts 5:32; Luke 11:13; Joh. 14:13 – 18, 26 – 27; Isa. 59:20; Heb. 5:7 – 9). God speaks from outside the body of Christians who are not filled with the Holy Spirit yet.

When we think that destruction from God has not gotten the attention of sinners, God is speaking even louder in a small low voice after the destruction. God's message of repentance is still being sent to sinners after destruction and natural disasters ends, but we must stand still and listen, sometimes while fasting and praying. There are plenty of plans and thoughts in the hearts of humans, but only God's plans will stand (Prov. 19:21). Not that Elijah served sin, but sometimes we must stand in awe of God, sin not, offer sacrifices of righteousness, put our trust in the Lord, and be still while we wait on the Lord (Ps. 4:3 – 5). Be still and know that God is God, and that he will be praised by real Christians among the heathen and throughout the earth. The Lord is with us and is our refuge. Again, God says, "Be still and know that I am God" (Ps. 46:10 – 11; 2 Chron. 32:7 – 8).

Moses said while slaveholders pursued him and the Hebrews, "Sand still, and see the salvation of the Lord. Hold your peace and the Lord will fight for you" (Exod. 14:13 – 14). God even told them when to travel and when not to travel while they journeyed out of slavery (Num. 9:16 - 23). Like when the Lord delivered them to the promised land in the midst of adversity, he will deliver you to a wealthy place, which includes a wealth of health, peace, love, forgiveness, financial stability, and life (Ps. 66:8 – 12; 2 Cor. 6:1 – 10; Col. 3:16; 1 Tim. 6:17; Prov. 13:7; Rev. 3:15 – 22; Joh. 14:1 – 3; Matt. 30:19 – 34; Jer. 29:1 – 11; 3 Joh. 1:2).

However, the Israelites in the wilderness complained against God and against Moses after seeing many miracles. And the New Testament tells us that their mistakes and blessings are for our warnings and examples, and to take heed or we who think that we stand will also fall like them. But God leaves us a way to resist temptation if we allow him to do so (1 Cor. 10:1 – 13; Joh. 17:14 – 19; James 4:7).

Stand fast in the liberty by which Christ has made us free, and do not be entangled again with the yoke of bondage, including the bondage of being a slave to sin (Gal. 5:1; Rom. 6:15–17; 1 John 5:14–17; Rev. 3:15–19; Matt. 12:33; Ps. 66:16–20; 2 Pet.2:18 – 22; 1 Sam. 15:24; 2 Kings 17:7 – 8, 13 – 14, 20; Isa. 57:10 – 13).

They who the Son of God set free, are free indeed (Joh .8:30 – 36). Therefore, stand fast in one spirit and one mind (Phi. 1:27; 1 Cor. 1:10; 2:9 – 16; Rom. 15:5 – 6).

You will not need to fight in this battle. Stand still and see the salvation of the Lord (2 Chron. 20:17).
And listen (Neh. 8:1 – 12).
And consider the wondrous works of God (Job 37:14).
My heart is fixed in God. I will sing and give praise (Ps. 57:7; 108:1).
Trusting after hearing evil news (Ps. 112:7).
Keep your mind stayed on God (Isa. 26:3 – 4).
Grow roots and bear fruit in the Lord (Isa. 37:31).
Stay upon your God.(Isa. 50:10).
In well doing (Gal. 6:9).
Grounded and settled in the Lord (Col. 1:21 – 23).
In confidence and trust in the Lord (Heb. 3:6, 14).
Until Christ comes (2 Pet. 3:8 – 14).
In the doctrine of God Almighty (2 Joh. 1:8 – 13).
Hold on to holiness and sanctification until judgment day (Rev. 22:5 – 21).

See also *HOLD ON; PATIENCE; WITH.*

SORROW

Grief, affliction, mourning; distress, sadness, and sometimes guilt. Christ was despised and rejected, a man of sorrows, and familiar with grief. He carries our grief and our sorrows. He was wounded for our transgressions; he was bruised for our iniquities. He was chastised so that we can have peace, and by his whippings and beatings we are healed. We like sheep have gone astray, we have turned to our own way, and the Lord has laid on Christ the iniquity of us all. He was oppressed and he was afflicted (Isa. 53). Christ has experienced what we have experienced, but without sinning in the process, and another difference is that he suffered and died for our sins as though he was guilty of sin, so we must live for Christ as living sacrifices while enduring some pain, sorrow, and suffering, like him (Heb. 4:15 and Heb. 2:16 – 18; Rom. 12:1; Luke 17:7–10).

The scripture says that he died for our iniquity, even the iniquity that we bring upon ourselves, yet we do not seek him like we should. This sometimes causes God to say to us, "Why do you cry about your affliction? Your sorrow is incurable. Because of the multitude of your iniquities, and because your sins have increased, I have done these things to you" (Jer. 30:15). Iniquity separates us from the Lord and sometimes forfeit our blessings (Isa. 59:2; Jer. 5:25; Num. 14:11 – 19 – 20; 24:11; Josh. 7:7 – 13).

David prayed a beautiful prayer when he repented for his terrible sins (Ps. 51). A lot of our sorrows come from our love of money, from lusting, or from our attempts to obtain ungodly earthly possessions that have caused many people to be pierced through with many hurtful sorrows (1 Tim. 6:9 – 10). Some money and certain riches are deceitful, just as dating the wrong person can be deceitful and lead to a marriage and divorce that causes painful sorrows (Matt. 13:3 – 9, 18 – 23). When God gives us money or any gift, no sorrow or variation comes with it (Prov. 10:22; James 1:16 – 17). Sometimes sorrows come to us because of something that other people did to us.

Some Christian children are rebellious, but rarely does a parent have a child who is defiant, embarrassing, and rebellious when they are raised in the Lord, and are chastised, led, guided, rewarded, loved, and nurtured. But if parents do not do these things, children are likely to bring sorrow to the heart of the parents (Ps. 119:136; Prov. 13:24; Heb. 12:5 – 6).

We are living in the last days, and these days will only get worse and worse, and are only the beginning of sorrows (Matt. 24). In these last days, the Bible says, "Draw near to God, and he will draw near to you. Cleanse your hands, you sinners, and purify your hearts, you double minded" (James 4:8). And after we endure and go to heaven, there will be no more sorrow, crying, pain, nor death (Rev. 21:4).

We must not drown ourselves in sorrow while living on earth, because sorrow of the heart breaks the spirit (Prov. 15:13). The positive spirit of a person will sustain them in sickness, but who can bear a broken or negative spirit (Prov. 18:14). The Bible says, "A merry heart does good like medicine, but a broken spirit dries the bones" (Prov. 17:22; 18:14). Therefore, humble yourself under God, and he will lift you up in due time (James 4:9 – 10). God will comfort you and cause you to rejoice and not be sorrowful (Jer. 31:12 – 13). Because the Lord is the Father of mercies, and the God of all comfort, who comforts us in all our tribulation, that we may be able to comfort people who are in any trouble, with the comfort that we ourselves are comforted by God (2 Cor. 1:3 – 4; 1 Thess. 5:11). And the ultimate level of godly comfort is to not only allow God to dwell with you, but inside of you in the form of the Holy Ghost, who is the Comforter from heaven (Joh. 14:16 – 26; 15:26 – 27; 16:7 – 16; Acts 9:31; Ps. 94:19; 2 Thess. 2:16 – 17; 2 Pet. 2; Jude 1).

God gives us eternal salvation in heaven, and he gives us the Comforter while we are on earth when we obey him (Acts 5:32; Luke 11:13; Joh. 14:13 – 18, 26 – 27 and Joh. 1:1, 14; Col. 3:16; 1 Joh. 2:5, 7, 14; Heb. 5:7 – 9).

When we are going through trials and tribulations, we should occasionally try not to cause others to be sad like we are, or they may not be able to help us, and the supporters must not discourage people who are suffering by saying that they are doing worse than they really are (2 Cor. 2:1 – 4). We must count it all joy when we have problems, and even be festive at times, because the joy of the Lord is our strength (Neh. 8:10; James 1:15 – 18).

Christ was deeply sorrowful and distressed before he was tried, wrongfully convicted, crucified, and executed, but he told God, "Not as I will it, but your will be done," and his disciples were so sorrowful that it caused them to sleep while they should have been watching for the enemy (Matt. 26:36 – 39; Luke 22:39 – 46; Isa. 53).

Sometimes we become sad after God shows us what our labor and duty is for him. And we must be careful how we ask God to reveal things to us, because the revelation may not be pleasant, and if God showed himself to us personally, we would not live to tell anyone, because if we see God before we go to heaven we will surely die (Exod. 33:17 – 23; Num. 20:12; Deut. 3:23 – 28). Some of God's revelations could still frighten us nearly to death, but they could certainly cause us to be afraid, reluctant, sick, and sorrowful like so many people in the Bible who were called to do a great service for God (2 Cor. 6:1 – 10; Jer. 45; Dan. 7:28; 8:27; 10:8 – 9; Rev. 1:17; 10:9 – 11; Matt. 13:1 – 23).

The revelation may not be a mysterious apocalyptic revelation, but it could be as obvious as a service for the Lord that requires labor or standing for the Word of God and the truth during persecution. And sometimes that causes sorrow.

When God gives us plenty of wisdom, plenty of grief will eventually happen, therefore people who increase knowledge also increase sorrow (Eccles. 1:18). David cried because the people of the land would not obey the Word of God (Ps. 119:136). But the Bible tells us to rejoice when we are persecuted for God's sake, and that they who live godly in Christ Jesus shall suffer persecution (Matt. 5:1 –11; 2 Tim. 3:11 – 13; Ezek. 14:6 – 11; Heb. 3:7 – 13; Ps. 38:9 – 22; Jer. 15:15 – 21; Rev. 12:7 – 17; Joh. 16:20).

It is best to suffer sorrow like Christ, and not like a sinner, a criminal, or a non-believer (1 Pet.4:12-19; 2 Tim. 2:8 – 9; Job 36:21; 1 Pet. 3:14 – 17). Christ must not carry the sorrowful, grief stricken cross alone, and he will not leave us alone, nor forsake us (Matt. 8:16 – 17; Luke 14:27; 1 Pet. 2:24; Isa. 42:16 – 21; 63:9; Heb. 13:5 – 6).

However, we must labor for the Lord and not grieve about it (Heb. 13:17). People who inherit eternal life in heaven with no pain, suffering, tears, nor sickness, shall enter heaven after plenty of tribulation on earth (Acts 14:21 – 22; Rev. 21:1 – 8; Luke 22:39 – 46). We must be willing to do what God instructs us to do no matter how it makes us feel, or we cannot be his disciple (Luke 9:57 – 62; 14:27). Apostle Paul wrote, "We boast of you among the churches of God for your patience and faith in all your persecutions and tribulations that you endure, which is the manifest evidence of the righteous judgment of God, for which you also suffer. Since it is a righteous thing with God to repay with tribulation people who trouble you, and to give you who are troubled rest with us when the Lord is revealed from heaven with his mighty angels, in flaming fire taking vengeance on people who do not know God. And on those who do not obey the gospel of our Lord Jesus Christ. These shall be punished with everlasting destruction when Christ comes in that day, to be glorified in his saints. Therefore, we also pray for you that our God will count you worthy of this calling" (2 Thess. 1:4 – 12).

Ezra said, "And at the evening sacrifice I arose up from

my heaviness; and having rent my garment and my mantle, I fell upon my knees, and spread out my hands unto the Lord my God" (Ezra 9:5). The Apostle Paul said, "But I determined this with myself, that I would not come again to you in heaviness" (2 Cor. 2:1). Be afflicted, and mourn, and weep. Let your laughter be turned to mourning, and your joy to heaviness (James 4:9). In this day you greatly rejoice, if only for a season, and if need be, you accept heaviness from many trials and temptations (1 Pet. 1:6). This is the day that the Lord has made, we will rejoice and be glad in it (Ps. 118:24).

And sorrow of mind (Deut. 28:65).
Sorrows of hell compassed me (2 Sam. 22:6).
I bore him with sorrow (1 Chron. 4:9).
From sorrow to joy, and from (Est. 9:22).
Sorrows in his anger (Job 21:17).
Many sorrows shall be to the (Ps. 32:10).
Strength labor and sorrow (Ps. 90:10).
Affliction, and sorrow (Ps. 107:39).
He adds no sorrow with it (Prov. 10:22).
Laughter the heart is sorrowful (Prov. 14:13).
By sorrow of the heart the (Prov. 15:13).
A fool does it to his sorrow (Prov. 17:21).
Godly knowledge increases sorrow (Eccles. 1:18).
All his days are sorrows (Eccles. 2:23).
Sorrow and sighing shall flee (Isa. 35:10).
You shall lie down in sorrow (Isa. 50:11).
A man of sorrows, acquainted (Isa. 53:3).
Griefs, and carried our sorrows (Isa. 53:4).
Shall cry for sorrow of heart (Isa. 65:14).
Your sorrow is incurable (Jer. 30:15).
Shall not sorrow anymore (Jer. 31:12).
Rejoice from their sorrow (Jer. 31:13).
Replenished every sorrowful (Jer. 31:25).
Added grief to my sorrow (Jer. 45:3).
Any sorrow like unto my sorrow (Lam. 1:12).

Heart of the righteous sorrow (Ezek. 13:22).
This is only the beginning of sorrows (Matt. 24:8).
Were exceedingly sorrowful (Matt. 26:22).
He began to be sorrowful (Matt. 26:37).
Soul is exceedingly sorrowful (Matt. 26:38).
Sorrow shall be turned into (Joh. 16:20).
As sorrowful yet rejoicing (2 Cor. 6:10).
Should have sorrow upon sorrow (Phil. 2:27).
That you sorrow not, even as (1 Thess. 4:13).
Pierced themselves through with many sorrows (1 Tim. 6:10).
Much torment and sorrow (Rev. 18:7).
And shall see no sorrow (Rev. 18:7).
Neither sorrow nor crying (Rev. 21:4).

See also *MORE THAN YOU CAN BEAR; ADDICTIONS; MENTAL HEALTH; HOPE; WITH; ADVERSITY; JOY; HAPPINESS; WORRYING; DEPRESSION.*

SUCCESS

Success is given by Christ, and without Christ you can do nothing, unless it is evil success (Joh. 15:1 – 12). Do not brag about your success, because God gave you the ability to do it, and at times, he does it completely for you without you knowing what you want or need for your own life (Ps. 39:9; 115:1 – 3; Isa. 26:12).

Do not be arrogant; let another person brag on you, and never your own mouth, a stranger, but never your own lips, because God puts down one person and lifts up another (Prov. 27:2; Ps. 75:4 – 7. Christ was born for the falling and rising again of many people, while Christ and those people are spoken against (Luke 2:34). Listen to good advice and try to have a plan A and a plan B, or you could fail. Plan C would be to make adjustments while still pushing towards the high calling of God through Christ Jesus (Prov. 15:22; Phil. 3:13 – 18). We must be wise in business deals, and diligent as ants (Prov. 6:6). But anything done without faith in Christ is sin (Rom. 14:23).

See also *CONFIDENCE*.

TESTS

To prove. Sometimes God allows adversity to test us and to see if we will obey his Word during adversity and persecution (2 Chron. 32:31; Deut. 8:2; Dan. 11:32 – 35; Judg. 2:20 – 23; 3:1, 4 – 11; Ps. 95:8 – 11).

Sometimes God makes it hard to accomplish things so that we will not say that we alone did it (Deut. 8:14 – 17). Christ is the Son of God and he obeyed Father God, but Christ the human, the Son of man who walked the earth, was tested, and tried (Isa. 28:16; Luke 4:1 – 13). God allowed the devil to test the very righteous man named Job (Job 1; Job 2 and Job 42). Jeremiah said that God tested his heart and knows him (Jer. 12:3 – 4). Abraham was tested by God when God asked him to sacrifice his only son, but God stopped him after he saw that Abraham was faithful to the Lord to do it (Heb. 11:17 – 19; Gen. 22). God sent a messenger of the devil to afflict Apostle Paul, but Paul said that when he was weak, God was strong for him, because the Spirit of God carried him (2 Cor. 6 – 10). Even though Christ is the Son of God, he learned obedience through suffering (Heb. 5:7 – 9; Luke 2:7; 4:1 – 21; 9:58; Matt. 2:13 – 15).

The Bible says, "It is good that I was afflicted, so I could learn God's ways" (Ps. 119:64 – 72). David said after he repented for his terrible sins, "You have tested my heart, you have visited me in the night, you have tried me and have found nothing wrong. Uphold my steps in your paths, that my footsteps may not slip" (Ps. 17:3 – 6; 94:18 – 19). Ultimately, the Lord will never totally leave nor forsake us (Joh. 14:18, 27; Heb. 13:5; Isa. 42:16 – 21). However, if you forsake the Lord, and serve the world, and serve people and things that the world has made into idol gods, the Lord will turn, hurt, and consume you, after he has done good to you (Josh. 24:20). If you forsake God, he will forsake you until you repent or until he is ready to pursue you for his calling and his purpose, if he calls you while you are rebelling against him. But many are called, few are chosen by God (Matt. 8:11 – 12; 20:16; 22:14; 2 Chron. 15:1 – 8; 24:20 and 1 Chron. 28:9).

To the faithful, God will protect you from temptation that he allows throughout the entire world, to test people who love worldly matters (1 Cor.10:1-13; Joh.17:14-19; Re.3:10-13; James4:7; Luke 4:1-13.

Count it all joy when you face different temptations, knowing this, that the test of your faith teaches us to be patience, and gives us a crown of life (James 1:3, 12 – 27). There are people in the Bible who asked God to test them, and to try their hearts, to know their thoughts, and to see if any wickedness was in them (Ps. 26 and Ps. 139:19 – 24). God tells us to try and test the spirit of other people and of churches, to see if they are truly of God (Jer. 6:16; 1 Joh. 4:1; Rev. 2:2 – 11; Rom. 12:2). If there are blemishes, wrinkles, and spots, leave that church and find a sanctified church, because we are sanctified through the truth (Joh. 17:17 – 20; Eph. 5:25 – 27; 1 Thess. 5:16 – 22).

God also tests ministers (1 Cor. 3:5 – 17; 1 Tim. 3:1 – 7). Deacons and other church officials should also be proven before they lead and before they even become deacons. And both ministers and deacons are supposed to have a sanctified and holy household at home including how they raise their children before they become deacons and ministers (1 Tim. 3:1 – 13). Joshua the righteous servant of the Lord said, "As for me and my house, we shall serve the Lord" (Josh. 24:15).

Sometimes we must search and examine our own ways and turn back to the Lord (Lam. 3:40). The New Testament says examine and test yourselves to see if you are truly in the Christian Faith (2 Cor. 13:5). This could reassure yourself that you are not a hypocrite or reprobate (Rom. 1:18 – 32; 2 Thess. 2:10 – 15; 8:13 – 14; 1 Pet. 2:6 – 8; 1 Pet. 2:6 – 8; 2 Tim. 3:1 – 8;

Tit. 1:16; Ps. 81:10 – 12, 15).

When people say, "I will serve the Lord until I die," or, "I will die for the Lord," or, "If I never get what I want in life I will still serve the Lord," or, "I am going to run on to see what the end is going to be," sometimes God causes them to prove that they mean what they said, and his test could be extremely long. The Apostle Peter told Christ that he would die for the Lord, but Christ told Peter that he will deny the Lord three times before sunrise. When faced with the fear of being arrested, falsely accused, beaten, and killed like Christ, Peter disowned Christ. After he realized that he had condemned and forsook Christ, Peter cried and wept extremely hard (Matt. 26:66 – 75). If you have a heart and a mind to promise God that you will stand with him regardless of anything, you should go ahead and make the promise to the Lord. Because to want to say it, but not say it, is the same as saying that you will not stand with the Lord through hard times, persecution, trials, tests, and against people who claim that they can live a life contrary to the Word of God, and who call good, evil, and evil, good (Isa. 5:20–25; Ps. 50:21; Mal. 2:17; Jer. 44:16, 28–29; Isa. 5:11 – 14; Ezek. 33:30–33).

In addition to the scriptures above, God says that it is best to not promise him that you will stand with him forever than to make the promise and not keep the promise. But again, if you feel like making that promise, you would be denying Christ if you refuse to make the promise or fail to make the promise. Christ says that if anyone comes after him and deny not themselves daily, and deny other humans, when necessary, they cannot be his servant (Eccles. 5:1 – 7; Deut. 23:21 – 23; Num. 30:2; Prov. 20:24 – 25; Jer. 42:1 – 6, 21 – 22; 2 Pet. 2:23; Luke 9:23–26).

Several scriptures say that God tries the heart, but the following scripture says that he tries the heart and has pleasure in people who are righteous (1 Chron. 29:17). The Bible does say that if we confess with our mouth and believe in our heart, we shall be saved. But God tries the heart, so it is not as easy as it sounds. Therefore, God does not always test the heart in an easy way. The Bible says that God tests our hearts like a hot fiery furnace and like a hot refiner tests silver and gold to determine its strength, value, and purity (Prov.17:3-4; Ps.12:6-7; 66:10-12; Zech.13:9). After our faith is tested by spiritual fire on earth, we come out more precious than pure gold, if we pass the test (1 Pet. 1:3 – 25). While suffering the loss of his children, health, and wealth, Job said, "Oh that I knew where I might find God, that I may come even to his seat. But he knows the way that I take, and when he has tested me, I shall come forth as gold" (Job 23:3 – 17). Hallelujah. Amen. But who may abide the day of God's coming? And who shall stand when he appears, now, or on judgment day? For he is like a hot refiner, and he shall purge and purify the children of God like silver and gold, that they may offer unto the Lord an offering in righteousness (Mal. 3:2 – 3). Hallelujah. Amen. Again, God tests the heart, but he rewards everyone according to their works, and brings us out of the test into a wealthy place (Jer. 17:10; Ps. 66:10 – 12). The ultimate wealthy place is in heaven where streets are paved with gold, (Rev. 21:21). There are many mansions and many treasures in heaven, but there is also wealth on earth that includes a wealth of health, peace, safety, security, protection, and obedient offspring (Ps. 66:8 – 12; 2 Cor. 6:1 – 10; Col. 3:16; 1 Tim. 6:17; Prov. 13:7; Rev. 3:15 – 22; Joh. 14:1 – 3; Matt. 30:19 – 34; Jer. 29:1 – 11; 3 Joh. 1:2).

Christ left his riches in glory to come to earth and suffer in poverty so that we can be rich in various ways (2 Cor. 8:9; Phil. 4:19; Lev. 12:6 – 8; Luke 2:21 – 24; Rom. 15:1 – 3).

God searched out the promised land for the Israelites in the Old Testament (Ezek. 20:6). But in the new promised land of heaven, God is preparing a place for us that includes mansions, streets paved with gold, and no sickness nor death (Joh. 14:1 – 3; Isa. 25:8; Rev. 7:17; 21:4). God told Daniel after Daniel saw visions of the coming of Christ and the end of the world, "Go your way, Daniel, for the words are closed and sealed until judgment day. Many shall be purified, cleansed, and tried, but the wicked shall do wickedly, and none of the wicked shall understand, but the wise shall understand" (Dan. 12:8 – 13). It is impossible to deceive God's highly anointed saints who some versions of the Bible call "elect" saints, and for the elect's sake, these evil last days shall be shortened. And if God did not shorten these days, no one would be saved (Mark 13). God's way is perfect, and his Word has been tested and is proven (Ps. 18:30).

The Lord tests righteous people (Ps. 11; Jer. 20:1 – 13).
But the Lord tests the heart (Prov. 17:3).
God tests the mind and the heart (Jer. 11:18 – 20).
Deceitful hearts (Jer. 17:9 – 10).
Great trial of affliction (2 Cor. 8:1 – 7).
Faith until death (Heb. 11:30 – 40).
God tries preacher's heart (1 Thess. 2:3 – 6).
Fiery trial which is to try you (1 Pet. 4:12).

See also *MORE THAN YOU CAN BEAR; WITH; VICTORY; WORRYING; ADVERSITY; PATIENCE; ALONE.*

TODAY

It is usually not good to procrastinate, but it certainly is not good to procrastinate regarding the saving of your soul. Wherefore, as the Holy Ghost says, "Today if you hear my voice, harden not your heart as in the provocation, in the day of temptation in the wilderness when the Israelites tempted God. So, God swore in his wrath that they would not enter his rest. Take heed, lest there be an evil heart in you to lead you away from the living God" (Heb. 3:7 – 19; 4:1 – 2). When Paul ministered unto Felix, he foolishly told Paul to go away until another day (Acts 24:24 – 25).

Do not brag about tomorrow, because you do not know what a day may bring (Prov. 27:1). One rich man in the Bible harvested his farm and thought that he would take it easy for the winter, but God said, "You fool, tonight you shall die and lose your soul" (Luke 12:16 – 21; 1 Thess. 5:1 – 11; 2 Pet. 3:10 – 18; Job 24:13 – 17).

What profits a person if they gain the world and lose their soul (Mark 8:34 – 38; Matt. 24:3 – 14; Job 27:8 – 23; 1 Thess. 2:2; 2 Tim. 1:12; James 1:8 – 27)?

Obviously, God can say what he will do today, tomorrow, the next day, or any day, but we must say, "If the Lord wills it," when we speak about what may happen tomorrow, because to count tomorrow without acknowledging that God must grant us that new mercy the next morning, is evil, and to know to do good but not do it is sin. Almost everyone in the world is guilty of this sin (James 4:13 – 17; Isa. 33:2; Lam. 3:21 – 23; Luke 13:31 – 33; Lev. 5:1; Prov. 3:27 – 29).

The Bible tells us to not say, "Why were the former days

better than the present day?" That would not be wise (Eccles. 7:10). God wants to do a new thing in your life (Isa. 43:18 – 19). Eyes have not seen, and ears have not heard what God has for people who wait on him (1 Cor. 2:9; 1 Pet. 1:8; Phil. 4:4 – 7; Isa. 64:4 – 8; Ps. 31:19; Luke 19:33 – 42; Jer. 33:3).

For the record, new things to us are not new to God, because in God's eyes, there is nothing new under the sun (Eccles. 1:9 – 11; Ps. 147:5; Prov. 3:19 – 20).

It is certainly sinful to drink alcohol excessively and say that you will do it again tomorrow (Isa. 56:12). To non – believers who live every day for what it is worth, while saying that they only live once, the Apostle Paul said, "If they believe that there is no resurrection to a better and eternal life, they may as well eat, drink, and live like they will die tomorrow," and they just might die tomorrow with such an anti – God attitude (1 Cor. 15:32).

Christ, the same yesterday, today, and forever (Heb. 13:8). But that pertains to his mercy, and to his holding us accountable for our actions. Some people live every day for what it is worth, they live in jeopardy every hour, and they eat and drink because they think that they could be dead tomorrow. That practice and thought process is sin, but if you live life to the fullest while glorifying God every day and resist the pleasing of your sinful flesh every day, you please the Lord, because the Spirit is against the flesh, and the flesh is against the Spirit. This cannot be stated enough (1 Cor. 15:30 – 34; Isa. 22:12 – 14; Gal. 5:16 – 26; 6:7 – 8, 14; 1 Pet. 2:11 – 12; 4:1 – 6; 1 Thess. 3:3).

God tells us to eat, drink, and be happy, but whatever you do, even when you eat and drink, do all things to the glory of God, and for his purpose and his pleasure (1 Cor. 10:31; Rev. 4:11; Eccles. 5:18 – 20; 8:15; 12:13; Luke 12:16 – 21).

This is not to say that we should live every day for what it is worth and not plan for the future, but Christ tells to not worry about tomorrow because today's evil is enough to worry about, and that God will always provide daily for people who serve him in righteousness and who trust in him (Matt. 6:24 –

34). David said, "I have been young and now I am old, but I have never seen the righteous forsaken, nor their children begging for bread" (Ps. 37:25; 71). Christ also instructs us to pray while saying, "Give us this day, our daily bread" (Matt. 6:9 – 13). That bread is not only edible, food, but the bread of life which is Christ, and Christ tells us, "They who come to me shall never hunger, and they who believe in me shall never thirst" (Joh. 6:35). Thus, although we must eat food to live, the Bible says that we cannot live by bread alone, but by every Word that proceeds out of the mouth of God (Luke 4:4; Exod. 24:7; Deut. 4:1 – 9). So, the Word of God is spiritual bread, the bread of life, and Christ is the living bread (John 6:35, 41, 48, 51). Although we may be sick or weak in the body, our spirit should be renewed every day, because our present troubles are small compared to the prize that we cannot see and that we shall receive (2 Cor. 4:16 – 18). We must wait on Christ like others wait for the morning to get what they want, and if they do not get what they want in the morning, they wait for another day (Ps. 130:5 – 6).

The following scriptures are examples of how we procrastinate after God warns us, and after he blesses us (Gen. 19:14 – 26; Num. 13:25 – 33; 14:1 – 24).

See also *PATIENCE; WORRYING.*

VICTORY

We all must keep faith in Christ while knowing that some of us will not receive the victory until we go to heaven, just as people in the Old Testament knew that they were serving the Lord but would not receive their reward until after Christ was born, killed, and raised from the dead thousands of years later, so they waited on Christ to be born but they died before Christ was born (Heb. 11:30 – 40). Esther stood with God, and said regarding the threats to her life, "If I perish, I perish" (Est. 4:16). But God gave them the victory and turned their sorrow to joy (Est. 9:22). We overcome all things by the blood of the Lamb of God who is Jesus Christ, and by the word of our testimony (Rev. 12:11; 1 Joh. 5:1 – 4). This literally means that we are not only conquerors, but we are "more than" conquerors through Christ who loves us (Rom. 8:26 – 39; Rev. 6:2; 2 Cor. 2:14; Prov. 16:32; Eccles. 7:19).

No weapon formed against us shall prosper, because if God is for us, who can be against us (Isa. 54:17; Jer. 29:1 – 11; 1 Chron. 12:17; Ps. 109:1 – 13).

When God punished Israel for their sins by sending them into slavery, the slaveholders did not take the poor people nor did they take Jeremiah, because they served and trusted in the Lord through much pain and suffering. When Jeremiah lost confidence because how people treated him, God said that he would deliver Jeremiah and cause Jeremiah's enemies to treat him well in the time of evil and in the time of affliction, because Jeremiah put his trust in the Lord and served the Lord as a holy and sanctified servant of God (Jer. 15:10 – 11; 39:8 – 18; 40:1 – 7).

To God be glory/victory (1 Chron. 29:11).
Victory over enemies (Ps. 6).
Fearing God causes victory (Ps. 34).
God judges the earth (Ps. 98).
Victory over darkness (1 Joh. 1:4 – 9).
Strength to leap over walls (Ps. 18:29).
They who fear God (Eccles. 7:18).

See also *TEST; PROTECTION; KEEPER; ALONE; WITH; TRY CHRIST; PATIENCE; MORE THAN YOU CAN BEAR; ADDICTIONS; ADVERSITY; HOPE; HELP; HOLD ON*

WITH

In the Old Testament it was prophesized that Christ would be born unto a virgin, and his name shall be called Immanuel (Isa. 7:14; Matt. 1:23; Joh. 1:1 – 14). The name Immanuel is translated, "God with us." And the name of the new city of heaven shall be, "The Lord is there" (Ezek. 48:30 – 35). The name Yeshua, Jesus in English, was given to him by his mother Mary to conceal him from the public who would have put certain demands on the child before it was time for him to minister (Matt. 2:13 – 16; Rev. 12:1 – 8; Joh. 2:1 – 12). At least one other person was also named Jesus when Christ lived on earth, but his name was changed to Justus (Col. 4:10 – 11). Before Christ went back to heaven, he promised that he is preparing a place for us in heaven, that where he is, we shall be there too (Joh. 14:1 – 3; Heb. 11:15 – 16). And we shall see God like he is, and we shall be like him (Phil. 3:17 – 21; 1 Joh. 3:2; Ps. 17:14 – 15).

But to be like Christ in heaven, we must be like him on earth (Tit. 2:11 – 15). God says, "Even to your old age I am he, and even to gray hairs I will carry you. I have made you and I will bear you. I will carry you and deliver you" (Isa. 46:4; Ps. 71:9 – 14). For God is our God forever and ever, and he will be our guide until death (Ps. 48:14). Thus, God protects, directs, and corrects us. The Bible says regarding us going to heaven, "God shall dwell with them, they shall be his people, and God himself shall be with them and be their God. God shall wipe away all tears from their eyes, and there shall be no more death, neither sorrow, nor crying, neither shall there be any more pain, for the former things are passed away" (Rev. 21:2 –

4).

The Bible tells us that Enoch and Noah walked with God, and that they were sanctified men (Gen. 5:22, 24; 6:9). Regardless of how much God favors you and leads, guides, and protects you, it is best to say that God is close to you rather than saying that you are close to God. Sanctified simply means to be set apart for holy use, but people act as though the word "sanctified" and the sanctified lifestyle is undesirable and shameful (Joh. 17:17 – 19; Isa. 29:23; Heb. 2:11; 11:16).

Hundreds and hundreds of years before Christ was born unto a virgin on earth as the Son of man, he was in the wilderness with the Hebrews and Moses as God the Son while they were traveling from slavery in Egypt (1 Cor. 10:1 – 17; Ps. 66:8 – 12; Exod. 14:19 – 20; Deut. 32:4, 15, 18, 30 – 31, 37).

They tempted God by complaining and by saying, "Is the Lord among us or not" (Exod. 17:7; Ps. 78:10 – 72)? They caused God to be unpleased enough in the wilderness and in the promised land to destroy them, but God remembered his promises to them and would not destroy all of them, nor cast all of them out of his sight (Num. 14:11 – 20; 24:11; 2 Kings 13:23; Ezek. 20:13 – 17).

When you draw near to God, God draws near to you. Submit yourself to God, resist the devil and he shall flee from you. Cleanse your hands you sinners and purify your hearts you double – minded. Humble yourself in the sight of the Lord and he shall lift you up (James 4:7 – 10; Luke 4:1-13). Jeremiah told God,"You drew near on the day I called on you, and you said, 'Do not fear'" (Lam. 3:57). Sin causes God to be far away (Ezek. 8:6). But God is not far from either one of us when we live a holy and sanctified life, and when sinners seek the Lord and truly repent and turn away from their sins (Acts 17:26 – 27; Eph. 2:13; Jer. 23:23 – 24, 33). All of heaven rejoices when sinners repent and become a new creation, born again (Luke 15:1 – 10; Joh. 3:3 – 7; 2 Cor. 5:17; 11:1 – 4). Your salvation is nearer than when you first believed (Rom. 13:11; Isa. 46:13). God is near and justifies the righteous (Isa. 50:8). If you seek God with a loyal heart and a willing mind, he shall be found by you, but if you forsake him, he will forsake you (2 Chron. 15:1 – 8; 24:20; 1 Chron. 28:9; Luke 11:9 – 10; Matt. 11:28 – 30; Jer. 6:16; 23:33).

God says that he brings his righteousness near to us, it shall not be far away, and that his salvation shall not wait (Isa. 46:13). You will be able to say, "God is near who justifies me. Who will contend with me? Who is my adversary? Let us stand face to face" (Isa. 50:8). God says that the Holy Ghost will give you words to say when it is time for you to speak before crowds and authorities, but do not self – incriminate yourself by talking without having your lawyer present (Matt. 5:10; 10:16 – 20). Be slow to become angry, do not stay angry long, be slow to speak and quick to listen (Isa. 53:7; Mark 15:4 – 5; James 1:19 – 27; Prov. 14:29; 15:18; 16:32; 21:23 – 24; 25:8 – 10; Eccles. 3:1 – 8; 5:1 – 7).

Seek the Lord while he can be found. Call on God while he is near; call on God while he is calling you (Isa. 55:6; Lam. 3:57; Jer. 30:19 – 24). Often God's wondrous works declares his presence, therefore we should also declare God's blessings and works by glorifying God in testimonies and music (Ps. 75:1; 78:32; 118:17). Offer the sacrifice of praise unto the Lord (Ps. 4:5; Heb. 13:15). God says, "I create the fruit of the lips. Peace, peace, to them who are near and them who are far away, and I will heal them" (Is. 57:19). Regarding rebellious people, infidels, hypocrites, and anti – Christians, God says, "For the day is near, even the day of the Lord is near, a cloudy day. It shall be the day of the heathen" (Ezek. 30:3). The Lord also says, "For the day of the Lord is near unto all heathens. As they have done, so shall it be done unto them. Their reward shall be upon their own head" (Oba. 1:15). Therefore it is best for God to be near you in your righteousness than for him to visit you in your rebellious sin, or evil and wicked sin. Some people do not obey the voice of God, they do not accept correction from God, they do not trust in God, and they do not draw near to God (Zep. 3:2). We should draw near God with a true heart (Heb.10:22).

The Spirit of God came upon a man in the Bible and God said, "Why do you transgress the commandments of the Lord, so that you cannot prosper? Because you have forsaken the Lord, he has also forsaken you" (2 Chron. 24:20). God is with you as long as you are with him, and especially when you remain humble, but trouble comes to people who withdraw themselves from God (2 Chron. 15; and 2 Chron. 12:5 – 8; Ezra 8:21 – 23; Deut. 1:34 – 45; Josh. 24:15 – 25).

David said, "I have set the Lord always before me. Because he is at my right hand I shall not be moved" (Ps. 16:8). The book of Amos tells us to seek good and not evil, so that we will live, and the Lord of hosts will be with us" (Am. 5:14 –15). David also said, "I will set no evil thing before my eyes, I hate the work of them who turn aside, it shall not cleave to me. I will not know a wicked person" (Ps. 101:3 – 4). The book of Psalms also says, "Oh how I love your Word. It is my meditation all day. You Lord, through your Word made me wiser than my enemies. And your Word is forever with me. I have more understanding than my teachers and elderly people. I have kept my feet from every evil way and have not departed from your Word. I hate every false way" (Ps. 119:97 – 104). If you feel that God is not with you, or if God truly has casted you out of his sight, look again towards God's holy temple (Jon. 2:4). But it must be a holy and sanctified church, and if you do not know of a holy and sanctified church, fast, pray, and study the Bible for yourself, and seek heaven first. Because the Bible tells us that where your treasure is, and where your values are, there shall your heart be too, whether it is with holiness and the pursuit of heaven, or with worldly things (Matt. 6:19 – 21, 24 – 33; 19:16 – 30; Rom. 2:6 – 11; 8:5; Phil. 2:21; 1 Kings 3:7 – 15; Heb. 11:24 – 27).

As stated earlier, "The world loves its own people, places, and things, and a friend of the world is an enemy of God" (James 4:2 – 4; Joh. 1:10 – 12; 15:18 – 19; 1 Joh. 2:15 – 17; 3:13; Phil. 3:16 – 21).

Why is there in the hand of fools the purchase price of

wisdom when they have no heart for it (Prov. 17:16; 18:1 – 2)?

Sometimes God will draw near to you or call upon you without you drawing near to him first. But you must still call upon the Lord and respond to him while he is near (Isa. 55:6; Ps. 75:1; 78:32; 118:17; Luke 4:42; Joh. 16:7). Draw near to God with a true heart (Heb. 10:22). God says, "I was found by people who did not seek me. I said, 'Hear I am' to a nation not called by my name. I have stretched out my hands all day long to a rebellious people who walk in a way that is not good, according to their own thoughts" (Rom. 10:16 – 21; Ezek. 3:4 – 21; Isa. 65:1 – 2). The Lord God shall come with a strong hand, and his arm shall rule for him. His reward is with him, and his works before him. He shall feed his flock like a shepherd, and he shall gather the lambs with his arm, and carry them in his bosom, and gently lead parents who have young children (Isa. 40:10 – 11). But God's people sometimes say after the Lord has comforted them and had mercy on them, "The Lord has forsaken me, and my Lord has forgotten me." And God replies, "Can a woman forget her nursing child, and not have compassion on the child of her womb? Surely, they may forget, yet I will never forget you. I have written your name on the palms of my hands" (Isa. 49:13 – 16). God gathers his people like a hen gathers her babies, but people refuse to allow him to do so (Matt. 23:37). He wants to lead all people with gentle ropes like when pet owners walk their pets, and he stoops down to feed them with his hand (Hos. 11:4). But most people bite God's hands who feeds them. The Bible says, "Behold, the Lord's hand is not shortened that it cannot save. Nor his ear heavy that he cannot hear. But your iniquities have separated you from your God, and your sins have hidden his face from you, so that he does not hear your call" (Isa. 59:1 – 4; 64:4 – 8; Ps. 107:17 – 22; Mal. 2:2; Hos. 14:1). And crying out to the Lord while admitting your wrong but still not repenting may not get an answer from God (Jer. 14:7 – 12). The Lord has said and is still saying, "Just as I cried and they would not hear, so they cried and I would not hear, says the Lord of hosts" (Zech. 7:13). Also, whomever pretends that they do not hear the cry of the poor, they too shall cry one day and not be heard (Prov. 21:13). The Bible also says, "Even though the Lord is high, yet he considers the lowly, but the proud he knows afar off" (Ps. 138:6). God Almighty says, "Take heed to my rebuke, and surely, I will pour out my Spirit upon you, and make my Word known to you, but you refused. I have stretched out my hand and no one regarded. Therefore, I will laugh at your calamity. I will mock when your terror comes. When your terror comes like a storm and your destruction like a whirlwind, when distress and anger come upon you, then you will call upon me, but I will not answer. They will seek me early, but they will not find me. Because they hated knowledge and did not choose the fear of the Lord" (Prov. 1:20 – 33).

The Bible says, "Since the beginning of the world, mankind has not heard nor perceived by ear, neither has eyes seen, O God, besides you, what you have prepared for them who wait for you. But we have sinned. We are all an unclean thing, and our iniquities like the wind have taken us away. And there is none who calls upon you, that stirs up themselves to take hold of you. For you have hid your face from us because of our iniquities. But you O Lord are our Father, we are the clay, you are our potter, and we all are the work of your hands" (Isa. 64:4 – 8; 1 Cor. 2:9). But when people continue to refuse to hear God, and to even disregard his Word, God often blinds them from his Word (2 Cor.4:3 – 4; 2 Thess. 2:10 – 15). And the Lord even turns them over to a reprobate mind, which means that God is certainly not with them, because they take pleasure in unrighteousness and in disobeying God's Word (Rom. 1:18 – 32; 2 Thess. 2:10 – 15; 8:13 – 14; 1 Pet. 2:6 – 8; 2 Cor. 13:5; 2 Tim. 3:1 – 8; Tit. 1:16; 2 Thess. 2:9 – 12; Isa. 66:4; Ezek. 21:23 – 24; 1 Kings 22:23; Ps. 81:10 – 12, 15).

God said regarding Israel, and it pertains to the whole world today, "For as the girdle cleaves to the loins of a man, so have I caused to cleave to me the whole house of Israel and Judah, says the Lord. That they might be unto me a people, and for a name, and for a praise, and for a glory, but they would not hear" (Jer. 13:11). Therefore, God eventually casted Judah out of his sight like he did the other eleven tribes, but Christ, Mary, and Joseph were still born in the tribe of Judah hundreds of years later (Ps. 78:67 – 72; 2 Kings 17:13 – 23; 21:16; 23:27; Jer. 14:19; Hos. 5:5; 11:12).

Judah was also the tribe of Caleb, Daniel, Isaiah, Zephaniah; Hezekiah, Josiah, Shadrach, Meshach, and Abednego (Rev. 5:5; Gen. 49:1, 9 – 12; Ps. 78:67 – 72; Matt. 2:6; Heb. 7:14, Num. 34:19, Dan. 1:6; 6:13; Isa. 1; Zeph. 1; 1 Kings 13:2; 2 Kings 22:1).

The fool says in their heart that there is no God. They are corrupt and abominable. The Lord looks down from heaven to see if there is any who understands, who seeks God. They have all turned aside, and do not call upon the Lord. For God is with the generation of the righteous, and he is a refuge for the poor (Ps. 14). The Apostle Paul said regarding all the original apostles, "For we are not as many, who corrupt the Word of God, but as of sincerity, but as of God, in the sight of God speak we in Christ" (2 Cor. 2:17; 1 Tim. 2:1 – 3). Furthermore, "But we have renounced the hidden things of dishonesty, not walking in craftiness, nor handling the Word of God deceitfully; but by manifestation of the truth commending ourselves to every man's conscience in the sight of God" (2 Cor. 4:2). Christ wants to present you to God unblameable and unrebukable in his sight (Col. 1:22; 1 Thess. 1:3). We must do what is well pleasing to God in his sight, and to be in good sight with God is to be near him, with him, and in his presence (Heb. 13:21; 1 Joh. 3:22). But to rebel against God causes God to cast people out of his sight and out of his presence, or to be punished in his presence, just as the beast in the book of Revelation will be tormented in fire and brimstone in the presence of the holy angels and of Christ the Lamb of God (2 Kings 24:20; Eph. 1:4; Rev. 14:9 – 10). The Apostle John said that he saw the dead both small and great stand before God, and they are judged according to what is in the book of their works (Rev. 20:12). God says, "Fear you not me? Will you not tremble at my presence" (Jer.

5:22)?

Christ says, "Search the scriptures, they testify of me, and of your eternal life, but you will not come to me so that you will have eternal life" (Joh. 5:39 – 40; Luke 24:24 – 27, 32; Acts 10:43; 17:11). God keeps his obedient people as the apple of his eye, he has mercy on them when they make mistakes, and protects them under the shelter of his wings when they trust in him (Ruth 2:12; Ps. 17:5 – 9; 57:1 – 2 and Ps. 61). But God takes away his mercy from people who do not repent and turn from their sins (2 Sam. 7:15). God told Jeremiah that the people of Israel could not get him to change his mind about punishing them even if Moses and Samuel stood before him to plead for them (Jer. 15:1 – 6). And after God had sent Jeremiah to warn the people, God eventually told Jeremiah that the people could choose to return to the Lord, but that Jeremiah must not return to them (Jer. 15:19).

It is a sin to not pray for people, including your enemies (1 Sam. 12:23; 1 Tim. 2:1 - 2; Matt. 5:44 – 45. But God told Jeremiah at one point to not pray for the sinful people of the land, because he would not hear Jeremiah's prayers (Jer. 7:16; 11:14; 14:7 – 12). In another scripture God tells all of us that there is a sin unto death and a sin not unto death, and that we should not pray for the sin unto death because God knows that we will not turn away from that sin. But the sin that God tells us to pray for is the sin that we repent for and turn away from (1 Joh. 5:14 – 17; Jer. 7:16 – 20; 11:14; 14:11; Rev. 3:15 – 19; Matt. 12:33; Rom.6 :15 – 17; Ps. 66:16 – 20.

The Bible says, "If I regard iniquity in my heart, the Lord will not hear me. Blessed be the Lord who has not turned away my prayer, nor his mercy from me" (Ps. 66:18 – 20). God says that when he punishes people, lands, and nations for their sins, even if Noah, Daniel, and Job were in those lands and nations, their righteousness would only save them, and that their righteousness would not save their sons and daughters (Ezek. 14:12 – 20).

Christ laid down his life for his sheep and he knows his

sheep. Christ's true sheep know his voice, they will not follow another, and will even run from anything that is not of God (Joh. 10:1 – 5; Eph. 5:1 – 2). Christ says, "Come unto me, all ye who labor and are heavy laden, and I will give you rest. Take my yoke upon you and learn of me, and you shall find rest unto your souls. For my yoke is easy, and my burden is light" (Matt. 11:28 – 30). But most people will not walk in God's ways to find rest for their souls (Jer. 6:16). God says, "When you spread your hands, I will hide my eyes from you. Yes, when you make many prayers, I will not hear. Your hands are full of blood (including blood on the hands of lying ministers). Wash, and make yourself clean. Put away your evil doings from before my eyes. Cease to do evil. Learn to do good and seek judgment. Relieve the oppressed, judge the fatherless, plead for the widow. Come now, and let us reason together, says the Lord. Though your sins are as scarlet, they shall be as white as snow; though they are red like crimson, they shall be as wool. If you be willing and obedient, you shall eat the good of the land. But if you refuse and rebel, you shall be devoured with weapons, for the mouth of the Lord has spoken it" (Isa. 1:15 – 20).

God also says that he hides his face from people who not only worship other gods, but who honor idols such Christmas, Easter, and Halloween idols, and when people seek benefits through witchcraft, voodoo, black magic, and sorcery (Deut. 31:17 – 20; 32:15 – 20). God was with Josiah who was the greatest and most righteous king in the history of the world, and he did not serve nor honor idolatry, neither did he honor sinful kings, and he never departed from the Lord but obeyed the Word of God. And he prospered wherever he went (2 Kings 18:4 – 8).

Jeremiah said regarding the people of Zion, "Although they spread their hands wide, God is far from them, no one comforts them, and God has caused people around them to become their adversaries" (Lam. 1:16 – 17).

Christ says, "They who are not with me are against me" (Matt. 12:30; Mark 9:38 – 40). In every nation, whoever fears Christ and works righteousness is accepted by Christ (Acts 10:35). And he will fulfill their desire, hear their cry, and save them (Ps. 145:19). Regarding the people of any nation who fear God, the Bible says, "What nation is there that is so great, who has God so near to them, as the Lord God is in all that we call upon him for" (Deut. 4:7; Acts 17:25 – 27; Eph. 2:13)?

If you are risen in baptism with Christ, seek those things which are above, where Christ sits on the right hand of God. Set your affections on things above, not on things on the earth. For your sinful nature should be dead, and your life is hidden with Christ in God. When Christ, who is your life, shall appear, then shall you also appear with him in glory (Col. 3:1 – 4). The Bible says, "It is a faithful saying, 'If we are dead with Christ, we shall also live with him, if we suffer like Christ, we shall also reign with him, if we deny him, he shall deny us'" (2 Tim. 2:11 – 12). If we say we have fellowship with him, and walk in the darkness of sin, we lie, but if we walk in the light of God's Word, the blood of Jesus Christ cleanses us from all sin (1 Joh. 1:6 – 7 and Joh. 8:12). Christ says, "I stand at the door and knock, and if anyone hears my voice, and opens the door, I will come to them, and sup with them, and them with me" (Rev. 3:20; 21:3). Hallelujah. Christ is Lord of lords, King of kings, and they who are with him are called, chosen, and faithful (Rev. 17:14). Christ goes on to say, "I come quickly, and my reward is with me, to give to everyone according to their works" (Rev. 22:12). But even on earth, the Lord your God who is with you is mighty, he will save you, and will rejoice over you in gladness (Zep. 3:17). Be strong and of good courage, do not be afraid, because the Lord your God will be with you wherever you may go (Josh.1:9). God told Joshua after he succeeded Moses, that the Lord will be with him like he was with Moses (Josh. 1:5). However, even though God was with Joshua, the sins of the people under him caused God to not deliver some of their enemies of war into their hands, and God told them to cry out to their idols that they honored and see if the idols would save them (Judg. 2:17 – 23; 5:8; 10:14). It was due to idolatry and other sins after leaving slavery in Egypt and arriving in the promised land that God sent his people into slavery a second time, but in Babylon the second time (Neh. 9:36 – 37; 1 Kings 14:10, 15; 2 Kings 17; Ps. 106:24; Jer. 2:7; 6:10 – 12; Ezek. 36:16 – 38; Am. 7:10 – 17).

God sometimes caused poor people to not be taken into slavery, they instead inherited the property of the rich and prosperous people (Jer. 39:9 – 10). Some of the people who were taken even sinned while in slavery, but God was still merciful to bring them out (Ezek. 36:19 – 24, Zep. 1:9). The Lord is so powerful and merciful, that he freed them and turned around and used them to punish other nations for their sins. God told Israel, "With you I shall destroy nations, with you I shall destroy kingdoms, with you I shall break in pieces governors and rulers" (Jer. 51:18 – 24). And in other scriptures God speaks about how he returned ancient Israel to their promised land and punished other nations for how they treated the ancient Israelites, although ancient Israel was being punished by God for their sins (Ps. 14; Jer. 30:10 – 17; Zech. 8:1 – 8). The people of modern – day Israel are not the descendants of ancient Israel.

David was a king, and he at one point committed evil sins, but he repented and lived a sanctified and holy life (2 Sam. 11; 12:1 – 24; 15; 1 Kings 3:6; 14:8; 15:3 – 5). David wrote, "God rewarded me according to my righteousness and the cleanness of my hands in his sight. I have kept the ways of the Lord and have not wickedly departed from my God. I am also blameless before him, and I have kept myself from iniquity. God also brings down high looks" (Ps. 18:20 – 27; 2 Sam. 22:25). God says to people who he has punished and who have repented for their sins, "As I have watched over them to pluck up, to break down, to throw down, to destroy, and to afflict, so will I watch over them to build and to plant" (Jer. 31:28; 44:27). As stated earlier, Christ was born for the fall and rising again of many people (Luke 2:34).

When God is with us, then who can be against us (Rom. 8:31)? Who shall separate us from the love of Christ? Shall

tribulation, or distress, or persecution, or famine, or nakedness, or danger, or weapons? We must be persuaded that neither life nor death, nor angels nor principalities, nor powers,
nor present things, nor things to come shall separate us from
the love of God that is in Christ Jesus our Lord (Rom. 8:35 – 39).
But sin and iniquity can separate you from your God, and your
sins can cause God to hide his face from you, so that he does
not hear your prayers (Isa. 59:1 – 4; 64:4 – 8; Ps. 107:17 – 22;
Mal. 2:2; Hos. 14:1).

Christ is above all powers and principalities, and above all
gods and idols, and God Almighty has given Christ all power
in heaven, on earth, and beneath the earth (Matt. 28:18; 1 Cor.
15:24 – 28; Eph. 1:21 – 23; Phil. 2:9; Ps. 8; Heb. 2:5 – 9; Joh.
16:15).

The Bible says, "I called upon the Lord in my distress. The
Lord answered me and placed me in a broad place. The Lord
is on my side. I will not fear. What can humans do to me" (Ps.
56:4; 118:5 – 9). When I cry unto the Lord, my enemies shall
turn back. This I know, for God is for me. God is my defense
(Ps. 59:9). And when God is angry with nations and he sends
destruction, the Lord is with solid Christians, and he is our refuge (Ps. 46:6 – 7).

The Lord is with righteous preachers and judges who
have no respect of persons (1 Sam. 3:11 – 19; 2 Sam. 23:3; Judg.
2:18; 2 Chron. 19). And the Lord will not always allow your enemies to laugh at you and to anticipate your fall, but they shall
fall, and their laughing shall cease (Ps. 35:18 – 28). Although it
does not look like it sometimes, when we stand for righteousness and it seems like we are standing alone, there are more
angels with you than there are devils with the enemy, even if
you cannot see your help and protection from heaven (2 Kings
6:16 – 18; 2 Chron. 32:7 – 8; Ps. 34:4 – 15; Act 12:9 – 11; Num.
22:24 – 27, 32; Matt. 26:53; Luke 24:15 – 16).

Again, God says that when your enemies out number you,
do not be afraid, because your Lord God Almighty is with you
and will not forsake you (Deut. 20:1; 31:6). When you stand

for righteousness, you will often be alone in the beginning, but in the end, you will stand alone in victory. However, when people uphold wrong, they have plenty of support, but in the end, they shall look like a fool alone. With them is an arm of flesh, but with holy and sanctified Christians is the Lord God Almighty to help us and to fight our battles. God even turns supporters of your enemies against each other (2 Chron. 20:21 – 24; 32:8, 21). But if you rebel against God, the Lord literally says that he may fight against you (Jer. 21:1 - 7; 44:27; 50:6 - 7; Zec. 14:2 - 3; Lam. 3:3 - 5; Ezek. 16:37; 23:22).

In God I will praise his Word, in God I will put my trust. I will not fear what flesh and blood can do to me (Ps. 56:4). But we must pick our battles, because if God tells us to not challenge a certain enemy, we must obey the Lord, or the Lord will not be with us, and he may allow us to suffer loss (Num. 14:40 – 43; Deut. 1:42). And if God does instruct you to fight a battle, you must do so, even if it does not seem like you will win. Just as when an angel of the Lord appeared to Gideon and said, "The Lord is with you, you mighty man of valor" (Judg. 6:12). But Gideon said, "If the Lord is with us, why has all of this happened to us? And where are the miracles that our fathers told us about when the Hebrews were leaving slavery in Egypt? But the Lord has forsaken us." And the Lord said, "Go, have I not sent you? I am with you." (Judg. 6:12 – 16). God still works miracles, but we often do not see them in the same manner as the Hebrews saw in the wilderness, because God spoke to mankind in the Old Testament and in various times and in various ways through the prophets, but in these last days he speaks to us through his Son who is God the Holy Ghost, and the birth, life, ministry, death, resurrection, and ascension back to heaven of Christ are all the miracles that we need to believe in (Heb. 1:1 – 2). We must live by faith nowadays even more than people did in the Old Testament, and without faith it is impossible to please God (Heb. 11:6; and Heb. 6:1 – 6; Ps. 105; Isa. 63:8 – 14; Deut. 32:20).

Take heed, lest there be in any of you an evil heart of unbelief like the ancient Hebrews in the wilderness, in departing from the living God, and fail to enter God's rest (Heb. 3:7 – 12). To people who live holy and sanctified lives, God says that he sends his fear before them and confuses their enemies, chases their enemies away, and that he walks in their dwelling places, when that place is a holy dwelling place (Exod. 23:27; Deut. 23:14; Jer. 18:23). God says, "I will walk among you and be your God, and you shall be my people" (Lev. 26:12). God hides us in the secret place of his presence from our enemies (Ps. 31:20). Sometimes God the Holy Ghost walks with us himself, instead of angels walking with us, just as he walked with the apostles in secret after the resurrection (Luke 24:15 – 16). They who dwell in the secret place of the Most High shall abide in the shadow of the Almighty. I will say of the Lord, "He is my refuge and my fortress, my God, in him will I trust" (Ps. 91:1 – 2). Your enemies may fight against you, but they shall not prevail, because Christ is with you, to deliver you (Jer. 1:19). Sometimes our enemies fear us because they see that God is with us and departed from them, but we must still be humble and behave wisely (1 Sam. 18:12, 14; 28:15 – 16). God causes your enemies and non – believers to help you, but this does not mean that he is with your enemies, especially if their benefits come from sinful deeds (Job 8:20 – 22; Jer. 17:9 – 11). God is certainly with holy and sanctified Christians who help other Christians (Ps. 54:4; Gal. 6:9 – 10; Ps. 37). If anyone is not serving the Lord but are rebelling against the Lord and supporting anti – Christian practices, God certainly becomes their enemy and fights against them (Isa. 63:10). God will also sometimes cause your enemies to help you in times of dejection, adversity, and affliction (Jer. 15:10 – 11). Sometimes you must stand still and see the salvation of the Lord, because the battle is not yours, but the Lord, because he is with you (2 Chron. 20:14 – 17). For the eyes of the Lord run to and from throughout the whole earth, to show himself strong on the behalf of them whose heart is perfect towards him (2 Chron. 16:9). But notice that God told the king in this scripture that he had done foolishly, and as a result, there will be wars (2 Chron. 16:7 – 14). And just as God's eyes look throughout the earth for saints and sanctified Christians who show themselves strong, the devil roams the earth seeking whom he may devour, because he knows that his suffering is forever and he loves taking down with him as many people as possible (1 Pet. 5:8; Rev. 12:7 – 17; Job 1; 2:1 – 10; 3:16 – 22; 13:15 – 16; 42:11).

Now unto the Messiah who can keep you from falling and present you faultless before the presence of his glory with exceedingly joy. To the only wise God our Savior, be glory, majesty, dominion, and power both now and forever and ever. Amen (Jude 1:24 – 25).

The Word of God is a light unto your paths if you live by every Word of God, even if you are not able to do all of it, live by all of it (Ps. 119:105; Matt. 7:21 – 23; Luke 4:4; Exod. 24:7; Deut. 8:3; and Deut. 4:1 – 9).

We must put on the whole armor of God, which is the shield of faith, the breastplate of righteousness, the helmet of salvation, and the sword of the Spirit which is the Word of God (Eph. 6:10 – 17; 1 Thess. 5:8). God is our refuge and strength, a very present help in time of trouble (Ps. 46:1). Even when God chastises us, he is with us, because he could leave us alone and let us self – destruct. If God did not punish people, that would mean that God would cut off their life. Just as when God told the prophet Amos that he would no longer pass by the people, which meant that he destroyed them and their places of worship (Am. 7:8-9 and Am. 5:17; Nah. 1:9, 11 – 12).

Often God is far away from his sanctuary which is the church house, because of the sinful lifestyles of the church house members (Ezek. 8:6). But the Bible says that when God casted off the Israelites and scattered them among other nations due to their sinning, God said that he would be a little sanctuary for them in those strange nations (Ezek. 11:16). There is always hope in the Lord. Who knows, if you repent and trust in the Lord while he is unpleased with you, maybe God will pass by and leave behind a blessing (Joe. 2:12 – 14). And

God does not always pass by in a storm or in some violent way, but in your heart or in a small gentle voice (1 Kings 19:11 – 13; Isa. 30:21). It is your responsibility to hear God in any way that he calls and any way that he visits you or passes by you (Matt. 11:15; 13:9 – 16, 43; Luke 8:4 – 8; Rev. 2:7; 3:6, 20 – 22).

God says to people who have caused themselves problems or have self – destructed, "You have destroyed yourself, but in me is your help" (Hos. 13:9). The love, desire, or pursuit of money in an ungodly way often causes many painful sorrows (1 Cor. 6:9 – 11; 1 Tim. 6:9 – 10; 2 Kings 5:15 – 27). The Bible tells us that God chastises people who he loves, and if he does not chastise you, that means he is not with you because you are not serving him in righteousness, and he will allow the world and even the devil to punish you. Sometimes people's own sinful actions punish them (2 Cor. 6:9; Heb. 12:5 – 11; 1 Cor. 5:1 – 5). When God chastises us, we must be thankful, because his grace is sufficient, and he could have killed us or allowed us to be killed (2 Cor. 6:9; 12:6 – 10; Ps. 118:8, 18). And just because God gives people things and just because he allows some people to prosper financially through sinful ways of making money, that does not mean that he is with them. God gives blessings to the just and the unjust, the good, the evil, and the unthankful, simply because they are part of his creation (Deut. 9:4 – 7; 10:17 – 22; Ezek. 29:17 – 20; Matt. 5:43 – 48; Luke 6:35; Acts 14:8 – 18; Isa. 57:15 – 21; 64:4 – 8).

On judgment day and on the day of their death, it will be too late for the unjust, unthankful, and evil people to change and join Christ (Rev. 22:10 – 13). Because there will be a resurrection of the dead, both the just and the unjust (Acts 24:15). And the holy and just shall forever remain holy and just, but the unjust and filthy shall remain unjust and filthy (Rev. 22:10 – 13). The righteous shall rise to everlasting life, and the sinner shall rise to everlasting damnation (Dan. 12:1 – 3; Matt. 13:47 – 50; 25:31 – 46; Acts 24:15; Joh. 5:24 – 29).

Christ says that a person who does not serve him is like salt with no flavor, good for nothing, and should be thrown away and trampled. Like a vineyard that does not produce grapes even after the owner grows it with the best farming supplies, and like a fruit tree that does not produce fruit at all. People of that nature are worthless to God and could be destroyed by God (Matt. 5:13; 21:18 – 19; Isa. 5:1 – 7; Ezek. 15; 19:10 – 14; Hos. 10:1 – 2).

People know God or need to know God for themselves. But just because some people know him in sickness, trouble, or good times, or because he gave them a spiritual gift or good tangible gift, this does not mean that they know his expectations and standards, which are, "We must live by the whole Word of God, and no one can see God without holiness. Also, we must be a living sacrifice, holy and acceptable to God" (Rev. 20:6; Heb. 12:14 – 15; Rom. 12:1 – 2; Eph. 5:5 – 10, 25 – 27; 2 Tim. 2:19 – 26; Ps. 4:3 – 5).

We must seek first the kingdom of heaven and all its righteousness, regardless of how God has proven himself to be with us in good times and bad times. God being with a person occasionally on earth, and another person living a saved and sanctified life on earth, can be two different things. Because even righteous people just scarcely get into heaven. They who endure until the end shall be saved (Matt. 10:20 – 22; 24:13; Heb. 3:7 – 19; Joh. 6:26 – 29; Eccles. 9:11 – 12).

Let us cleanse ourselves from all filthiness of the flesh and spirit, perfecting holiness in the fear of God (2 Cor. 7:1; Rev. 22:10 – 13).

Some people who have less knowledge of the Bible are closer to God than some other people who have a wealth of knowledge. This is because some less knowledgeable people exercise more humility, meekness, fasting, sanctification, holiness, and love and fear of God. And another reason that being a preacher is a dangerous position is because the more they know the more they are held accountable (James 3:1; 1 Cor. 9:16). And with much wisdom comes much grief (Eccles. 1:18).

Where two or three people are gathered in Christ's name, there Christ will be with them (Matt. 18:15 – 20; 2 Chron. 26:3

– 21; Acts 12:12; 20:36; 21:5; 2 Chron. 20:13 – 14; Zep. 3:17).

Even Christ, in his distress and suffering before death felt that God had forsaken him while he was on the cross (Matt. 27:46). That happened after he passed all the tests of temptations from the devil (Matt. 4:1 – 10; Luke 4:1 – 14; Joh. 16:32). Elijah did not think that the Lord was still with him, but God confirmed that he was with Elijah (1 Kings 19; Rom. 11:1 – 5; 1 Kings 18:26 – 32). Jeremiah felt the same way one time, but God showed up and confirmed his presence with Jeremiah as well (Jer. 15:10 – 21; 20:14 – 18; 38:6 – 13; Lam. 1:12; 3:17 – 66). Other servants of the Lord also thought at times that God was not with them (Ps. 88). God did not answer the prayers of King Saul anymore because of sin (1 Sam. 15:35; 28:6). And the Lord took his mercy away from Saul (2 Sam. 7:15). God answers prayers according to the idols in a person's heart, and people separate themselves from God when they set up idols and display idols (Ezek. 14:2 – 11). Sometimes God will withdraw himself from sinful people, even people who have sinful thoughts (Lam. 5:20 – 22). God alienated himself from Israel because of their physical sexual immorality and because of them being spiritual whores when they dealt with idols and anti-god nations and policies (Ezek. 23:1 – 18; Hos. 9:15 – 17). The Word of God says, "They shall seek the Lord, but they shall not find him, because he has withdrawn himself from them." God goes on to say, "I will return to my place, until they acknowledge their sins and seek my face. In their affliction they will seek me early" (Hos. 5:3 – 6, 15; Jer. 23:39 – 40). And one reason that nations and sections of nations suffer so much death and destruction is because of sin, even the sins of so – called Christians, and the failure of the people to repent and acknowledge God while they live and attempt to live a holy and sanctified life (2 Chron. 7:14; Matt. 13:14 – 15; Luke 19:37 – 42; Isa. 6:8 – 10; Lev. 20:6 – 27; 26:3 – 6; Deut. 28; 29:2 – 6, 22 – 29; 1 Kings 8:32 – 40).

God is very poetic with his words at certain times. For example, he uses the word "early" very eloquently when he says that he rises early in the morning to call people, to teach people, to send his righteous ministers to teach people, and to give instructions, but the called people refuse to hear God. They instead reject God and turn their back and their face away from God, his Word, and the holy and sanctified lifestyle (Jer. 7:13, 25; 25:3 – 5; 29:19; 32:33; 35:14 – 15; 44:4). When rebellious sinners refuse and deny God after he says that he rises early to try to save them, they in their punishment seek God early, but sometimes he does not hear them until he knows that they are serious about changing their ways and are not simply seeking God for relief from their punishment, adversity, and affliction (Hos. 5:3 – 6, 15; Ps. 78:34; Prov. 1:28; 1 John 5:16–19).

Some people think that when God sends what we call natural disasters, God did not send those things to punish rebellious and hardhearted sinners. They even say that if God did those things as a form of punishment, why didn't people change? But God himself says that even after he punishes most people they still rise early and corrupt their doings (Zep. 3:7). God does not always punish us to force us to change, but the primary purpose of punishment is to reward wrongdoings with pain, setbacks, loss, and sometimes even death, and we know that if God punishes a person with death, they have no chance at changing. The wages and reward for sinning is death (Rom. 6:23 and Rom. 1:18 – 32; 2 Thess. 2:10 – 15; 8:13 – 14; 1 Kings 13:11 – 24; 1 Cor. 11:23 – 30; Ezek. 7:13; 18:4; 33:11, 19 – 20; Deut. 30:19 – 20; Job 20:11; 24:19; 36:5 – 13; Ps. 1:5 – 6; Prov. 19:5, 9; 21:16; 27:20; 30:15, 16; Isa. 5:14; 13:9; Josh. 7:1 – 13; 1 Chron. 10:13 – 14; Rev. 2:23; Matt. 18:11 – 14; Lam. 3:31 – 33; 1 Tim. 2:4; 2 Pet. 3:9; Luke 13:1 – 5).

Some people do search for God wholeheartedly, just as when Isaiah told God that he would seek the Lord early. And God says, "I love people who love me, and they who seek me shall find me, when they seek me with their whole heart" (Prov. 8:17; Isa. 26:9; 55:6). God is near people who repent, are humble, and who have a heart and spirit of love, awareness, and fear towards the Lord (Ps. 34:18).

Therefore, the Lord says, "Behold, I even I, will utterly forget you and forsake you, and the city that I gave you and your fathers, and will cast you out of my sight" (Jer. 7:15; 23:39; 2 Kings 17:18, 20, 23). Yet instead of repenting and living a sanctified and holy life, many people say, "O God, you have casted us off and broken us down. You have been displeased. Restore us again! You have made the earth terrible and shown your people hard times. Will the Lord cast us off forever, and no longer favor us? Have his promises failed? Has God forgotten to be gracious? Has he in his anger shut up his tender mercies" (Ps. 60:1 – 3; 77:7 – 9)? Some people would rather say this or assume or pretend that God is with them while they live in sin, instead of doing what God instructs so – called Christians to do. And that is, repent, seek Christ, and turn from their sinful ways, and God will heal the land (2 Chron. 7:14). But the leaders of the land judge for bribes, ministers teach for pay, prophets prophesize for money. Yet they lean on the Lord and say, "Is not the Lord among us? No harm can come upon us" (Mic. 3:11). But God says, "Be ye holy, for I am Holy" (1 Pet. 1:14 – 16; 1 Tim. 2:8).

No one can see God without holiness (Rev. 20:6; Heb. 12:14 – 15; Rom. 12:1 – 2; Eph. 5:5 – 10, 25 – 27; 2 Tim. 2:15).

God himself says that there are people who draw near to him with their mouth and honor him with their lips, but in their works and deeds they are far from him, and their fear towards him is taught to them according to the commandments of humans (Isa. 29:13; Mark 7:6 – 7; Col. 2:22; Eph. 4:14; 1 Cor. 2:9 – 16; Tit. 1:14; Jer. 12:2; Ezek. 33:31; Joh. 7:18).

Not everyone who mentions God's name shall be saved. God will say to them on judgment day, "Depart from me you worker of iniquity." But they who do the will of God shall be saved (Matt. 7:21 – 23; Mic. 3:11). The book of Malachi says, "You have wearied the Lord with your words. Yet you say, how have we wearied him? When you say everyone who does evil is good in the sight of the Lord, or where is the God of judgment" (Mal. 2:17). There are also people who do not believe in God, or who acknowledge that there is a God but believe that God is not Almighty and that he neglects us and has forsaken the earth, or that Christ's promise to return on judgment day will not happen (Ezek. 8:12; 9:9; Jer. 12:4; Isa. 40:27; Ps. 94:1 – 11). But God says that he is not slack in keeping his promise, and that it is not his will that anyone should perish, and that he is longsuffering towards us, and hopes that everyone repents and be saved. Furthermore, Christ's return shall come like a thief in the night, when you least expect it, and the earth shall be destroyed along with non – believers and people who believe but did not serve the Lord in holiness and sanctification (2 Pet. 3:3 – 4, 9 – 10). Until Christ returns, God says, "My eyes are on all their ways, they are not hidden from my face, nor is their iniquity hidden from my eyes. I will repay them double for their sins and iniquities, and for their abominations and idols" (Jer. 16:17 – 18; Ps. 21:7 – 15).

God does not need to see what sinners every day do if he chooses not to, because sinners own actions punish them, in addition to God and his angels punishing them, but the Bible tells us that God never withdraws his eyes from the righteous (Job 36:7 – 19; Ps. 125:4 – 5). If you do not inquire of God for healing but inquire of other gods, idols, and humans, it is not because God is not in the land, because he is everywhere, but maybe he is not with you because you are not with him (2 Kings 1:1 – 8.

Christ rebuked the cities where most of his mighty works had been done, because they did not repent (Matt. 11:20). But Nineveh did repent in Jonah's day, and the residents of that city shall help judge the world on judgment day, but a greater person than Jonah is here now, and this is Christ Jesus (Matt. 12:41).

When God gives peace, no one can make trouble, and when God hides his face no one can find him, whether it is against a nation or a single individual human (Job 34:29). Also, when God is with you, there is nothing anyone can do about it, but when God curses a person, they are cursed indeed, and nothing can be done about it until that person seek God's face with repentance, occasional fasting, and prayer (Matt. 17:14 – 21; Acts 19:14 – 18; James 5:16). We must be free indeed, not cursed indeed, and they who the Son set free are free indeed (Joh. 8:34 – 36; Rom. 6). For thus says the High and Lofty One, who inhabits eternity, whose name is Holy, "I dwell in the high and holy place with people who have a contrite, humble, poor, and broken spirit. To revive the spirit of the humble and the heart of the contrite ones. For I will not contend or be angry forever, or the souls which I created will fail." But because of sin God becomes angry and strikes people with affliction and adversity and hides his face in his anger. The church house is not the body of Christ, but the body of Christ are holy and sanc-tified human church members. Our bodies are temples of God for God the Holy Ghost to dwell in on earth, and when people defile their bodies and God's temples, God destroys those human bodies (Luke 17:20 – 21; 1 Cor. 6:9 – 20; and 1 Cor. 3:16 – 23; Eph. 2:19 – 22; Rom. 6:23; Heb. 3:4 – 19; 4:1; Rev. 21:22 – 27).

And when we defile the church house of God, the Lord often turns his face away from that church house (Ezek. 7:22). But God sees everything and will heal us from our sin, sick-ness, affliction, and adversity (2 Sam. 12:7 – 14; Job 31; Jer. 16:17). Christ forgave and healed a paralytic, and the Bible says that the power of God was present to heal (Luke 5:17). Peace, peace to them who are far off and to them who are near, says the Lord. But the wicked is like the troubled sea. There is no peace, says my God, for them who do wickedness (Isa. 57:15 – 21).

The Bible tells us that God departed from Sampson when he chose to sleep with a heathen woman who cut his hair and robbed him of his physical strength (Judg. 16:19 – 31). The book of Psalms also tells us of how God withdraws from his anointed people sometimes, due to sin (Ps .89:38 – 52). God never totally or utterly forsakes us (Neh. 9:31; Ps. 119:8). Christ is merciful and will never leave nor forsake, and the Lord is your helper, do not fear humans (Deut. 4:31). Be strong and of good courage, fear not, nor be afraid of people, for the Lord your God goes with you, and he will not fail you nor forsake you, and God will even fight for you against your enemies, to save you (Deut. 20:4; 31:6). God says, "I will bring the blind by the way that they knew not. I will lead them in paths that they have not known. I will make darkness light before them, and crooked things straight, and not forsake them. They will be turned back and ashamed who trust in idols and who say to idols, you are our gods" (Isa. 42:16 – 17). Spiritually speaking, God asks regarding non – believers, hypocrites, weak, wretched, and so – called Christians, "Who is spiritually blind and spiritually death but my servants and my messengers" (Isa. 6:8 – 13; 29:9 – 14; 42:18 – 20; 1 Cor .2:11 – 16; 2 Cor. 4:3 – 4; Joh. 9:39 – 41; Matt. 13:10 – 17).

If you return to God, he will return to you, no matter what sins you have committed (Matt. 12:31). For your Maker is your husband, the Lord of hosts is his name, and your Redeemer the Holy One of ancient Israel. The God of the whole earth is his name. For the Lord has called you as a woman forsaken and grieved in spirit, and as a young wife who has been refused by her husband. God says, "For a small moment I have forsaken you, but with great mercies I will gather you. In a little wrath I hid my face from you for a moment, but with everlasting kindness I will have mercy on you, says the Lord your Redeemer" (Isa. 54:4 – 10). Christ will not leave us as orphans, but he sends the Holy Ghost to help and comfort us (Joh. 14:15 – 27; 15:26 – 27; 16:7 – 16; Acts 9:31; Ps. 94:19; 2 Thess. 2:16 – 17; 2 Pet. 2; Jude 1).

The only people who receive the gift of the Holy Ghost dwelling inside of them are people who obey God (Acts 5:32; Luke 11:13; Joh. 14:13 – 18, 26 – 27 and Joh. 1:1, 14; Col. 3:16; 1 Joh. 2:5, 7, 14).

God the Holy Ghost will not dwell in unclean human bodies, but the devil with many of his demons will be more than happy to dwell inside of sinful people (Matt. 12:43 – 45; 2 Pet. 2:19). And the devil can dwell in your presence outside of your body too if you allow it (Luke 4:1 – 13; Ps. 109:6; Rev. 12:9 – 12; Job 1; 2:1 – 7; Zech. 3:1 – 3).

The Holy Ghost can be upon you without being in you, but it is best to be filled with the Holy Ghost and not simply have it dwell with you outside of your body (Luke 2:25 – 26). The Spirit of God came upon David when he was anointed, but David was not filled with the Holy Ghost because the Holy Ghost had not been given to anyone yet before Christ was born, died, rose from the dead, and went back to heaven (1 Sam. 16:13 – 14; Joh. 7:39; 14:16–26; 15:26–27; 16:7–16; Acts 9:31; Ps. 94:19; 2 Thess. 2:16–17).

Ezekiel was moved by the Spirit of God to go minister and to warn people, and he went in bitterness, but he said that the hand of God was strong upon him (Ezek. 3:14). Angels also dwell with us but not inside of us and will sometimes leave us according to the will of God, and due to sin (Ps. 34:4 – 15; Act 12:10 – 11). The Spirit of God leaves us from time to time for various reasons according to the will of God, whether you have sinned or not. And the Spirit of God often leaves us to test us (Luke 4:1 – 13; 2 Kings 20:1 – 7; 2 Chron. 32:22 – 31). So, it is best to have the Holy Ghost dwelling and living inside of you and not just dwelling with you outside of your body. The Bible says that the world cannot receive the Spirit of truth, because people of the world do not know Christ, but sanctified and holy Christians do know him, and he dwells with them and in them (Joh. 14:17). We must be born again of the water and of the Spirit (Joh. 3:1 – 7; Acts 2:36 – 39; 8:14 – 17; 10:47 – 48; 19:2 – 5). And they who worship God must do so in spirit and in truth (Joh. 4:23 – 24; Zech. 8:1 – 8). When the Holy Ghost dwells inside us, it comforts us and strengthens us (Luke 4:1 – 13; Joh. 14:16 – 26; 15:26 – 27; 16:7 – 16; Acts 9:31; 2 Pet. 2; Jude 1).

The Holy Ghost also speaks through us when we may not know what to say while teaching and preaching, and while being persecuted for righteousness' sake, and while speaking before earthly authorities (Jer. 20:7 – 12; Matt. 5:10; 10:16 – 20; 1 Pet. 3:14; Isa. 58:1 – 2).

God loves sinners too, but willful sin separates people from God, just as a married couple may still love each other, but problems in the marriage may cause them to separate. God says that he is married to the backslider (Jer. 3:6 – 15, 22; Hos. 1:2; 14:4 – 6; Rom. 1:18 – 32; 2 Thess. 2:10 – 15). Therefore, God could spiritually divorce rebellious sinners, but sinning against him can certainly cause him to separate from rebellious and hardhearted sinners (Isa. 50:1). The Bible says, "Indeed, people who are far from you shall perish. You have destroyed people who desert you for harlotry. But it is good for me to draw near to God, that I may declare all his works" (Ps. 73:23 – 28).

The Bible also says, "How great is your goodness that you have laid up for people who fear you and trust in you. You shall hide them in a secret place of your presence from the plots of humans and from the strife of tongues. Blessed be the Lord, for he has shown me his marvelous kindness. For I have said in my haste that I am cut off from your presence, but you heard my CRYING. Love the Lord all you saints, for the Lord preserves the faithful. Be of good courage, and he shall strengthen your heart, all you who hope in the Lord" (Ps. 31:19 – 24).

Let your conduct be without covetousness, be content with such things as you have. For Christ says, "I will never leave you nor forsake you, so you will be able to boldly say, 'The Lord is my helper, and I will not fear what humans shall do to me'" (Heb. 13:5 – 6).

Mankind disappoints God often to the point that it is like God having high expectations for us in a dream, but he wakes up to be displeased with what he sees. God despises no one without cause (Ps. 73:20; Job 36:5). However, God is so happy to help and heal us that it is like him waking up from sleeping and being very pleased (Jer. 31:25 – 26). Regardless of anything, when it seems like God is not with us, he does not slumber nor sleep while we suffer, but he is always in control, and the Lord is our keeper (Ps. 121).

God says, "O, that they had such a heart in them that they would fear me and always keep all my commandments, that it might be well with them and with their children for-ever" (Deut. 5:29). When we humble ourselves, God takes away much, if not all, his wrath that he had against us (2 Chron. 12:12). This pertains to entire cities and nations too. But some people continue to work against God and think that they pros-pered according to their anti – God practices more than they did while serving the Lord, but God says that he will watch over them for evil and not for good, and he will see whose word stands, his or theirs. The answer is that God will watch over them and punish them with adversity (Jer. 44:15 – 29). Speak-ing of God watching over people, two people in the Bible were about to part, and they prayed that God watch over them both until they met again (Gen. 31:44 – 49).

Hezekiah prayed to the Lord and wept bitterly after he learned that God would cut off his life, but God heard his prayer and added fifteen more years to his life and defended the city as well (Isa. 38:1 – 6). Because although God judges his people, he also has compassion on them when he sees that their strength is gone (Deut. 32:36; Isa. 40:27 – 31). But sin causes even the most courageous, strongest, and fastest person to fail and fall (Am. 2:10 – 16).

Do not think that it is a strange or uncommon thing to be tempted by sin, or that the blood of Christ has given you a pass to sin, because Christ was tempted just as we are tempted, but he did not sin. Therefore, we must go boldly before the throne of grace, so that we may obtain mercy and find grace to help in our time of need, and God will make a way for us to escape temptations (1 Cor. 10:13; Heb. 4:14 – 16; 1 Thess. 3:3 – 4; Luke 4:1 – 13; Eph. 3:20 – 21).

Cast all of your cares upon the Lord, because he cares for you, and again, know that you are not the only one going through adversity or affliction, but remember that the devil roams the earth seeking whom he may devour, because he is angry about going to hell forever (1 Pet. 5:8; Rev. 12:7 – 17; Job 1; 2:1 – 10; 3:16 – 22; 13:15 – 16; 42:11).

People do not have God when they make excuses about sinning and refuse to seek the Lord for strength to not sin (2 Joh. 8 – 11). Righteous Christians and holy and sanctified Christians suffer like Christ, but not like a sinner nor a criminal, and although sinners go to hell, and the dead in Christ shall rise first on judgment day, judgment starts at the church house and with Christians (1 Pet. 4:12 – 19). Do the things that you have seen in Christ, the prophets of the Old Testament, and in the Apostle Paul, and the Lord will be with you (Phil. 4:9). The grace of our Lord Jesus Christ be with your spirit (Gal. 6:18). The grace of the Lord Jesus Christ, and the love of God, and the communion of the Holy Ghost, be with you all. Amen (Rev. 22:21; 2 Cor. 13:14). To holy and sanctified people and people who desire to be holy and sanctified, Christ says, "I will be with you always, even until the end of the world. Amen" (Matt. 28:20).

Enoch walked with God (Gen. 5:24).
Noah walked walked God (Gen. 6:9).
God is with you in all that (Gen. 21:22).
Will send his angel with you (Gen. 24:40).
I will be with you, and I will bless you and your seed (Gen. 26:3).
Not fear, for I am with you (Gen. 26:24).
If God will be with me (Gen. 28:20).
The God of my father has been with me (Gen. 31:5).
The Lord was with Joseph (Gen. 39:2).
The Lord was with him and made all that he did to prosper (Gen. 39:3).
The Lord was with Joseph (Gen. 39:21).
The Lord was with him (Gen. 39:23).
I die, but God will be with you (Gen. 48:21).
Certainly I will be with you (Exod. 3:12).
The Lord is with us, do not fear (Num. 14:9).

Lord will not be with you (Num. 14:43).

Lord his God is with him (Num. 23:21).

Forty years the Lord has been with you. You lacked nothing (Deut. 2:7).

Lord your God is with you (Deut. 20:1).

God goes with you, to fight (Deut. 20:4).

God goes with you and will not fail you nor forsake you (Deut. 31:6 – 8).

There is no strange god with God Almighty (Deut. 32:12).

There is no god with me (Deut. 32:39).

As I was with Moses, so will I be with you (Josh. 1:5).

God is with you wherever go (Josh. 1:9).

Lord was with Joshua and his fame grew throughout the nation (Josh. 6:27).

Neither will I be with you anymore (Josh. 7:12).

The Lord will be with me .(Josh. 14:12).

The Lord was with them (Judg. 1:22).

Lord was with the judge and delivered them out of the hands of their enemies (Judg. 2:18).

The Lord is with you (Judg. 6:12).

If the Lord be with us, why then has all this befallen us (Judg. 6:13)?

Surely I will be with you (Judg. 6:16).

The Lord was with him (1 Sam. 3:11 – 19).

God is with you (1 Sam. 10:7).

I will not return with you because you have rejected the Word of the Lord (1 Sam. 15:26).

The Lord is with him (1 Sam. 16:18).

Lord was with him (1 Sam. 18:12, 14).

Lord was with David (1 Sam. 18:28).

For the Lord is with you (2 Sam. 7:3).

God will be with you (2 Sam. 14:17).

I will be with you (1 Kings 11:38).

They that be with us are more than that be with them (2 Kings 6:16 – 18).

The Lord was with him (2 Kings 18:4 – 7).

God's hand might be with me and keep me from evil (1 Chron. 4:9 – 10).

The Lord was with him (1 Chron. 9:20).

Lord of hosts was with (1 Chron. 11:9).

The Lord be with you (1 Chron. 22:11).

Is not the Lord your God with you (1 Chron. 22:18)?

God, will be with you (1 Chron. 28:20).

With us for our captain (2 Chron. 13:12).

Lord was with him (2 Chron. 15:9).

With you in judgment (2 Chron. 19:6).

Lord shall be with the good (2 Chron. 19:11).

Lord will be with you (2 Chron. 20:14 – 17).

More with us than with him (2 Chron. 32:7).

With him is an arm of flesh (2 Chron. 32:8).

With us is the Lord God (2 Chron. 32:8).

Meddling with God who is (2 Chron. 35:21).

God who is with me (2 Chron. 35:21).

I will teach you by the hand of God. All that is with the Al-Mighty I will not conceal (Job 27:11).

When the Almighty was yet with me (Job 29:5).

He who is perfect in knowledge is with you (Job 36:4).

With kings are they on the throne (Job 36:7).

For thou are with me Lord (Ps. 23).

Dwell with God forever (Ps. 23).

Lord is with them who fear (Ps. 25:14).

His song shall be with me (Ps. 42:8).

Lord of host is with us (Ps. 46:7, 11).

I am continually with you (Ps. 73:23).

My mercy shall be with him ((Ps. 89:24).

I will be with him in trouble (Ps. 91:15).

They may dwell with me (Ps. 101:6).

They are ever with me (Ps. 119:98).

With him is plenteous (Ps. 130:7).

Awake, I am still with you (Ps. 139:18).

His heart is not with you (Prov. 23:7).

His reward is with him (Isa. 40:10).

Fear not, for I am with you (Isa. 41:10).
Waters, I will be with you (Isa. 43:2).
Fear not, for I am with you (Isa. 43:5).
Our transgressions are with us (Isa. 59:12).
With you to deliver you (Jer. 1:8).
I am with you to save you (Jer. 15:20).
With me as a mighty terrible (Jer. 20:11).
I am with you (Jer. 30:11).
I am with you to save you (Jer. 42:11).
For I am with you (Jer. 46:28).
With you I will destroy (Jer. 51:20).
Shall know that the Lord their God am with them (Ezek. 34:30).
Judah yet rules with God (Hos. 11:12).
God shall be with you (Am. 5:14 – 15).
Walk humbly with your God (Mic. 6:8).
We will go with you because we heard that God is with you (Zech. 8:23).
With him of life and peace (Mal. 2:5).
God with us (Matt. 1:23).
They who are not with me are against me (Matt. 12:30).
How long shall I be with (Matt. 17:17).
I am with you always, even until the end of the world (Matt. 28:20).
He might be with him (Mark 5:18).
How long will I be with (Mark 9:19).
Highly favored, the Lord is with you. Blessed are you among women (Luke 1:28).
Hand of the Lord was with (Luke 1:66).
You are they who have continued with me in my temptations (Luke 22:28, 40 – 44).
The Word was with God (Joh. 1:1).
He who sent me is with me (Joh. 8:29).
With him when he called (Joh. 12:17).
The light with you (Joh. 12:35).
Make our abode with him (Joh. 14:23).

Because I was with you (Joh. 16:4).
The Father is with me (Joh. 16:32).
Be with me where I am (Joh. 17:24).
Is accepted with him (Acts 10:35).
For God was with him (Acts 10:38).
Hand of the Lord was with (Acts 11:21).
Am with you, and no man (Acts 18:10).
Was with you in weakness (1 Cor. 2:3).
Therein abide with God (1 Cor. 7:24).
God who was with me (1 Cor. 15:10).
Be present with the Lord (2 Cor. 5:8).
Workers together with him (2 Cor. 6:1).
To die and live with you (2 Cor. 7:3).
Love and peace shall be with (2 Cor. 13:11).
With me in the gospel (Phil. 4:3).
God of peace shall be with you (Phil. 4:9).
Yet am I with you in the spirit (Col. 2:5)
Be dead with Christ from the rudiments of the world (Col. 2:20).
If you are risen with Christ, seek those things that are above (Col. 3:1).
Your life is hid with Christ (Col. 3:3).
Appear with him in glory (Col. 3:4).
Will God bring with him (1 Thess. 4:14).
Together with them in the clouds (1 Thess. 4:17).
Ever be with the Lord (1 Thess. 4:17).
Lord be with you all (2 Thess. 3:16).
If we be dead with him (2 Tim. 2:11).
We shall also live with him (2 Tim. 2:11).
Shall also reign with him (2 Tim. 2:12).
With them who call on (2 Tim. 2:22).
Only Luke is with me (2 Tim. 4:11).
No man stood with me (2 Tim. 4:16).
Lord stood with me (2 Tim. 4:17).
Christ be with your spirit (2 Tim. 4:22).
Grace be with you (2 Tim. 4:22).

Have fellowship with us (1 Joh. 1:3).
Is with the Father, and with (1 Joh. 1:3).
With his Son Jesus Christ (1 Joh. 1:3).
Fellowship with him, and .(1 Joh. 1:6).
One with another, and (1 Joh. 1:7).
Walk with me in white (Rev. 3:4).
Sup with him, and he with (Rev. 3:20).
One hour with the beast (Rev. 17:12).
They who are with him are called (Rev. 17:14).
Tabernacle of God is with (Rev. 21:3).
He will dwell with them (Rev. 21:3).
My reward is with me (Rev. 22:12).
Christ be with you all (Rev. 22:21).

WORRYING

To torment oneself with or to complain about cares or anxiety, or to suffer from disturbing thoughts (Heb. 2:15; 1 Joh. 4:18). God does not want us living in fear, bondage, or torment. Worrying can cause you to lose your appetite, among other things, while asking God to answer your prayers (Ps. 102:1 – 4). Worrying can also cause loss of sleep and insomnia, but God says that he gives sweet sleep (Ps. 127:2 and Ps. 4). It is understandable to have anxiety sometimes when faced with pressure or things that can be detrimental to you or yours. Christ himself had a moment of anxiety before he was arrested by Roman soldiers to be falsely tried, crucified, and executed (Luke 22:39 – 46). Christ was in deep sorrow and distress, even extreme sorrow, unto death, but he concluded that God's will be done, and not his own will (Matt. 26:36 – 39). In normal or even mildly extreme situations, Christ says why worry, because worrying cannot add to your physical stature or bank account, or anything that is in need, and when you face times when even the little things are out of your control, why worry about the bigger problems (Luke 12:25 – 26; Matt. 6:19 – 34). The Bible also tells us to have a humble heart, to watch what your eyes desire, and to not get involved with things over your head, or too deep and profound for you (Ps. 131:1). Let God deal with that, because the Bible says that the Spirit of God within us searches the deep things of God (1 Cor. 2:4, 9 – 10, 13 – 16; Ps. 92:5; 1 Chron. 28:9).

Worrying can also cause depression, so it is important to encourage people who are suffering with anxiety and worrying (Prov. 12:25). We often must be still and let God, be still and let go, be still and see the salvation of the Lord (Exod. 14:13; 2 Chron. 32:7 – 8). God says be still and know that he is God (Ps. 46:10 – 11). The Bible tells us to humble ourselves under the mighty hands of God so that he can lift you up and settle you in due time, and cast all your cares upon the Lord, because he cares for you (1 Pet. 5:6 – 11). The Bible says, "Rejoice in the Lord always. Again, I say, rejoice! Have anxiety for nothing, but pray about everything, and express thanksgivings to God. Let your requests be made known to God, and the peace of God that surpasses all understanding, will guard your heart and minds through Christ Jesus" (Phil. 4:4 – 7).

In terms of worrying about the coming of the Lord, Christ says that the prophecies in the following scriptures must be fulfilled first about the antichrist, hypocrisy, persecution, death, destruction, false prophets, and false ministers, but let not your heart be troubled, neither be afraid (Matt. 24:3 44; Joh. 14:1, 27; 2 Thess. 2:1 – 12).

It is impossible for the world to deceive God's sanctified Christians (Matt. 24:24; Rev. 12:9; 20:3, 8, 10). When Christ was born, Herold, a heathen king was greatly troubled, along with all of Jerusalem (Matt. 2:1 – 4). And he tried to kill the baby Jesus Christ to prevent Christ's ministry by killing all the first – born males in the land with hopes of also killing Christ, but obviously his attempts failed to prevent Christ from being born (Matt. 2:13 – 16; Rev. 12:1 – 8). Christ's second coming will not be prevented either, and sinners should be worried about his return, or about them dying in sin before Christ comes the next and final time, because we will rise from the grave the same way that we died, either holy, righteous, un-righteous, or filthy (Rev. 22:10 – 13; Acts 24:15; 1 Pet. 3:18; Dan. 12:1 – 3).

In terms of self – afflicted sin and living on earth, God asks, "Why are you crying about your affliction? I have done these things to you because of your many sins, and because your sins have increased" (Jer. 30:15). God does have great con-cern for his sin sick people, and he expresses his care and concern by having mercy on them (Jer. 31:20). But if their own self – inflicted anxiety, worrying, adversity, and affliction does not cause them to repent, God turns them over to a reprobate mind because they refused the joy, peace, and prosperity of the Lord. God tells us to not envy people who have temporary peace and troublesome prosperity that comes from the world (Jer. 12:1 – 3; Mal. 3:13 – 18; Deut. 23:5 – 6; Ps. 73:1 – 12; Prov. 23:17).

The joy of the Lord is your peace and strength, and you do not need to worry about it ever causing you trouble or backlash (Ps. 4:7; Neh. 8:10; James 1:15 – 18; Joh. 14:27). But some people become so accustomed to pain, suffering, adversity, affliction, and setbacks that they no longer seek the Lord for help (Rom. 1:18 – 32; 2 Thess. 2:10 –15; 2 Thess. 2:9 – 12; Isa. 66:4; Ezek. 21:23 – 24; 1 King 22:23; Tit. 1:16; 2 Tim. 3:1 – 8; Ps. 81:10 – 16).

BONUS READINGS

Coronavirus (COVID-19)

Baptism

Confessing with Your Mouth, Believing in Your Heart, and Calling on the Name of the Lord

CORONAVIRUS (COVID-19)

In March of 2020, there was a global outbreak of Coronavirus (also called COVID-19). It may have happened because many people, including some Christians accepted; embraced; and supported homosexuality, abortions, and late-term abortions. We do know that those abominations, murders, and evil, wicked sins were legalized on a global scale; and only a few years later, there was a global outbreak of Coronavirus, which was something the world had never seen or heard of before, just as global and worldwide acceptance of anti-God practices were legalized globally like never before.

We do know that God promises to not allow disease, affliction, and adversity in our lands when we obey his Word; and that if we do not obey his Word, God says he allows prolonged disease and sickness in the land and even new diseases and illnesses that are not written in the Bible (Exod. 15:26; Deut. 7:12–15; 28:58–61; Rev. 2:18–29; Rom. 5:9; Jer. 30:12–15; Ps. 38; 107:17).

Most pandemics and natural disasters are a result of God being displeased with our sinful actions. Many people live by laws and practices that they made or supported; and that results in pain, natural disasters, bad weather, sorrow, sickness, disease, death, and destruction (2 Kings 17:19; Ps. 28:4–5).

Most people did not acquire the Coronavirus. God is too gracious and merciful to allow that to happen. But he does have a way of getting everyone's attention, instilling fear in everyone, and causing almost everyone to pray unto him, but some people are too hard-hearted to pray. God punishes people harder who do not take heed to his rebuke and warnings and who do not choose the fear of the Lord (Prov. 1:28–30). The Lord will take sickness out of the land when people turn again to him, confess his name in righteousness, pray, repent and turn away from their rebellion (Exod. 23:25; Deut. 7:15; 28; 29:2–6; 2 Chron. 7:14; Matt. 13:14–15; Luke 19:37–42; Isa. 6:8–10; Lev. 20:6–27; Jer. 4:22).

We should not be surprised when we see and hear of new diseases, destruction, and death because the Bible says that in these last days, dangerous and perilous times will continue to happen due to sin, hypocrisy, blasphemy, and rebellion and that our generation will experience more tribulation and trouble than the world has ever known or will ever hear of again. Because most people do not accept the love of the truth of God's Word (Matt. 24:21; Mark 13:19; Dan. 12:1; 2 Thess. 2; 1 Tim. 4:1–3; Mic. 5:2, 4, 15).

The last days for most of us are the days before we die because most people will not live to see the last day of the earth's existence (2 Tim. 3:1–7; 1 John 2:18). But God allows most of us to die sooner or later because most of us must die to get to heaven unless we are alive on the last day of the earth's existence. Saved people who are alive on the last day of the earth's existence will be instantly transformed into angels without ever dying (1 Thess. 4:13–18; 1 John 2:18).

Not everyone who died from COVID-19 is going to hell and not everyone who died from COVID-19 was an enemy of God. But people who support worldly anti-God laws, practices, and policies are enemies of God (James 4:4; John 1:10–12; 15:18–19; 1 John 2:15–17; 3:13; Phil. 3:16–21).

If anyone thinks that COVID-19 had nothing to do with mankind legalizing homosexual marriages and abortions, including late-term abortions, then do they think that God will never punish the world for that level of rebellion, blasphemy, and hypocrisy? God says, "Shall I not visit the earth for these sins?" (Prov. 19:23; Jer. 5:9, 29; 14:10). Sin separates us from our God (Isa. 1:15; 59:1–2; 64:4–8; Ps. 107:17–22; Mal. 2:2).

Some humans try to void God's Word, and that causes God to have a controversy with the inhabitants of the land and causes humans to not be able to go to work so God can work (Ps. 119:126; Job 37:7; Hos. 4:1–2). And if COVID-19 is not one of God's ways of punishing the world for embracing abortions and homosexuality, that only means that harder times are coming because God shall act regarding abortions and homosexuality. And Christ says that the tribulations, troubles, and diseases that we suffer are only the beginning of sorrows (Matt. 24:3–8). Some of those sorrows have come to past already during times like World War I and World War II, but the Bible says that times will be harder and harder, and that trouble in our generations are only the beginning of sorrows (Matt. 24:3–8). God's Word will never return to him void. God eventually does exactly what he says he will do, whether he promises to send blessings or death and destruction (Isa. 14:24; 46:9–10; 55:10–11; Jer. 23:20; Ezek. 5:13; 6:9–10; 12:21–28; 22:14; 24:13–14; Dan. 9:12–14; Matt. 24:32–44; 2 Pet. 3:6–14; 2 Kings10:10).

Several scientists in April 2020 said that COVID-19 was not man-made, but that it did probably originate in China. Most people know that China was and maybe still is an extremely anti-Christ nation. Therefore, God may have used COVID-19 to punish them although some people believe that China created the virus to decrease their extremely large human population. Hopefully, it was not made by humans on purpose with evil intentions, but if it was made by humans, the Bible says that God made everything, even wicked people, for the day of evil (Prov. 16:2–7; Isa. 45:5–7; Lam. 3:37–40). In other words, God sometimes uses evil inventions to punish people because the inventions are accessible to him, even if he did not create them himself. Those same scriptures also say that people who invent wicked things shall not go unpunished, and by the fear of the Lord, people depart from evil and that when a person's ways and works please the Lord, God makes even their enemies to be at peace with them (Prov.16:2–7).

The government of New York boldly embraced almost every anti-God law and practice that mankind created, and that is one reason they suffered so much. Louisiana also had a high number of COVID-19 cases, and they suffer a lot in Louisiana from hurricanes, floods, and other forms of adversity because Louisiana is basically the modern-day magic, sorcery, voodoo, and witchcraft capital of the United States. Mardi Gras crowds are believed to be the reason that COVID-19 cases were so high in Louisiana, but Mardi Gras itself is anti-Christian. Mardi Gras originated with pagan and heathen ties and is a time when people make one last effort to indulge in eating, drinking, and sinning before the celebration of the life, crucifixion, death, and resurrection of our Lord and Savior Jesus Christ. Mardi Gras ends on Fat Tuesday, and people have historically repented for their sins the following day on Ash Wednesday, which is the first day of Lent and the beginning of the preparation for Holy Week, Passion Week, Passover week, resurrection week, and Resurrection Day, erroneously called Easter by most people.

The harder people speak and stand against God, the harder his punishment is toward those people (Ps. 90:11; Jude 1:14–25). Therefore, it is no coincidence that American and European nations suffered the most from COVID-19. It is one thing to be a non-Christian, but it is a lot worse to be a hypocrite Christian. At least non-Christians in their nations do not pretend to be Christians, and God says that many so-called Christians are worse than people who do not claim to be Christians (Jer. 2:32–33; 5:28–31; 2 Chron. 33:9; Matt. 5:19; 23:15; 2 Kings 21:10–12; Lam. 4:6; Ezek. 16:47–48; 1 Tim. 5:8; 1 Cor. 5:1).

God says that he will heal the land if people who are called by his name shall pray, repent, and turn from their wicked ways (2 Chron. 7:13 – 14; Isa. 6:8–10; Ezek. 33:31; Matt. 13:14–15; Luke 19:37–42; Deut. 29:2–6). Killing unborn babies and supporting that practice is evil and wicked.

Remember, just as our leaders can cause great peace and

prosperity in the land, our leaders can also cause God's wrath to strike the land. Just as was the case when the land suffered a great famine during the days of King David. David prayed to God, and God told David that the famine was punishment for the sins of King Saul, who was David's predecessor (2 Sam. 21:1). And it is highly likely that COVID-19 happened because of the wicked abortion and homosexual laws that President Barack Obama and other world leaders legalized.

Noteworthy, after the Lord finally ended the global pandemic, worldwide inflation struck the earth to the point that most people said it sometimes felt and looked like a recession. This happened because many people did not repent and turn to the Lord during the pandemic, even though God spared their life.

BAPTISM

FAILING TO BE BAPTIZED PROPERLY COULD BRING DAMNATION TO YOUR SOUL

Baptism is to wash away sins by being immersed in water, signifying the death, burial, and resurrection of Christ (Rom. 6:1–5; Col. 2:12; 2 Tim. 2:11).

To bury your sins in water while you rise out of the water to newness of life, becoming a born-again Christian, a new creature, and new creation (John 3:3–7; Rom. 8:5–14; 2 Cor. 5:17; 1 Pet. 1:23).

The Bible says that soap and water cannot wash away our sins (Jer. 2:22; Matt. 23:27–28). But the Spirit of Christ, the blood of Christ, and water together washes away our sins, and the Bible says that these three agree as one (1 John 5:6–8). We must also allow Christ to give us the Spirit of the Holy Ghost, also called the Holy Spirit. Because Christ says we must be born again of the water and of the Spirit, or we cannot go to heaven (Acts 2:36–39; 8:14–17; 10:42–48; 19:1–6; John 3:3–7; Mark 16:16; Rev. 21:8, 27; 22:14 – 15).

REPENTANCE

We should repent while being baptized. We get baptized to try to go to heaven, not only for healing, earthly possessions, or problem-solving. These things will be added at some point in your sanctified life, and they are sometimes added immediately after baptism (Matt. 6:31–34). When we truly repent, we repent unto life (Acts 11:18). Because godly sorrow causes repentance unto salvation, but worldly sorrow causes death (2 Cor. 7:9–10; Ps. 38:15–18; 85:8; Ezek. 18:21–22).

Therefore, true repentance gives us life everlasting in heaven (Gal. 6:7–8; Matt. 19:29; Luke 14:26–27; 18:29–30; Deut. 33:9).

Jesus preached repentance while he was on Earth and after he went back to heaven when he revealed himself to John. He says that he gave certain people time to repent, but they did not repent and that they will be punished with great tribulation and death unless they repent (Rev. 2:19–23).

WHY ARE THERE SO MANY DIFFERENT FORMS OF BAPTISMS?

Baptism in water has become a very controversial subject, but it should not be, because God is not the author of confusion (1 Cor. 14:33; Heb. 6:1–6). There is one Lord, one faith, one baptism (Eph. 4:4–6). So, why do Christians have so many ways of baptizing? All methods of baptism do not mean the same, because the Bible says that there is only one baptism (Eph. 4:4–6). Some people baptize in the name of the Lord Jesus Christ, some people sprinkle water, some people pour water, some people baptize in the name of the Father, and of the Son, and of the Holy Ghost, and some people say we do not need to be baptized at all to be saved. We should speak the same thing, have the same mind, and the same judgment, without division (1 Cor. 1:10).

There is only one interpretation of God's Word. Two people cannot have two different interpretations of the Word of God (2 Pet. 1:20; 1 Cor. 14:36). You are either right or wrong, because the Word of God is of no private interpretation, and it is not revealed to only one person (2 Pet. 1:20; 1 Cor. 14:36).

Considering that there is only one baptism, then sprinkling (aspersion), and pouring (affusion), it is not right, because it is not enough water to cover the whole body. Thus, all sins are not washed away, and you may not be filled with the Holy Spirit. The Spirit, water, and blood agree as one (1 John 5:6–8). Also, sprinkling and pouring is not in the Bible.

WHY DO SOME PEOPLE SAY THAT WE ARE NOT REQUIRED TO BE BAPTIZED?

A preacher once said, and many inaccurate preachers since that time have said, that we do not need to be baptized in water at all because the Bible according to him says we are baptized in the blood of Jesus and not in water. But as stated before, the Bible says the blood and water agree as one (1 John 5:6–8). Heb. 10:22 says, "Let us draw near God with a pure heart in full assurance of faith…and having our bodies washed with pure water." And yes, the Bible says that we are washed by the blood of Jesus Christ, but the Bible also says that we are washed by water and that the Spirit, water, and blood agree as one (1 John 5:6–8; Rev. 1:5; 7:14).

John the Baptist baptized a multitude of people including Jesus, and Peter and the apostles baptized three thousand people in one day during the first ever baptism after the resurrection of Christ (Matt. 3; Acts 2:36–47). John the Baptist refused to baptize Jesus because he felt that he was not worthy to baptize Jesus, but Jesus told John the Baptist that he must baptize him to fulfill all righteousness (Matt. 3). Therefore, to be baptized in water is right, and it is ordained by God. If being immersed in water is not important, why was John the Baptist baptizing people in the Jordan River (Matt. 3:1–6)? If sprinkling and pouring is right, why did John go to the town of Aenon to baptize people? The Bible says that John baptized people in the town of Aenon because there was plenty of water there (John 3:23). Why did Philip baptize the eunuch in water (Acts 8:38)? Notice the preacher got in the water with the person who was being baptized (Acts 8:38). The preacher did not send someone else into the water to do the baptizing for him while he prayed from outside of the water, like some preachers do nowadays. Why did Jesus himself get fully immersed in water (Mark 1:9–10)? Are we not all supposed to do everything like Jesus did? Some people nowadays say that baptizing in water puts too much emphasis on ceremonial means. But Jesus says that if you do not believe and get baptized as he and the apostles did, you shall be damned (Mark 16:16; Acts 2:38; 8:14–17; 10:47–48; 19:2–5; John 3:3–7; Rev. 21:8, 27; 22:14–15).

Most preachers who do not believe in baptism have large churches and do not want to take the time to baptize all their people. If getting wet is a problem for the minister, he can wear a waterproof suit. Why didn't the apostles baptize by sprinkling and pouring but instead baptized everyone by getting in the water with them, and fully immersing the new believer in water and raising them back up out of the water (Acts 2:38; 8:14–17; 10:47–48; 19:2–5)?

A LIST OF THE MANY THINGS THAT WERE DONE IN THE NAME OF THE LORD

Colossians 3:17 commands us to do all things in the name of Jesus, whether it is in word or deed. We preach in Christ's name (Luke 24:47; Acts 9:27–29). We speak in the name of the Lord (James 5:10). We preach in the name of the Lord (Jer. 26:11, 16). We teach in Christ's name (Acts 4:16–20). And the apostles were forbidden and nearly killed for teaching in Christ's name (Acts 4:28, 33). We command in Christ's name (2 Thess. 3:6). We cast out devils, do miracles, and give to others in Christ's name (Mark 9:38–41; Acts 16:16–18; Heb. 6:10).

The devil is subjected unto us through Christ's name (Luke 10:17). We receive children in Christ's name (Mark 9:37). We ask the Father for things in Christ's name (John 16:23–24). We ask God for healing in Christ's name (Acts 3:1–6, 12, 16). We give thanks in Christ's name (Eph. 5:20). We anoint and pray for the sick in Christ's name (James 5:13–15). Our help is in the name of the Lord (Ps. 124:8). We even suffer for the sake of righteousness in the name of Christ (Acts 5:38–42). We are washed, sanctified, and justified in the name of Jesus, but by the Spirit of God. It is that same one Spirit but a new name (1 Cor. 6:9–11).

We are supposed to celebrate Christmas in Christ's name,

but the love of the world and the love of money have caused many Christians to not say Merry Christmas during the entire Christmas season, but they instead say Happy Holidays and Seasons Greetings. Instead of saying, "It was the night before Christmas," they say, "It was the night before gifting." And instead of saying, "The twelve days of Christmas," they instead say, "The twelve days of gifting." Instead of continuing to say Christmas break, the world is now saying winter break. Therefore, we should be happy to be baptized in Christ's name, and to not be baptized in Christ's name is to take his name out of the baptism too, just as Christ's name has been taken out of the Christmas season by many people (John 3:3–7; Acts 2:38–39; 8:14–17; 10:47–48; 19:2–5; Rom. 8:5–14).

We lift our hands in Christ's name (Ps. 63:4). All means all (Col. 3:17). The Holy Ghost comes in the name of Jesus (John 14:25, 26). Saved people rise in the resurrection by the name of Jesus (2 Cor. 4:14; 1 Cor. 15:25, 28). Elijah built an altar in the name of the Lord when he put the prophets of Baal to shame (1 Kings 18:26–32; 19:15–18; Rom. 11:1–5).   Peter said, "Get baptized every one of you in the name of Jesus Christ for forgiveness of sins" (emphasis added) (Acts 2:38).

Again, he said every one of you, not just the Apostolic Church, Baptist, Catholic, Church of Christ, Church of God in Christ, Pentecostal, Presbyterian, or anti-Christian groups; but every one of you must be baptized in the name of Jesus Christ (Acts 2:36–39; 8:14–17; 10:42–48; 19:1–6; John 3:3–7).

Even in the Old Testament, people did things in the name of the Lord, but not in the name of the Father, because Father is a title, not a name. They blessed in the name of the Lord (2 Sam. 6:18; Deut. 10:8; 1 Chron. 23:13; Num. 6:23–27). They ministered in the name of the Lord (Deut. 18:5, 7). They walked in the name of the Lord (Mic. 4:5; John 8:31–47). They rejoiced in the name of the Lord (Ps. 89:16). Zechariah and Haggai prophesied in the name of God (Ezra 5:1). The people set up their banners in the name of the Lord (Ps. 20:5). Just as some people do not baptize in the name of the Lord, they do not bless you in the name of the Lord either (Ps. 129:8). If you do not do all these things in the name of the Lord Jesus Christ, you have limited power (Acts 3:16). Moses was not allowed to go to the promised land because he did not speak to the rock in the name of the Lord (Exod. 17:7; Num. 20:7–13; 27:14; Deut. 6:16; Ps. 106:32–33). By not speaking to the rock in the name of the Lord, Moses did not believe God and did not sanctify God in the presence of the people (Num. 20:12). The same applies when people do not believe the one baptism. When you pray, you are not going to pray to the Son or Holy Ghost, because they are titles, not names. You are going to pray to the Father, which is a title also, but in Christ's name (John 16:23–24). We pray unto the Father in the name of Christ. We start our prayers by saying "Father God," and we end our prayers by saying, "In Christ's name. Amen." To not use the name Christ is having a form of godliness but denying the power thereof, and ever learning but never able to come to the power of the truth (2 Tim. 3:5).

MANY MINISTERS DO NOT BAPTIZE IN THE NAME OF THE FATHER, AND OF THE SON, AND OF THE HOLY SPIRIT

Speaking of what Jesus and the apostles did, Christ told them in Matt. 28:19 to baptize in the name of the Father, and of the Son, and of the Holy Ghost. Why didn't they do that? Were they disobedient? In Acts 2:38, when the original apostles did it for the first time after the resurrection, they did it in the name of Jesus Christ. As a matter of fact, no one in the Bible was ever baptized in the name of the Father and of the Son and of the Holy Ghost. Every time someone in the Bible was baptized after the resurrection of Christ, they were baptized in the name of Jesus (Acts 2:36–39; 8:14–17; 10:42–48; 19:1–6; John 3:3–7).

The Apostle Paul asked, "Is Christ divided? Was Paul crucified for you? Or were you baptized in the name of Paul?" (1 Cor. 1:13). No, they were all baptized in the name of Jesus (1 Cor. 1:13). Jesus baptized no one, but the apostles did the work for him, and they all baptized people in Christ's name (John

4:2). So why are most preachers nowadays not baptizing like the apostles did in the Bible (Acts 2:36–39; 8:14–17; 10:42–48; 19:1–6; John 3:3–7)?

John the Baptist preached the baptism of repentance for the remission of sins (Mark 1:4). In Acts 2:38, Peter preached a similar sermon when he said, "Repent, and be baptized every one of you in the name of Jesus Christ for the remission of sins, and you shall receive the precious gift of the Holy Spirit." God himself says that Jesus was sent for the remission of our sins and to teach us about salvation (Luke 1:76–78). Christ purchased us with his blood, so shouldn't we be baptized in his name? But some people deny Christ who purchased them, even in baptism (1 Cor. 3:9; 6:13–20; 7:21–24; Acts 20:28; 2 Pet. 2:1–2; Deut. 32:6).

THE "TRINITY" IS NOT IN THE BIBLE, SO WHERE DID IT COME FROM?

In AD 325, the Catholic Church held its first council of Nicaea. The Council was organized by Emperor Constantine and maybe the pope. At this council, bishops, priests, and certain pagan religious leaders came together to discuss their baptisms and the trinity, among other false doctrines. This controversy began in the second century. Before that time, the word trinity was not used because it is not in the Bible. Thus, it was never used among the original apostles and apostolic followers. It was introduced by theologians of the second century to try to explain the oneness of the Father, the Son, and the Holy Spirit. The answer is in Col. 2:8–9 when the scripture says, "Beware, lest anyone spoil you through philosophy and vain deceit, after the tradition of men... For in Jesus dwells all the fullness of the Godhead bodily" (emphasis added).

And in 1 John 5:7, the scripture says, "These three are one," meaning the Father, Son, and Holy Ghost are one. Christ says that whoever receives him also receives Father God Almighty (Matt. 10:40). Arius, a deacon of Alexandria, held that the Son was subordinate to the Father. The council ruled that the Father and the Son were equal and condemned Arius and the Arians. Later, at the Council of Constantinople in 381, 150

Catholic bishops determined that the Holy Ghost would be considered a Third Person of God. This is how mankind decided to start using the word trinity, a word that is not in the Bible.

No African nations were invited to the council where the manmade trinity was created. The baptism in the name of the Father, and of the Son, and of the Holy Ghost is a white peoples' baptism that was performed during slavery and that originated in the political institution of Christianity, 325 years after the resurrection. Compare that to only 50 days after the resurrection when the first baptism was performed by the black Hebrew apostles. Christianity is a white anti-Christ religion that supports slavery, oppression, sharecropping, ethnic cleansing, genocide, and Apartheid, and is opposite of the Christian Faith of Holiness and Sanctification (James 3:17 – 18; Isa. 61:1 – 3; Luke 4:16 - 21; James 1:26 – 27; 1 Tim. 1:8 – 10; Heb. 2:11; 12:14; Exod. 21:16; 23:9; Lev. 25:14, 17; Deut. 23:15 – 16; 24:7; 1 Peter 1:16).

THIS IS WHY PEOPLE LEARNED TO BAPTIZE IN THE NAME OF A MANMADE TRINITY

As with any Christian denomination, not all Catholics are bad and there are good and not so good people in every denomination. Romans changed the names of the days of the week and the names of the months of the year in honor of idol gods and goddesses. Before that, God himself named the months of the year. Roman Catholics changed the word Passover to the word Easter, which is in the King James Version of the Bible only one time and should not be. Roman Catholics apparently changed the baptism in one part of the Bible from being baptized in Christ's name to being baptized in the name of the Father, and of the Son, and of the Holy Spirit. The original apostles never baptized anyone that way, but everyone in the Bible was baptized in the name of Christ (Acts 2:36–39; 8:14–17; 10:42–48; 19:1–6; John 3:3–7).

Therefore, just as we call the first and second day of the week Sunday and Monday, for example, even though they are named for the so-called sun god and moon god, a lot of people get baptized in the name of the Father, and of the Son, and of the Holy Spirit because it is embedded in people's minds and hearts. Being baptized in the name of the Father, and of the Son, and of the Holy Spirit has become just as common and easy to do as saying Sunday and Monday although those days and all days of the week honor idol gods. But the saving of a person's soul from hell should cause people to want to be baptized correctly (John 3:3–7; Acts 2:36–39; 8:14–17; 10:42–48; 19:1–6).

Christ died for all people, so those of us who are living should no longer live for ourselves, but for Christ who died for us and rose from the dead (2 Cor. 5:15; 1 John 2:2–4; Acts 17:26; Heb. 2:9; Rom. 5:6–9; 8:32; Isa. 53; John 11:47–57; Acts 10).

As stated earlier, the Bible says that there is no private or misinterpretation of the Word of God, we are either right or wrong (2 Pet. 1:20; 1 Cor. 14:36). But there are a few mistranslations of terms in the King James Version of the Bible. Passover was replaced with Easter in Acts 12:4. Passover originated thousands of years before Easter. Passover was a holy day, while Easter was, and still is, a pagan and heathen holiday in honor of a sex goddess. Most people try to celebrate them at the same time of the year, and some Christians participate in the evil rituals. It is all right to celebrate the death, burial, and resurrection of Jesus; but the original purpose of Easter was to honor an evil goddess. Whoever added Easter to the Bible may be on their way to hell, according to the following scriptures: Rev. 22:18–20 and Deut. 4:1–4 and 12:32. Therefore, we know the term Easter should not have been put in the Bible by man, and it is possible that the baptism in the name of the Father, and of the Son, and of the Holy Ghost should not have been placed in the Bible either. Evidence of Easter being recklessly included in the King James Version of the Holy Bible is that most Bible scholars and publishers do not include it in other versions of the Bible because most people know better than to replace the word Passover with the word Easter. But most people are reckless and neglectful on a yearly basis when they celebrate Easter during Passover and on Resurrection Day even though most of them have learned better. Popes of the Catholic

Church also changed the calendar from the Julian calendar that was named for Julius Caesar to the Gregorian calendar named for Pope Gregory XIII. And the customs and traditions of the holidays that were taken from pagans and heathen religions were added to Christianity by the Catholic Church, but Christianity is not the same as the Christian Faith, because Christianity has always been a political entity (Isa. 61:1 – 3; Luke 4:16 – 21; 1 Tim. 4:1 – 3; 6:9 – 10, 21; Acts 6:7; Rom. 1:5; 16:25 – 27; James 2:1 – 10; Phil. 1:27; 4:2, 22; Matt. 20:24 – 28; Gal. 3:28; Col. 3:11 – 15; Rev. 5:9; 7:9; 14:6).

Just as people are accustomed to saying Easter instead of Passover, Resurrection Day, or resurrection week, they are also accustomed to being baptized in the name of the Father, and of the Son, and of the Holy Ghost, instead of being baptized in Christ's name, the person who died for their sins (Acts 2:36–39; 8:14–17; 10:42–48; 19:1–6; John 3:3–7).

The Bible says there is one Lord, one faith, and one baptism (Eph. 4:4–6). But Acts 2:38 and Matt. 28:19 mention two different baptisms. The original apostles only baptized in Christ's name (Acts 2:36–39; 8:14–17; 10:42–48; 19:1–6; John 3:3–7).

So, it is possible that Roman Catholics put Matt. 28:19 in the Bible, but the apostles are accurate. Any church that does what popes and priests initiated and not what the apostles initiated are inaccurate (Eph. 2:20; Acts 2:36–39; 8:14–17; 10:42–48; 19:1–6; John 3:3–7).

They are trying to obey what Jesus said in Matt. 28:19, but are disobeying him, because the apostles nor anyone else in the Bible were ever baptized according to what is written in Matt. 28:19. If Roman Catholics did not put in the Bible the baptism in the name of the Father, and of the Son, and of the Holy Spirit and that Christ really did say that, it means that in the New Testament, God goes by the name of Christ. Christ says that he came in his Father's name (John 5:43; Rev. 14:1). Jesus says that the works that he does, he does them in his Father's name, because the Father is in Christ and Christ is in the Father (John 10:25, 37–38). And it was not the Son who did the works, but the Father (John 14:10). Either way, Jesus said that we will believe and keep his Word through what the apostles teach us (John 15:20; 17:20). What the apostles wrote should mean more than what Roman Catholics and popes wrote, and if Catholics indeed did write a false baptism in the Bible, then that would not be the true way. The Bible says the true way shall be evil spoken of (Acts 19:1–9; 1 Pet. 4:14; 2 Pet. 2:1–3). Jesus also told the apostles that whosoever shall not hear them are in more trouble than the people of Sodom and Gomorrah, the two cities that God destroyed because of sin (Mark 6:11). He told the apostles to teach and preach what he told them (Matt. 10:27). The apostles were eyewitnesses, and we should take heed and be mindful of them (Acts 4:32; 2 Pet. 1:16–19; 3:2; Heb. 2:3–4).

The apostles are only telling us what they saw and heard Christ do (1 John 1:1–4; Acts 1:1–3, 8, 22; 2:32; 3:14–15; 4:18–20, 33; 5:28–29, 32; 10:39–48; 13:31; 22:14–18; 26:16; Luke 1:1–4; 10:23–24; 24:34–53; 1 Cor. 9:1–2; Matt. 13:10–17).

Luke said he and the apostles were eyewitnesses from the beginning of Christ's ministry (Luke 1:1–4). They saw him alive for forty days after he rose from the dead by many infallible proofs (Acts 1:1–3; 2:32). They ate and drank with him after he rose from the dead (Acts 10:40–48; Luke 24:34–53). While eating with the apostles, Christ opened their understanding and told them that they are eyewitnesses and to go preach repentance and remission of sins in Jesus's name among all nations, beginning in Jerusalem (Luke 24:46–49). After Christ's Resurrection, the Word of God was not first taught at Nicaea, Constantinople, or Rome. The apostles saw and heard things that righteous people, prophets, and kings did not see, and Christ said that people are spiritually blind who do not obey what the original apostles wrote (Matt. 13:10–17; Luke 10:23–24; 2 Cor. 2:17; 4:2–5).

The apostles were beaten and commanded not to speak in the name of Jesus, but they still taught and preached Christ daily in the temple, in houses, and publicly (Acts 5:40–42;

20:19–27). Moses said, "I know that the Lord has sent me to do all these works, for I have not done them of my own mind" (Num. 16:28). Paul spoke similar words regarding himself (Gal. 1:10–12). Even Christ himself said that his doctrine is not his own, but God's, and that people who speak of themselves, seek their own glory; but they who seek the glory of God is true and has no unrighteousness in them (John 7:14–18). Jesus said that he did nothing of himself, but he did only what he saw his Father do (John 5:19). And the apostles only did what they saw Christ do.

REJECTION OF THE BAPTISM IN CHRIST'S NAME IS ANTICHRIST

If we do not acknowledge the name of Christ in baptism, that omission is a version of the antichrist, because we would be saying that we do not need the name Christ. When you acknowledge the Son, you automatically have the Father (1 John 2:18, 22–23). What hinders you from being baptized properly (Acts 8:36–39; Gal. 5:7)? To be baptized in the name of Jesus, or of the name of Christ, or of the name of the Lord Jesus Christ, fulfills the Father, the Son, and the Holy Spirit (1 John 5:7). To be baptized otherwise is to reject Christ's name, being a form of the antichrist, but most people do not intend to be antichrist and do mean well when they are baptized improperly (1 John 2:18). But to be baptized in the name of the Father, and of the Son, and of the Holy Ghost does not fulfill any scripture, any prophecy, or any washing away of sins because the name "of" Christ was not mentioned (Acts 2:36–39; 8:14–17; 10:42–48; 19:1–6; John 3:3–7).

There is power in the name of Jesus, and demons tremble at the name of Christ (Luke 10:17; James 2:18–20; Mark 1:23–28; 3:9–12). So, if you really want to be saved from your sins and empowered by the Holy Ghost, which is also the Holy Spirit, to overcome any weaknesses, demons, or sinful habits, being baptized in the name of Christ gives you that power and it fulfills the Father, the Son, and the Holy Spirit (1 John 5:7). The word Christ is the European version of the Hebrew word Messiah (Dan. 9:25–26; John 1:41; 4:25).

When people believe in Christ and are baptized, their vile, immoral, and wretched bodies become new and part of his glorious body (Eph. 2:19–22; Ps. 118:22; Matt. 21:42; 1 Pet. 2:7; Acts 4:11–12).

Christ is a tried stone, a precious cornerstone, and a sure foundation, built on the foundation of the prophets and the apostles, Christ being the chief cornerstone who holds up all the weight (Isa. 9:6–7; 28:16; Rom. 15:1–4). But people who reject the baptism in Christ's name are rejecting the cornerstone of the building of Christ and that cornerstone has now become the chief cornerstone in heaven, on earth, in hell, in our personal lives, in our families, in our schools, and even in prisons when we accept Christ fully. And how can we accept Christ fully if we refuse to be baptized in his name? The stone that the builders rejected has now become the chief cornerstone. When people reject the baptism in Christ's name, they too reject the chief cornerstone who is Christ. Nor is there salvation in any other, for there is no other name under heaven given among mankind that saves us (Acts 4:10–12; Eph. 2:20; Ps. 118:22; Matt. 21:42; 1 Pet. 2:6–7; Isa. 28:16).

God gave Christ all power in heaven, on earth, beneath the earth, and in hell and a name above all names, and that is another reason that being baptized in the name of Christ fulfills everything, including the Father, Son, and Holy Ghost (1 Cor. 15:24–28; Eph. 1:21–23; Col. 2:10; Phil. 2:9; Ps. 8; Heb. 2:5–9; John 16:15; Matt. 28:18).

THE FIRST BAPTISM IN HISTORY

Peter and John said they would not obey man more than God (Acts 4:19–20). But Catholics go to priests to ask for forgiveness, which is not necessary, but people who are not Catholic obey Catholic baptisms, putting themselves in the same jeopardy as Catholics, who now have a different Bible than what other Christians use. Once again, most Catholic people are good people, and non-Catholic people who allow non-Catholic ministers to tell them that they are saved because they simply believe, confess, and call on the Lord are equally in error as when Catholic people unnecessarily confess their sins to a priest with hopes to be forgiven by God. Jesus says, "If you keep my commandments, you shall abide in my love, even as I have kept my Father's commandments, and abide in his love" (John 15:10). And it was at Jerusalem that Peter and the apostles started the first church by baptizing three thousand people in the name of Jesus (Acts 1:4–5, 8–9; 2:38). Peter told them what Jesus commanded him to do, that repentance and forgiveness of sins should be preached in Jesus's name unto all nations. And when Peter performed the first baptism, he baptized the people in the name of the Lord Jesus Christ for the forgiveness of their sins (Luke 24:47; Matt. 28:19; Acts 2:38–39). This word had been preached and the baptism had been performed to the entire world by the apostles by AD 62, which was about thirty years after Christ went back to heaven (Col. 1:23; Acts 2:36–39; 8:14–17; 10:42–48; 19:1–6; John 3:3–7).

Thus, God visited the Gentiles to take out of them a people

for his name (Acts 15:14).

THE APOSTLES ONLY BAPTIZED IN CHRIST'S NAME

Luke put everything in order (Luke 1:1). And he wrote the book of Acts where all people were baptized in Christ's name (Acts 2:36–39; 8:14–17; 10:42–48; 19:1–6; John 3:3–7).

And Jesus after going back to heaven showed John a revelation and told him to write the book of Revelation, a book most of us do not understand entirely (Rev. 1:10–19). The Apostle Paul knew a man who he could not figure out if the man was an angel or not. Paul said this man saw things in heaven that he was not allowed to talk about (2 Cor. 12:2–4). The apostles knew men and heavenly spirits like that, so they certainly knew more than we know. Who are you going to believe, them or present-day preachers? They said that they heard Jesus, saw him, and handled the Word of life with their hands (1 John 1:1–3; Phil. 2:14–16). The Word is God (John 1:1; Rev. 19:13). The apostles stood in the temple and taught the word of a sanctified life (Acts 5:20; John 17:17–19; Isa. 29:23).

Jesus is the image of the invisible God (Col. 1:15). One apostle said if you know God, you will hear their doctrine, and if you refuse to hear them, you have the spirit of error (1 John 4:6). Another apostle said if a man or an angel teaches you anything other than what the apostles taught, let it be accursed (Gal. 1:8–9). Paul said there is no other gospel than what they have taught (Gal. 1:6–9). In other words, preachers who baptize in the name of the Father, and of the Son, and of the Holy Ghost are accursed. This does not mean that they are not good people of God, because we all serve the same God (Mal. 2:4–10), but only if we do everything in Christ's name (Col. 3:17, 23; 1 Cor. 10:31). Christ says no one comes unto the Father without going through him first and that it is impossible to honor God without honoring him. And we cannot get to Christ without following the apostles' doctrine (John 14:1, 6; 5:22–23; Matt. 10:40; Acts 4:12). There is only One God and One mediator and advocate between God and humans, and that is Jesus Christ (1 Tim. 2:5; 1 John 2:1). Christ also told the apostles that anyone who receives the apostles receives Christ and whosoever receives Christ receives the Father (Matt. 10:40). Christ told the apostles, "I am the way, the truth, and the life, and no one comes unto the Father but by me. If you know me, you know my Father also, and have seen him," (John 14:1–7). Anyone who attempts to come unto the Father other than going through Christ first, that person is a thief and a robber, (John 5:22–23, 36–38; 10:1–17, 24–29; 12:26; 14:1, 6; 18:37; Acts 4:12; 2 John 1:9).

People will die in their sins if they do not believe in Christ (John 8:21–24). For through Christ, descendants of ancient Jews and Gentiles have access by one Spirit unto the Father (Eph. 2:18). The Father sent the Son to be the Savior of the world (1 John 4:14). Although Christ had not been born into the world yet, when the Hebrews left slavery in Egypt and wandered in the wilderness, the people in the wilderness served the same God, ate the same spiritual meat, drank the same spiritual drink, and drank of the same spiritual Rock that followed them—that Rock was Christ—but God was not pleased with most of them, and they were destroyed by God (1 Cor. 3:5–17; 10:1–13). Therefore, not every Christian is a servant of the Lord, because some people only benefit from God's protection and prosperity while not standing for the Word of God (Luke 4:4; Exod. 24:7; Deut. 4:1–9; 8:3). The Bible speaks of an eloquent man, mighty in the scriptures, instructed in the way of the Lord, being fervent in the spirit, who taught diligently the things of the Lord, and spoke boldly about the baptism; but Aquila and Priscilla took him aside and taught him the way of God more accurately (Acts 18:24–26). The same thing is happening nowadays. There are good preachers in the word who do not baptize in the name of Christ, but they should allow someone to teach them more accurately so they can teach their congregation more accurately. There are also preachers who are lying hypocrites but who tell the truth in some cases. Paul did acknowledge them as prophets, but he said they needed rebuking sharply, because they ruin whole families (Titus 1:11–13). Paul said to do those things that you have learned, received, heard, and seen in him and the God of peace shall be with you (Phil. 4:9; 2 Tim. 3:10) and to teach no other doctrine (1 Tim. 1:3). He also said that God made him an example to us and that if you are otherwise minded, God will reveal Paul's doctrine to you (Phil. 3:17). Paul went on to say that his life, baptism, and ministry are a pattern to people who should hereafter believe (1 Tim. 1:16). That is because he was called to be a witness unto all people of what he had seen and heard (Acts 22:15–16; 1 John 1:1–3; Phil. 2:14–16). This is why Paul said, "Be ye followers of me, even as I also am of Christ. Remember me in all things and keep the ordinances as I delivered them to you" (1 Cor. 4:15–16; 11:1–3; Phil. 3:17).

The apostle's doctrine is our example (Phil. 3:17; 1 Thess. 1:5–7). Paul also said, "You are saved, if you keep in memory what I preached unto you, otherwise you have believed in vain" (1 Cor. 15:1–2). Christians often talk about the scripture that says we are to forget the things that are behind us and press toward the mark of the prize of the high calling of God in Christ Jesus. But they often fail to mention the following verses that say, "Let us therefore, as many as be perfect [or blameless] … Let us walk by the same rule, let us mind the same thing" (Phil. 3:13–18). Paul also said, "The things that you have heard of me among many witnesses, the same commit to faithful people, who shall be able to teach others also" (2 Tim. 2:2). The Bible says mark people who do what the apostles did, and to do otherwise is to be an enemy of the cross of Christ (Phil. 3:16–18). It also says, "Mark people who cause divisions and offences contrary to the doctrine which ye have learned from the apostles and avoid them" (Rom. 16:17). The scripture goes on to say that people who are not on the foundation of the apostles use good words and fair speeches to deceive the hearts of simple-minded people (Rom. 16:18). The Bible says that the apostles are of God and they who know God hears them and they who are not of God hears not the original apostles. "Hereby know we the spirit of truth, and the spirit of error" (1 John 4:6). The apostles said, "Keep and hold the traditions which ye have been taught, whether by word, or our letter" (emphasis added) (2 Thess. 2:15). They also said, "God called you by our gospel" (emphasis added) (2 Thess. 2:14).

We are not called by the pope's or any Protestant preacher's doctrine. Paul said God shall judge the secrets of people by Jesus Christ and according to the gospel that Paul taught (Rom. 2:16). The Apostle John testified and wrote of the things he saw Jesus do, and we know that John's testimony is true and is more credible than the pope's, any priest, or any non-Catholic preacher (John 21:24). That which they have seen and heard they declared those things unto us (1 John 1:3). Jesus says that the apostles bear witness of him because they were with him from the beginning (John 15:27).

The Bible says that people who reject the Word of God will be destroyed but people who fear God shall be rewarded (Prov. 13:13). Jesus also says that whosoever hears the apostles, hears him, and whosoever rejects what the apostles said and did rejects Christ, and they who rejects Christ rejects God who sent Christ (Luke 10:16). Some people may say that they do not reject Christ, but if anyone refuses to be baptized in Christ's name, they are rejecting Christ, even if they do not mean to reject him. And when you teach people about Christ and they reject your wisdom, it is not you they reject, but they reject God (1 Thess. 4:3–8). Isaiah prophesized that Jesus will be despised, rejected, and acquainted with grief and sorrow (Isa. 53:3; Luke

22:39–46). Jesus was rejected in his own hometown (Luke 4:16–32; 9:51–58). Christ's own biological brothers did not believe in him at one point (John 7:1–8). Ultimately, Jesus came unto his own people including the ancient Jews, and his own people did not receive him (John 1:10–14; Acts 13:26–31; Luke 24:44–49).

Paul said that we should know the commandments that they gave us from Jesus (1 Thess. 4:2). Peter said of Paul that God gave him wisdom to write parts of the Bible and that all his writings are true, and some things are hard to be understood. But only unlearned and unstable people wrestle with Paul's teachings and other scriptures, to their own destruction (2 Pet. 3:14–17). John said that he was a witness to the documenting of the Word of God and of the testimony of Jesus Christ and of all things that he saw (Rev. 1:1–2; John 1:34). Are you going to believe some modern-day Protestant preacher, reverend, priest, or pope instead of believing the apostles who ate, drank, laughed, and cried with Christ? The apostles said that the people received the word that they taught not as if it was from man, but as it is in truth, the Word of God (1 Thess. 2:13). Paul was called to preach to the Gentiles, and he did not talk to the apostles for any instructions; he received instructions directly from Christ (Gal. 1:11–24). He went to Jerusalem after three years of working with the Gentiles, stayed only fifteen days talking to Peter, departed, and returned fourteen years later (Gal. 2:1, 2–10, 18). Without any instructions from Peter who performed the first ever baptism in Christ's name, Paul still preached that people should be baptized in the name of Jesus without Peter telling him to do so (Acts 19:1–6).

The Bible teaches us to withdraw ourselves from anyone who does not obey the apostles' doctrine and who does not teach their tradition (2 Thess. 3:6–7). According to the Bible, people who do not understand the apostles' doctrine are possibly blind and lost, and the apostles said that they did not handle the Word of God deceitfully, nor did they corrupt the Word of God (2 Cor. 2:17; 4:2–5; Matt. 13:10–17; Luke 10:23–24).

Jesus commanded the apostles on what to do after his departure, just as Moses commanded Joshua. Joshua left nothing undone of all that the Lord commanded Moses, but people were disobedient (Josh. 11:15; Deut. 34:9). Just as most people do not follow what Jesus commanded Peter to do, and that is to baptize everyone in Christ's name (Acts 2:36–42; Matt. 16:18).

CHRIST GAVE THE APOSTLES MORE AUTHORITY THAN ANY PREACHER

Jesus told the apostles that whosoever sins they forgive, let it be forgiven, but whosoever sins they retain, let it be retained unto them (John 20:22–23). That is because Christ gave them the keys to heaven, the keys being the Word of God. Christ told Peter, "Upon this rock I will build my church, and the gates of hell shall not prevail against it. Whatever you bind on earth shall also be bound in heaven, and whatever you set free on earth shall be free in heaven" (Matt. 16:18–19). When we obey the apostles, we are freed from sin, but if we disobey the apostles, we are bound to sin and hell unless we repent (Matt. 16:18–19). And the Word of God will never be bound (2 Tim. 2:9). "Upon this rock I will build my church," Peter accepted that authority and started the first church by baptizing three thousand people in the name of Jesus and they stayed in the apostles' doctrine (Acts 2:36–42; Matt. 16:18).

When Peter started the first church and baptized the first people of the church, he spoke these words, "Repent and be baptized, every one of you, in the name of Jesus Christ for the remission of sins, and you shall receive the gift of the Holy Ghost." That is your key to the gates of heaven and the gates of hell cannot prevail against it (Matt. 16:18; Acts 2:38; John

3:3–7). If we do not deny the name of Jesus and keep his Word, the door to heaven will be open, even if you have only a little strength, but Christ will say to hypocrites, "Depart from me, you worker of iniquity" (Matt. 7:21–23; Mic. 3:11; Luke 13:24–27).

THERE IS ONLY ONE CHURCH, ONE FOUNDATION & ONE BODY OF CHRIST

The baptism in Christ's name that Peter performed on the day of Pentecost is the rock that people are rejecting and disallowing (Acts 4:10–12; Eph. 2:20; Ps. 118:22; Matt. 21:42; 1 Pet. 2:6–7; Isa. 28:16).

And people who accept the baptism in Christ's name allow Christ to be the chief cornerstone and pillar in their life, holding up their entire life (Matt. 16:18; 1 Pet. 2:6–8; Acts 2:36–39; 8:14–17; 10:42–48; 19:1–6; John 3:3–7).

God says, "I lay in Zion a chief cornerstone, elect and precious, and they who believes in him will by no means be put to shame. Therefore, to you who believe, he is precious, but to they who are disobedient, the stone which the builders rejected has become the chief cornerstone, and a stone of stumbling and a rock of offense." They stumble, being disobedient to the Word (1 Pet. 2:6–8; Luke 4:4; Exod. 24:7; Deut. 4:1–9; 8:3).

There is only one church in the entire world, and it is the one that the apostles established when Peter and the apostles baptized three thousand people in Christ's name in one day (Acts 2:36–39; 8:14–17; 10:42–48; 19:1–6; John 3:3–7).

It does not really matter what the name of a church is, but

the church must be based on the apostles' doctrine, according to what Christ tells us (John 14:1, 6; 5:22–23; Matt. 10:40; Acts 4:12).

The church is the one body and foundation of Christ, and we cannot join the body of Christ or get on the foundation of Christ without being baptized in his name, and without becoming Christ's bride, but we cannot become his bride without being baptized in his name (Matt. 9:15; 2 Cor. 11:2–3; Eph. 5:23, 27; John 3:3–7; Acts 2:36–39; 8:14–17; 10:42–48; 19:1–6).

There is only one body and one foundation. "Therefore, thus says the Lord God, behold, I lay in Zion for a foundation a stone, a tried stone, a precious corner stone, a sure foundation" (Isa. 28:16). Another foundation can no one lay than what is already laid by Jesus Christ and the apostles (1 Cor. 3:11). We must all be on that same one foundation and part of that same one body of Christ. And the foundation of God stands sure, having this "seal," them who are his. "Let everyone who names the name of Christ depart from sin" (2 Tim. 2:19; 2 Cor. 1:21, 22; Eph. 1:13; 4:30).

God also uses a "seal" to identify his people in the book of Revelation (Rev. 7:4; 9:4). There is only one Spirit, one foundation, one body, one God and Father of all, who is above all, one Lord, one faith, and one baptism (Eph. 4:4–6).

PREVENTING PEOPLE FROM BEING BAPTIZED IN CHRIST'S NAME IS ANTI-CHRIST

People sometimes say that they will run on in Christ's name, but it is best to also be baptized in Christ's name if you plan to run for Christ in his name. Christ says, "Do not fear any of the things you are about to suffer. The devil will even throw some of you in prison to test you. Be faithful until death, and I will give you the crown of life" (Rev. 2:10). Paul, while in prison, was faithful until death and believed until he was executed that he would be set free (2 Tim. 4:9–18). The name of Christ is the door, and Christ says that his people will not follow another person or another god (John 10:7–9). And denying his name causes the door to close shut (Matt. 7:21–23; Mic. 3:11; Luke 13:24–27).

A good example is when Jesus spoke to the hypocrite lawyers about the persecution and killing of the prophets (Luke 11:46–52). He told them, "You have taken away the key to knowledge. You did not enter in yourself and hindered other people from entering" (Luke 11:52). The same applies to people who do not allow others to be baptized in Christ's name. Some pastors have learned better and know that the baptism in

Christ's name is the one and only true baptism, one Lord, one faith, one baptism, one Spirit, one body, one hope, and one God (Eph. 4:4–6). But they refuse to teach this true way to their congregation because they fear being rejected and that the people will resist change.

BRIDES TAKE THE NAME OF GROOMS & PROPER BAPTISM GIVES US CHRIST'S NAME

When we are baptized, we become a bride of Christ. But brides are supposed to take the name of the person they have married (Rev. 19:7; 21:2; 22:17; Isa. 54:4–10; Jer. 31:27–37; Matt. 9:15; 25:1; John 3:29; 2 Cor. 11:2–3; Eph. 5:23).

When we backslide, or deny Christ's name, fail to stand for the Word of God, refuse to stand with Christ, or are ashamed of the Word of God in the presence of others, the Bible says that is the same as Christ's bride playing the role of a whore (Jer. 3:6–15, 22; Hosea 1:2; 4:15–16; 14:4–6).

Jesus says that he is coming back for people with his name (Rev. 22:4). The following scriptures are additional scriptures that say when we are baptized in Christ's name, we become married to Christ (2 Cor. 11:2; Jer. 3:14; 31:32; Isa. 62:4–5).

How can you be married to someone without having their name? When people are born into this world, they should take their earthly father's last name (Gen. 48:15–16). When we get baptized, we should become born again and accept our heavenly Father's name. You do this by getting baptized in his name, which is Christ, and by receiving the Holy Ghost (John

3:3–7; Acts 2:36–42; 8:14–17; 10:47–48; 19:2–5).

When we receive Jesus and believe in his name, we have the power to become the sons and daughters of God (John 1:12). How can you become his son or daughter without having his name. Unless someone thinks that it is possible to be a bastard child of God. We know that it is impossible to be a bastard child of God. We are either a child of God, or a child of the devil (John 8:36–45; Mic. 4:5; 1 Tim. 5:15). And we know that being baptized in Christ's name causes even people who were born out of wedlock to no longer be a bastard (Heb. 12:4–8).

CHRIST'S NAME IS ABOVE EVERY NAME IN HEAVEN, EARTH, & HELL

Jesus has a name above every name that is named, in this world and in the world to come (Eph. 1:21; Phil. 2:9). Christ's name is above the name of any angel, even the great ones like Michael and Gabriel (Heb. 1:4–5). Every knee shall bow at the name of Christ (Phil. 2:10). His name is above any form of Jehovah, Yahweh, Allah, Muhammad, Buddha, pope, priest, father, rabbi, elder, bishop, monk, or reverend. His name is far above all principalities, dominions, and powers. He is head over all things (Eph. 1:20–22). And all judgment is now in the hands of Christ and not in the hands of God so that everyone should honor the Son of God (John 5:20–27). This is another reason that we should do all things in Christ's name (Col. 3:17). Christ says, "Everything that the Father has is mine" (John 16:15). Even hell belongs to Christ. Jesus has the keys to hell and death, and just as Satan will not work against himself, he will not build a hell for himself either (Rev. 1:18; 20:10; Luke 17:19–26; Matt. 12:22–28).

In Matt. 28:18, Jesus says that he has all power in his hands. Does this mean that God is now weak? When Christ's name became a name above all names, did God give him a name above his own? No, because they have the same name in the New

Testament (John 5:43; 10:22–33). Nor is there salvation in any other name (Acts 4:12; 1 Tim. 2:5; 1 John 2:1; John 5:20–27).

GOD THE FATHER, GOD THE SON, GOD THE HOLY GHOST WERE IN CHRIST, BEING ONE

The apostles baptized in Christ's name because they knew that Jesus was telling them that the Father, Son, and Holy Ghost are the same Spirit but a different revelation of God (1 John 5:7; Acts 2:36–39; 8:14–17; 10:42–48; 19:1–6).

"There is one body and one Spirit, even as you are called in one hope. One Lord, one faith, and one baptism" (Eph. 4:4–6). How can God still be above all if he gave all power to Christ? The answer is that the Father, Son, and Holy Ghost have the same name in the New Testament and in our generations. The Bible says that there is only one Spirit, one body, one Lord, and one God and Father of all, who is above all and through all and in you all (Eph. 4:4–6; Zech. 14:9; John 5:43; 10:25; 14:26; 1 John 2:23; 5:7–8).

Therefore, the Father, Son, and Holy Ghost are the same Spirit (1 Cor. 15:24–28; Phil. 2:5–11; Ps. 8; Heb. 2:5–9; 4:12; Matt. 28:18; Rev. 1:16; 2:12–16; 19:15, 21; Eph. 1:20–23; 6:10–20; Col. 2:10; John 16:15, 21)?

Jesus was God incarnate, meaning Jesus was God in the flesh (John 1:1–14). Christ was the image of the invisible God (Col.

1:15). God the Father, God the Son, and God the Holy Ghost were all in Jesus; and when Christ went to the wilderness to be tempted by the devil, he was full of the Holy Ghost, thus the Holy Spirit was in him (Luke 3:21–22; 4:1). But the Holy Ghost had not been given to anyone else yet (John 7:39). Christ was filled with the Holy Ghost because God was in Christ (2 Cor. 5:19). Daniel had an excellent spirit in him, but the Holy Ghost had not been given yet, so he had a good "spirit" with a lowercase "s." The same applies to Caleb who was one of two people who God allowed to go to the promised land out of thousands of people, because he had a different spirit than the other people, with a lowercase "s" (Num. 14:24). After Jesus resisted the temptation of the devil, he returned to Galilee in the "power of the Spirit," with an uppercase "S" (Luke 4:14).

FATHER, SON, AND HOLY GHOST ARE TITLES, NOT NAMES

If the Catholic Church did not write the so-called trinity in the Bible and Christ really did command us to be baptize in the name of the Father, and of the Son, and of the Holy Ghost, notice that He said name and not names. Father, Son, and Holy Ghost are titles, not names. Col. 2:8–10 tells us to beware of philosophy and traditions of humans. To baptize in the name of the Father, and of the Son, and of the Holy Ghost is simply man's tradition, because no one in the Bible ever did it (Acts 2:36–39; 8:14–17; 10:42–48; 19:1–6; John 3:3–7).

If you went to the bank and tried to deposit money into your father's and son's bank account, the banker would ask you, "What is your father's and son's name?" This is what happens when people baptize in the name of the Father and of the Son and of the Holy Ghost. They try to acknowledge, honor, and respect all three, but no name is stated. The Bible says when we acknowledge the Son's name, we automatically acknowledge the Father and the Holy Spirit, and that the Holy Spirit is sent to us in Christ's name (John 14:26; 1 John 2:23). Christ says, "I come in my Father's name, but you do not receive me. If another comes in his own name, you will receive him (John 5:43).

THIS IS WHY THE FATHER, SON & HOLY GHOST ARE ONE

Colossians 2:9 says in Jesus dwells the fullness of the godhead bodily, meaning in Jesus dwells the Father, Son, and the Holy Ghost (1 John 5:7). Just as the Father, Son, and Holy Ghost are complete in Jesus, you are complete in him if you are in his name (Col. 2:10). Father, Son, and Holy Ghost could also be a precept or short parable. Jesus often spoke in parables, and in parables, he uttered things that had been secret from the foundation of the world (Matt. 13:34–35). We know that the Spirit of God the Son was with God the Father, before the foundation of the world (Gen. 1:26; 1 Cor. 10:1–17; Ps. 66:8–12; John 17:5, 24; Heb. 1:1–2; 2 Tim. 1:9; 1 Pet. 1:20; Rev. 3:14).

David quoted by the Holy Ghost, "My Lord said to my Lord, 'Sit on my right side until I make your enemies my footstool'" (Mark 12:36). The word "Lord" is capitalized when referring to both the Father and the Son. David spoke by the Holy Ghost hundreds of years before Jesus was born. All the prophets spoke by the Holy Ghost (2 Pet. 1:20–21). Mary was pregnant by the Holy Ghost. But was not Mary pregnant by God? She was pregnant by God the Holy Ghost (Matt. 1:18). When Elisabeth was pregnant with John the Baptist, she met Mary, and the baby in Elisabeth's stomach leaped for joy while Elisabeth was being filled with the Holy Ghost. The baby leaped because God the Holy Ghost was present (Luke 1:39–44). Even John's father was filled with the Holy Ghost before the birth of

Jesus (Luke 1:67). God the Father sent God the Holy Ghost in God the Son's name, and his name is Christ (John 14:26). But didn't Jesus say that he came in his Father's name (John 5:43; Luke 13:35; 19:37–38)? How can the Father send the Holy Ghost in the Son's name if the Son came in his Father's name? This is because in the New Testament, the Father, Son, and Holy Ghost come in the name of Christ, the one who suffered and paid the price to inherit all of the Father's equal authority, power, and possessions (John 16:15; 1 Cor. 15:24–28; Eph. 1:21–23; Matt. 28:18; Col. 2:10; Phil. 2:9; Ps. 8; Heb. 2:5–9; Matt. 28:18).

Christ told Father God, "I have manifested your name unto the men who you have given me out of the world… and they have kept your Word" (John 17:6). This is because the Father, Son, and Holy Ghost are one Spirit, with the same name. Christ says that whoever receives him also receives Father God Almighty (Matt. 10:40). The Bible says, "O Lord, there is none like thee, neither is there any God besides thee, according to all that we have heard with our ears" (2 Sam. 7:22; 1 Chron. 17:20). Jesus said too, "The Lord our God is One Lord" (Mark 12:29). And the people said, "Yes, he is one God, there is none other but him" (Mark 12:32). Zechariah prophesized and said that the Father shall be pierced on the cross and they shall look at the Son hanging there bleeding (Zech. 12:10). How can the Father be pierced with a spear, and it be the Son too without them being the same Spirit? The prophesy was fulfilled in John 19:34–37 and Rev. 1:7. Even before the natural birth of Jesus, the Prophet Zechariah said that God shall be one Lord and King of the Earth, and his name one (Zech. 14:9). Paul wrote of different gifts that God gives us, and the gifts come from the same Spirit, the same Lord, and the same God who works all in all (1 Cor. 12:4–6). And again, the word Spirit is capitalized, signifying God Almighty, and the scripture says that the Spirit, our Lord, and our God are the same Spirit. The Lord our God is one Lord (Deut. 6:4). The Lord is God, and there is none else (1 Kings 8:60). The Father is how God revealed himself in the Old

Testament, except in the fiery furnace when the image of the Son of God appeared in the furnace with Shadrach, Meshach, and Abed-Nego (Dan. 3:25). In the New Testament, God revealed himself as the Son, but now that Jesus has gone back to heaven, God reveals himself as the Holy Ghost, without image. When God the Son visits the earth nowadays, his visits bring destruction, wrath, chastisement, punishment, and someday soon the end of the world (1 Cor. 15:24–28; Heb. 4:12; Rev. 1:16; 2:12–16; 19:15, 21; Eph.6:10–20).

God the Holy Ghost visits the earth as the Comforter in the name of Christ, and as a protector and strengthener. And the Holy Ghost completely dwells inside of the body of righteous people (John 14:16–27; Acts 5:32; Col. 2:10). In the Old Testament, the people begged to hear Moses because if God the Father had returned, they knew they would die (Exod. 20:18, 19; Deut. 5:23–26), just as in Ezekiel's day. God used Ezekiel to warn the people before he killed them, but he did not visit the earth himself (Ezek. 3:4–21). When God walked the earth, he revealed himself as the Son. Now he reveals himself in the form of the Holy Ghost. God the Father will not be manifested again until judgment day. Then God will be all in all, and all power goes back into the Father's hand (1 Cor. 15:23–28). The Father is God in creation, the Son is God in redemption, and the Holy Ghost is the Comforter, strength, and power sent from heaven in the name of Christ, even at this present time (John 14:16–27).

When Jesus told the apostles to baptize in the name of the Father, and of the Son, and of the Holy Ghost, he was telling them to simply say Christ, or Jesus Christ, or the Lord Jesus Christ, and that covers everything, because when we acknowledge the Son, we automatically acknowledge the Father (1 John 2:22–23; Mark 9:37; Matt. 10:40). Scriptures says, "Whosoever denies the Son, the same person has not the Father, but they who acknowledge the Son has the Father also" (1 John 2:23). When God talked to Christ, Father God called the Son God, and at another time, the Son was called Lord (Heb. 1:8;

Mark 12:36). God told Christ, "Your throne, O God, is forever and ever (Heb.1:8). The Bible says that this is a mystery, but that there should still be no controversy, the Bible also says that God was received up to heaven after the resurrection (1 Tim. 3:16). Jesus says that when they saw him, they were looking at the Father and that he and the Father are one (John 10:30, 38; 12:44–45; 14:6–10; 17:21–23). Christ says that whoever receives him also receives the Father (Matt. 10:40). The Apostle John said that they who abides in the doctrine of Christ, they have both the Father and the Son, and if anyone comes to you and brings not this doctrine, receive them not in your house, or you become partaker of their evil deeds (2 John 8–13). If anyone happens to hate Christ, they also hate the Father, so non-Christian religions cannot claim to love God if they do not embrace Christ (John 15:23).

A certain singer once said that the Father, Son, and Holy Ghost became one in the New Testament. But they were always one, because in John 17:5, Jesus asked God to glorify him with the glory that they had together before the world was created. Jesus was even named "Jesus" before he was conceived in Mary's womb (Luke 2:21). Isaiah 42:8 says that God will not give his glory to another. If God gave Jesus all power and a name above all names, how can Jesus not have his glory (Eph. 1:20–23)? Jesus said, "Father, glorify your name." And God said, "I have glorified it, and will glorify it again" (John 12:28). Christ told God, "Holy Father, keep through your own name the apostles who you have given me, that they may be one, as we are" (emphasis added) (John 17:11).

Jesus told God in the very next verse, "I kept them in your name" (John 17:12). Jesus tells us to ask for things in his name so the Father can be glorified in the Son. That is one reason we pray to the Father in Christ's name (John 14:13). If they had glory together before the world was created, why does Isa. 43:10–11 say that there was no God before God and that there will not be one after him? Those same scriptures tell us that God alone is our Savior because the Savior Jesus and the Savior

God are the same Spirit. Again, John 14:13 tells us to ask in his name, and he will give it to us so that the Father can be glorified in the Son. Therefore, when we are baptized in Christ's name, the Father is gloried in the Son. Eph. 3:9 says that this is a mystery, which was hid in God from the beginning of the world. It goes on to say that God created all things by Jesus Christ, because they are one. God made all things through Christ, but God also says that he made all things by himself (Isa. 44:24). Christ says, "Do you not believe that I am in the Father and the Father in me? The words that I speak to you I do not speak of myself, but the Father who dwells in me does the works" (John 1:1–14; 14:10). God was in Christ (2 Cor. 5:19). Psalms 136:4 says that God alone does the wonders.

THE BABY JESUS WAS CALLED FATHER AND GOD

The Prophet Isaiah said, "Unto us a child is born, and his name shall be called Mighty God and Everlasting Father" (Isa. 9:6). If the baby was to be called Father and God, then the baby and the Father must have the same Spirit, name, and authority (Isa. 9:6). Peter tells us to be mindful of the Old Testament prophets and the commandments of the apostles (2 Pet. 3:2). We know that the world was not worthy of Jesus, but he died for us anyway (1 John 2:2–4; Acts 17:26; Heb. 2:9; Rom. 5:6–9; 8:32; Isa. 53). The Bible tells us that the world was not even worthy of the prophets and apostles (Heb. 11:36–38; James 5:5–11). So, who are you going to believe, man's doctrine or the prophets and apostles?

WE MUST BE BORN AGAIN OF THE WATER & OF THE SPIRIT TO GO TO HEAVEN

In the Old Testament, God said, "My Spirit shall not always strive with humans, because they are flesh" (Gen. 6:3). We must be born of the water and of the Spirit or we cannot go to heaven (John 3:3–7), born again, a new creature, not of the will of the flesh, blood, or mankind, but of the will of God (John 1:10–13). Because flesh and blood cannot enter heaven (John 3:3–7; 1 Cor. 15:42–52; Gal. 5:16, 24–25; 1 Thess. 4:14–17).

And they who sow to the flesh shall of the flesh reap corruption and problems, but they who sow to the Spirit shall of the Spirit reap everlasting life (Gal. 6:7–8, 14). We reap what we sow, in every aspect of life, good or bad (Rom. 2:4–11; Gal. 6:7–10).

In the Old Testament, the people served God in sincerity and truth, because the Holy Ghost had not yet been given (Josh. 24:14; 1 Sam. 12:24; 1 Kings 2:4; 3:6). But now that the Holy Ghost is a gift, we must worship God in spirit and in truth (John 4:23–24; Zech. 8:1–8).

We must compare spiritual with spiritual, because natural-thinking people cannot understand the things of the Spirit of

God, because it is foolishness to them, but sanctified Christians have the mind of Christ (1 Cor. 1:10; 2:9–16; Rom. 15:5–6).

FATHER, SON & HOLY GHOST HAVE THE SAME NAME

"In the beginning was the Word, and the Word was with God, and the Word was God" (John 1:1, 14; 1 John 5:6–8; Job 27:11; Prov. 8:22–36).

Even in the New Testament, Jesus's name is called the Word of God (Rev. 19:11–13). This is because when Christ was born on earth, the Word was made flesh and dwelt among mankind (John 1:14; Heb. 2:14–15; 1 Tim. 3:16; Phil. 2:5–11; Col. 1:15).

Again, Jesus is the image of the invisible God (Col. 1:15). John the Baptist was a cousin of Jesus who was born before Jesus was born, but John said that Jesus was before him and that he did not foreknow Jesus (John 1:29–31). And John said that Christ must increase and that he and we must decrease (John 3:28, 30–31). Jesus told the ancient Jews that he was before Abraham. This proves that Jesus and God have and are the same Spirit (Eph. 2:18). Abraham was before Moses and David, but Jesus was before them all, because Jesus Christ is God's New Testament's name. Jehovah is God's Old Testament name (Exod. 6:3; Ps. 83:18). But now Christ is the name that God ordained for salvation in the New Testament, and there is no other name whereby we must be saved (Acts 4:12; John 14:4–6; 1 John 2:1).

"Thou shalt not take the name of the Lord in vain, for the Lord will not hold people guiltless who takes his name in vain" (Exod. 20:7). Jesus says that the law and the prophets of the Old Testament were preached until John the Baptist started preaching, but since that time, the kingdom of God must now be preached (Luke 16:16). Thus, in this generation, no one comes unto the Father unless they use the name Jesus and that if anyone tries to reach God in any other way, they are a thief and a robber (John 5:22–23, 36–38; 10:1–17, 24–29; 12:26; 14:1, 6; 18:37; Acts 4:12; 2 John 1:9).

Christ says we will die in our sins if we do not wear the name Christ in holiness, sanctification, and righteousness (John 8:21–24). Through Christ, descendants of the Jews and Gentiles have access by one Spirit unto the Father (Eph. 2:18). Jesus says we should honor him as we honor the Father and that if we do not honor the Son, we do not honor the Father (John 5:22–23). However, supporters of the trinity may say that they use that same scripture to honor the Father, Son, and Holy Ghost. But Jesus Christ says that he declared unto us God's name (John 17:26). Therefore, God's New Testament name is Jesus Christ. If anyone disagrees, they should tell us what name Christ was referring to when he said that he declares to us God's name and that he came in his Father's name (John 10:25; 17:26). As stated earlier, Christ says that he came in his Father's name and most people do not receive him and that when another person comes in their own name, people receive them (John 5:43). Prov. 30:4 asks, "What is God's name, and what is his Son's name?" They both are named Jesus in the New Testament because they are the same Spirit (Eph. 2:18). Jesus also says, "Anyone who believes in me, believes not in me, but in God who sent me." This means they who believe in Jesus's name believe not in Christ's name, but in the name of God (John 12:44). Christ also says that when people saw him, they saw God who sent him (John 12:45). This is one reason that the name "Immanuel" means "God with us" (Isa. 7:14; Matt. 1:23).

In the Old Testament, God revealed himself by the Holy Ghost through the prophets, but now God speaks by Jesus through the Holy Ghost in righteous teachers (2 Pet. 1:20–21; Heb. 1:1–2). God spoke to people in the Old Testament by prophets, but in these last days, God speaks to us by his Son Jesus Christ, whom he has appointed as the heir of all things, by whom God also made the entire universe (Heb. 1:8–12). God said unto the Son, "You are God," and that the Son made the heavens and the earth (Heb. 1:8–12). How is that possible? Did God make the earth? Yes, he did, but he made it with the one Spirit of the Father, Son, and Holy Ghost (1 John 5:7). Father God says, "Thus says the Lord, your Redeemer, and he who formed you from the womb. I am the Lord who makes all things, who stretches out the heavens all alone, who spreads abroad the earth by myself" (Isa. 44:24). Jesus, now being in the image of God's person, cleansed and purged us from our sins and sat on the right hand of the Majesty, meaning the right hand of royal power (Heb. 1:3). There is also a scripture that simply says, "Christ the power of God" (1 Cor. 1:24). We are baptized into Christ by one Spirit (1 Cor. 12:12–13). If Christ is one and if we are baptized into one Spirit, with a capital S, then that one Spirit is the Father, Son, and Holy Ghost all in one name. As many as have been baptized into Christ have put on Christ (Gal. 3:27; Rom. 6:3–4). There is no other way to become heirs to the promise because people who have been baptized into Christ have put on Christ (Gal. 3:26–29). How can you be baptized into Christ without being baptized in his name? How can you put on Christ without wearing his name, as in marriage (2 Cor. 11:2; Jer. 3:14; 31:32; Isa. 62:4–5)?

There is no condemnation to people who are in Christ Jesus (Rom. 8:1). Once again, how can you be in Jesus if you were not baptized in his name? Even the 144,000 virgin saints in the book of Revelation will have the Father's name written on their forehead (Rev. 14:1). And what is his name? Jesus! In Rev. 3:12, Jesus says that he will write his God's name upon us. Then he says he will write his new name upon us. God's New Testament name is Jesus, unless you think that he is going to write two different names on you. If you believe that, why didn't he say that he will also write the Holy Ghost's name on you? It is because the Father, Son, and Holy Ghost are under the same name

(1 John 5:6–8). We all will have one name written on our foreheads, the name Jesus (Rev. 22:4). The Bible says in Eph. 3:14–15, "I bow my knees unto the Father of our Lord Jesus Christ, of whom the whole family in heaven and earth is named." John 14:26 tells us that God will send the Holy Ghost in Christ's name, because God, Christ, and the Holy Ghost have the same name. The Father, Word, and Holy Ghost are one (1 John 5:7). The Word was God in the beginning, and the Word became flesh (John 1:1, 14; 1 John 5:6–8; 1 Tim. 3:16).

So, God, the Word who is the Son, and the Holy Ghost are one (1 John 5:7). The word trinity is not in the Bible! Man made it up. The closest thing to trinity in the Bible is in 1 John 5:7, and it says that these three are one. Peter told the ancient Jews that they had crucified both Lord and Christ, both Father and Son (Zech. 12:10; John 19:37; Acts 2:36). The Lord our God is one Lord (Deut. 6:4). The Lord is God, and there is none else (1 Kings 8:60). Jesus said as well, The Lord our God is One Lord (Mark 12:29). And the people said, "Yes, he is one God," and that there is none other but God (Mark 12:32). After doubting the resurrection, Thomas ended up calling Jesus his Lord and his God (John 20:24–29).

WHAT HAPPENS TO INFANTS & PEOPLE WHO CANNOT BE BAPTIZED?

The Bible tells us that some people become so sick that they cannot pray for themselves and that the Spirit of God prays for them (Rom. 8:26–34). This is one way that people who are not baptized in Christ's name can go to heaven, and God will also save some people no matter how they are baptized or not baptized, because he is merciful and gracious (Rom. 8:26–34). But God's ultimate plan is for all people to be baptized in the name of his Son who died in our place (John 3:3–7; Acts 2:36–39; 8:14–17; 10:42–48; 19:1–6; Rom. 8:5–14).

Jesus was baptized by John the Baptist (Matt. 3). Some people believe that Jesus was baptized by John the Baptist for people who cannot get baptized themselves due to illness, incarceration, or isolation from the true Word of God, as in some places, or because they died as an infant. That may or may not be true, but if that is the case, everyone who is free to get baptized must do so. But people who cannot get baptized because it is beyond their control to do so, they can use the scripture that says that they are saved when they believe, confess, and call on the name of Christ (Rom. 10:9–10, 13). And in the case of babies, it does not take spiritual sense to know that babies go to heaven. Common sense tells us that. However, what some people may not understand is that it is not easy for most people to confess Christ during persecutions. Remember the Parable of the Sower that talks about people who accepted Christ speedily, but when persecution and tribulation came because of the Word of God, and the cares of this world and the deceitfulness of riches overtook them, they denied Christ (Matt. 13:1–23; 1 Tim. 6:6–12). Most people will be in position to be baptized, and sick people who are able to be baptized in Christ's name after being baptized in the name of the Father and of the Son and of the Holy Ghost should not refuse to be baptized over again in Christ's name. Why wouldn't a person make sure that they are baptized correctly before they die due to illness? Often in life, when doing something will help but not hurt or hinder, then we should certainly do it (Acts 2:36–39; 8:14–17; 10:42–48; 19:1–6; John 3:3–7).

God will forgive some people even if they are not baptized properly or not baptized at all, because the Lord has mercy on whom he will and he hardens whom he will (Rom. 9:14–21; Prov. 21:1; John 9:39 – 41). When God hardens the heart of some people instead of having mercy on them, that means that they have sinned so wickedly that God is sending them to hell, and that he is not allowing them to turn to him with a mind to live holy. And God knows that most evil-hearted people will not turn to him wholeheartedly anyway. But most of us must be signed, sealed, and about to be delivered. In other words, our names must be signed in the Book of Life, the book must be sealed, and we must be on your way to heaven, daily (John 6:26–27; 1 Cor. 9:2; 2 Cor. 1:21–22; Eph. 1:13; 4:30; 2 Tim. 2:19).

We must be confirmed, preserved, and blameless (1 Cor. 1:8; 1 Thess. 5:23). Your name must not only be on the church roll, but in the Book of Life (Isa. 44:5). If you put money in a savings account, that money is being saved. If you put money on a bench at the bus stop, it will most likely be lost. Someone may give the money back to you because that happens sometimes, but not often. The same applies to people who are not saved by being signed, sealed, and delivered in the Book of Life (Rev.

20:12–15; Heb. 12:23; Mal. 3:16).

The grace of God that brings salvation has appeared to all people (Titus 2:11–15). Do not receive the grace of God in vain, because our God is a consuming fire and a jealous God (2 Cor. 6:1–10; Heb. 12:28–29; Jude 1:4; Deut. 4:24).

Grace, which is undeserving love and blessings, has been benefited by every human being and grace will save some people who did not serve the Lord their whole life, because first shall be last and last shall be first (Matt. 19:29–30; 20:15–16; Luke 2:34; 13:23–30; Ps. 75:6–7).

It is everyone's decision to take advantage of God's grace. Do not think that anyone is saved because God has healed them or delivered them from trouble. Jesus healed people all the time in the Bible, but that did not mean that they were saved. Jesus told them after he healed them, "Sin no more, or a worse thing will happen to you" (John 5:1–14; 8:3–12; Matt. 11:20–24; 12:43–45).

But some people immediately followed Jesus after he healed them (Matt. 20:34; Mark 10:52). We must be strong in the grace of God, not weak, and not use grace as an excuse to sin (2 Tim. 2:1).

WE ARE BORN IN SIN, BUT AREN'T BABIES BORN INNOCENT?

Jesus says he shed his blood for the remission of sins (Matt. 26:28; Acts 2:38). And because Christ died for our sins, we must repent for the remission of sins (Acts 2:36–39; 8:14–17; 10:42–48; 19:1–6; John 3:3–7).

This means that your willful sin, sins from mistakes and errors, sins committed unaware, and the sins that you inherited from Adam are forgiven after you are baptized in the name of Christ. It has been said that we are born into sin. How can this be when we have done no good or bad in the womb, or as newborn babies (Rom. 9:11). The Bible says that God made everyone righteous, but mankind has made so many wicked inventions that influence people to sin (Eccles. 7:26–29; Ps. 33:13–15).

We are born into Adam's sins. If you do not get baptized in the name of Christ, you still have Adam's sins, no matter how you repent for your own sins. By Adam's disobedience, everyone became guilty of sin, because Adam ate of the tree of knowledge causing all of us to know that we did something wrong when we sin, and our knowledge of sin causes us to die like Adam and Eve died. But by the obedience of Jesus, everyone has the chance to live a righteous life and to live forever (Rom. 5:12–21; 1 Cor. 15:20–21). Christ died and rose from the dead for you! When you repent, you repent for your sins, and when you get baptized in the name of Jesus, the Lord washes away the sins of Adam and your own sins. At that point, you are a new creature—you are born again. The old you and Adam's sins are dead, and all things are new (Rom. 6; 1 Pet. 1:23; 1 John 2:29; 5:4, 18). People who commit sin are of the devil, just as Eve obeyed the devil when she convinced Adam to eat of the tree of knowledge (1 John 3:8–10). Sin is of the devil and not of God (1 John 3:8–10; John 8:34–47; 1 Tim. 5:15). They who are born of flesh is flesh, like Adam, and they who are born again of the water and of the Spirit are spirit, like Christ (John 3:1–6; Rom. 8:5–14). Christ died for all people, so they who live should not live unto themselves, but unto Christ who died for them and rose again (1 John 2:2–4; Acts 17:26; Heb. 2:9; Rom. 5:6–9; 8:32; Isa. 53; John 11:47–57; 2 Cor. 5:15; Acts 10).

We must live a holy and sanctified life separated from the things of the world (John 17:14–19; 15:18–19). "An unjust person is an abomination to the righteous, and the righteous is an abomination to the wicked" (Prov. 29:27). True religion is to go unspotted from the world (James 1:26–27; Isa. 1:15 – 20). "Let us cleanse ourselves from all filthiness of the flesh and spirit, perfecting holiness in the fear of God" (2 Cor. 7:1). Without holiness, no human can see God (Heb. 12:14–15; Rom. 12:1–2; 2 Tim. 2:15).

A friend of the world is God's enemy (James 4:4; John 15:18, 19; 1 John 3:13; Rom. 6; 8:1–16; Gal. 5:16–26; 1 Pet. 2:11; 1 Cor. 1:10; 2:9–16; Rom. 15:5–6).

CHILDREN AND BAPTISM

Concerning children, Jesus says that we should not forbid children to be baptized (Matt. 19:13–14). If kids are to be baptized, they must be immersed in water like Jesus and everyone else in the Bible (Acts 2:36–39; 8:14–17; 10:42–48; 19:1–6; John 3:3–7).

Sprinkling and pouring is not a proper baptism, and it was never done in the Bible. Kids must be old enough to understand that they must strive to not commit willful sin anymore (Mic. 2:1; Ps. 19:12–14; Rom. 1:18–32; 2 Thess. 2:10–15).

We are all saved by grace, but Rom. 6:1–6 tells us that grace shall not always continue and that we should remain new creatures after we are baptized into Christ. Parents and pastors often baptize children too young, and they later go out and sin again willfully, and the Bible tells us that there remains no more sacrifice for sin when we sin willfully after learning the truth (Heb. 10:26–29). Jesus says that if a person starts to build a building, they must finish it, or other people will mock and laugh (Luke 14:26–30). The same applies to us when we are baptized. We must finish what we started, in holiness and sanctification. The Bible says that it is best not to get baptized in the first place if we do not plan to live free of habitual and willful sin (Heb. 10:26; 2 Pet. 2:19–22; Rom. 1:18–32; 2 Thess. 2:10–15).

Those same scriptures tell us that when people are baptized and later backslide, they will end up in worse shape than before. The Bible tells us to sin no more or a worse thing will happen to us (John 5:14; 8:3–11; James 5:13–20; 2 Pet. 2:20; Isa. 57:11–12).

So, we need to be careful about baptizing children before they understand what they are doing. It is okay to have them blessed or christened, as Jesus was when he was an infant, but notice that Christ did not get baptized during his christening (Luke 2:25–39). Jesus was not baptized until he was thirty years old (Luke 3:21–23). If a child is christened, it is about equal to being blessed, and the child will still need to be baptized in the future, as Jesus was. If children are truly ready to be baptized, do not forbid them (Matt. 19:14). Not only does this save their souls, but also it prevents them from being natural bastards if they were born out of wedlock, and spiritual bastards if they were born in wedlock to unsaved parents. Even kids who were born in wedlock to unsaved parents are spiritual bastards, until they and/or their parents get baptized properly (1 Cor. 7:14; 2 Cor. 6:14–18; Heb. 12:8).

Before Christ died for our sins, a bastard was not allowed to enter the congregation of the Lord (Deut. 23:2). Kids are often baptized without understanding and without true repentance. They often sin willfully later in life and live in sin for years. Jesus says this is like a dog returning to eat its own vomit (2 Pet. 2:20–22). Kids who do not know the difference between good and evil will go to heaven anyway if they should die (Deut. 1:35–39; Matt. 19:13–14). Even in the Old Testament, only people with understanding were held responsible for what the preacher was saying (Neh. 8:1–3). And all the children and teenagers were allowed to go into the promised land when their parents were not allowed (Num. 32:11–12). There is no such thing as kids needing to be baptized to wash away sins that they inherited from their parents (Exod. 32:30–35; Ezek. 14:12–20; 18:14–32).

Kids should not be baptized to take the place of the circumcision, because circumcision is spiritually no longer needed (Col. 2:11; 1 Cor. 7:19).

CHRIST IS HOLY AND SANCTIFIED LIKE WE SHOULD BE

Christ commands that we live in true holiness and right-eousness "all the days of our life" (Luke 1:74–75; Eph. 4:21–32).

It is written, "Be ye holy, for I am holy" (1 Pet. 1:14–16; 1 Tim. 2:8; Eph. 5:25 – 27; Rev. 20:6).

Righteous God loves righteousness (Ps. 11:7). The Holy Scripture says, "Let no one deceive you, they who live right-eously are righteous, for God is righteous, and they who sin are of the devil" (1 John 3:5–10). God is righteous, and everyone who strives to live right is born again (1 John 2:29; 3:7). God gives the Holy Spirit to people who obey him (Acts 5:32; Luke 11:13; John 1:1, 14; 14:13–18, 26–27; Col. 3:16; 1 John 2:5, 7, 14).

We must get rid of anger, wrath, malice, blasphemy, and filthy words (Col. 3:8). God says, "I the Lord speak righteous-ness, I declare things that are right" (Isa. 45:19; Ps. 19:8). The Bible says that we must be holy in all manner of conversation (1 Pet. 1:15; 1 Cor. 15:33; 2 Pet. 3:10–12; Ps. 19:12–14; Prov. 8:5–8; 1 Cor. 15:33; Eph. 4:21–32; Isa. 33:15–16; Mal. 2:5–6).

PEOPLE WHO DO NOT OBEY THE APOSTLES' DOCTRINE ARE SPIRITUALLY BLIND

The Bible says that if the apostles' doctrine is hidden, it is hidden from people who are lost (2 Cor. 4:3–5). God has hidden this from some wise and prudent people but revealed it to many babes and common people (Matt. 11:25; Luke 19:37–42; 1 Cor. 1:26–32).

If you do not obey God's Word, he will blind you, or allow the devil to blind you, and cause you to not understand it (John 12:40; 2 Cor. 4:4; Eph. 4:18).

Blessed are you whom God has caused to understand (Matt. 13:10–17). The Bible says in all your getting, get understanding (Prov. 4:7; Jer. 9:23–24). May the Lord Jesus Christ continue to bless all people who are not baptized in Christ's name, and who reject the baptism in Christ's name and his solid foundation, strong cornerstone, and pillar (Isa. 28:16; Ps. 118:17–24; Matt. 21:42; Acts 4:10–11; 1 Pet. 2:6–7).

WHY DOES GOD WORK IN THREE REVELATIONS & MANIFESTATIONS OF HIMSELF?

Why did God choose to operate as one Spirit with three different revelations of himself? It is brilliant of Father God to operate this way. God the Son sets examples for us with no excuses. The invisible things of God from the creation of the world are clearly seen, being understood by the things that are made, even his eternal power and "Godhead" so that people are without excuse (Rom. 1:18–32; Col. 2:9; Acts 17:24–31).

God the Son was preordained before the foundation of the world but manifested in these last days for our sake (1 Pet. 1:20). Father God operates as God the Holy Ghost so he can be our Comforter, in the name of Christ, and a protector and strengthener who remains on earth with us to our benefit (John 14:16–26; 15:26–27; 16:7–16; Acts 9:31; Ps. 94:19; 2 Thess. 2:16–17).

The revelation of God the Father, God the Son, and God the Holy Ghost also allows God to be in heaven, on earth, and throughout the entire universe, including all galaxies, planets, stars, and moons at the same time (1 Pet. 3:18–20; 2 Pet. 2:4–9; Ps. 8; Matt. 10:32–33; 12:50; 16:17; 18:10, 14; 23:9).

God the Father sent God the Son in the form of flesh and blood to be an example to us on how to serve only one God who is God Almighty and to serve him without honoring idols because idolaters will not inherit the kingdom of God (Eph. 5:5; 1 Cor. 6:9; Rev. 21:8, 27; 22:14–15; Gal. 5:19–21; 1 Sam. 15:23; Col.3:1–6).

God the Son is also our confirmation, proof, and validation of the resurrection of the dead of not only Christ but of all dead people when Christ returns (Acts 24:15; Dan.12:1–3; Matt. 13:47–50; 25:31–46; John 5:24–29; Rev. 22:10–13; 1 Cor. 15:20–28).

God the Father also reveals himself as God the Son to illustrate to his creation how we should live and how we should honor our parents and to be obedient to godly parents (Eph. 6:1–4; Col. 3:18–20; Exod. 20:12) and how good children can someday inherit the possessions and power of their parents to work hard in life to achieve their goals and to do well with their inheritance (Prov. 13:22; John 16:15; Luke 15:11–32).

God the Son also teaches married couples how to love, honor, support, and respect each other as husband and wife, being one flesh, just as the Father, Son, and Holy Ghost are one Spirit. Christ also illustrates to us how the church, the family, and certain organizations can consist of many members, but we should still operate as one (Rev. 19:7; 21:2, 9; 22:17; 2 Cor. 11:2–3; Eph. 4:4–6; 5:23, 27; Isa. 54:4–10; Jer. 3:6–15, 22; 31:27–37; Hosea 1:2; Ps. 73:27–28).

God the Son is also an example of how to resist temptation, to be humble, to forgive, to be compassionate, how to be tolerant of other people, how to be merciful, to give, to help people, and to love one another, including our enemies. God the Son showed us how to resist temptation when the devil offered Christ fame, riches, power, and earthly kingdoms, but Christ used Bible scriptures to rebuke the devil, and so should we (Luke 4:1–21). The life of God the Son teaches us how to handle adversity, affliction, false accusations, poverty, homelessness, persecution for living godly, to not oppress people, and how to deal with being an oppressed person like Christ was oppressed (2 Cor. 8:9; Phil. 4:19; Lev. 12:6–8; Luke 2:21–24; 9:58; 21:36–37; 22:39–46; Matt. 25:31–46; Isa. 53).

Christ also teaches us how to handle not being physically attractive, and the Bible tells us that Christ was not physically attractive nor was he handsome (Isa. 52:13–15, 53; Heb. 2:16–18; 4:15; 1 Pet. 2:22).

God the Son chose not to visit the earth as a handsome man because people would have favored him for good looks and not because he is the Son of God. And he did not visit the earth as a middle – class person, a rich person, or a powerful politician because people would have favored him for those reasons. Job was more one of the most righteous people to ever live, and he was wealthy, but his example of a sanctified life was not as strong as God visiting the earth as the Son of God; neither was Job's sacrifice nor suffering as great. God the Father knew that people who seek him will respect God the Son, and they live more righteously because of God the Son's examples than the examples of Job and other righteous people in the Bible.

CHRIST & GOD ARE ONE, SO WHAT HAPPENED TO CHRIST'S HUMAN BODY AFTER HE WENT TO HEAVEN?

Another question that some people may ask regarding Father God operating as one Spirit with three different revelations of himself is, "If God and Christ are the same, what happened to the human body of Christ?" When Christ died, rose from the dead, and went back to heaven, the same thing probably happened to his body that happens to our body when we die; it is dissolved, and we become absent from the body but present with God (2 Pet. 1:12–15; 3:10–18; 2 Cor. 5:1–10).

Our "spirit" goes back to God who gave it, just as God the Son's "Spirit" returned to heaven from whence he came (Gen. 2:7; 7:22; Eccles. 12:7; Job 27:1–6; 34:14–15; Dan. 5:23).

The human body of Christ did have a human side, or a human element, and it was characterized when God the Father sometimes refers to Christ as the Son of David and the Son of Man. This is done because Christ was the son of Mary and the adopted son of Joseph and because he was a descendent of

David, according to the flesh, according to his human side. Christ declared to be the Son of God with power, according to the "Spirit" of holiness (Matt. 9:6, 27; 15:22; 16:13; Rom. 1:3–4; Dan. 7:13–15).

There is one mediator between God and mankind, the man Jesus Christ, but the man Jesus Christ operated with the Holy Spirit of the one God Almighty inside of him (1 Tim. 2:5; 1 John 2:1; 5:7; Gen. 17:1).

Another characterization of the human side of Christ happened before he was arrested and on the cross when Christ asked Father God to remove his pain, suffering, and eventual death. At that moment, he suffered from anxiety to the point that sweat fell from his body like drops of blood, but the human side of Christ was obedient to Father God and said to God the Father, "Not my will, but your will be done" (Matt. 26:36–42; Luke 22:39–46).

God the Son would not have been worried about what humans would do to him when they arrested him because he is God. That was the human side of Christ suffering from anxiety. He later said to God the Father while on the cross, "Into your hands, I commit my 'spirit'" (Luke 23:44–46). Then he took his last breath and died. In this instance, "spirit" is spelled with a lowercase "s." When the word "Spirit" is spelled with an uppercase "S," the term always refers to only God the Father, God the Son, and God the Holy Spirit. When spelled with a lowercase "s," the term "spirit" refers to our spirit that is inside of our bodies and to all other spirits. Therefore, the human body of Christ was a vessel and temple for God the Son to dwell in, and when the human body of Christ died, his "sprit" returned to God who gave it. And while the dead human body of Christ was in the grave, the "Spirit" of God the Son visited a God made prison for "spirits" and preached to the "spirits" who disobeyed God when Noah preached to them before God destroyed the earth by water (1 Pet. 3:18–20; 2 Pet. 2:4–9).

Angels who went against God are also in a dark God made prison and in chains made for spirits (Jude 1:5–6; Rev. 9:11;

12:7–12; Luke 10:17–20; Col. 2:18; Rom. 8:38–39; Matt. 9:34; 12:24; 25:41; 1 Pet. 3:18–20; 2 Pet. 2:4).

God hid the dead body of Moses, seemingly because some people would idolize Moses's body just as some people preserve and idolize the bodies of certain other people who lived when the Bible was written. Even though God hid the body of Moses, the "spirit" of Moses appeared to Christ on earth and talked with Christ (Matt. 17:1–13). Also, when the "spirit" of Moses met with Christ, the "spirit" of Elijah was also in the meeting. Elijah's body was taken to heaven by God in a whirlwind hundreds of years before Christ ministered on earth, and Elijah's body was not found either even though a group of fifty men searched for him throughout the mountains for three days (2 Kings 2:1–18). Melchizedek had no mother or father, but he appeared on earth and disappeared from earth according to the will of God, and there was never a baby Melchizedek nor a dead body after his departure (Heb. 7:1–3). But there was a baby Jesus, although there is not a dead body of Jesus after Christ went back to heaven. Christ did not glorify himself to become High Priest, but God said to him, "You are my Son. Today I have begotten you." God also says in another place, "You are a priest forever after the order of Melchizedek," who in the days of Christ's flesh, when he had offered up prayers and supplications with strong crying and tears to God, who was able to save him from death and was heard because of his godly fear, though he was a Son, yet he learned obedience by the things that he suffered. And having been made perfect, he became the author of eternal salvation to all who obey him, called of God a High Priest, "after the order of Melchizedek" (Heb. 5:5–10). God, who at certain times and in different places, spoke in the past to humans by the prophets, but in these last days, God speaks to us by his Son, through whom he made the worlds. Having become so much more than the angels as he has, by inheritance, obtained a more excellent name than them. To which of the angels did God ever say, "You are my Son, today I have begotten you?" (Heb. 1:1–2, 4–13). God did not put the world to come in subjection to angels. But one testified in a certain place, saying, "What is man that God is mindful of him, or the son of man that God visits him? God made him a little lower than the angels. God crowned him with glory and honor and set him over the works of his hands. God has put all things in subjection under his feet." In that, he put all in subjection under him; he left nothing that is not put under him. But now, we see not yet all things under him. But we see Jesus, who was made a little lower than the angels for the suffering of death, crowned with glory and honor, that he, by the grace of God, should taste death for every human (Heb. 2:5–10). It does not matter what happened to the human body of Christ after God the Son went back to heaven to rule the entire universe just as it does not matter what happened to the bodies of Moses, Melchizedek, and Elijah. God uses people as holy vessels and temples that will be dissolved and go back to the dust after death. All that matters is that Christ rose from the dead, and that when we rise from the dead, our soul and "spirit" goes to heaven, where our one God of the Father, Son, and Holy Ghost is on the throne, and these three are one (1 John 5:7–8). The Bible says that Christ returned to heaven and sat on the throne of God and on the right-hand side of God the Father (Rom. 8:34; Col. 3:1–2; Heb. 1:3, 13; 8:1; 10:12; 12:2; 1 Pet. 3:22).

But in the book of Revelation, John saw only One on the throne (Rev. 4:2). John also said that the One who he saw was the Son of God, and that Christ told him, "I am the First and the Last, who was dead but is now alive forevermore. Amen. I have the keys of hell and death (Rev. 1:11–19; 22:13). How can Father God be the first and the last and besides the Father there is no God if Christ is also the first and the last and is called God (Isa. 41:4; 44:6; 48:12; Heb.1:8)? The answer is that they are the same Spirit, and God reveals himself in our day and age as God the Son and as God the Holy Ghost and with the same name (Zech. 14:9; John 5:43; 10:25; 14:26; 1 John 2:23). As stated earlier, all power is in the hands of God the Son who now visits the earth to call people to holiness and to chastise, to destroy, and to punish (1 Cor. 15:24–28; Phil. 2:5–11; Ps. 8; Heb. 2:5–9; 4:12; Matt. 28:18; Rev. 1:16; 2:12–16; 19:15, 21; Eph. 1:20–23; 6:10–20; Col. 2:10; John 16:15).

God the Holy Ghost is with us always, even until the end of the world, and is our Comforter, guidance, power, protection, and strength, in the name of Christ (Matt. 28:19–20). It has been erroneously said that the original apostles baptized people in the name of the Lord Jesus Christ during the first ever baptism to start the first ever church congregation to try to get the ancient Jews to accept Christ (Acts 2:36–47). That is not true. About three thousand people were baptized in Christ's name on that one day, and additional people were baptized daily. Peter told them that the baptism in Christ's name and the gift of the Holy Ghost is for the ancient Jews, their children, and to everyone, even people in faraway nations (Acts 2:36–47; 8:14–17; 10:47–48; 19:1–10; John 3:3–7).

Also, the Apostle Paul baptized Gentiles in the name of the Lord Jesus Christ even though he had never met Peter nor any of Christ's original apostles. Paul did not meet Peter until three years after he started baptizing Gentiles in the name of Christ. Therefore, Paul was not taught by any human to baptize people in Christ's name, but Christ himself taught Paul to baptize people in the name of the Lord Jesus Christ (Gal. 1:11–24; 2:1, 7–10; Acts 19:1–10; John 3:3–7).

Therefore, the baptism in Christ's name was not performed only to convince the ancient Jews to accept Christ. But it may be that Christ revealed himself standing on the right hand of the glory of God to convince certain ancient Jews of Christ's resurrection when Stephen being full of the Holy Ghost saw Jesus the Son of man in the sky (Acts 7:51–60). Obviously, Stephen did not see God because no one has seen God and lived. Secondly, Stephen only saw the glory of God, and he did not see a throne like John saw when John saw One on the throne (Rev. 4:2). Thirdly, Stephen saw a revelation of Christ standing at the right hand of God, which could mean the right hand of power, like in other scriptures that say, "Christ, the power of God, and the wisdom of God," and that Christ sat on the right side of the Majesty, and Majesty means royal power (Heb. 1:1–3; 8:1; 12:2; 1 Cor. 1:22–24; Col. 3:1–2; Eph. 1:19–23; Ps. 8:9).

The Prophet Micah also spoke of God the Son having the power of the majesty of the Lord. Micah said hundreds of years before Christ walked the earth, "But you, Bethlehem, though you are small, yet out of you shall come the one to be ruler in Israel, whose goings forth are from of old, from everlasting. He shall stand and feed his flock in the strength of the Lord, in the majesty of the name of the Lord His God. And they shall abide. For He shall be great to the ends of the earth" (Mic. 5:2–4). God the Son now has all power in his own hand, so there is no need for him to physically or literally sat on the right side of God the Father on the throne. God the Son went to heaven and sat on the right hand of the power of God the Father, meaning omnipotent power being one God, just as John saw God the Son on the throne as one God (Rev. 1:11–19; 4:2). Jesus says, "You will see the Son of man sitting at the right hand of the Power and coming on the clouds of heaven" (Matt. 24:27–44; 26:64). Christ says that if anyone is ashamed to stand for his Word, he will be ashamed of them when Christ, the Son of man, comes in the glory of his Father with the holy angels (Mark 8:38). Therefore, when Stephen saw the Son of man standing on the right hand of the glory of God, he saw Jesus, the Son of man, standing on the right hand of the Power of God and of the glory of God (Matt. 26:64; Mark 8:38; Acts 7:51–60).

"LET US MAKE MAN IN OUR OWN IMAGE," WAS SPOKEN TO WHO?

When God said in Genesis 1:26, "Let us make man in our own image," who was he talking too? Bible scholars from several denominations have opinions. Some people believe that God was talking to himself. Some people believe that God was talking to himself with God the Son in his distant future plans because he knew that he would send Christ as a sacrifice for the people who he created and love. Other people say that he was talking to angels. And some people say that he was speaking directly to his Son, Christ. It is amazing how many Christians from different denominations agree that God was talking to himself or to God the Son as part of the one Godhead (Rom. 1:18–32; Col. 2:9; Acts 17:24–31).

Many of those same people do not baptize in Christ's name, and they try to acknowledge a trinity that they admit is not in the Bible. The answer to the question is that God the Father was talking to God the Son and to himself because they are the same one Spirit and have the same one name in our generations (Zech. 14:9; Eph. 4:4–6; John 5:43; 10:25; 14:26; 1 John 2:23; 5:7–8).

The earth, all other planets, and the entire universe was made by God the Father through Jesus Christ (John 1:10; Heb.

1:2; 11:3; 1 Pet. 1:20).

There is only one God, of whom are all things, and one Lord Jesus Christ, through whom are all things (1 Cor. 8:6). As stated earlier, God the Son was preordained before the foundation of the world but manifested in these last days for our sake (1 Pet. 1:20). God says, "Beside me there is no God and no Savior, and before me there was no God formed, and neither shall there be after me (Isa. 43:10–11; 44:6; Deut. 6:4; James 2:19; Jude 1:25; Mark 12:29; John 10:30).

Christ also says that he is the beginning and the ending, the first and the last (Rev. 1:8, 11; 21:6; 22:13). Therefore, God and Christ are obviously one. Christ is the mediator between Father God and humans (1 Tim. 2:5). The Bible says that a mediator cannot be a mediator of one, but that God is still one (Gal. 3:20; 1 Cor. 8:6; Acts 4:12). To clarify, it is impossible for a mediator to be the middle – person between God and humans because the mediator is God himself. God the Son and God the Holy Ghost are revelations of God the Father, but the same one Spirit and the same one name (Eph. 4:4–6; Zech. 14:9; John 5:43; 10:25; 14:26; 1 John 2:23; 5:7–8).

David said by the Holy Ghost, "My Lord said to my Lord, 'Sit on my right side until I make your enemies my foot-stool'" (Mark 12:36; Acts 2:34–35). Again, God the Father was speaking to God the Son, or to himself, which is the same. And just as the capitalized word "Spirit" refers to only God the Father, God the Son, and God the Holy Spirit, the capitalized word "Lord" also refers only to God. Every knee shall bow, and every tongue shall confess that Jesus Christ is Lord, to the glory of God the Father (Phil. 2:5–11). At another time, when God talked to Christ, Father God told Christ that the Son is God (Heb. 1:8). God told Christ, "Your throne, O God, is forever and ever" (Heb.1:8). Once again, God is talking to himself as God and to God the Son as the same one God (Gen. 1:26; John 1:10; Heb. 1:2; 11:3). And when Christ says that people who over-come shall sit with him on his throne just as he sat with his Father on the Father's throne, that scripture mirrors and reflects another scripture that says, "No one comes to God the Father without going through God the Son" (Rev. 3:21; John 14:6). How can we sit on a separate throne with the Son of God after God the Son delivers the kingdom of heaven into the hands of God the Father and after all power goes back from God the Son to God the Father when the earth is destroyed? In other words, even if the Father and the Son were two different Spirits, Christ would not be on a throne in heaven because all power goes back into the hands of the God the Father when the earth is destroyed. All things including God the Son will be subject to God the Father, and the Father will be all in all, (1 Cor. 15:24–28). There is one body and one Spirit, one Lord, one faith, one baptism, one God and Father of all, who is above all and through all and in you all (Eph. 4:4–6).

God the Father gave God the Son a name above every name, and that is because they have the same name, which is Jesus Christ (Zech. 14:9; Phil. 2:5–11; John 5:43; 10:25; 14:26; 1 John 2:23; 5:7–8).

It is impossible for God the Son to have a name that is above God the Father. The prophet Zechariah prophesized of the coming of Christ when he said, "The Lord shall be King over all the earth. In that day it shall be—the Lord is one, and his name one" (Zech. 12:10; 14:9; John 19:31–37; Rev. 1:4–8).

God the Son now has all power and authority, and that does not mean that God the Father is weak, sick, dead, lazy, or have taken a back seat to what goes on in heaven, earth, hell, and the entire universe, but it is impossible for Christ to have all power, and Father God still be omnipotent, omnipresent, and omniscient without them being the same one Spirit (Col. 2:10; 1 Cor. 15:24–28; Phil. 2:5–11; Eph. 1:20–23; 4:4–6; 6:10–20; Matt. 28:18; Heb. 2:5–9; 4:12; Rev. 1:16; 2:12–16; 19:15, 21).

God Almighty is mysterious, and he would not be Almighty God if he was not mysterious. The Bible says, "Without controversy, great is the mystery of godliness." The Bible says that God's ways are past finding out, and that his ways and thoughts are much higher than ours (Rom. 11:33; Isa. 55:8).

God was manifest in the flesh, justified in the Spirit, seen of angels, preached to the Gentiles, believed on in the world, and received up into glory (1 Tim. 3:16). The Apostle Paul also wrote, "To him who is of power to establish you according to my gospel, and the preaching of Jesus Christ, according to the revelation of the mystery, which was kept secret since the world began, but now made manifest, according to the commandment of the everlasting God, made known to all nations for obedience of the faith—to the only wise God be glory through Jesus Christ forever. Amen" (Rom. 16:25–27). God is mysterious in many ways, but it is safe to say that the revelation of the Father, Son, and Holy Ghost was one of the mysteries kept secret since the world began because although the worlds were made through God the Son, God the Son was not manifested for thousands of years (1 Pet. 1:20; John 1:10; Heb. 1:2; 11:3; Col. 1:15).

But the first and second coming of God the Son was and is prophesized (Isa. 7:14; 9:6–7; 52:13–5, 53; Dan. 7:9, 13, 22; 9:24–27; 12:1–4; Gen. 49:9–10; Num. 24:17; Zech. 14:9; 1 Thess. 4:13–18; 1 Cor. 15:50–58).

The Apostle Peter said that some of the Apostle Paul's writings are hard to be understood, but that they are valid and righteous, that Christ shall return for people who are without spot and blameless, and that some people struggle with the apostles' doctrine to their own destruction (2 Pet. 3:14–16). God the Father made the world and all planets by God the Son (John 1:10; Heb. 1:2, 8–13; 11:3; 1 Pet. 1:20).

The Son is the image of the invisible God, the firstborn over all creation (Col. 1:15). Paul also said, "We speak the wisdom of God in a mystery, even the hidden wisdom, which God ordained before the world unto our glory, which none of the princes of this world knew. If they had known it, they would not have crucified the Lord of glory. But God has revealed them to us through his Spirit. For the Spirit searches all things, yes, the deep things of God. These things we also speak, not in words, which man's wisdom teaches, but which the Holy Spirit teaches, comparing spiritual things with spiritual. But the natural person does not receive the things of the Spirit of God because they are foolishness to them, nor can they know them, because spiritual things are spiritually discerned. Who has known the mind of the Lord that they may instruct him? But we have the mind of Christ (1 Cor. 1:22–24; 2:6–10; Luke 23:34).

The Apostle Paul wrote, "I was made a minister, according to the gift of the grace of God given to me by the effectual working of his power. That I should preach to the Gentiles the unsearchable riches of Christ, and to make all people see what is the fellowship of the mystery which from the beginning of the world has been hid in God, who created all things by Jesus Christ, to the intent that now the principalities and powers in heavenly places might be known by the church the manifold wisdom of God, according to the eternal purpose which he purposed in Christ Jesus our Lord" (Eph. 3:7–12). Furthermore, the Apostle Paul wrote, "I became a minister according to the stewardship from God, which was given to me for you, to fulfill the Word of God, the mystery which has been hidden from ages and from generations, but now has been revealed to his saints" (Col. 1:25–26). Paul also said that we wanted people to have a full assurance of understanding, to the knowledge of the mystery of God, both of the Father, and of Christ, in whom are hidden all the treasures of wisdom and knowledge (Col. 2:2–3).

WHAT IS THE NAME OF THE FATHER, SON, AND HOLY SPIRIT?

God went by a few names in the Old Testament, including God Almighty and Almighty God (Gen. 17:1; 35:11). The name God Almighty is not used in the New Testament of the Authorized King James Version of the Bible other than in the book of Revelation (Rev. 1:8; 4:8; 11:17; 15:3; 16:7, 14; 19:15; 21:22).

Therefore, the name God Almighty was used first in the book of Genesis, which is the first book of the Bible, and the book of Revelation, which is the last book of the Bible. The closest reference to the name God Almighty outside of the book of Revelation in the New Testament is one time when the Apostle Paul quoted God's words and referred to him as Lord Almighty (2 Cor. 6:17–18). Maybe Christ and the apostles never used the name God Almighty in the gospels because they knew that ministers would baptize people in the name of God Almighty instead of in the name of the Lord Jesus Christ (Acts 2:36–42; 8:14–17; 10:47–48; 19:2–5; John 3:3–7).

Jehovah is another name of God from the Old Testament and is written in only a few scriptures (Exod. 6:3; Ps. 83:18; Isa. 12:2; 26:4). Some versions of the Bible use the term Lord instead of Jehovah. The term Yahweh is used instead of Jehovah in some versions of the Bible and is often used in the Hebrew Bible. Hebrew letters have only consonants but no vowels, and over time, vowels were inserted to create the words Yahweh and Jehovah from JHVH and JHWH, thus also replacing the letter "Y" with "J" and creating the word Yahweh from YHWH and YHVH. Jehovah-jireh, Jehovah-nissi, Jehovah-shalom, and Jehovah-shammah are not names of God (Gen. 22:14; Exod. 17:11, 15; Judg. 6:24; Ezek. 48:35).

It should be noted that God's original chosen people the ancient Hebrews and ancient Israelites were blinded from the Christian Faith in part so God can call the entire world to repentance (Rom. 11:25–36; Isa. 55:8). If God had allowed ancient Hebrews, ancient Israelites, and ancient Jews to accept Christ, they would have stood against allowing other people to become Christians. Because for thousands of years, God taught ancient Hebrews, ancient Jews, and ancient Israelites to be separate from the rest of the world (Acts 10). There are other names of God in the Hebrew Bible, but God does not go by any of those names anymore. In our generations, God goes by the name Jesus Christ (John 5:43; 10:25, 30; 14:26; 1 John 2:23; 5:7–8).

Even in the Old Testament and in the Hebrew Bible, it was prophesized that "the Lord shall be King over all the earth. In that day it shall be—the Lord is one, and his name one." And that God shall be pierced while hanging on the cross (Zech. 12:10; 14:9; John 19:31–37).

Those prophesies were fulfilled when God the Son was pierced on the cross as King of the entire universe, (John 16:15; 19:28–37; Rev. 1:4–8; Col. 2:10; 1 Cor. 15:24–28; Phil. 2:5–11; Eph. 1:20–23; 4:4–6; Matt. 28:18; Heb. 2:5–9).

The name Immanuel had several purposes. One purpose was to indicate to the world that God is with us, just as Christ says that he is with us always, even to the end of the world (Isa. 7:14; 8:8; Matt. 1:18–25; 28:19–20). Also, the name Immanuel was given to conceal Jesus from people who would crown him too soon and from others who would crucify him too soon (John 7:1–9; Matt. 8:4; 16:20; 17:9; Mark 7:36; 8:30; Luke 8:56).

Also, to prevent the baby Jesus from being killed by an evil king who killed all the male children two years of age and younger to try to prevent the child Jesus from growing up

(Matt. 2:13–16; Rev. 12:1–8; Exod. 1:15–22; 2:1–10).

An angel told Joseph that the child's name is Immanuel to fulfill prophesy, but that same angel told Joseph to name the child Jesus, which was a popular name in those days, and it prevented the world from knowing that the child was really Immanuel (Matt. 1:18–25). There was a disciple of the Apostle Paul who was named Jesus, but they called in Justus instead of Jesus in honor of the Lord (Col. 4:11). Therefore, we baptize in the name of the Lord Jesus Christ because he is Lord of all (Dan. 9:25–26; John 1:41; 4:25).

Another name that God went by in the Old Testament was "I Am" (Exod. 3:13–15). Christ also says that he himself is "I Am" (John 8:58). That is because they are the same Spirit with the same name in the New Testament and throughout all generations after the New Testament was written. Father God, and God the Son is "I Am" because he is omnipotent, omniscient, omnipresent, one God, one Spirit, with one name (Eph. 4:4–6). When Moses asked God what his name is, God told Moses, "I Am That I Am." God went on to say that this is his name forever, and this is my memorial unto all generations (Exod. 3:13–15). Generations after God the Father said that God the Son is now "I Am." God the Son says, "I am with you always, even to the end of the world" (Matt. 28:20). "I am he, the Messiah, the Christ" (John 4:19–26). "I am the bread of life" (John 6:35, 48). "I am the bread which came down from heaven" (John 6:41). "I am the living bread" (John 6:51). "I am the light of the world" (John 8:12). "I am from above" (John 8:23). "I am not of this world" (John 8:23). "Before Abraham was, I Am" (John 8:58). "I am the door" (John 10:9). "I am the resurrection" (John 11:25). "I am the way" (John 14:6). "I am the truth" (John 14:6). "I am the life" (John 14:6; 11:25). "I am the true vine" (John 15:1). "I am Alpha and Omega" (Rev. 1:8). "I am he who lives" (Rev. 1:18). "I am alive forevermore" (Rev. 1:18). Father God says, "I am the Lord who heals" (Exod. 15:26). "I, even I, am he, and there is no God with me. I kill and make alive. I wound and I heal. Neither is there any who can deliver out of my hand" (Deut. 32:39). "I, the Lord, the first, and with the last, I am he" (Isa. 41:4). "I am he. Before me there was no God formed, neither shall there be after me" (Isa. 43:10). "I, even I, am the Lord, and beside me there is no savior" (Isa. 43:11). "Before the day was, I am he. And there is none who can deliver out of my hand" (Isa. 43:13). "I am the Lord, and there is no one else. There is no God beside me" (Isa. 45:5). "That they may know from the rising of the sun, and from the west, that there is none beside me. I am the Lord, and there is no one else. I form the light and create darkness. I make peace and create evil. I the Lord do all these things" (Isa. 45:6–7). "Even to your old age, I am he. I will carry you. I have made, and I will bear. Even I will carry and will deliver you" (Isa. 46:3–4). "Remember the former things of old, for I am God, and there is none else. I am God, and there is none like me" (Isa. 46:8–9). "I am for you, and I will turn to you" (Ezek. 36:9). I am the Lord who makes all things (Isa. 44:24). As you can see, the Father, Son, and Holy Spirit have the same name in our generations and have always been the same one Spirit. The rejection of the baptism in the name of the Lord Jesus Christ is deception by the devil who Christ says deceives the whole world because he knows that his time is short (Rev. 12:7–12; Luke 10:18).

Nowadays, Father God comes to us in the name of Jesus Christ (John 5:43; 10:25; 14:26; 1 John 2:23). And God the Holy Ghost, also called the Holy Spirit, always dwells on the earth, and he dwells inside the body of people who obey the Lord (Matt. 28:19–20; Acts 5:32; John 14:13–18, 26–27; Col. 3:16).

Our bodies are temples made for God to dwell in (1 Cor. 3:16–23; 6:9–20). When we are baptized in Christ's name, we become members of the household of God, built on the foundation of the apostles and the prophets, Jesus Christ himself being the chief cornerstone, and the stone that most people reject (Eph. 2:19–22; Ps. 118:22; Matt. 21:42; 1 Pet. 2:7; Acts 4:11–12).

There is one body and one Spirit, one hope, one Lord, one faith, one baptism, one God and Father of all, who is above all, and through all, and in you all who are filled with the Holy Ghost (Eph. 4:4–6). The Father, Son, and Holy Ghost is the great "I Am" because he is all in all, and there is no one else (Isa. 45:5–7; 46:8–9). There is only one God, of whom are all things, and one Lord Jesus Christ, through whom are all things (1 Cor. 8:6; 15:24–28). God said, "Let us make man in our own image, according to our likeness" (Gen. 1:26). But God also says, "Thus says the Lord, your Redeemer, and he who formed you in the womb. I am the Lord, who makes all things, who stretches out the heavens all alone, who spreads abroad the earth by myself" (Isa. 44:24).

CONFESSING WITH YOUR MOUTH, BELIEVING IN YOUR HEART, AND CALLING ON THE NAME OF THE LORD

BELIEVING AND CONFESSING, AND ACCEPTING THE LORD'S SUPPER UNWORTHILY

If all a person must do to be saved is believe, confess, and call on the name of the Lord, why does the Bible say that people become sick and sometimes die when they accept the Lord's Supper while living in sin (1 Cor. 11:23–30)?

WE MUST LIVE HOLY IN THIS PRESENT WORLD

We must also live godly and righteously in this present world (Titus 2:11–12). Remember, the Lord's Prayer says regarding God about us, "Your will be done on earth as it is in heaven" (Matt. 6:10). We must offer the sacrifices of righteousness and put our trust in the Lord while also offering the sacrifices of praise, and to give thanks unto the Lord (Ps. 4:5; Heb. 13:15).

BROKEN PROMISES TO GOD MAKE LIFE WORSE THAN BEFORE

God says it is better to not make promises unto him at all than to make promises and break them, because that could cause more problems in your life, even death (Eccles. 5:2–6; Deut. 23:21–23; Prov. 20:24–25; Jer. 42:1–6, 21–22; 2 Pet. 2:20).

If all we must do to be saved is confess, believe, and call on the Lord, why does the Lord say that we risk dying and going to hell if we do not keep our promises made unto him? "Whatsoever you do, do it wholeheartedly as unto the Lord, and not unto mankind or idols" (Col. 3:17, 23). We must seek glory from God alone, and glory from mankind will eventually come, if it is God's will (John 5:41, 44; 7:18; 12:42–43; 2 Cor. 3:1–4; 1 Thess. 2:4–6).

We must not live by bread or earthly desires and possessions alone, but by every Word of God (Deut. 8:2–3; Luke 4:1–4; John 6:27).

We are not to obey God's Word with partiality (1 Tim. 5:20–21). Jesus says that anyone who obeys his Word shall never die (John 8:51).

We must be doers of the Word and not hearers only (James 1:22–27; Matt. 13:1–23; Acts 17:11–12; Ps. 81:10–16; Jer. 15:15–21; Rev. 10:9–11).

LIVING IN THE FLESH IS WAR AGAINST THE BODY & SOUL

We reap what we sow, in every aspect of life, good or bad (Rom. 2:4–11; Gal. 6:7–10). When we sow to the flesh, we reap trouble to the flesh, but people who sow to the Spirit shall reap everlasting life in heaven (Gal. 6:7–8, 14). Therefore, we must worship God in spirit and in truth and not in the flesh or as a lover of the world (John 4:23–24; Zech. 8:1–8). People who live in the flesh cannot please God (Rom. 8:8). The Spirit is against the flesh and the flesh is against the Spirit (Gal. 5:16–26; 1 Pet. 2:11–12). Flesh and blood cannot inherit the kingdom of heaven, but walking in and living in the Spirit while you are alive allows you to go to heaven (1 Cor. 15:42–52; Gal. 5:16, 24–25; 1 Thess. 4:14–17; John 3:3–7).

When people fail to please God who is in heaven and are lovers of this current world, they are enemies of God (James 4:2–4; John 1:10–12; 15:18–19; 1 John 2:15–17; 3:13).

True religion is to go unspotted from the world (James 1:26–27; Isa. 1:15 – 20). When you become filled with the Holy Spirit inside of your body, greater is Christ in you than they who are in the world (John 16:33; 1 John 4:4). The fruit of the Spirit is goodness, truth, and righteousness and it is a shame to even speak of in a glorifying manner the fleshly sin that sinners do (Eph. 5:9–12). If a sinner does not repent, there shall be no reward for them, and their candle shall be put out (Prov. 24:20). Because to be worldly minded is death, but to be spiritually minded is life and peace, and if anyone does not have the Spirit of God, they do not belong to God (Rom. 8:5–10). We must abstain from fleshly lust that war against the soul (1 Pet. 2:11). "The human spirit is willing, but the flesh is weak" (Matt. 26:41). But if you allow Christ to do so, he will strengthen and settle you (1 Pet. 5:6–11; Ps. 3:5; 55:22).

SOME PEOPLE BELIEVE & CONFESS BUT ARE FULL OF THE DEVIL

There was a female in the Bible who was a worker of witchcraft, voodoo, sorcery, and black magic and she made plenty of money for people. She confessed with her mouth the Lord Jesus Christ and believed in her heart that God raised Christ from the dead, but she was possessed with a demon, so not everyone who confesses Christ is of Christ, but a lot of people are of the devil (Acts 16:16–24). People who sin are of the devil because sin is not of God, but of the devil (1 John 3:5–10; Prov. 11:31; 1 Pet. 4:18).

Not everyone who sins is possessed with a demon or the devil, but some people are possessed and do not know it" (Matt. 12:43–45; 2 Pet. 2:19). When you acknowledge the true Word of God, it is good if you can profess it while living a godly life. To confess is to simply speak, but to profess means to do, like when a person has a profession that earns them a paycheck (Titus 1:1). We should be doers of the Word of God (James 1:22–27; Matt. 13:1–23; Acts 17:11–12; Ps. 81:10–16; Jer. 15:15–21; Rev. 10:9–11).

John 3:15–21 says that God gave his only begotten Son, that whosoever believes in him should not perish, but have eternal life, and that Christ did not come to condemn the world, but to save it, and that they who do not believe are condemned. But the Bible also says that Christ is the light of the world (John 1:1–14; 8:12). And that people love darkness rather than light, and their love of darkness and sin shall condemn them (John 3:15–21). If you say you fear God and that you obey his voice, but you still walk in darkness, then you must reevaluate yourself (Isa. 50:10; 2 Kings 17:20–41). People who confess Christ must also keep his commandments (Dan. 9:4). Bible scripture says, "Let my heart be blameless regarding your Word, so I will not be ashamed" (Ps. 119:80).

CONFESSING CHRIST WHILE BEING AN OPPRESSOR & HIGH-MINDED

We cannot be right with God in our heart if our hearts are not right toward all people, all races, all socioeconomic statuses, all social classes, and with pets and animals (1 John 2:9–11; 3:13–15; 4:20; Prov. 12:10).

FEARING GOD CAUSES FORGIVENESS

God has mercy on us all, but he has more mercy on people who fear him (Luke 1:50). The Lord is near people who call upon him in truth and who fear and love him (Ps. 66:16–20; 115:11; 130:3–4; 145:17–21).

God's forgiveness toward us is meant to cause us to love and fear him, not simply believe, confess, and call upon him as a weak Christian or a hypocrite (Ps. 66:16–20; 130:3–4; 145:17–21). Blessed is everyone who fears the Lord. Their spouses and children shall be beneficial to them (Ps. 128). They who fear the Lord must also trust in the Lord, and he will bless those who fear him, both small and great, and their children (Ps. 115:11–18). The mercy of the Lord is forever on people who fear him, and on their grandchildren, when God's Word is obeyed (Ps. 103:13, 17–18). As a parent has pity on their children, the Lord has pity on people who fear him (Ps. 103:13). God says in the Old Testament that he has mercy on people who love him and keep his commandments (Exod. 20:6). And Christ says in the New Testament that we are his friends only if we do whatever he commands us to do (John 14:15; 15:14–15). We must live in the fear of God and in the comfort of the Holy Ghost (Acts 9:31). The Bible says that we begin to be wise when we learn to fear God (Ps. 111:10). The Bible also teaches us to ask God to establish his Word in us as servants and that we must be devoted to fearing God (Ps. 119:33–38). We must be servants of the Lord and not simply beneficiaries. We must be God's servants because he is not our servant. Therefore, if all we must do to be saved is believe in our heart that God raised Christ from the dead and confess that truth with our mouth, then why does the Bible also say that we must both love and fear the Lord (Luke 1:50; Deut. 5:10; 7:9; 13:4; Heb. 12:26–29; Ps. 66:16–20; 130:3–4; 145:17–21; Prov.16:6; Lev. 26:3–6; Dan. 9:3–19)?

Solomon prayed to the Lord and said, When the heavens are shut up and there is no rain because the people have sinned, when they pray and confess your name, and turn from their sin because you afflict them, then hear in heaven, and forgive the sin of your people, that you may teach them the good way in which they should walk, and send rain on your land which you have given to your people. When there is famine, disease, loss of crops, enemies, and sickness, and they pray with their hands speeded towards you, hear, answer, and forgive them according to their ways and according to their heart, that they may fear you all the days that they live. (1 Kings 8:33–40) God answers our prayers according to the idols in our heart, and idolatry is forbidden by God (Ezek. 14:1–11; 23:49; 1 Cor. 10:14; Gal. 5:19–26; Col. 3:5; 1 Sam. 15:23).

God takes pleasure in people who fear him and hope in his mercy (Ps. 119:132; 147:10–11). Therefore, although we must be wise enough to fear God, we all need mercy sometimes, and that is why David loved the Lord and expressed it repeatedly when he wrote the book of Psalms, but scripture also says that David feared the Lord (1 Chron. 21:27–30). In every nation, people who fear God and work righteousness are accepted by God (Acts 10:35). God is good and does good, and we should ask him to teach us his ways (Ps. 119:64–72). David asked the Lord, "Teach me your ways, so I will talk of your wondrous works. Remember, O Lord, your tender mercies, and your lovingkindness. For they have been from long ago" (Ps. 25:4–10; 119:12, 26, 33, 64, 66, 108, 124).

To people who obey God, they shall receive eternal life, glory, honor, and peace and there is no respect of persons with God, because we reap what we sow (Rom. 2:4–11; Gal. 6:7–10). When we tell people too often that God is good and that he forgives us, that does not cause most people to live right (Rom. 2:4–6; Isa. 57:10–11). Certain people in the Old Testament did not serve God wholeheartedly after he warned, punished, and destroyed millions of them (Isa. 1:5–9; 2 Kings 17; Hag. 2:17). And even though the pharaoh sinned more after he experienced God's punishment in the days of Moses, God still had the last word (Exod. 9:33–35). We must tell people how good, gracious, merciful, and long-suffering God is and warn them about his wrath and displeasure with our sinful ways. People do not have a problem believing that God forgives us, because if Christ had not died for our sins, we would have been dead a long time ago. Maybe people tell other people about the goodness of God more than they tell them about the wrath or displeasure of God because sometimes it seems as though God is not near while they are suffering or feeling alone. But God is always in control, and not even a single bird falls from the sky without God doing it or allowing it (Matt. 10:28–31; Luke 12:6–7). God hears our cry and is long-suffering while he waits for us to finally repent, so we must be long-suffering and faithful toward him while we wait on him (Luke 18:7–8; Isa. 42:14). Love suffers long (1 Cor. 13:4). None of us suffers longer than Christ. When Christ suffered, he committed himself to God, and so should we (1 Pet. 2:19–25). By God's mercy and truth, our sins are forgiven, but we must depart from sin because we also fear God (Prov. 16:6). When God holds his peace through grace and punishes us lightly, that does not cause some people to fear him (Rom. 2:4–6; Isa. 57:10–11). Most people want to hear that God is good and that he does not punish us. However, God himself says that his goodness toward us does not cause us to fear or obey him, but that it should (Isa. 57:11–13; Hosea 3:5). God says he will forgive our sins and cleanse us of our sinful acts if we allow him to do so, and when people hear the good that God does toward us, they shall fear God for his goodness and the prosperity that he provides (Jer. 33:8–9). God is good, but that same good God will send many people to hell. God is good, but how good are you to God? On judgment day, God will say to you, "Well done, my good and faithful servant" (Matt. 25:23). And you shall receive a crown of life because those of us who are with Christ even in hard times are called, chosen, and faithful (Rev. 2:10; 17:14). On the other hand, God will say to people who call on the Lord and who confess his name but still live in sin and iniquity, "Depart from me, you worker of iniquity" (Luke 13:22–30; Matt. 7:21–23). We must love, trust, and fear God and not just simply love him for his goodness (Heb. 12:26–29; Isa. 66:1–2; Deut. 5:29; Exod. 20:20; Ps. 115:11; Prov. 22:4; 23:17; Mal. 2:5–6).

FAITH WITHOUT WORKS IS DEAD & BELIEVING WITHOUT OBEYING IS DEAD

To believe is to accept as true, to commit, and to have faith (John 20:30–31). For yet a little while, Christ who shall come will come and not wait any longer (Heb. 6:1–6; 10:35–39; 11:1, 6; Luke 18:1–8).

To believe is to have faith, and to have faith is to believe. But faith and belief without works is dead and meaningless, and faith without good works cannot save you (James 2:13–26). The just shall live by faith, and it is impossible to please God without faith (Rom. 1:16–18; Hab. 2:4; Gal. 3:11), for we walk by faith, not by sight (2 Cor. 5:7). If anyone draws back or backslides, God has no pleasure in them (Heb. 10:38; Rom. 1:16–18; Hab. 2:4; Gal. 3:11).

Therefore, let us draw near Christ with a true heart. Let us hold fast the profession of our faith without wavering, having been washed with pure water in baptism, for Christ is faithful who promised us all things, even eternal life. Let us love one another and do good works toward all people, not forgetting to assemble and to warn one another even more as judgment day, our dying day, and as our birthdays approach (Heb. 10:22–25).

BEING TOO STUBBORN OR TOO SICK TO CALL ON THE LORD

It is best to live right and call on the name of the Lord daily with a pure heart while following righteousness, faith, love, and peace, fleeing youthful lusts (2 Tim. 2:22; Job 27:8–23; Prov. 3:5–8).

After we believe in our heart and confess with our mouth, a sinful heart must depart from us (Ps. 101:3–4). Some people cannot call on Christ because they are presently doing something sinful. And some people did not have time to call on the Lord before death because they died suddenly. And yet others are too hard-hearted and stubborn to call on the Lord while they are on their deathbed. But for people in trouble who call on the Lord, God is merciful and gracious to save their soul and their body, and if they should still die, they could go to heaven, which is the ultimate goal (Rom. 8:26–34).

Calling on Christ can indeed save you, but unless we are too ill, mentally, or physically, to serve the Lord, simply calling on Christ may not save us. And people who are too sick to call on the Lord for themselves, if they were already a saved saint of God, the Holy Ghost prays for them with heavenly groanings that we do not understand on earth. God who searches the heart knows what the mind of the Holy Spirit is because the

Holy Spirit makes intercessions for the saints according to the will of God. All things work together for the good of people who love God and are called according to his purpose, and God justifies and glorifies them as saints (Rom. 8:26–30). Therefore, those wonderful scriptures do not pertain to just any person who called on the name of the Lord before they became sick. Also, God hardens whom he will and has mercy on whom he will, so some terminally ill people will receive mercy, while others will not repent because God hardens their heart, mainly because he knows that they will not repent anyway, or that God has already made up his mind to send them to hell (Rom. 9:11, 14–21; Exod. 9:12–18; 10:27; 14:8; 33:19; Ps. 105:24–45; Prov. 21:1; Isa. 24:1–3; 63:16–19; Josh. 11:16–20; Matt. 20:1–16; Zech. 10:6; Gen. 19:12–25; John 9:39 – 41).

GRACE DOES NOT MEAN THAT WE SHOULD BE A SLAVE TO SIN

The Bible says, "Shall we sin willfully because we are under grace? God forbids" (Rom. 6:1–3). We are justified by Christ, but Christ is not the minister of sin (Gal. 2:17). God asks, what sin have people found in him that causes them to sin (Jer. 2:5)? "Know ye not that you are slaves to whomever you obey, whether of sin unto death, or of obedience unto righteousness? God be thanked, that you were the servants and slaves of sin, but you have obeyed from the heart the truth that has been delivered unto you" (Rom. 6:15–17; 1 John 5:14–17; Rev. 3:15–19; Matt. 12:33; Ps. 66:16–20).

The key words are "heart" and "obeyed." If you build again the sin that you turned away from, you make yourself a sinner again (Gal. 2:16–18). If you live in darkness after confessing Christ, you lie to yourself and do not practice the truth (1 John 1:6). If we say we know Christ and do not obey his Word, we are liars. People who say they abide in the Lord ought to live as Christ lived (1 John 2:4). Do not receive the grace of God in vain, nor take grace for granted (2 Cor. 6:1–10). The Bible tells us to be strong in the grace that is in Christ Jesus and not to be weak in Christ's grace (2 Tim. 2:1). Grace does not allow us to sin (Jude 1:4). God says, "Let us have grace," but we must still serve God acceptably with reverence and godly fear, because our God is a consuming fire and a jealous God (Heb. 12:28–29; Deut. 4:24). No one can see God without holiness, and we can fail the grace of God (Heb. 12:14–15; Rom. 12:1–2; 2 Tim. 2:15).

OBEDIENCE IS BETTER THAN SACRIFICE

Obedience is better than sacrifice, unless we offer the sacrifice of righteousness and put our trust in the Lord (1 Sam. 15:22; Rom. 12:1 – 2; Matt. 9:10 – 13; 23:23; Prov. 21:3; Ps. 4:5; 40:6 – 8: Hos. 6:6; Mic. 6:7; Heb. 13:15).

To make sacrifices such as giving to the church and to the poor, for example, but continuing to live in sin, those kinds of sacrifices are not better than obedience to the Lord. Jesus was obedient and a sacrifice as well, including not only when he suffered and died but also when he left his riches in heaven to live in poverty on earth for our sake (2 Cor. 8:9; Phil. 4:19; Lev. 12:6–8; Luke 2:21–24; Rom. 15:1–3).

SATAN BELIEVES AND CONFESSES BUT SATAN ALSO FEARS GOD

Some people say that all you must do to be saved is to confess and believe. Satan confesses and believes that Jesus is the Son of God, but Satan trembles at the name of Jesus, and so should we (James 2:18–20; Mark 1:23–24; 3:11–12; Luke 10:17).

Satan is more powerful than most humans, who should also fear God (Eph. 6:11–17; Isa. 66:1–2). After hearing the Apostle Paul, Felix trembled, but he told Paul that he would talk to him later (Acts 24:25–26). When you believe, you must also speak the truth (2 Cor. 4:13).

THE DEVIL IS THE FATHER OF HABITUAL, REBELLIOUS AND WILLFUL SINNERS

Although Jesus was accused of having a demon, he was never possessed with a demon (John 8:48–49; 14:30). But Satan did try to tempt Christ, to no avail (Luke 4:1–13). Jesus says that he did nothing of himself, but he did only what he saw his Father do (John 5:19). Christ says that he speaks that which he has seen in his Father, and sinners and hypocrite Christians do those things that they have seen in their father, the devil, and the lusts of the devil they will do, because they are of the devil and are not of God (John 8:34–47; 1 Tim. 5:15; 1 John 3:5–10; Prov. 11:31; 1 Pet. 4:18).

GOD TESTS THE HEART, SO BE CAREFUL HOW YOU CLAIM TO HAVE A GOOD HEART

If living a righteous life is not important, why did God say that people who influenced many others to live right shall shine like stars when they get to heaven (Dan. 12:1–4; Prov. 11:30)?

God says in the Old and New Testaments that he tries the heart (Jer. 11:20; 1 Thess. 2:4). Because the heart can be deceitful above all things and desperately wicked, therefore the Lord searches our heart (Jer. 17:9–11). God knows the secrets of the heart (Ps. 44:20–21; 2 Chron. 6:30).

God knows the imaginations and thoughts of the heart. God will bring to light the counsels of the heart when he comes (1 Chron. 28:9; 1 Cor. 4:5), because most people's ways are right in their own eyes, but God examines the heart (Prov. 21:2). The Hebrews while leaving slavery in Egypt returned to Egypt in their hearts (Acts 7:38–39). The Lord says that he searches the heart and inner body, and he gives unto everyone according to their works (Rev. 2:21–26; Jer. 17:9–11; 21:14; 32:19; 1 Kings 2:44).

Sooner or later, Christ will try you to see if your heart can stand for all the Word of God, because we must live by every Word of God (Luke 4:1–4; Exod. 24:7; Deut. 4:1–9; 8:2–3).

Thus, we must do more than simply believe, confess, and call on the name of the Lord (Rom. 10:9, 13). Even if we cannot obey every Word of God, we must accept the entire Word of God and stand for and support every Word of God and not reject it or support antibiblical laws, practices, and lifestyles. Christ was tested by God in the wilderness and God allowed the devil to tempt Christ, but Christ quoted scripture when he rebuked the devil (Luke 4:1–4). And God led the Hebrews in the wilderness to humble them and allowed them to hunger to test their heart, whether they would keep his commandments or not, and to teach them that they must not live by food and earthly possessions alone, but by every Word of God (Deut. 8:2–3; Luke 4:1–4).

There is a generation that is pure in its own eyes but is not washed from its filthiness (Prov. 21:2; 30:12; Deut. 12:8). The Bible says, "Do good, O Lord, to those who are good, and to those who have a righteous heart" (Ps. 125:4–5). To hypocrites, habitual and willful sinners, to atheists, and to anti-Christians, the Word of God says, "As silver, brass, iron, and tin is gathered into the furnace to melt it, so will I gather you in my anger and in my fury, and I will leave you there, and melt you" (Ezek. 22:20). The refiner is for silver and the furnace for gold, but the Lord tests the heart to see if it is pure and if it can stand God's tests, like refiners and furnaces test silver and gold (Prov. 17:3). Christ says that they who come to him must worship him in spirit and in truth (John 4:23–24; Zech. 8:1–8). God desires truth in the inward parts of our body, the heart (Ps. 51:6). God's Word is truth, and we must be sanctified through the truth (John 17:17, 19; Col. 1:5–6; 1 Thess. 2:13). Christ gives eternal salvation to people who obey him (Heb. 5:7–9). God gives the Spirit of truth, which is the Holy Ghost, to people who obey him, and the Holy Ghost strengthens us (Acts 5:32; Luke 11:13; John 14:13–18, 26–27).

God tries the heart, and he has pleasure in people who are

righteous (1 Chron. 29:17). Trust in the Lord with all your heart and lean not to your own understanding. In all your ways acknowledge him, and he shall direct your paths. Be not wise in your own eyes, fear the Lord, and depart from evil. It shall be health to your navel, and marrow to your bones (Prov. 3:5–8; 2 Chron. 31:21; Num. 15:39–41; Jer. 29:11–13).

The navel in this scripture also indicates the inner being and the heart (Prov. 3:5–8). The Bible also says that the Word of God is sharper than any two-edged sword, cutting deep into the bone marrow, soul, and spirit and is a discerner of the thoughts and intents of the heart (Heb. 4:12). The book of Psalms tells us that when our hearts are not right with God, his blessings are limited, and we could be faced with years of trouble and even death (Ps. 78:32–41). What is in your heart will come out, whether it is God, self, or the devil (Matt. 12:34; 15:15–20; John 2:24–25; Ps. 51:1–6; Prov. 23:6–7; Jer. 17:9–10; Isa. 59:12; 1 Cor. 2:4; 1 Thess. 1:5).

WHAT IS IN YOUR HEART WILL COME OUT

God told the prophet Ezekiel to listen to him carefully and to take his word to heart (Ezek. 3:10). Where your treasure is, so will your heart be also, whether that treasure is heaven, good things, or sinful things (Matt. 6:19–21, 24–33; 19:16–30; Rom. 2:6–11; Phil. 2:21; Heb. 11:24–27).

Christ says that we must love him with all our heart, all our soul, and with all our mind (Matt. 22:37–39; Deut. 6:5). The Bible tells us, "Rejoice young people, in the time of your youth, and let your heart be joyful in your youth, and walk in the ways of your heart, and in the sight of your eyes. But know, that for all these things, God will bring you into judgment" (Eccles. 11:9; 12:13–14; Rom. 2:16).

Every idle word that we speak shall be judged by God, and our spoken words justify us or condemn us, just as hypocritically confessing Christ with our mouth condemns us (Matt. 12:36–37). Before Christ died for all people, God choose the ancient Israelites, ancient Jews, and ancient Hebrews unto himself to be a holy people, separate from the rest of the world (1 Kings 8:53; Exod. 19:5; Deut. 14:2; 26:18; Ps. 135:4; Titus 2:14; 1 Pet. 2:9; 1 John 2:2; Acts 17:26; Heb. 2:9; Rom. 5:6–9; 8:32; Isa. 53).

Not only did God eventually accept and bless all nations, but he also said that all nations will be punished with ancient Israel, because those nations were unholy, but ancient Israel was unholy in the heart and resisted the Holy Ghost (Jer. 9:25–26; Acts 7:51). God wants to put a new spirit in us, replace the stony and hard heart, and give us a spiritual heart of flesh, that we may walk in his Word, keep his Word, and be doers of his Word, and we shall be his people, and he shall be our God (Ezek. 11:19–20; 36:23–27). Remember, we must be doers of the Word and not just hearers (James 1:22–27; Matt. 13:1–23; Acts 17:11–12; Ps. 81:10–16; Jer. 15:15–21; Rev. 10:9–11).

The lamp of the body is the eye. Therefore, when your eye is good, your whole body is full of light, but when your eye is unholy, your body also is full of darkness and evil (Luke 11:33–36). Jesus says, if your hand, foot, or eyes cause you to sin, spiritually cut them off, because it is better to live a life without hands, feet, and eyes than to have your whole body cast into hell (Matt. 18:8–9). What is in you will come out, whether it is good or bad (Isa. 59:12; 1 Cor. 2:4; 1 Thess. 1:5; Matt. 12:34; 15:15–20; Ps. 51:1–6; Prov. 23:6–7; 27:19; 1 Sam. 24:13).

WE MUST SUFFER LIKE CHRIST & NOT LIKE A SINNER

We must not join the body of Christ only for blessings, but to also be Christlike, which means we must also suffer like him and carry our own cross, or we cannot be his disciple (Luke 14:26–27; Deut. 33:9). The Bible says, "We should have confidence in the day of judgment, as he is, so are we in this world" (1 John 4:17). And just as an African man helped Jesus carry his physical cross, Christ will help you carry your cross of adversity, affliction, persecution, sickness, and suffering but you must live and sometimes suffer like Christ (Mark 15:21). Christ suffered for us, leaving us an example, that we should follow his steps (1 Pet. 2:21). We are the children of God only when we obey him and when we are holy, sanctified, and separate from the world (Acts 5:32; Luke 11:13; John 14:13–18, 26–27; Phil. 2:15; 1 Pet. 1:13–17; Rom. 8:1, 5–14; 2 Cor. 6:17–18; Deut. 32:4–5).

Christ says whoever obeys him is his mother, brother, and sister (Matt. 12:46–50; Mark 3:31–35). Also, being children of God, if we want to share Christ's glory, we must also share his suffering (Rom. 8:16–17). And we must be obedient and holy (Acts 5:32; Luke 11:13; John 14:13–18, 26–27; 1 Pet. 1:13–17).

Most people seek their own desires and not the things that are of Jesus Christ (Phil. 2:21; 1 Tim. 6:9–10; James 3:13–16; John 5:41, 44; 1 Cor. 13:5).

The Apostle Paul chose to live and suffer like Christ, and he said, "Things that were gain to me, I counted as a loss for Christ's sake. And I count all things as a loss for the excellency of the knowledge of Christ Jesus my Lord, for whom I have suffered the loss of all things, and count them as dung, that I may win Christ. Not having my own righteousness, but the righteousness that is of God by faith, that I may know him, and the fellowship of his suffering" (Phil. 3:7–11; 2 Tim. 1:12).

While Job was suffering, his wife told him to curse God and die to end his suffering, but to curse God is a sin that resulted in immediate death in the Old Testament (Lev. 24:10–15, 23). Job told his wife and friends that we must not expect only good from God and that although it seemed like God was killing him, Job said, "Yet will I still trust in him" (Job 2:8–10; 13:15–16). Before God tried and tested Job's heart by making him sick, killing his children, and destroying his wealth, Job prayed regularly for his children's safety, but God still tested his heart by killing his children (Job 1:1–5).

To be afflicted or to face adversity from God can sometimes be a blessing, as was the case with David. He said that it was good that he was afflicted so he could learn God's ways (Ps. 119:71). Jeremiah said that his ministry caused him to receive affliction from God because of God's wrath on other people and that his affliction made his skin, flesh, and bones feel old (Lam. 3:1–4). Jesus witnessed a good confession while he was being tried and crucified before Pontius Pilate, and Jesus instructs us to keep his commandment without spot, unrebukable, until his return (1 Tim. 6:13–14). David was a king, and he at one point committed terrible sins, but he repented and lived a sanctified and holy life, being a new creature, and being once again first with God (2 Sam. 11; 12:1–24; 15; 1 Kings 3:6; 14:8; 15:3–5).

David wrote, "God rewarded me according to my righteousness and the cleanness of my hands. I have kept the ways of the Lord and have not wickedly departed from my God. I am also blameless before him, and I have kept myself from iniquity. God will save his afflicted people, but he brings down high looks" (Ps. 18:20–27). The same applies to the church of God because Christ is returning for a church without spot, wrinkle, or blemish (Eph. 5:1–28; 1 Pet. 1:13–19; 2 Pet. 3:1–14; 1 Tim. 6:3–16; Jude 1:22–24).

True religion according to the Bible is to go unspotted from the world and to help the fatherless and the widow in their affliction (James 1:26–27; Isa. 1:15 – 20). Christ says to not only believe in him, but also to suffer for his sake (Phil. 1:29). So as you can see, to "believe" also means to "obey" Jesus and live a sanctified and righteous life, separated from willful sin (John 17:17–19; Isa. 29:23; Heb. 4:14–16; 10:26; Mic. 2:1; Ps. 19:12–14; Rom. 1:18–32; 2 Thess. 2:10–15).

SOME PEOPLE GO TO HELL AFTER BELIEVING, CONFESSING & CALLING ON CHRIST

Not everyone who says, "Lord, Lord," shall enter the kingdom of heaven, but they who do the will of God shall go to heaven (Matt. 7:21–23; Mic. 3:11). Blessed are they who always practice righteousness" (Ps. 106:3; 119:20). Some people flatter God with their mouth and lie to him with their tongue (Ps. 78:36). We must receive the Word of God in our hearts after we hear it, and people usually do what is in their heart, because where your treasure is, there shall your heart be too (Ezek. 3:10; Luke 12:32–34; Rom. 2:6–11; 1 Kings 3:7–15; Heb. 11:24–27).

Jesus told Nicodemus that we must be born again of the water and of the Spirit, or we cannot go to heaven (John 3:1–7). The Bible says, "If we sin willfully after we have received the knowledge of the truth, there remains no more sacrifice for sins, but there is only a fearful expectation of judgment and fiery punishment. They who broke Moses' law died without mercy under two or three witnesses, how much sorer punishment for those who have trodden underfoot the Son of God, and counted his sanctified blood an unholy thing, and did it despite the Spirit of grace? It is a fearful thing to fall into the hands of the living God." (Heb. 10:26–31; Exod. 20:18–19; Deut. 5:23–26; Mic. 2:1; Ps. 19:12–14).

Remember, the people in Moses's time begged to hear Moses after initially rebelling against Moses, because if God had spoken to them, they knew they would have surely died (Exod. 20:18–19; Deut. 5:23–26).

The Holy Scripture says, "God's voice shook the earth in the Old Testament, but during these last and evil days, he will shake heaven and earth, because God is a consuming fire, and a jealous God, whose name is Jealous" (Deut. 4:24; Exod. 34:14; Heb. 12:26–29).

When we believe, we must also believe that there is a heaven being prepared for us (John 14:1–4) and that God could destroy us and send us to hell if we do not obey him, because scripture says that God is faithful to do good toward us (1 Thess. 5:24; Isa. 11:4–5; Deut. 7:9; Ps. 31:21–24).

Scripture also says that God is faithful to send sinners to hell (Rev. 20:5–8), because when God says it, he will do it (Isa. 46:9–10; 55:11; Jer. 23:20; Ezek. 24:13–14). The Bible even says, "Whoso is wise, and will observe God's mercy, goodness, and his punishments, they shall understand the lovingkindness of the Lord" (Ps. 107). Unwise people do not think that God can be good, merciful, and terrible too; but the Bible tells us that in his punishing wrath, God can be terrible (Exod. 34:10; Deut. 7:21; 10:17; Neh. 1:5; 4:14; 9:32; Job 37:22; Ps. 47:2; Jer. 20:11).

Destruction from God happened with the ancient Israelites in the wilderness and with the people of Noah's day, and in Sodom and Gomorrah when even angels were destroyed because they did not believe that God would do it (2 Pet. 2:1–9; Jude 1:5–7; Rev. 12:9). The Holy Scripture also says that people did not believe Moses and the prophets, and some people nowadays will not believe that they can go to hell even if someone returned from hell today to warn them (Luke 16:19–31; Acts 13:41). Christ returned from heaven to warn the earth while simultaneously saving the souls of people, healing them, and delivering them. Christ even asked one man how he can believe heavenly things if he did not even believe what Christ said about earthly things (John 3:12–13). Judgment day, which is for most people, the day that we die, because we will rise from the dead in the same sinful or righteous condition that we were in when we lived (Rev. 22:10–13).

WE MUST BE CHRIST – LIKE ON EARTH TO BE LIKE CHRIST IN HEAVEN

When we get to heaven, we shall see God like he is, and we shall be like him (Phil. 3:17–21; 1 John 3:2; Ps. 17:14–15). But we cannot be like him in heaven if we do not strive to be like him on earth (Titus 2:11–12; Matt. 6:10; 1 Cor. 6:9–11; 1 Tim. 6:9–10; 2 Kings 5:15–27).

When God walked the earth in the human body of Christ, God said and is still saying to the entire world that he will not ask us to do or to suffer anything that he did not experience himself, but yet without sinning himself (Heb. 2:16–18; 4:14–16; Num. 23:19; 1 John 3:5; Ps. 92:15; 1 Pet. 2:21–23; Gal. 2:17).

We were made in the image of God, and we must retain that image while we live (Isa. 43:7, 20–22; Gen. 1:26; 1 Cor. 11:7; 15:47–55; Phil. 2:6–11; James 3:9).

GOD DOES NOT HEAR THE PRAYERS, CALLS & CRYING OF SOME PEOPLE

God says that sometimes before we call, he will answer, and while we are yet speaking, he will hear, but this is mainly in reference to righteous people (Isa. 65:24). God does hear the prayers, crying, and calling of sinners too, but only regarding earthly help and necessities, because the Bible says that God does not hear the prayers of sinners when it comes to repentance, unless they are truly repenting wholeheartedly (Job 8:20; 35:13; Prov. 1:28–30; Jer. 14:7–12; Mal. 2:17; John 9:24–33).

David said, "I cried unto God with my mouth. If I regard sin in my heart, the Lord will not hear me. But God has heard me, he has attended to the voice of my prayer. Blessed be God who has not turned away my prayer, nor his mercy from me" (Ps. 66:16–20). God told Job's friends that he would hear Job's prayers, but not their prayers (Job 4:1–8; 32:1–10; 34:34–37; 42:7–9).

Some people do not feel that they must repent because they think they are not doing anything wrong or that their wrong is not as bad as other people's. But God says, "I listened and heard, but they do not speak right, no one repented of their sin and wickedness, and they say, 'What have I done?' Everyone turns to their own way of doing things" (Jer. 8:6). Some people do not pray, repent, or call on the name of the Lord until they are in trouble or when God chastises them (Isa. 26:16; 1 Kings 8:32–40). The Lord said by the mouth of Isaiah, "God's hand is not shortened that it cannot save, neither is his ear closed that it cannot hear, but your sins have separated you from God, and he will not hear your prayers" (Isa. 59:1–4; 64:4–8; Ps. 107:17–22; Mal. 2:2; Hosea 14:1). Just as God did not answer the prayers of King Saul anymore because of sin (1 Sam. 28:6). God told the Prophet Jeremiah, "I know the thoughts that I think towards you, thoughts of peace, and not of evil, to give you an expected end. Then shall you call upon me, and pray unto me, and I will hearken unto you. And you shall seek me and find me when you search for me with your whole heart" (Jer. 29:11–14). But notice that God had already punished those people very hard (Jer. 29:10).

So, as you can see, believing in your heart, confessing Christ with your mouth, and calling on the name of the Lord is not all we must do to be saved; but you must do those things in righteousness or at least start trying to live right after doing those things. Talk is cheap. To clarify even further, the Bible says that there is a sin unto death and that people should not pray about it. And there is a sin not unto death, and people should indeed pray about it (1 John 5:16–19). When we pretend to repent, God does not hear those prayers, and those sins can cause us to die in sin, but when we repent sincerely and wholeheartedly, God hears us and that is the sin not unto death (1 John 5:16–19; Jer. 7:16–20; 11:14; 14:11; Rev. 3:15–19; Matt. 12:33; Rom. 6:15–17).

Sinners who humble themselves and admit their wrong even if they do not have the strength to turn away from their sins are more likely to be heard and answered by God than sinners who say that God forgives us for everything while proudly living in sin (Luke 18:9–14; 23:39–46). God, in his grace and mercy, blesses ungodly people, and some of them still make plans against him (Hosea 7:15). But people who strive to live righteously always are favored by God, their prayers are heard at all times even if they do not get the answer that they want, and they will also inherit eternal life (Ps. 106:3; 119:20). Jesus says that if you forsake all and follow him, you shall receive in return a hundred times that which you lost in this life but expect persecutions on earth, followed by eternal life in heaven (Mark 10:28–31; Job 1; 2:1–10; 13:15–16; 42; 1 Cor. 7:25–34; Luke 14:25–27, 33).

When Jesus healed and delivered sinners in the Bible, he told them to go and sin no more or a worse thing will happen to them (John 5:14; 8:3–11). If after people escape the pollutions of the world and become entangled again in the world, their latter end will be worse than the beginning (2 Pet. 2:20; 1 John 5:4–5). The way of a sinner is hard (Prov. 13:15; Jer. 40:3; 44:23).

IT WILL BE TOO LATE TO CALL ON GOD ON JUDGMENT DAY

It was made very clear in the book of Acts that Jesus was sent to save and bless us and that we are to repent, turn away from our sins, and be converted or that same Jesus could destroy us (Acts 3:19–26). And Jesus himself says that he will not hear sinners on judgment day and that there will be weeping and grinding of teeth (Matt. 8:11–12; 13:38–43; Luke 13:24–28).

On judgment day, the Bible says, "They who are holy and righteous shall still be holy and righteous, and they who are filthy and unrighteous shall still be filthy and unrighteous. It will be too late to call on the Lord." Furthermore, Christ says, "I come quickly, and my reward is with me, to give to everyone according to their works" (Rev. 22:10–13; Acts 24:15; 1 Pet. 3:18; Dan. 12:1–3; Ezek. 18:19–32; 2 Thess. 1:4–12).

CHRIST IS ASHAMED OF PEOPLE WHO ARE ASHAMED TO CRY OUT UNTO HIM

Jesus says that people who do not openly acknowledge him and openly stand for the truth on earth, he will not stand for them before his Father in heaven and that he will be ashamed of them before God (Mark 8:38; Matt. 10:32–33). We must not even be ashamed to confess and call on the name of Christ in the presence of kings and other politicians (Ps. 119:46–47; Jude 1:3). God blesses us in the presence of our enemies and nonbelievers, and we must likewise stand for his Word and bless Christ in their presence (Ps. 23; 31:19; 1 Pet. 3:15). "Be steadfast, unmovable, always abounding in the work of the Lord, knowing that your work is not in vain in the Lord" (1 Cor. 15:58). The Apostle Paul was chosen to suffer great things for Christ's name before the ancient Jews, Gentiles, kings, and politicians (Acts 9:10–16). The Bible says, "The Lord is on my side, I will not fear. What can humans do to me? The Lord is for me. Therefore, I shall see my desire on those who hate me. It is better to trust in the Lord than to put confidence in mankind and in politicians" (Ps. 56:4; 118:6–9). Blessed are they who are not offended in Christ (Matt. 11:6). And when Christ delivers people and sets them free from sin, sickness, bad habits, and bondage and afterwards they return to their sinful lifestyle, they crucify Christ over again and put him to an open shame (Heb. 6:1–6).

YOUR HEART SHALL BE WHERE YOUR VALUES ARE

The Bible says, "If you are currently risen with Christ, seek those things which are above, where Christ sits on the right hand of God. Set your affections on things above, not on things on the earth" (Col. 3:1–2). "The way of life is above to the wise, that they may depart from hell beneath" (Prov. 15:24). The Bible says, "Where your treasure is, there shall your heart be also" (Matt. 6:19–21, 24–33; 19:16–30; Rom. 2:6–11; Phil. 2:21; Heb. 11:24–27).

If your treasure is in heaven, there shall your heart presently be also, and your soul will be there in the future for eternity (Matt. 6:21). But if your treasure is sinful, you and your heart shall be among those sinful things. Many people seek their own desires and not the things that are of Jesus Christ (Phil. 2:21; James 3:13–16). God told one hardworking man that he would die, because the man pursued earthly possessions and was not equally rich toward God (Luke 12:16–21; Isa. 40:21–25). If your actions and heart are right with God, putting God first, you are safe with God, but even if your actions are right and ungodly things are in your heart, God answers your prayers according to those things in your heart that you put before him, which is idolatry (Ezek. 14:1–11; 23:49).

SOME PEOPLE DO NOT CRY OUT TO GOD BECAUSE OF FEAR OF LOSING HUMAN FAVOR

Jesus tells us to believe and confess, because some people will try to believe without confessing and without openly praising his name, because they love the praise of mankind more than the praise of God (John 12:42–43). Paul said, "I am not ashamed of the gospel of Christ, for it is the power of God unto the saving of your soul. The just shall live by faith. For the wrath of God is revealed from heaven against all ungodliness and unrighteousness" (Rom. 1:16–18; Hab. 2:4; Gal. 3:11; Heb. 6:1–6; 10:38; Acts 20:19-20, 27; 2 Tim. 1:12).

Romans 10:10 says to believe with the heart unto righteousness and to confess and repent unto salvation. Several versions of the Bible erroneously changed the meaning and wording of the previously mentioned scripture, except the New King James Version and the King James Version, which is also the only Bible that is called the Authorized Version. In support of the original wording and meaning of Romans 10:9–10 of the Authorized King James Version of the Bible, holy scripture says that we must repent unto salvation, or otherwise, we are faced with death (2 Cor. 7:10). Many ministers have been misleading people by telling them that they are saved when they simply confess with their mouth and believe in their heart. Those ministers have blood on their hands from when struggling, physically ill, mentally ill, slaves of sin, wretched, low confidence, low self-esteem, arrogant, or hypocritical people die in their sins while thinking they were saved because a minister told them that all they must do to be saved is confess and believe. Even newcomers to the Christian Faith who want to live right have been deceived by these ministers. All people should read other parts of the Bible as well or the whole Bible if they can find the time and desire to read the whole Word of God because we must live by every Word of God (Luke 4:4; Exod. 24:7; Deut. 4:1–9; 8:3).

Another scripture in the New Testament tells us that some of the ancient Jews and some Gentiles searched the scriptures daily to see if what the apostles wrote was true. Then they "believed" after embracing other parts of the Bible as well (Acts 17:10–12). God, Christ, the prophets, and the apostles taught and wrote a lot more than Romans 10:9–10, 13. Paul said in Titus 1:1 that he acknowledges and confesses the truth, but it is done in godliness. Besides, if you believe in your heart, you should do right, because what is in your heart will come out, good or bad—just as when a person lusts after a married woman in their heart, it is adultery, because he did wrong in his heart (Matt. 5:27–29; 2 Pet. 2:14; Prov. 23:7; Jer. 17:9–11; Exod. 20:17; James 3:13–16).

The Spirit of God and Word of God, which are the same, helps us to discern the unholy thoughts and intentions of the hearts of others (Heb. 4:12; 1 Cor. 12:10; Eph. 6:17).

ASK GOD WHAT ELSE THAT HE WANTS YOU TO DO

God told Ezekiel, "Receive into your heart all my words" (Ezek. 3:10). Expecting to go to heaven after simply confessing, believing, and calling on Christ is like a kid going to school without completing assignments but still expecting to be promoted to the next grade. When Jesus blinded Saul in the New Testament, converted him to the Christian Faith, and later changed his name to Paul, Christ told him, "Arise, be baptized, and wash away your sins, calling on the name of the Lord" (Acts 22:16). Paul believed in his heart, confessed with his mouth, and called on the name of the Lord but he was still baptized (Act 9:20–24). Paul also instantly said, "Lord, what do you want me to do?" (Acts 9:1–6). We must do a lot after we confess with our mouth and believe in our heart.

WE MUST REPENT & LIVE A HOLY & SANCTIFIED LIFE

The Bible says that we must be sanctified after we repent (Acts 26:18) and that all people everywhere must repent (Acts 17:26, 29–31). Sanctified means to be set apart and set aside for holy use (Ps. 4:3–5; Heb. 12:14–15; Rom. 12:1–2; 2 Tim. 2:19–26).

Jesus asked God to, "Sanctify the people through your truth. Your Word is truth. And for their sakes I sanctify myself, that they also might be sanctified through the truth" (John 17:17–19; Isa. 29:23). Do not be ashamed to be sanctified, because God who sanctifies us is not ashamed to call the sanctified his own people (Heb. 2:11; 11:16). But if we are ashamed of Christ and his sanctified Word, then Christ will be ashamed of us before his Father on judgment day (Matt. 10:32–33; 1 Thess. 2:2; 2 Tim. 1:12; Rev. 3:1–6).

It is the will of God what we be sanctified and holy, and sex sins can cause us to not be sanctified (1 Thess. 4:3–8). People who reject this doctrine do not reject mankind who teaches this, but they reject God who commands this (1 Thess. 2:2; 4:3–8; John 17:17–19; Isa. 29:23; Heb. 2:11; 11:16; Matt. 10:32–33; 2 Tim. 1:12; Rev. 3:1–6).

God wants to sanctify you wholly so your whole spirit, soul, and body will be preserved blameless unto the coming of our Lord Jesus Christ (1 Thess. 5:19–23). Jesus told Paul that he would be sent to the Gentiles (Rom. 11:13) and that he would "open their eyes, turn them from darkness to light, and from the power of Satan to God, that they may receive forgiveness of sins, and inheritance with those who are sanctified by faith in Jesus Christ" (Acts 13:45–52; 26:17–18). The Word of God is good if a person uses it righteously. Know this, the law is not made for a righteous person, but for the lawless, disobedient, ungodly, sinners, unholy, profane, murderers, manslayers, whoremongers, sex outside of marriage and premarital sex, liars, the perjured, and anyone else who is contrary to the Word of God (1 Tim. 1:8–10). Peter shamefully used profanity when he denied Jesus and he swore while saying he did not know Jesus (Matt. 26:66–75). But after he repented with tears, he served the Lord in complete sanctification and labored in the Lord until his death (Matt. 26:66–75; John 21:12–19). David also sinned a terrible sin when he took a man's wife, impregnated her, and had her husband killed, and God punished David terribly. But after accepting his punishment and after repenting, David served the Lord in complete sanctification until his death (2 Sam.11; 12:1–24; 15:1–30; 16:5–14, 21–22; 17:15–22; 18; 1 Kings 15:3–5; Ps. 118:18; Isa. 55:3; Acts 13:34).

David and Peter both served the Lord in sanctification before their great sins, and after their great sins, they did not make any more sinful mistakes, and they died in holiness and sanctification (Rev. 22:10–13; Acts 24:15; Dan. 12:1–3; Ezek. 18:19–32; 2 Thess. 1:4–12).

This is one reason that Jesus told people after he healed and delivered them, "Sin no more or a worse thing will happen to you" (John 5:14; 8:3–11; James 5:13–20; 2 Pet. 2:20; Isa. 57:11–12).

So, people nowadays cannot use David and Peter as an example of how God forgives heathens, infidels, anti-Christians, sinners, hypocrites, and evil and wicked people, unless those people become a true servant of the Lord. Jesus says that we are the salt of the earth but that if salt loses its flavor, it is good for nothing and it is thrown out and trodden under the foot of humans (Matt. 5:13), just as vines and branches that do not produce good fruit are cast into the fire (Isa. 5:1–7; Ezek. 15; 19:10–14; Hosea 10:1–2). People should not look at the sins and forgiveness of David and Peter as excuses for sinning while hoping that they receive that same forgiveness, although God will give us the true mercies of David, and of Peter, if we repent (Isa. 55:3; Acts 13:34). But we should try to live like Christ, Enoch, Methuselah, Mordecai, Melchizedek, Noah, Job, Isaiah, Jeremiah, Daniel, Anna, Esther, Ezra, Nehemiah, the Apostle Paul, Elijah, Elisha, John the Baptist, the Apostle John, Joshua, Caleb and certain others. Some of the original twelve apostles cannot be mentioned with the names of the aforementioned people, because even though they walked with Christ and saw the miracles, Judas betrayed Christ and the other ten ran away and forsook Christ when he was arrested (Mark 14:44–50; Matt. 26:66–75). Christ told them that they would forsake him, because he knows everything—past, present, and future—and they told Christ that they would not, but they did (Matt. 26:30–31; Ps. 147:5; Prov. 3:19–20; Deut. 31:14–23). Job's life and how he handled adversity, sickness, suffering, and temptation was one of the best examples in the Bible of how to live a righteous, holy, and sanctified life while accepting God's will. And he remained righteous even after God killed his children, destroyed his wealth, and took away his health with several terminal illnesses and after his wife condemned him to die and told him that his sick breath stank (Job 1; 2; 4:1–8; 13:15–16; 19:17; 24:1–11; 27:1–6; 29; 31; 32:1–10; 34:34–37).

To see what the apostles saw and to live as they lived is a great service on their part, and a lot of Christians are more like the ten apostles and like David who loved the Lord but made terrible mistakes. Ten of the apostles, eleven including Judas, physically walked with the Lord but still did not serve God as wholeheartedly as the prophets of the Old Testament did who never saw God or the Son of God. Jesus told the apostles, "Blessed are they who have not seen and still believe" (John 20:24–31).

Most Christians nowadays have not denied Christ as Peter

did or have killed a woman's husband because they desired the husband's wife, but some Christians still have denied Christ or have been anti-Christian in one way or another. And it is true that God will forgive the worst of us, but to not serve Jesus wholeheartedly after we repent is not an option. Jesus says they who he has forgiven for a few sins love him little, but they who have been forgiven for plenty of sins love him much more (Luke 7:40–48). Saul, who was later called Paul, lived an anti-Christian life; but after Jesus converted him, he labored hard for the Lord and never backslid or forsook the Lord like David and Peter did. In his humility, Paul said he was less than all the original apostles, even though he labored more than all of them (1 Cor. 15:9–10). That is because God forgave Paul for a lot of sins, so Paul labored a lot for the Lord after being saved (Luke 7:40–48). King Hezekiah and King Josiah were not as famous as David and Solomon but were much more righteous (2 Kings 18:4–7; 23:25), Josiah being the most righteous. We should try to be like these sanctified people who were living sacrifices and labored for the Lord. God says that he will wash us whiter than snow even though our sins are as red as scarlet and crimson, but he also tells us to put away evil from before his eyes, cease to do evil, and learn to do good and he will reason with us (Isa. 1:16–20; Rev. 7:14). Our reasonable service is to be a living sacrifice unto the Lord, holy and acceptable unto God (Luke 17:7–10; Rom. 12:1; Eccles. 12:13–14; Deut. 10.12–14; Heb. 12:26–29).

As stated earlier, God says to holy and sanctified people who have labored in his name, "I know your works. Behold, I have set before you an open door, and no one can shut it. You have only a little strength remaining, but you still have not denied my name, and you have kept my Word" (Rev. 3:8). Some Christians go to church on a regular basis and are deacons, mothers of the church, and even ministers but they use profane words in their speech. However, the Bible tells us to rid ourselves of anger, wrath, malice, blasphemy, and filthy words and to let all our conversations be holy (Col. 3:8; 1 Pet. 1:15; 2 Pet. 3:10–12;

Ps. 19:12–14; 1 Cor. 15:33; Eph. 4:21–32; Isa. 33:15–16; Mal. 2:5–6).

BELIEVING, CONFESSING & CALLING ON GOD MUST INCLUDE BAPTISM

Romans 10:9, 13 says, "If you confess with your mouth the Lord Jesus and believe in your heart that God raised him from the dead, you shall be saved. For whoever calls on the name of the Lord shall be saved." But the Bible also says that people who are his and let everyone who confesses the name of Christ depart from sin (2 Tim. 2:19). Many shall be called, but few shall be chosen (Matt. 20:14–16). No one can see God the Father except they go through God the Son, and no one gets to Christ without living by what the original apostles did and wrote, all of it, not just what is so beautifully and graciously written in the tenth chapter of Romans (John 5:22–23; 14:1, 6; Acts 4:12; Matt. 10:40).

False prophets, hypocrite preachers, and unwise preachers are telling people that all they must do to be saved is believe in their heart and confess with their mouth and they shall be saved (Rom. 10:9, 13). To say that only believing and confessing will save you without living right has become one of the biggest lies in history. A preacher in 2014 said that people do not have to be baptized in the name of Jesus Christ like Peter and Paul commanded (Acts 2:36–39; 8:14–17; 10:42–48; 19:1–6; John 3:3–7).

The preacher said that Peter and Paul were trying to get the ancient Jews to accept Jesus. That same preacher said that we do not have to be baptized at all and that to simply believe and confess the name of the Lord will save us. The truth is that the scriptures speak to all of us and we must fulfill both scriptures to be saved. We must believe, repent, confess, call on God, be baptized in Christ's name, be filled with the Holy Ghost, and continue to believe, confess, and call on the name of Christ (Acts 2:36–41; Rom. 10:1–3, 8–14; 1 Kings 8:33–34).

The Apostle Peter reminded the ancient Jews that whosoever calls on the name of the Lord shall be saved. He then performed the first baptism by baptizing about three thousand people in the name of the Lord Jesus Christ after they repented for their sins (Acts 2:21, 36–47). Jesus says that we cannot go to heaven unless we are born again of the water and of the Holy Spirit (John 3:3–7). The people in Matt. 7:21–23 confessed but did not obey and were cast away by Jesus. Being baptized symbolizes the death, burial, and resurrection of Christ (Rom. 6:1–5; Col. 2:12; 2 Tim. 2:11). And when you go down into the water in Christ's name, you are spiritually dying, burying your sins and your former self in the water, and rising out of the water as a new person, just as Christ rose from the grave with all power (Col. 2:10). Christ himself was baptized by John the Baptist who had already baptized a multitude of people while they confessed their sins to God (Matt. 3). Peter and the apostles baptized three thousand people in one day (Matt. 3:1–11; Acts 2:36–47). Some preachers say baptism places too much emphasis on ceremonial means, and those preachers usually have very large congregations and simply do not want to get in the water to baptize a lot of people every week. But Peter performed the very first baptism after the resurrection of Jesus, and he patiently baptized about three thousand people in one day (Acts 2:36–41). Peter may have had help, but three thousand were baptized. In Acts 10:40–48, the people believed and were filled with the Holy Ghost, but Peter still commanded them to be baptized in the name of the Lord. The scripture states, "Can anyone object to them being baptized in water and receiving the Holy Ghost, like we have?" (Acts 10:47–48). Yes, the Bible does say, "Whosoever believes in Jesus shall receive forgiveness of sins" (Acts 10:43).

Paul met a group of Christians who believed but had not been baptized, nor did they have the Holy Ghost. Paul then baptized them in the name of Jesus, and they were filled with the Holy Ghost (Acts 19:1–6). Paul himself was told to call on the name of the Lord, but he was also told to be baptized (Acts 22:16). The Apostle Paul said that people who call on the name of Christ should also be sanctified, (1 Cor.1:2). And to be sanctified is to be set aside for holy use by God and to be separated from worldly matters (John 17:17–19; Isa. 29:23; Heb. 2:11; 11:16; 1 Thess. 4:3–8; 5:19–23).

A man in the Bible believed that Jesus is the Son of God and the man himself said, "Here is water. What prevents me from being baptized?" The scripture states, "Philip said, 'If you believe with all your heart, you should be baptized.' And he answered and said, 'I believe that Jesus Christ is the Son of God,' and they both went down into the water, and Philip baptized him" (Acts 8:36–38). A prison guard was told by Paul and Silas to believe, and he and his family shall be saved, but that same family was also baptized in the name of the Lord Jesus Christ, just like all the original apostles were baptized (Acts 2:36–41; 8:14–17; 10:42–48; 16:25–34; 19:2–5; John 3:3–7).

If a preacher is telling you that obeying only Rom. 10:9–13 will save you, they are lacking wisdom, or they are a lying false prophet. Some preachers stand in the presence of thousands and thousands of people and even more thousands on television and on the Internet and tell them, "Raise your hands and repeat after me." After they recite Romans 10:9, the preacher then tells the people that they are saved, born-again, part of the body of Christ, and on their way to heaven. That is not true, and it is best for a person to voluntarily give their life to Christ and to recite those scriptures and not repeat what a minister says who does not know if the person means what they say or not. We must openly confess Christ and believe in him before and after baptism. They who believe and are baptized shall be saved, but they who do not believe shall be damned (Mark 16:16; Rev. 21:8, 27; 22:14–15).

So obviously, if you believe, you must also get baptized (Mark 16:16). If you believe and do not confess and repent, you may go to hell (Mark 8:38; Matt. 10:32–33; Acts 17:26, 29–31).

Simply confessing and believing will not save you, because repentance and proper baptism is also required. Notice that all the people in the Bible were baptized in the name of Jesus and not in the name of the Father, and of the Son, and of the Holy Ghost (Acts 2:36–44; 8:14–17; 10:40–48; 19:1–6; John 3:3–7).

The Bible says we must live by every Word of God and not just by the part that says that we are saved when we believe, confess, call on God, and are baptized in the name of the Father, and of the Son, and of the Holy Ghost (Luke 4:4; Exod. 24:7; Deut. 4:1–9; 8:3). Those scriptures are in the Bible, but so are thousands of other scriptures, including the ones that say we must live right and that we must be baptized in the name of Christ like the apostles were baptized (Acts 2:36–41; 8:14–17; 10:42–48; 19:2–5; John 3:3–7).

No one can truly confess Jesus but by the Holy Ghost (1 Cor. 12:3). Jesus also says they who believe in him shall receive the Holy Ghost (John 7:37–39). But in Acts 5:32, when the Holy Ghost had been given to the apostles, they said Jesus shall give the Holy Ghost to people who obey Christ. "'Christ the Redeemer shall come to people who turn from sin,' says the Lord" (Acts 5:32; Luke 11:13; John 14:13-18, 26-27; Heb. 5:7-9; Isa. 59:20).

So, as you can see, to "believe" means to "obey" Jesus and live a sanctified life (John 17:17–19; Isa. 29:23). People who sin are of the devil because sin is of the devil and not of God (1 John 3:8–10; John 8:34–47; 1 Tim. 5:15).

We must be separated from willful sin (Heb. 10:26; 4:14–16; Mic. 2:1; Ps. 19:12–14; Rom. 1:18–32; 2 Thess. 2:10–15).

The Bible says that at the very first baptism, the people believed, had all things in common, and were baptized in the name of Jesus (Acts 2:36–44). If any preacher tells you that simply believing and confessing will save you, they are limited in wisdom, or they are a lying false prophet or a hypocrite preacher. Rom. 10:10 tells us to believe unto righteousness and to confess unto salvation, just as 2 Cor. 7:10 says that we should repent unto salvation, or we will die.

The Bible says that God will speak peace to his people, but they must not turn again to folly (Ps. 85:8; 2 Cor. 7:10). Again, the Bible also says that the Lord knows people who are his and let everyone who confesses the name of Christ depart from sin (2 Tim. 2:19; James 2:7). Flee youthful lusts and follow righteousness, faith, love, and peace with people who call on the Lord with a pure heart, daily (2 Tim. 2:22; Job 27:8–23; Ps. 1; Prov. 3:5–8).

Luke 1:50 says God's mercy is on people who fear him. Hezekiah walked before the Lord in truth and with a perfect heart and did that which was good in the sight of God (2 Kings 20:3). David asked God to cleanse his "heart" from willful, unwilful, and unknown sins so he will be acceptable in the sight of the Lord (Ps. 19:12–14). The Lord's eyes run to and from throughout the earth; to show himself strong on behalf of people whose heart is perfect toward him (2 Chron. 16:9). And God knows that Satan works hard against strong Christians who obey God's Word and who live and suffer like Christ (Rev. 12:17).

Josiah and Hezekiah were the two most righteous kings in the Bible, second and third behind King Jesus (2 Kings 18:4–7; 23:25). Josiah turned unto the Lord with all his heart, soul, and might (2 Kings 23:25). In the New Testament, Christ also commands us to serve the Lord with all our heart, soul, and mind (Matt. 22:37). Just as God's eyes searches the earth for people who serve him with a perfect heart so he can be strong for them, the devil roams the earth like an angry lion seeking to devour weak Christians and anti-Christians (1 Pet. 5:8). As state earlier, a certain woman in the Bible told Jesus, "Blessed is the womb that bore you, and the breast that you sucked." Jesus replied, "Blessed are they who obey the Word of God" (Luke 11:27–28). Jesus says that anyone who obeys his Word shall never die (John 8:51).

Hypocrite preachers tell the people what their itching ears want to hear, while the preacher denies God who called them, and the truth shall be evil spoken of by the congregation (2 Tim. 4:2–3; Prov. 17:3–4; 2 Pet. 2:1–2). They will be punished along with the false prophet (Ezek. 14:10; Jer. 23:34–39; Hosea 4:9). And the hypocrite teacher will certainly bear the judgment of God (Gal. 5:7–10).

If people are going to live by the part of the Bible that says we are saved when we believe and confess, then they should obey the rest of the scripture as well. They should obey the part that says we must live by God's righteousness and not our own (Rom. 10:1–3, 9–10). To believe is to have faith, but faith without works is dead, and faith without works cannot save you (James 2:13–26; Matt. 7:7; Mark 2:1–5). Paul said, "According to the faith of God's elect people, and the acknowledging of the truth which is after godliness" (Titus 1:1). To acknowledge means to confess, accept, or admit the truth of. Again, Jesus says, "People draw near unto me with their mouth, and honor me with their lips, but their heart is far from me. In vain do they worship me, teaching for doctrines the commandments of humans" (Mark 7:6–7; Col. 2:22; Titus 1:14; Jer. 12:2; Ezek. 33:31; John 7:18; 1 John 3:18; 1 Thess. 2:4–6, 13).

They disregard God's Word and live by the statutes that they made (2 Kings 17:19; Ps. 28:4–5). Isaiah also said the same thing in the Old Testament (Isa. 29:13; Eph. 4:14; 1 Cor. 1:10; 2:9–16; Rom. 15:5–6).

The book of Malachi says, "You have wearied the Lord with your words. Yet you say, how have we wearied him? When you say people who do evil are good in the sight of the Lord," (Mal. 2:17). Jesus is the savior of all people, especially of those who truly believe (1 Tim. 4:10).

To the pure, God will show himself pure, but to the sinful, he will show himself as a punishing judge (2 Sam. 22:27; Ps. 18:26). Blessed are the pure in heart, for they shall see God (Matt. 5:8). The commandment of the Lord is pure, rejoicing the heart and enlightening the eyes (Ps. 19:8). The Bible says that whoever shall call on the name of the Lord shall be saved (Joel 2:32; Acts 2:21; Rom. 10:13). This is true, but you must be trying to live a holy and sanctified life as well. When the Bible says that whoever shall call on the name of the Lord shall be saved, that scripture is written in the same chapter of the Bible as the scripture that says that we must be baptized in the name of the Lord Jesus Christ and receive the gift of the Holy Ghost (Acts 2:21, 36 – 44; John 3:3 – 5). So, we must delight in the Lord and call on him always, not just in times of need (Job 27:8–23; Prov. 3:5–8).

False preachers, false prophets, and lying preachers are abusing and misusing the scriptures that say we are saved when we confess and believe, and it is getting worse and worse. Gospel musician Kirk Franklin said on his radio show in 2016 that people can consider their house clean because they listened to his radio show play music. That was one of the biggest lies ever told by a musician. God told Hezekiah to get his house in order because his death was near, but Hezekiah repented in tears, humility, and in fear of God and as a result he lived fifteen more years (Isa. 38). We also must take heed to the whole Word of God (Luke 4:4; Exod. 24:7; Deut. 4:1–9; 8:3). We must not live by the commandments of mankind as with Kirk Franklin's false statement (Mark 7:6–7; Col. 2:22; Eph. 4:14; 1 Cor. 1:10; 2:9–16; Rom. 15:5–6).

People who live by Kirk Franklin's words and the words of false prophets and lying preachers disregard God's Word and live by the statutes that humans made (2 Kings 17:19; Ps. 28:4–5).

People who believe that all they must do to be saved is to confess with their mouth and believe in their heart are making mention of God's name, but not in truth nor in righteousness

(Isa. 48:1; Rom. 10:9–10, 13; Heb. 6:1–6). The Bible also says that we must not simply believe in our heart, but that we must praise the Lord with uprightness of heart, while we learn God's righteous judgments (Ps. 119:7). It is time to awake out of sinful sleep, spiritually lazy sleep, and acts of omission toward God because our salvation and our judgment day are closer than when we first believed. "The night is far spent, the day is at hand, let us therefore cast off works of darkness, and let us put on the armor of light. Let us walk honestly, as in the day, not in partying, drunkenness, sexual sins, evil conduct, fighting, and jealousy. Instead, put on the Lord Jesus Christ, and make no provisions for the flesh, to fulfill lusts" (Rom. 13:11–13; Gal. 5:13). For most people, judgment day is the day that they die and not on the last day when God destroys the earth (Rev. 22:10–13; Acts 24:15; 1 Pet. 3:18; Dan. 12:1–3; Ezek. 18:19–32; 2 Thess. 1:4–12).

There is a book of our works being recorded in heaven, and God judges us based on what is in the Book of Works, and that determines if he writes our name in the Book of Life in heaven forever (Rev. 3:1–6; 20:12–13; Phil. 4:3; Mal. 3:16).

Believing and confessing are only the first steps (Rom. 10:9, 13). Those scriptures sometimes refer to various situations in life, mainly people who are sick and bedridden and cannot be baptized due to their illness and any other person who cannot get to a body of water such as some prison inmates and when people would like to give their life to Christ and are making plans to be baptized in the very near future. In defense of Romans 10:9 that says we are saved when we simply believe, confess, and call on the name of the Lord, Peter said the same thing in Acts 10:42–48; but Peter also said in those same scriptures that we must be baptized in the name of Jesus Christ and receive the gift of the Holy Ghost (Acts 2:36–44; 8:14–17; 10:40–48; 19:1–6; John 3:3–7).

BLESSINGS DO NOT ALWAYS MEAN THAT A PERSON IS SAVED

Before Jesus died, rose from the dead, and ascended back to heaven, he only ministered to the ancient Jews. Christ sent Paul to the Gentiles, and God told Peter to accept the Gentiles, but that was after Christ went back to heaven. Before that time, an unsaved woman approached Jesus and asked that he heal her daughter. Jesus told her that he did not come to minister to people who were not of the ancient Jews, and why should he take from God's children and give to dogs? The woman told Jesus that even dogs eat of the crumbs that fall from the children's table. At that point, Jesus granted her request (Matt. 15:21–28). As you can see, just because a sinner receives things from God, that does not mean that God is pleased with them, and it does not mean that sinners are saved. Now that Christ is calling all people to repentance, why wouldn't he bless sinners (Acts 17:26, 29–31)? Do you give only to your most obedient child and not give to the disobedient child occasionally? The child who is more obedient to God and to parents should receive the most and on a more regular basis, but you cannot totally disregard the disobedient child. You must give them things at times to show them that you love them, but that does not mean that you are pleased with their disobedience. Therefore, God's blessings shine on the just and the unjust, the good, the evil, and the unthankful but that does not mean that unthankful and unjust people are going to heaven (Deut. 9:4–7;

10:17–22; Ezek. 29:17–20; Matt. 5:43–48; Luke 6:35; Acts 14:8–18; Ps. 17:13–15; Neh. 9:35–39; Ps. 145:9–10).

OBEYING ONLY THREE VERSES OF THE BIBLE DOES NOT SAVE YOU

When people say that "all you have to do to be saved is to believe," they are like lazy people who have a new job and say all they must do is a little work. We should not look for the least amount of anything regarding God, and to do our very best towards God is our reasonable service, while also being a holy living sacrifice unto Christ (Rom. 12:1; Luke 17:7–10). And obedience is better than sacrifice, because God desires righteousness towards him and mankind, and mercy towards other people more than he desires sacrifice (1 Sam. 15:22; Rom. 12:1 – 2; Matt. 9:10 – 13; 23:23; Prov. 21:3; Ps. 4:5; 40:6 – 8: Hos. 6:6; Mic. 6:7; Heb. 13:15).

Even if we cannot live up to all of God's high standards and high expectations, the Lord still has very high standards and expectations, not low ones (Heb. 4:12; Rev. 1:16; 2:12, 16; 19:13; Matt. 10:34–39; 1 John 5:12; Eph. 6:17; John 1:1).

Why should we expect to do little obedience toward God but receive plenty of blessings from God? We are supposed to be servants of the Lord, and he is not our servant. God should not have to continue to wait on us, and wait for us, and to give us everything we need while we do little toward him. Obedience is better than sacrifice and is our minimum service and requirement (1 Sam. 15:22; Rom. 12:1 – 2; Matt. 9:10 – 13; 23:23; Prov. 21:3; Ps. 4:5; 40:6 – 8: Hos. 6:6; Mic. 6:7; Heb. 13:15).

CONFESSING WITH YOUR MOUTH, BELIEVING IN YOUR HEART

The Bible says that God requires all people everywhere, in every nation, to repent and turn away from their sins and God shall judge the world in righteousness on judgment day (Luke 24:46–49; Acts 14:8–18; 17:26, 29–31). Therefore, it is a terrible lie when people say that all you must do to be saved is to believe, confess, and call on the name of the Lord (Rom. 10:9, 13).

Some Protestants claim that Catholics are not aligned with the Bible, especially when Catholics go before a priest to confess their sins and to ask for forgiveness as though the priest is God. But when Protestant preachers stand before multitudes of people and tell them that they are saved after they simply recite Romans 10:9–10, 13, they mislead millions of people yearly. God says in the Old Testament and Christ says in the New Testament that we must live by every Word of God (Luke 4:4; Exod. 24:7; Deut. 4:1–9; 8:3). This does not mean that we are able to obey all of it, but we must acknowledge, stand for, and live by all of it while confessing that we must not live in or support sin. Jesus says that he wishes people were cold or hot, because if we are lukewarm, he spits us out of his mouth. God chastises people who he loves, and they must repent and turn away from their sins or they will be lost in their sins to the grave and to hell. Because people who obey sin are servants and slaves of sin, and they are not servants of Christ (Rev. 3:15–19; Rom. 6:15–17).

We must be on fire for the Lord after we confess and believe, otherwise we are cold and lost. Christ seeks us to save us but to only confess, believe, and call on him in times of need is to be lukewarm, and God rejects and spits out lukewarm people. Jesus also says, "Either make the tree good and its fruit good, or make the tree bad and its fruit bad, because a tree is known by the fruit it produces" (Matt. 12:33). Even a child is known by their ways, whether they are pure or right (Prov. 20:11). "Blessed are they who hunger and thirst for righteousness, for they shall be filled" (Matt. 5:6; Ps. 42:1–3; Prov. 15:8–9; Rev. 21:6–8; 22:13–21).

Some people make themselves rich but have nothing because they are empty, blind, miserable, and unsaved; but some poor people are rich with salvation, sanctification, holiness, happiness, good health, good children, peace, wisdom, necessities, strength, safety, and protection (Prov. 13:7; Rev. 3:15–22). Some of God's people live like Christ lived on earth, in tribulation and poverty, but are still rich (Rev. 2:9). God fills hungry people with good things, but he sends ungodly rich people away empty (Luke 1:53). Notice that the scripture did not say that hungry people are filled with food, but with good things, whatever those things may be. God fills people who hunger with whatever good thing their soul hungers for, but sometimes we must seek God and not simply wait on him to show up—seek and you shall find (Luke 11:9–10; Matt. 11:28–30; Jer. 6:16). Rebellious people shall seek but not find, and they shall call on God, but he will not answer, because they did not choose the fear of the Lord (Luke 6:25; Prov. 1:28–30). In the Old Testament, God says that the sins of some people are written upon the tables of their heart with an iron diamond-tipped pen (Jer. 17:1). But God is asking us to write his Word in our hearts and minds (Prov. 3:3; Jer. 31:33; 2 Cor. 3:2–3, 7).

Everyone who forsakes the Lord shall be ashamed, and they who depart from the Lord shall be written in the earth, meaning in the grave and not written in the Book of Life, because they have forsook the Lord, who is the fountain of living water (Jer. 17:13; John 7:37–39; Rev. 22:18–19; Rom. 1:24–25; Deut. 4:2; 5:22; 12:32; Ezra 6:11; Prov. 30:5–6; Eccles. 3:14–15).

REFERENCES

The Holy Ghost, also known as the Holy Spirit
The King James Version of the Holy Bible

BACK COVER SUMMARY

During hard times when it is an additional challenge to read through the many chapters of the Bible for answers to your problems, this book lists topics in alphabetical order that will comfort you and guide you to supporting scriptures and revelations to help strengthen you and to help open doors for you through Christ. When you think that you have done all that you can do but nothing seems to work, this book explains how, when, and why God is with you. When you may be uncertain, lacking confidence, lacking necessities, questioning God, giving up hope, or feeling that dreams and goals are fading fast, this book provides support with holy scriptures that gives you many reasons to keep going and to not give up. If you are already living in peace and prosperity, this book prepares you for future times when God will test and try you, and for when God allows the devil to tempt and try you, just as Christ was tempted. When Christ resisted the devil's temptations, the devil fled from Christ, but only for a season and with plans to return one day to tempt and to try again. Some of the strengthening and supportive topics are: Abandonment, Accusations, Addictions, Adoptions, Adversity, Alone, Anxiety and Depression, Betrayal, Blessings, Child Abuse, Child Support, Children's Prayer, Comfort, Courage, Crying, Encouragement, Enemies, Failure, Favor, Foster Care, Happiness, Help, Joy, Keeper, Mental Health, More Than You Can Bear, Outcast, Patience, Protection, Rejection, Reward, Stand Still and Know That I Am God, Sorrow, Success, Tests, Victory, With, and Worrying. The author has published six books. May the Lord Jesus Christ bless you while you read, overcome, grow, and prosper.

ABOUT THE AUTHOR

Elijah Paul

Elijah Paul has published six books and is a Christian minister who has been in the ministry since the 1990's. All the author's initial developments of his books began by the direction of God Almighty as part of a much larger book nearly twenty-three years before he published his first book. The Lord showed the author the original vision that caused him to begin writing, and God gave additional visions through the years as the Lord revealed them to the author. The original work was written over a twenty-two-year period and consists of more than 1,400 pages and more than 2,000 topics. The author's original vision from God included a vision of a number 2, which caused the author to assume that the larger book would be published after two years of writing. As years passed, the author became worried that he was not fulfilling God's work and that pursuing advanced college degrees and handling adversities, afflictions, trials, and tribulations were delaying the larger book's completion date. As more years passed, the author assumed that the number 2 that he saw in the vision must have involved the number 12 which is a significant number in the Bible, but after the larger book was still far from being completed after twelve years, the author assumed that the vision of the number 2 must have been twenty years. And after twenty years of writing, the author felt that he had failed to fulfill God's calling and purpose. But when the larger book was finally finished after twenty-two years of writing, the author realized that the number 2 that he saw in the vision was twenty-two years and also the year 2020. After twenty-two years of writing, God finally revealed to the author that the larger book will never be published as one huge book, but that several smaller books will be published from the original larger book. The first smaller book was taken out of the larger book and published in the year 2020. Therefore, the fulfillment of the vision of the number 2 is twenty-two years to finish writing, and the first book was published in the year 2020. The author plans to spend the rest of his life publishing books from his twenty-two years of documenting revelations from Christ.

BOOKS BY THIS AUTHOR

Slaveholders, Churches & Colonists Changed The Bible. The Greatest Identity Theft In History. Black Jews & Black Egyptians Changed To White

The Recrucifixion Of Christ By Barack Obama & Christians Who Support Homosexuality & Abortions (Sold At Walmart.com, Google Play, Apple Books, Barnesandnoble.com, Booksamillion.com, Thriftbooks.com)

Favor Of God, Forgetting Your Past, Remembering Where God Brought You From

God Is With You In Hard Times When You Think That He Is Not

One Lord, One Faith, One Baptism, All Questions Answered With Scriptures

Crucifixion Of Christ By President Obama

www.ingramcontent.com/pod-product-compliance
Lightning Source LLC
Chambersburg PA
CBHW051937090426
42741CB00008B/1176